GET YOUR WRITS OUT!
Another Dose Of The Alternative Football Press

edited by

Martin Lacey

with material from

Rodney Rodney
King Of The Kippax
The Hanging Sheep
Voice of the Valley
Through The Wind & Rain
Out Of Court
A Load Of Bull
The Lad Done Brilliant
Brian Moore's Head Looks Uncannily Like London Planetarium
The Crooked Spireite
A Kick Up The R's
Brian
Hull, Hell and Happiness
On Cloud 7
Blow Football

Thanks also to

City Gent
John Mulcreevy

First published 1991 by
Juma, 44 Wellington Street, Sheffield 1

ISBN 1 872204 02 3

Two years ago I wrote an introduction to 'El Tel Was A Space Alien', the first ever compilation of football fanzines. At that time I felt it necessary to begin with an explanation of exactly what fanzines were and how they started. These days such basics are obsolete.

Nobody who goes to football matches can be unfamiliar with the fanzine seller, a cheery optimist standing out in all weather apologetically trying to sell something which, he's keen to stress, isn't the programme, but is a lot more interesting than the programme. By now your curiosity will have got the better of you; you've bought your first fanzine; you've discovered it's actually pretty good; you've got hooked.

Even a substantial number of people who never go to football will know about football fanzines, since the 'fanzine phenomenom', as it's invariably - and fairly accurately - described, has been the subject of innumerable features in every section of the media. Fanzines have become an institution, an industry. Their passion and outspoken nature has made them popular with the fans, and in many cases equally unpopular in the boardroom and the committee room. Fanzines have been threatened, banned and sued, in some cases merely for daring to criticize. It is the proud boast of my own 'Elmslie Ender' that we are Britain's most banned fanzine, prohibited from sale at (at last count - we're not sure how far the ban extends down the non-league pyramid) a staggering 212 grounds, for reasons which in retrospect seem trivial beyond belief. If we're the most banned, the Brighton fanzine 'Gulls Eye' has suffered the most expensive backlash: left with a bill for £6000 in legal fees after being forced to apologise in court for a slur on the club's directors. Yet fanzines have continued to criticize, have stood up for the paying supporter and in some cases have won acceptance and respect where they once faced animosity and mistrust.

The clubs and authorities certainly have good reason to be wary of the fanzines.In football there is no democracy; to quote the Clash "All the power's in the hands of the people rich enough to buy it", people who have in the past controlled the majority of what supporters read through the official programme and official newspapers may have difficulty coming to terms with an influential independent voice scrutinizing and criticizing their actions. But even the most thick skinned director knows that, unlike a supermarket where the customers go elsewhere if they don't like the way it does business, football clubs rely on an illogical brand loyalty which is more akin to religion than business. So fans have a right to their say and the sooner that is more broadly accepted the better.

In sheer numbers the growth of fanzines has been staggering. The best barometer of this is the godfather of most of the new breed, When Saturday Comes, which over five years of publication has continued to pay homage to its roots by including reviews of new fanzines and a monthly alphabetical listing. In December 1986 there were eight in the list; by September 1987, just 15, the Elmslie Ender included. Then it took off. The typeface became progressively smaller in order to fit the listing into a page; in 1990 they gave it up as a hopeless task and split the list into two alphabetical sections in alternate months, then three. How much longer they will fill valuable ad space with this information is unknown, but When Saturday Comes has done its bit and more. There are now hundreds of football fanzines around the country and still more starting every week.

While we are handing out the plaudits a mention, too, is due to Sportspages bookshop in Charing Cross Road, not least because the owner John Gstaad complained bitterly that it wasn't mentioned in the last volume! Sportspages have stocked virtually every football fanzine ever produced, initially on a virtually non-profit basis. As the publications became more numerous and took over ever more expensive West End retail floorspace so they had to become more hard-headed about it; nevertheless, Sportspages' generous terms and prompt payment have been of immense help to everyone they deal with.

It would be untrue to say the growth has been entirely positive. Two years ago virtually every fanzine would include a page of near sycophantic reviews of other publications, something which was forgiveable because, in early 1989, you would be hard pressed to find a fanzine which wasn't genuinely worthwhile. These days instead you'll find an article bemoaning the current state of the 'scene'. And they're not just bitter because their clique is no longer so exclusive. Standards have declined. The unwritten code of the pioneering fanzines that being 'alternative' meant being self-conciously anti-racist, anti-sexist, anti-homophobic has been seriously breached by a minority. Often malice is not intended, but if fanzines are to be seen as an ethical alternative to the clubs' propaganda and the tabloids' sensationalism then they have a responsibility to look carefully at what they're saying. The line between humourous disrespect of opposing teams and their fans and pointless provocation is also too frequently crossed. Profit used to be a dirty word in the fanzine world, or at least those fanzines which did make a profit were committed to using it for the good of their club, not to line individuals' pockets. The writers did it all for love.

The last couple of years have seen the rise of the 'professional' fanzine - and this doesn't refer to the likes of *When Saturday Comes* which would long ago have sunk under the weight of its own success if it hadn't been professional, but fanzines which are started for the sole purpose of making money for the editor/publisher. There are fanzines run by people who don't even support the team they're writing about, or didn't before they jumped on the fanzine bandwagon. Not so long ago I was asked for advice about starting a football fanzine. This is something I'm always willing to give, both in my capacity as a printer, as I hope to get some work out of it, and as a fanzine writer, because it's my hobby. I was stunned when he dropped into the conversation, without a hint of irony, the admission that he didn't actually know anything about football, and did I think this would be a problem?

The period since '*El Tel....*' has been an eventful one for the game, and hopefully one in which a corner has been turned. The greatest cause for celebration has been the abandonment of the ID card scheme. It would be nice to report that the government finally paid heed to the fans, the fanzines, the FSA and common sense; as we all know in fact it took the deaths of 95 people and a judicial enquiry to make them admit the obvious.

Nevertheless, the end of the Thatcher/Moynihan era, while depriving fanzines of some choice subject matter, has ushered in a new era of optimism. Just a year ago the idea that 10 Downing Street might be occupied by a football fan would have seemed fantastic, and even if John Major may not be the sort of fan who'd travel to a midweek fixture at Hartlepool or stand on a rain soaked terrace in a January gale, and even if he is overplaying his man-of-the-people credentials with an eye on an impending election, he's made his bed and must lie in it. He cannot now afford to show indifference to the fate of the game.

The shock of Hillsborough and gratitude at the rescinding of the ID card threat meant opposition to the all-seat stadia proposal was slow to get off the ground. If all seat meant all-safe, all-comfortable, all-new, all-well appointed then it might be a good idea. But it is doubtful whether even the top clubs can live up to these ideals, never mind the Halifax's and Maidstone's. The Taylor report failed to explain how simply closing the terraces or bolting benches onto them would make football grounds any safer or pleasanter. Thankfully, this now seems to have been acknowledged and the threat is receding.

The 1990 World Cup was also a positive boost for the English game. Not because England managed to finish fourth in what was, in truth, an appallingly mediocre tournament, but because the media decided to reverse the usual set-'em-up-knock-'em-down process, as the failure-hungry hacks gradually came to terms with the awful reality that England might actually win the World Cup and their papers faced being left behind in the tide of patriotic fervour. No doubt as the European Championship progresses they will once again be ready to pounce on the merest hint of fallibility and distort every instance of an Englishman so much as passing wind in public on foreign soil into a major case of hooliganism, but for the time being there's an uneasy truce. The benefits are that the England team are household names for the first time in twenty years, and heartily though we may be sick of Gazza, when such things are rekindling interest in the game among the pre-teen generation raised on computer games and american football it would be stupid to moan too loudly.

This book is the second in a series. It may well be the last. When I started work on '*El Tel Was A Space Alien*' I felt I had some crusading purpose, to bring fanzines to a wider audience. That has certainly been achieved, though not in any major part by me. The circulations of many individual fanzines are larger than the print run of this book. Nevertheless, so many people told me they enjoyed '*El Tel...*' and asked me when Volume 2 would be published that I think I can honestly say this book was brought to you by public demand. Fanzines are here to stay.

MARTIN LACEY

chapter I

RODNEY, RODNEY!

ISSUE TWO

40 P

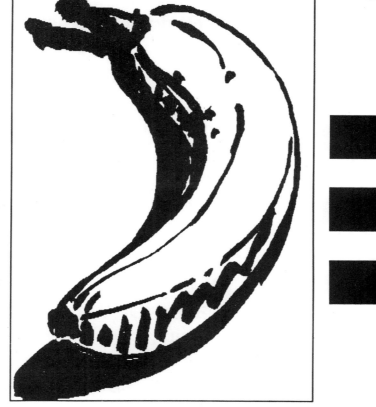

The Banana   Phenomena

Oh Blimey! It's Frank Sidebottom

Football in The 1990's. What Chance?

Rodney, Rodney! is a general interest Fanzine based in Manchester, originally inspired by Rodney Marsh. Choosing not to dwell on the ugliness of soccer sectarianism, it covers the usual fanzine topics.

Rodney, Rodney! rose from the ashes of an ill-managed and under resourced record label called Ugly Man Records in September 1988. Having lost copious amounts of money bringing out records that people could not find in the shops it seemed a natural progression into the world of alternative football publishing. In awe of the likes of Absolute Game and When Saturday Comes, dazzled by the writing, amazed by their depth of knowledge, Rodney, Rodney! was an attempt to emulate. In the 7 issues that have ensued we have improved with every issue, which says an awful lot about the first issue rather than the seventh. The most striking feature of early issues was the occasional and inexplicable disappearance of words. Our word processor could have benefited from a slightly more thorough operator. The readers entered sweepstakes to see how many mistakes would appear in the next issue. The contributors seethed and some left. The magazine became infrequent as external projects tended to get in the way. In May '89 we released a compilation LP protesting against the dreaded ID. We also arranged a Benefit gig starring the Icicle Works in aid of Hillsborough vicyims. Football books by Frank Sidebottom followed. All these activities diverting us away from the steady flow of fanzine prose. All this has been rescued by the appointment of Chris Salt as official editor. Rodders is now appearing in all the usual fanzine haunts on a regular two monthly basis. The quality of the writing is improving and it's presentation too.

If you want to know more about Rodney Rodney and the myriad of activities that it covers drop us a line. and if you enclose a stamped addressed envelope with enough stamps on it you can have a whole load of back issues for nothing.

POLICE TO SPONSOR LEYLAND/DAF RIOT VAN TROPHY

The Italians are being thorough in their preparations for the World Cup. Recently a party of Carabinieri has been over in this country on a fact finding mission. Our Midlands correspondent was on hand.

It's a Saturday in March and Wolves are entertaining Leeds United in an all-ticket second Division promotion clash. It is not a sell out because ticket sales were stopped earlier in the week on police advice to allow for the possibility that forgeries are in circulation. (no forged tickets were found).

It will have been made clear to the Italian visitors that segregation and saturation are the bywords when policing such a 'high risk' game. A massive police presence makes itself known in the town (the West Midlands Police already being well practised in the art of harassing pre match drinkers), as well as outside and inside the ground. Your correspondent notes the deployment of ten riot vans, twelve horses and well in excess of a hundred police officers. The re-assurance provided to the spectators by this vast expenditure on overtime is furthered by being regularly buzzed by the "hooli-copter".

Saturation policing having been achieved your correspondent now looks to segregation. The visiting fans are tucked safely behind their fences separated from harm by an extensive no man's land, helpfully marked on the map on their tickets. But wait, what's this? A group of Leeds followers are being led into the section of terracing reserved for home supporters - by the police. Cue, violence, arrests, ejections and a kick off delay.

Now I wonder what our visiting fact finders have discovered after their day at Molineux. Certainly there has appeared to be evidence of the kind of tribal violence that they will have been forewarned about. But they will have been told that such outbursts are very much a rarity these days? Or will they have been encouraged to get their retaliation in first and adopt the heavy handed policing methods advocated in the West Midlands? Were the police simply proving their incompetence by shepherding the visiting supporters into the home section or was there a point being made? Your correspondent remains unsure but is confident that the carabinieri will have returned to sunnier climes with a less than positive view of English Supporters.

Your Midland Correspondent

---

crowd took up the chant of "nazis Raus!", and visibly wilted at the sight of the skull and crossbones flag. So did the H.S.V. Skinheads at the derby; some of them were responsible for killing two Turkish 'Gastarbeiter' not so long back.

Over to my left is an Irish Tricolour tastefully embellished with an Ireland football scarf next to one with the local anarchosyndicalists' red star on black background. Most of the Flags - all big and home made - are in St Pauli brown and white, and the only Union Jack has 'Sex Pistols' hand sewn into it. It's bearer is a serious Rotten clone.

As popular as flags are hand-held mopheads made out of shredded paper - during Volker's walkabout the entire bunker end seems to be populated by Harpo Marx clones doing that deranged HM head dance thing. Fans push past me carrying bin liners full of the stuff to distribute like Christ's loaves and fishes to all the waiting Marxists.

The Werder team stroll onto the sward for a pre match jog, resplendent in pink and turquoise day-glo tracksuits which make Franz Beckenbauer's dug-out wear look positively tasteful. Ugghh! Yeuch! Aaagghh! this is hard kitsch! A muffled chant of 'Vac-er-da' rises up from the boys from Bremen, two thousand strong, finding their voices at last. They've segregated theselves behind one goal like we used to, well clear of the most vociferous areas of home support, but there are pockets of brown and white even amongst the boys from Bremen. Street on derby day. Hardly anyone is joining in my neighbour's response - "Was ist Grun und stinkt wie Fisch? - Werder Bremen", mostly because they also come from a port but also because no-one hates Werder; they are a kind of Forest, with a record of low-budget success. Germany rejoiced when they pipped the despised Bayern for the title two years back, but even so .....those tracksuits!

For 'Die Profis mit Herz' (that's 'heart' and nothing to do with the sponsors renting out motors) this is the 'difficult' second season. The St Pauli Phenomenom was the main talking point in the last Bundesliga term, in which the so-called championship contenders meekly surrendered the title to a worse than par Bayern. The team's style rocked the Bundesliga like Wimbledon's did our First Division, by running for each other and not being over-respectful to skillful opponents.

The deterministic, elitist West German football mentality dictates that promoted clubs get relegated in their first season and that hardly anybody wins away from home. To quote Corporal Jones for the second issue running 'they don't like it up 'em!' and this was borne out when Bayern Munich's management launched a formal complaint after their 0-0 draw at Millerntor, meaning to the League about the St Pauli fans being too close to the pitch. 'Typically, too, the Hillsborough disaster 'could not have happened anywhere in Germany apart from St Pauli' according to the German press.

Complaints too from the League about Millerntor being unsegregated (the only one), but because there has been no trouble to speak of, no action was forthcoming, which allowed the club to spend its profit instead on floodlights (not new floodlights - just floodlights!)

When the teams finally came out Werder had mercifully swapped their turquoise and pink for green and white. Most of the game was played out to the accompaniment of chanting which swept right round the tight arena - 'Zan - Pow - Lee' to British ears. The female fans - at leats 25% of the crowd by my reckoning - were every bit as passionate as the menfolk, which sheds some light on all this trendy nonsense about needing to sanitise and seat crowds in order to attract 'families'. This is not the only modern myth exploded by the St Pauli phenomenom. H.S.V. represent just about everything which the British Press, the Government, the League and the F.A. want to 'modernise' our clubs into becoming, but they mean nothing in Hamburg. On the contrary, St. Pauli has soul; an anti establishment soul which has breathed fresh life into and bred many imitations within the Bundesliga. Unlike inflatables, the bubble is yet to burst. Fan culture is developing as never before - even Eintracht Frankfurt fans have adopted the skull and crossbones flag, and, overall, Bundesliga gates are up a quarter of a million on last season.

As I was getting the beers in at Millerntor at half time I spied someone running up the stairs to the terraces with a T Shirt on his back which read "No one likes us, we don't care - Millwall". "Very apt, 'arry," I mused. I suppose it is the nearest we come.

Final Score: St Pauli 0 Werder Bremen 0

The Double Agent

Rodney, Rodney! is planning a weekend excursion to Hamburg for a match during April , quite possibly over Easter anybody interested drop us a line.

RODNEY, RODNEY!

ZAN - POW - LEE

Eine Grundübung beim FC St. Pauli. Die Spieler suchen direkten Kontakt zu den Fans.

Imagine a club with a catchment area which combines Belfast's Falls Road and the Liverpool docks together with London's Soho and Notting Hill. Imagine it has a tight little ground next to Blackpool Pleasure Beach.

Imagine this ground has no segregation, but anybody making monkey noises at the opposition's black players is intimidated into silence by hundreds of Punk anarchists chanting "Nazis Out"

Imagine that the keeper takes the field giving the clenched fist salute and goes on demonstrations to support local squatters.

Imagine the club thanks its fans for their loyalty by subsidising two special trains to the last away game of the season at less than a third of the normal fare and by selling beer at 25p a pint after the final home game.

Imagine a new religion for the alienated, the unemployed, the hilarious and the left.

Its easy if you try........go on! ....read on.

The St. Pauli experience begins with a stroll through Hamburg's 'Dom', one of the world's biggest fair-grounds. The outrageous sights, sounds and all the smells of the fair set you up just nicely for the carnival atmosphere at St Pauli home games, but the ground itself is hidden behind a giant slab of concrete - the bunker built as a refuge from Mr Churchill's saturation bombing. It's about five stories high and topped with a six metre thick concrete roof. Hamburg has loads of these, many serving nowadays as rehearsal venues for Heavy Metal Bands (Residents Associations eat your hearts out)

St Pauli's Millerntor ground lies betwixt this bunker and the Holsten Wall, built many centuries past to keep out the Danes from the neighbouring town of Altona (trans: All Too Near). In days of yore the tiny dwellings of the poor cuddled vainly up to the outside of this same city wall, but when the Danes came a-rootin an' a lootin' it was the little guys who copped for it. Unlike the proper Burghers within, the Hanseatic Oi Polloi got neither civic status nor the civic protection that went with it.

Likewise F.C. St. Pauli, the unwanted gatecrashers in the Bundesliga, the inner city urchins with no stars and no high rollers. Civic status is reserved for Hamburger S.V., ex-European Champs and big league perennials - H.S.V. get to play in the 60,000

capacity municipal concrete bowl. St. Pauli get Millerntor

"Tor - Tor - Mill-ern-tor" sing the home fans ('Tor' is the German word for 'Goal' as well as 'Gate') rounding the bunker, followed by "wir wollem keine - Bayern Schweine" (use your imagination) and the international "Ole - Ole, Ole......". No Werder Bremen fans in sight yet. No turnstiles either, just a gap in the boundary fence where the steward ex-changes your ticket for a red card (to wave when St Pauli players get fouled) and in you go.

Then.......TOTAL, COMPLETE CULTURE SHOCK!..... a young woman - in jeans - gives me a body search, as thorough as the ones we know and love over here, but with none of the attendant feelings of hu-miliation or insult. She's not police, but an ordinary member of the supporters' club. In fact, I do not see a policeman all afternoon.

Culture Shock Nummer Zwei : the b-beer t-tent under the stand! While I am stood there catching flies my minders are up the steps to claim a place on the terrace; only then will an emissary be sent for the beers. I soon see why - apart from the seats the ground is 95% full, and there is still an hour to go before kick off.

At first, second and third glance I can't quite believe that this place holds 20,551 even with the ten rows of recently added seats perched precariously on scaffolding right behind us. Still less do I credit last season's home average gate - 20,848 - until my minders explain that St Pauli were made to play their home derby against H.S.V. in the concrete bowl. 53,960 turned up to see a draw.

Last season was their first in the top flight for 10 years and lessons had been learned from that catas-

trophe. Back then, the club opted to play at the concrete bowl, miles from their community, and spent too many Marks on so-called stars deemed essential to survival in the big league. Big crowds never materialised and the 'team' of big names was crap - they didn't just go down, but bust as well, and ended up in an amateur league (so there's hope Newport!) before putting together a revival, bit by bit.

Understandably, then, this time around the club did not flee its nest, did not buy any stars, and budg-eted for a 14,000 average crowd it worked - they finished 10th, 6 places behind H.S.V., but overshot their gate projection by 50%! H.S.V. got the 14,000 average gate!

Instructive, eh? Meanwhile, H.S.V. fans sulk in corners about how only half the Millerntor faithful understand the laws of the game. Maybe they have a point, of sorts - a lot come along to be part of the street theatre - type terrace culture and community pride which infuses Millerntor on match days.

St Pauli isn't just sailors, ships and the Reeperbahn. Mention the 'Hafenstrasse' to any German and his/ her brain pans up newsreel footage of hundreds of leather-jacketed, visored, anarchosyndicalist squat-ters pouring out of the tenements on St Pauli's 'Harbour Street' to do battle with the police. The Hamburg senate wants to knock down this old quarter for 'redevelopment', but St Pauli and the neighbouring districts of Altona and Eimsbuttel make up a left wing city within a city, and the 'Haf-enstrasse is their Orgreave. The Skull and Cross-bones flag at the front of me on the terrace is their symbol. Around it are gathered leather jackets sprouting hair of every hue. St Pauli is their club.

And here cometh their man - Volker Ippig, Keeper of the Net and Keeper of the faith. The crowd go gaga as Volker strides out for his solo 'pitch inspec-tion', which consists mainly of repeated exchanges of clenched fist salutes between their man and all those in the crowd who were with him on the last 'Hafenstrasse' Solidarity Demonstration. This is way beyond hero worship; it is closer to the bond between Liverpool players and people in those dark days after Hillsborough. It is an affirmation of community.

The unsegregated Werder fans are respectfully silent during this ritual. even the harder boys amongst them would not dream of crossing the 'Hafen-strasse' street fighters of TV News fame. The only hint of trouble throughout the whole of last season was when the right wing Borussen Front travelled up from the Ruhr when Dortmund visited. England fans will remember this scum from'88. At Millerntor they ran into a wall of noise as the entire

RODNEY, RODNEY!

I'm not a racist but I once sat in front of one at a football ground.... it all happened at a recent Friday night game in the North West. Sat on the next to back row of the stands in front of the DJ's box, I specifically remembered the man on the mike wishing the visiting fans a warm welcome and safe journey home. It struck a chord so I turned to look at the announcer. The game commenced and sad to say we were positioned within earshot of a regular Mr Knowledgeable. He showed a breathtaking knowledge of the visitor's team, knowing all their names. The No 4 for the visitors was a very combative and aggressive character and soon incurred his wrath. The player's style was pugnacious to say the least, but the basis of the smartarse's problem was the colour of No 4's skin. What started off as light but irritating " watch the coloured gentleman' progressed to the more offensive repertoire of the racist. When the home team brought on their "psycho" who proceeded to dump the No.4 on the pitch he's only black'. After another heated meeting of the minds the referee brought the players together to shake hands. "Now wash your hands' chipped up our friend. On turning round I came to the reality that our foul mouthed racist buddie was in fact the man with the "good night God bless' sincerity for the visiting fans at the start of the game. This explained his expert knowledge of the London Visitors ("Cockney Gits' as he called them out of the confines of his glass box). What made the whole episode a hundred times sadder was the sniggering members of the junior supporters' club four rows in front who probably see the mindless drivel we had to endure as the norm and in future years will treat the people who sit in front of them with the same. No Future!!

"A WOMAN'S PLACE IS IN THE BOUTIQUE"

During last season the wife of Blackpool F.C.'s Chairman was excluded from Tranmere Rovers' boardroom and macho talking shop. Sheffield Wednesday even have their women's hideout, the 'Blue Room', surely a a misnomer. In commenting on the possible role of women in football, nay society as a whole, the gypsyesque Ron Atkinson quipped that 'Women should be in the kitchen, discotheque and boutique'. And probably in that order, eh, Ron? Ron's no doubt stuck in the some social timewarp too as to the shopping habits of women. How

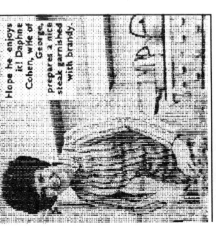

Hope he enjoys it! Daphne Cohen, wife of George, prepares a nice steak garnished with brandy.

many boutiques do you see these days?

Anyway picture the scene ten minutes before kick off in the dressing room of a struggling second division outfit. The 'Boss' is extolling the virtues of cool mediation and clear heads before her motley collection of troglodytes go out to confront the raw boned collection of extras from the production company down the road (the opposition).

'Be calm, be confident, be fulfilled.'

No it's not the resurrection of Mal(Practice) Allison within the grit and gristle of the English Football League, Soccer for Thinkers (Pelham Books 1967) but an extract from 'The Manageress' Channel 4's recently concluded six rounder.

Cheri Lungi, as Gabriella Benson represents post feminist woman's charge into our male dominated physical play ground. Prompted by her ex-Italian international footballing Father (cum property speculator) she takes on the role of nurturer and childminder to a scheming, cigar smoking wide boy chairman and the usual collection of working class lads with nouveau riche spending habits (the team).

Ms Benson, in conjunction with her reluctant but honest coach Eddie 'players today don't know they're born' Johnson, set about changing results , tactics and attitudes.

During the course of the season we're taken on a Charlie Cooks Tour of soccer's less desirable aspects, 'Character forming racial abuse!!' from home supporters, the dubious managerial practices of the ex manager 'that bastard Jacksaw' Freddie Taylor, players indulging their talents off the field with under age schoolgirls, avaricious private box developers, mountains of beer consumed by culturally unfulfiled Gladiators and the extra marital affairs of club employees.

What of some of the players?

Gary Helliwell: Club Captain, experienced functional midfield metronome and professional beer drinker.

Jim Wilson: Literally dies with his boots on after mirroring the gambling obsessions of Stan Bowles and yes you guessed it, his wife's sleeping with the ex manager and the Vice Chairman. But, relief all round, not at the same time.

Charlie O Keefe: Philandering goal scoring paedophile.

Club Hardman: Whose name and talent escape me, a tough and brave player who

kicks the weaker opponents but has a heart of gold and a mentally retarded son.

The Graduate Footballer: Approves wholeheartedly with the Boss's appointment, reads the Guardian and patronises his fellow professionals. He suggests to one of his more gullible team mates that the Football League has introduced a new competition for the middle two teams of each of the four divisions. The trophy being the Dalkon Shield, another case of barriers to entry into the European competition perhaps.

Perry Gardner: Helmut Haller goal scoring specialist and 'fanny Merchant'. The seminal savage boot of FOUL no 30, June 1975 described the fanny merchant as, a highly skilled player in terms of ball skills, but lacking the will orb the ability to kick opponents. Therefore likely to be put out of the game by a competent Ball winner e.g Stan Bowles was called a fanny merchant by Jack Charlton.

The supporters are seen as being racist, semi literate disposable and invisibly lost in a sea of animated extras witnessing bouts of Don Howe stunt arranged plays. Alas a thoroughly depressing first half performance.

Who can save the team and the series from such cynical scriptwriting? Well our fanny merchant pops up with two late winners and Ms Benson fights off the property speculators whilst at the same time re affirming that the real power in the game lies on the terraces and on the pitch. She cites the late Don Revie as her main influence, a 'good man who cared' the first manager to mother his team. Women in Football? Well there's always hope given the continuing success of the Dalkon Shield.

Bernard Lisewski

RODNEY, RODNEY!

WHEN IRISH EYES ARE SMILING...

(They're secretly smirking at us!)

I want to take you on a journey through a country, which many people may not have visited. It's the beautiful Emerald Isle. Famed for its writers and artists, its blarney and Guiness. Home to many rock stars, Van Morrison and U2, Chris De Burgh and Bob Geldof. Together I think that we'll find a few surprises. My guide will not be justice to the delights of this hallowed nation. For reference please consult the map.

All geography students will be familiar with the conundrum; which country has the largest capital city in the World? Ireland because it's capital is always Dublin. Less well known however is a small village to the south of Fair City, nestling on the coast, called Preston. This was the birth place of Ireland's most talented defender of the Eighties, Mark Lawrenson.

Moving Southwards towards Wicklow, we pass through the small village of Liverpool from which another national hero, John Aldridge was born. Many visitors would progress further to the home of the exquisite crystal in Waterford, but few would spot the small market form of Barnsley en route, whence its most famous son Mick McCarthy strode to fame with Manchester City, Celtic and Eire. On the outskirts of Waterford lies Maidstone, the birth place of Ireland's dynamic midfield player Andy Townsend.

Moving west from Waterford we encounter Cork and Bantry Bay, a south westerly area which has been a rich hunting ground for national supremo, Jack Charlton, himself from Ashington, Co Cork. Among his national squad other Corkers are Kevin Sheedy of Builth Wells, John Sheridan of Manchester and Chris Morris of Newquay, the three villages which encircle Killarney.

Twixt Killarney and Limerick lie some delightful places which have unearthed further soccer genius, most notably the sleepy hamlets of West Ham and St. Paul's Cray whose sons have been the gaelic heroes Chris Hughton and Tony Cascarino. Our feast in this vernal land would be replete only with visits to Galway and Athlone, which lie on the axis across the island from the capital. A path, which must have been trodden by midfield ace, Ray Houghton on his way from Glasgow to his

Galway school.

Travelling worth through Sligo and the Blue Letter Mountain into Co Donegal, even more of the splendours of this magical isle unfolds. Little wonder that it inspired Gerry Peyton from the tiny fishing village of Birmingham to the great goalkeeping heights he has achieved.

Our coastal route has netted some rich picking which I'll repeat for your enjoyment.

	GERRY PEYTON (BIRMINGHAM)	
CHRIS MORRIS (NEWQUAY)	MARK LAWRENSON (PRESTON)	MICK McCARTHY (BARNSLEY)
		CHRIS HUGHTON (WEST HAM)
RAY HOUGHTON (GLASGOW)	ANDY TOWNSEND (MAIDSTONE)	JOHN SHERIDAN (MANCHESTER)
		KEVIN SHEEDY (BUILTH WALLS)
	JOHN ALDRIDGE (LIVERPOOL)	TONY CASCARINO (ST.PAUL'S GRAY)

A gaelic treat for Irish eyes! If you want a substitute try Paul McGrath of Ealing in Co. Tipperary.

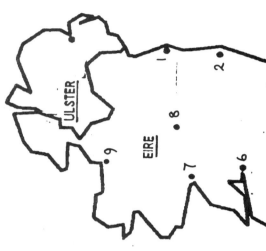

KEY

1. Dublin
2. Wicklow
3. Waterford
4. Cork
5. Killarney
6. Limerick
7. Galway
8. Athlone
9. Sligo

RODNEY, RODNEY!

Ask the Expert

In this issue we play host to Alf Bones, ex-pro with Scarthorpe Rovers and Madchester Albion. Alf passes on his tips in his own irrepressible fashion.

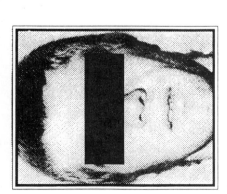

Dear Alf
I am a 14 year old defender who regularly comes up against centre forwards a good six inches taller than me. Obviously I find that I'm beaten in the air every time any advice?

Robert Stevens, Nottingham.

Dear Rob
Try and time your jumps so at the very least you manage to put your opponent off. Another tip is to learn to anticipate the destination of your opponents header - interception is always effective. If all else fails though, squeeze him by the knackers until he sings like Jimmy Somerville.

Dear Alf
Could you settle an argument between me and my dad are having? He says you were sent off 22 times in your career I reckon it's only 20. Who's right? Also, my dad wants to know have you ever had a lobotomy?

Simon Nicholls

Dear Simon
The answer to that last question is no, I haven't - I don't like French food. But dad is right about the sendings off. And don't forget the 71 Bookings, 5 Charges of bringing the game into disrepute, 3 court appearances, and two prison sentences. Read all about it in my new book ''Breakin' Bones''.

"Play acting is spoiling the game"

Dear Alf
Were you disappointed when only 2,000 people turned up for your testimonial match?
Alison Mackay, Yeovil

Dear Alison
To be honest, I was more disappointed that only 2 players turned up, you only find out who your true friends are, when your looking to get hold of 50 grand, tax-free to open a sports shop or fashion boutique.

Dear Alef
What's your opinion on the professional foul rule?
Ross McGillis

Dear Ross
I've always stuck to it wherever possible. ha..ha..only joking. I think that rule has killed the game stone dead; well at least it's limited my game.

RODNEY, RODNEY!

6

THERE'S ONLY FIVE PETER GRUMMITTS......

In the beginning there was the old cigarette card - a packet of ten 'players', a portrait of Tom Finney to make up the team and a guarantee of chronic bronchitis within ten years. Since the late 60's, Panini have had the market sewn up with their slick stick-it-in-your-glossy-album operation. But in between these two disparate ages, there has been life for the football card collector. Ah yes, the golden (bubble gum) age of football cards.! Let us enter the wonderful world of six Andy Lockheads, eight John Kayes, ten Terry Hennesseys, a dozen Len Badgers and five Peter Grummitts....

God bless America - the old tart introduced the bubble gum card to the country on the back of such imported TV faves as Batman, the Man from U.N.C.L.E. and the Monkees. Whadaya know, next thing the film star features of Bill Foulkes and Brian Labone were being packaged in the same glamorous style. Suddenly the Ted Helmsley's (*) of this world were being projected to star status courtesy of bubble gum cards, the least desirable footballers became the most desirable of schoolboy commodities.

Eyes and skies of the photo portrait used to be made bluer by the artist's pen. The whole sweet smelling package was a million miles away from a rain soaked, wind swept Saturday afternoon 0-0 draw. The sweet smell? well that was the bubble gum, a thin strip of pink that lost its sickly taste within fifteen seconds of vigorous chewing. There were days when our street was littered with a thousand little pink strips that had been immediately jettisoned from freshly opened packets of 'Football Stars'.

The main force behind this revolution was a company called A & B C, not surprisingly, an American company. The cards themselves were manufactured in England - how else could they obtain all the precious information that graced both sides of the cards? On the front, name, club, and position. On the reverse, a full pen pic revealing height, weight, but alas not favourite meal and pop group (the latter was probably 'Dire Straits' even then). The bottom panel on the reverse either had a quiz with magic rub-in answer, or a remarkable fact about the card's particular player, e.g. Bobby Charlton - "Did you know that Bobby is a football idol throughout the world?" Educational as well as exciting.

These cards became an addiction. We'd beg steal or borrow to be able to get a 'fix' of four or five packets. But 'bulk purchases' were often the guarantee of disappointment and you merely topped up your supply of 'swaps'. Certain combinations of players re-appeared in the same batch of packets - we were sure that John Osborne of West Brom and John Sissons of West Ham had something going together. Still, the thrill of opening a card wrapper had us hooked. The excitement of ripping the wax paper to reveal a George Best or an Eddie Gray could be counted as an early sexual experience. There developed a second transfer market at street level. In one particular set, Allan Clarke, who had become the game's most expensive player, was worth at least a Gordon Banks, a Billy Bremner and a Denis Law - his was a unique card that had been given a one off amendment - 'Leicester City transferred to Leeds United!' Jon Sammels of Arsenal on the other hand was worth sod all; art imitating life?

Of course, the magic disappeared as seasons went on. Other collectibles came along; wall posters from Tiger & Jag and Scorcher; League Ladders from Shoot; tacky medals and statuettes from the petrol companies; soccer stamps from The Sun and, most significantly the introduction of stickers and albums. Two last ditch attempts at prolonging the craze are however, worthy of mention. Anglo cards of Halifax issued the 'learn the game with the stars' series that saw the usual garish colour portraits replaced by wonderfully crap illustrations; 'pass snide remarks at the referee the Johnny Giles way' was a particular favourite. A&BC like the masters of tack that they were came up with autographed Black & White portraits - we soon doubted their authenticity when we saw that Ian Ure's signature was a beautifully flowing affair rather than a scribbled cross.

The end of the bubble gum card craze in general, signalled the end of the sixties and the end of a kind of innocence. Though more American in essence than 'Mom's apple pie', it turned our national sport into a glamorous, star studded fantasy. Let's face it. Tommy Smith never looked so good.

(*) Ted Helmsley, swift of foot full back of Sheffield United and er Sheffield United

THE BUBBLE GUM CARD TEAM (the cards that wouldn't go away)

Peter Grummit (Sheff Weds/Notts Forest)
Peter Rodrigues (Leicester City)
Ted Helmsley (Sheff Utd)
Jim McCalliog (Sheff Weds)
Ron Wylie (Birmingham City)
John Kaye (W.B.A.)
Dick Krywicki (Huddersfield Town/W.B.A.)
Bobby Tambling (Chelsea)
Andy Lockhead (Burnley)
Len Glover (Leicester City)
Peter Grummit (Sheff Weds/Notts Forest)

Any swaps get in touch with Craig Ferguson c\o us.

RODNEY, RODNEY!

The papers were full of the story, it was on the news, everyone concerned was talking about it....."The return of the Messiah"

Unfortunately I had no idea who the Messiah or Stokoe were. Paul my boyfriend could hardly contain himself. I approached him as he leapt about the living room and tentatively queried who Stokoe was. - I must point out that Paul is normally a level headed human being, until you mention SUNDERLAND - he stopped jumping and looked at me dumb founded. At this moment I realised Sunderland fan he went on to tell me who Stokoe is; he spared no detail of Stokoe's achievements. Was that all?... a football manager, why the hysterics. He asked me to go the match with him, no one else was going, and in the circumstances, I agreed, it seemed the least I could do.

THE CRACK OF DAWN

The big day arrived Saturday, Bradford City v. Sunderland. I got up at the crack of dawn and rushed around trying to get everything organised before I caught the bus to meet Paul at the train station. I was half an hour late and boy was he annoyed! I could tell by the way he kept clenching and unclenching his hands. We had missed the train and would have to get a later one. This meant less drinking time. Eventually we boarded the train and off we went. Paul started to look out of the window and back at me, sweat breaking out on his forehead. I sat in guilty silence. I silently prayed the train would hurry up .

Once in Bradford we made our way towards the ground, on foot. I am known for my aversion to walking but after arriving late at the station I thought better about complaining. We found a little pub near the ground. It was full of football supporters, both Bradford City and Sunderland. We got a drink and started talking to some Bradford fans. The other three discussed the various positions of teams in the league and the talked about the forthcoming match. Evidently it was a pretty big game for both teams. Anticipation was beginning to mount and I was quite enjoying all the pre-match premonitions and forecasts.

TEN TO THREE

As we approached the gates of the Bradford City ground I was overcome with excitement. I could not wait to see 'the Messiah'. We went through the gates and followed everyone else into the stand. I looked at the clock - Ten to Three, ten minutes to go. I fidgeted and looked around at my fellow supporters; they looked like ordinary human beings, not the thugs I had been led to believe all football fans were.

They all went wild! They were jumping around, whistling, waving their arms about and chanting "Stokoe" to the tune of "Amazing Grace". I looked for 'the Messiah'.

"Where is he? Where is he?" I asked Paul. He pointed to this little old man with a wizened face wearing a shabby sheepskin and a dirty old trilby hat.

"Is that him Have I come all this way to see him?" The bubble of excitement had burst. The match kicked off amid the usual shouts and cheers. I will not bore you with the details - I cannot remember them to be honest - but it is sufficient to say that Bradford scored three goals and Sunderland only two.

HERDED OUT

As we left the ground I looked around at the dejected faces of the Sunderland ranks. We were herded out of the ground; most of the fans filed quietly on to the coaches. We moved towards the railway station. The journey home was a quiet affair with Paul in a desolate mood, sinking further and further into depression.

I tried to cheer him up by saying it was only a game of football. When he glared at me I guessed it was the wrong thing to say.

Sally Bond

RODNEY, RODNEY!

big five?!!, big shmive!

in depth report by frank sidebottom.

hello fantastic footballing fans,............
.... frank sidebottom here actually,.....
and every now and then we hear or read yet
another thing about a "super league" with
the "**big five**",.... and if you ask me,........
i think the whole idea is **bobbins**.

for a start who <u>are</u> the "big five"?
well we all know just 'who' consider that
they 'are' "big five", but on 'what' do they
base that?, it can't be on current form
as that would not include manchester utd.
who seem to always be mentioned in a 'big
five', and should this 'super league' have
been formed in 1960, burnley, wolves and
leicester city would've been in it. now i
know everyone automaticly thinks of the
'big five' including liverpool....but they
were not even in division 1 in 1960!

so.... how do we decide who are "big five"?
on current form southampton are in!, or
maybe it should be on attendances, which
would put manchester city in, or if it's
on grounds then sheffield wednesday are
in, or if it's size of shorts then my team
the timperley big shorts are in..!

so you can see the problem.   i mean spurs
always consider themselves "big five" but
man city push them into 6th place on crowds,
wednesday push them into 7th with a better
ground and they only hang on in 8th place
due to paul gasgoins shorts being bigger
than mine!

and anyway, who in their right mind would
want to see spurs v man united week-in
week out...., and imagine if you came
bottom of the "big five" league !?!?
but what most teams would give to be 5th
in division 1,!.

also it would mean the loss of the 'giant-
killer' which makes football so so fantastic,
and how can the two big north east clubs
be excluded, or sheffield united (the 1st club)
who started it, or **blackburn** who have won
loads or notts forest or northwich victoria
who have the oldest ground..?, give me the
"quite big 92" anyday with the thought
that streetly celtic (currently bottom) of
the midland combination league only have
417 teams to climb above to be in the
"big five" themselves. (only a thought
but the chance is there).

so come on martin edwards, you know the 'big
five' is so that united only have 4 other
teams in the way of your title, and come
on terry venables, just because you spent
your way in, and come on kenny...is the
"big five" so you avoid the re-match with

alty f.c.?. and be realistic george graham,
how can you have a knock-out cup with
5 teams in?, unless say everton get a bye
to the final, and the other 4 play to see
who meets them.!?.

no,... i am totaly against a "super league",
infact put division one back to 22 clubs,
and remember readers there is only **one**
'big five',...and that's jackie charlton!

above — big 5...... little ½.

chapter 2

WHY CITY?

In the beginning, back in 1955.... It was the birth of rock'n'roll, Blackboard Jungle, Rock Around The Clock.... and the rebirth of the Maine Road Blues with.... The Revie Plan.

I was 11 and a goalie at the time. My dad was Irish and a Bolton supporter. He sometimes took me to Burnden Park and cruelly made me stay 'til the final whistle. My eldest brother was a latent Blue and my elder brother a teddy boy (now a director of his own firm!) so he didn't support anyone except the local Palais! They all pulled my leg about City, including my elder sister, but it was good grounding. I became a goalie because I was useless as an outfield player so I was stuck in goal for the bomb site 20 a side games. I made one stupendous save which I knew nothing about as my style was to march up and down from one set of coats to the other. Whilst on the march the local star whacked in a shot which caught my left kneee in the ascendancy and the ball flew off back down the pitch apace to everyone's delight and amusement, and I made the position my own!

City had just reached Wembley (and beaten United three times in the season), they also had the best goalie around, Bert Trautmann, and the fact that he was a German just added to the mystique. The other local clubs had lousy goalies, United had Ray Wood (an English international!?) and Bolton had Ken Grieves, an Australian Lancashire cricketer, so it was no contest. I became a Blue and Bert was my role model and hero. I failed him badly!

By this time I was at secondary school in Salford, a Reds stronghold (until they all moved to London) and the only Blue in a class of 40. I learnt early on that most if not all Reds are obnoxious, arrogant and conceited which is why they're nicknamed 'The Rags'. It's not just a play on words but means Red Arrogant Gits and no self respecting Manc. would want to become one. Basically we can take it (and dish it out a bit) but they like to dish it out but can't take it, typically running on the pitch in 1974 to stop the game when we were winning 1-0.

There it is then, the question that's on all outsiders' lips, answered in one(?) paragraph. That's why there's so many Blues.

THE GOOD & THE BAD & THE ....!?

So, I've seen the good times, Wembley (often), the Championship, Europe, great players, big wins..... and the bad times, relegations, drubbings, lousy players.... times when I'd start a new job with the resolution of not admitting to being a Blue, until of course I met my first ally, and it took a long time to realise that the above was governed by the way in which the club was run.

From an early age, 14/15, I was always one of those who wrote in to the papers and this lasted well into my mid life crisis. I don't know why? If anything remotely funny or controversial struck me I'd dash off a letter or, with the help of my wife Sue, a cartoon to the local media, a fine moment (?!) being Tommy Doc. showing a card we'd sent him on his prediction incapability on TVAM in '85. Being into memorabilia and old programmes helped too. Poem and 'greatest team' competitions were naffly entered and won and by 86/87 we'd (Sue was well and truly roped in by now) a dossier worthy of a fanzine. Unfortunately we'd never heard of them.

I remember being on the platform waiting for the 'Special' train at Watford after yet another away defeat in '85 surveying the sad faces of the Blues fans and thinking 'These boys (and girls) need their own mag to cheer 'em up a bit on their travels', but never quite got round to producing the goods.

A 'Friends of Manchester City' organisation was attempted in '86 and I put together a 'Best of King of the Kippax' (used the pseudonym then aswell) but it never got off the ground.

At the time I was enjoying reading 'Attila' in the News on Sunday and at the same time I got hold of the first two issues of 'When Saturday Comes' off a friend and I was hooked. In the summer of '87 I joined the F.S.A. and met folk of the same ilk, particularly Ged O'Brien, Mike Van Vleck of 'Heartbeat' and Martin Gordon of 'Just Another Wednesday' (this blokes a doctor and he doesn't feel daft doing a mag so why should I?) Then followed some contributions to a City fanzine, which just beat me to it, and then an invitation from 'When Saturday Comes' for an article duly printed in October '88 and I was away.

KING OF THE KIPPAX ARRIVES!

I was always fired up by injustice, and Heysel, Moyny, the European Championship media coverage and the ID cards proved to be the final straw(s). The existing City zine couldn't cope with 20 pages of material from me per month and I disagreed with the editorial view plus we were too vulnerable with only one zine. So 'King of the Kippax' was envisaged in embryo. Naively I thought that it wouldn't be too much different than bringing work home, sets of minutes, specifications etc. but it's a whole new ball game.

Everyone now knows that 'The Kippax' is City's equivalent of 'The Kop' and after a few days of arguing with the co-editor, Sue, we decided to call the mag 'King of the Kippax' instead of 'Kippaxed'. It's still a sore point, I can tell you, and was nearly the end of a wonderful relationship! Not a month goes by without this voice piping up 'See, told you we should've called it "Kippaxed" '.

WHAT'S IT ALL ABOUT?

I was more interested in hitting the major issues rather than slating the club (plenty to go at on both counts though) and also providing a homourous and informative mag and maybe giving a positive approach to our quest to return to Div. 1 'cos we'd had a bad start.

So the main thrust of the mag was to look forward to games and awayday facilities with ground diagrams etc. , to look back at what actually happened, (where is this hooliganism?), sound off at the ID cards proposal, back to Europe etc. and promote the F.S.A., and it's pretty well stayed like that. No gimmicks, just an attempt at a good mag. Hopefully! It's a very personal mag and the only 'royal' one in the business, from one of if not THE oldest editorial team!

Anyway my mate Tony said he could get 500 copies done fairly cheaply so in September '88 I put together KK1 aiming for 16 pages but achieving 18 then finishing up with 20. I decided to charge 50p but my best stuff had gone elsewhere so I wasn't confident of selling a lot, and 500 was a lot!

LIFT OFF

KK1 was launched at Barnsley. I knew I'd have a captive audience in the car park on the approach to the away end but very nearly bottled out and went in without selling. I thought 'Who's interested in my views?' (KK1 was virtually all my own) but I'd served my time with the media, took a deep breath. thought of the printing costs I had to clear, sold about 80 and felt like a real (but conspicuous) king, for a day at least.

The 500 went fairly quickly with a bit of help from my friends and another batch was printed to tide us over till KK2 came out. For this one we borrowed a few hundred quid off the bank, interviewed Jim Reeve of Piccadilly Radio, shopped around for proper printing and increased the run to 2000.

Since then we've gone from strength to strength, with contributions pouring in, thankfully, and a regular 'crew' helps out with the selling. It's a kitchen table production, generally starting after 9 p.m. when the youngest, Alex, gets to sleep (not easy with three others pounding about).

WE ARE FAMILY!?

The whole family is drafted in. My wife Sue does the cartoons and artwork, Marnie (21) does the typing, as does Marie, my mother-in-law. Kaye (14) types and sells, Danny (19) sells and even our Alex (4) has shifted a few! Method in my (pre-vasectomy) madness!

Since we started City's gone up, ID cards have gone (so far), we're back in Europe, we've had the horror of Hillsborough and the all seater stadia proposal now hovers. Also we've been invited onto TV, been on the radio and interviewed for the local papers, met and mingled with City and media 'stars' old and new and made many new friends. It never ceases to amaze us!

Of the future? It'll be more of the same whilst thirsting for new 'angles'. We hope to keep it going with maybe more frequent or bigger issues but we're never ever satisfied and will always strive to improve while retaining its homespun character.

So what's the best thing about doing a fanzine? Certainly seeing fans reading it and getting a laugh gives us a buzz and providing a platform for fans views and experiences which otherwise they wouldn't have is important as is prodding the consciences - forget the local papers and the programme. Yeah forget that!

A DIRTY WORD (PROFIT!)

Any profits made are used to improve the fanzine and this summer we were able to invest in a word processor - just in time as our second hand typewriter finally gave up the ghost. Running costs are mounting though, postage, printing, stationery, outlets etc., everyone wants a little bit more and football itself is getting dearer by the season. There's only two prices to charge to make things easy for street selling, 50p or £1. Why doesn't this government bring out the 75p coin? Whenever possible we produce 'bumper' issues for no extra charge and subscribers benefit from extra editions without any increase in fees. From time to time we make donations to charities, the FSA, Mandy Turner Appeal, Junior Blues etc.

And what do the club think, after all KK's fairly genteel and our club's not too bad with the fans, with the Junior Blues organisation, a decent supporters and travel club and admission prices among the cheapest in the country plus a chairman who despite everything is approachable? Very wary. Very wary! And so they should be! Secretly of course, they love it (!???) It's now actually 'made' the souvenir shop.

As we enter our third year of office there's no loss of interest or enthusiasm but panic sets in regularly!

DAVE WALLACE

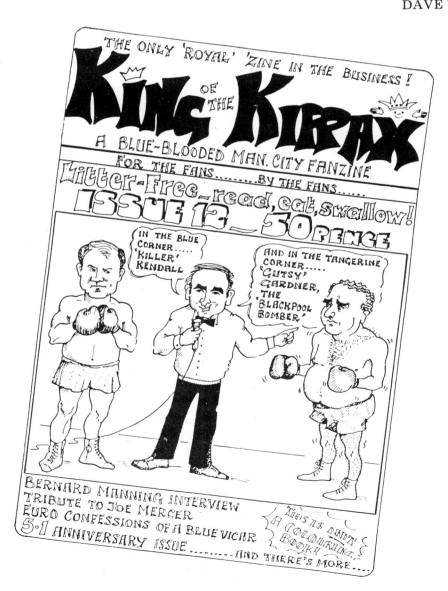

PHANTOM of the FFF Forest

(OR "YOU DON'T HAVE TO BE MAD TO BE A GOALIE — BUT IT SURE HELPS!")

SIT DOWN

'Sit down Sir' said the police chief .....
'He can't f____ing well allow that can he?'
'I wouldn't have thought so sir'
But he did.

Well the arguments raged and everyone added
their two penneth - Jimmy Greaves, Neil Midgley,
Elton Welsby, to name but a few and there was
much sniggering and smirking going on from
people who should've known better.

TURDS TRICK

So, was it a piece of quick thinking and slick
opportunism, or ungentlemanly conduct, a foul
or even a turds trick?

Definitely the latter, it was the sort of
professional foul you wouldn't normally expect
from a team like Forest - I thought that
Cloughie may have run on and clipped the lad's
earhole, but no.

Anyway, no way was it a goal and I wouldn't
like us to score 'goals' like that would you?

Gifford gave the game away when he said
'Dibble was about to throw the ball up in the air
to clear it' - and that's the crunch, because
Andy DIDN'T throw the effing thing up, it was
knocked out of his hand whilst he was in
possession and I doubt if Gifford or even the
linesman actually SAW the incident.

So it shouldn't have counted, but who am I to
judge?

UNIQUE POSITION?

Well let me tell you I'm in a unique position
because not only was I once a goalie (of sorts)
I've also been a referee. Additionally I'm
completely open and honest, fairminded, unbiased
and to clinch it in a previous life I might well
have been a Roger Gifford or even a Gary Crosby *HEAD*
(but I doubt it!) - so it wasn't a goal, Courtney
was right and that's final.

Can we have our extra point back please?

MEN HAD BALLS &

THOSE WERE THE DAYS(!?)

To judge the situation objectively though you've
got to go back to the days when men were men,
fair was fair, balls had laces (?!) Rock'n' Roll
was King and policemen, players and even
managers were older than yourself.(well myself)

Yes, I'm talking about the mid-50's that
wonderful era when the Blues beat the Reds
three times in a season and reached Wembley
twice, lifting the cup in '56.

I'm talking of the time when Everton supporters
ripped the coach doors off steam trains and
Teddy Boys wrecked cinemas as Blackboard
Jungle and Rock around the Clock hit town.

Yes, it was an era when everyone behaved
impeccably and soccer was a family game (are
you kidding) when Maggie lived in a corner
shop and even before the landlady of a well
known Manc hostelry on Liverpool Road went bent
(if she was ever straight!?)

I'm talking of the days when Bert broke his
neck in the cup final, Ray Wood had his jaw
broken the year after and Harry Gregg was
bundled into the net by 'Sir' Nat the year after
that as were goalies up and down the country,
and Jimmy Greaves, no doubt, still thought they
were over protected.

EUROPE HERE WE COME

It was also the time when we entered European
competition and T.V. coverage of soccer increased.

Now most continental teams used to cheat like
buggery, one way or another (no wonder we
dropped our hoolies on them) but one thing they
didn't do was challenge goalies, even though
they didn't half fanny about a lot in the box,
timewasting etc. No, they reckoned that
football should be played by skilful use of hand(?!)
and foot (occasionally sticking the boot in) and
goalies should be left to clear the ball so that
play could recommence. All that *THE* charging
nonsense ever did was cause aggro on and off
the field and lead to disputed goals.

CONT....

PHANTOM OF THE FOREST.

Don't get me wrong it should still be a mans
game (except at O/T !?) Maybe Dibs was a bit
dozy - maybe Lake and Hendry should've
warned him of the phantom - didn't Crosby try
something similar in the first half - didn't
Billy Whitehurst try it on for Hull at Maine Road
last season?
50-50 balls should still be challenged and there's
been times - like Chelsea's first goal last
season when Dixon should've finished in the back
of the net instead of the ball.

CHANGE THE RULES

Anyway, they then started messing about with
the rules cos of the timewasting, backpassing
etc instead of getting to grips.
Bert looked majestic bouncing the ball and
booting it or throwing it upfield. Thankfully he
was never made to roll it along the floor and
pick it up quickly as some forward steamed in.

It was after this in the mid-60's when the rules
changed, that I decided to pack in the game (it
also coincided with our championship season!) -
you try rolling the ball out on some wild hill
with the slope and a gale force wind against you,
in 6" of mud with the local nutter trying to kick
a lump out of your best bits whether in
possession or not - and having to miss the
bopping at the Plaza yet again with the latest
injury.

Other rule changes followed including that one
where if the goalie handled the ball outside the
box, he got sent off!

I remember, almost, but not quite, writing to
Peter Fox, the Stoke goalie after he suffered
as above and threatened to pack the game in.

Over the last 30 years whilst Brucie and
Beasant have recently exploited the drop back
goalie theme, unnecessary rule changes have
generally turned many modern goalies into
ungainly poseurs what with those flashy jumpers
an all!

So let's go back to letting em bounce the ball
then clearing it and little toadies like Crosby
can fade away and fester.

Dibs is far too good a goalie to let it bother
him for long, but I tell you what, wouldn't it've
been nice just for once for us to go down to
the other end & pop a couple in!

"The Biggest Name in World Football"	
A.C.Milan?	They bought Marco van Basten and won the European Cup in 1989.
Napoli?	They bought Diego Maradona and won the Italian League in 1989.
Real Madrid?	They bought Hugo Sanchez and won the Spanish League in 1989.
NO!	
Manchester United	They bought Ralph Milne and won the English League in 1967.

---

26) SAT. FEBRUARY 17TH: QPR (AWAY)
or: F.A.CUP 5TH ROUND

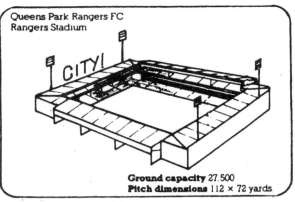

Queens Park Rangers FC
Rangers Stadium

Ground capacity 27.500
Pitch dimensions 112 × 72 yards

Off to London again, three years to the month,
doesn't time fly, since our last visit to Loftus Rd.
Anyone remember? It was an eventful occasion
when rumours were rife about the Fulham/Rangers
merger, successfully quelled by a well organised
FSA campaign including a sit down protest on
the pitch before the game and at half-time.
Their 'official' supporters club being in favour
of the 'merge' we understand.

'Where were you at Maine Road', the City fans
chanted, pause, 'You were watching Fulham!'

Anyway we lost on the plastic pitch 1-0 and you
have to go back to our first visit in 50/51 for
a win: Overall it's 1 win, 4 draws and 5 losses
in the 10 visits, so we're definitely due a result.

Now Loftus Road is a cracking little ground which
has been completely redeveloped carefully and
sensibly stage by stage so as not to financially
cripple the club. An example to all.
There's a double decker behind each goal, one
for us one for them, a full length main stand
with executive boxes below the upper tier and a
full length single tier stand on the opposite
side. (Now that is interesting -Ed!)

The plastic pitch has gone and there's four
modern floodlight poles which act as a landmark
every time you pass through to the South of
London.

Look out for this fella!

TO DAY THE Ranger
IS AMONGST YOU IN
DISGUISE —

— HE MAY BE NEXT TO YOU!

Fanzines are: In the loft and A Kick Up The R's

KING OF THE KIPPAX

Steamy Saturdays with James H.

HEARD ABOUT THE CITY FANS AT CHELSEA?

Did you see the programme on Women's football recently?

It seemed to confuse Women playing soccer (did you see the City girls?) with women attending matches as a dilution to hooliganism. What an insult. Highlight of the programme for me was the interview with David Dent of the Football League on the invitation/ban of women to 'the Boardroom'. Anyway, I couldn't stop the other-half putting pen to paper, the whole blinking family's at it now......

WOMEN IN FOOTBALL? Spare me please. Leave me my Saturday afternoons of peace and quiet - tuned in, turned on to James H Reeve. Don't make me be a part of some mad "social engineering" scheme, providing a buffer between one set of hooligans and another.

Sort out the crowd control problems, seating arrangements (or not) toilets and snack bars FIRST and I just might be tempted to come along- provided, that is, that all matches are played in good weather, and I can secure suitable finance ("Oh no, mum, not my money box again!")

Don't get me wrong. I love watching football or, to be more accurate, I love watching the footballers (it's the thighs.....!!) (Sexist-Ed) But the price I'm asked to pay in terms of physical discomfort, monetary hardship and ultimate sacrifice of 'an afternoon to myself' is too much to bear.

And then there's the kids. Funny, but I've never managed to have the sort of children who happily spend an afternoon in a crummy, low budget creche with total strangers. I'm not saying they're "clingy" but Velcro come to our house to field test their products. Funny too, that creches are only mentioned in terms of women attending football matches! Why haven't there been such things from day one so that fathers can bring their children?

Fellers, you've brought your present problems upon yourselves. You wanted your precious football to be a predominantly male domain. You tolerated the filth, and added your own few quarts of urine. You devoured with gusto the "scabby dog" fare. You have all pushed and shoved in your time, shouted obscenities, insulted and abused your rivals/ referees/ players/managers and chairmen.

Please don't expect women to come in and clear up your mess. We do it the other six days a week - leave us alone on Saturday afternoons- James H.will do fine whilst you're away!

(Other Ed's note:The decree nisi's in the post and let's hope they bring back Mike Sweeney!)

MANCUNIAN HOTLINE ... ...

United fans now dress in Manchester City shirts (the colour of the new away strip, would you believe, is sky blue)

UNITED OFFICIAL: Hello, it's me again, I've got a question.
CITY OFFICIAL: What's that?
UNITED OFFICIAL: Well I think I know the answer but they've made me ask it.
CITY OFFICIAL: Go on then
UNITED OFFICIAL: Well, promise first that you won't go on and on about us never having an original thought in our heads whatsoever.
CITY OFFICIAL: What do you mean?
UNITED OFFICIAL: You know about when we've nicked all your players so we could win a trophy, then nicked one of your old boys as manager, and then played at Maine Road and then we played our Euro ties under your floodlights and then we nicked Salford's nickname, the Red Devils and then Spurs' glory glory song and then.....
CITY OFFICIAL: Get on with it man
UNITED OFFICIAL: Well, we've got this lovely new away strip... it's...it's...... gorgeous, very Laura Ashley, I think he's wonderful don't you just like Bryan.....
CITY OFFICIAL: What colour is it?
UNITED OFFICIAL: Well, it's sort of a pastel shade y'know, in fact it's, it's well it's sky blue and white, you'll love it......
CITY OFFICIAL: What's the question?
UNITED OFFICIAL: Derby day, we'd like to play in it so come on, know your place and be a sport you can play in maroon....
CITY OFFICIAL: Sod off!

KING OF THE KIPPAX

Listened to bits of a recent midday radio programme/phone in when a certain prospective Chairman of a certain football club was being interviewed and it really got on my zits when he said repeatedly that the club in question were 'The Greatest Club in the World' (not this one again - Ed!)

Anyway, no expense was spared to track down this famous person and take him to task on this issue and he finally agreed to be interviewed by 'KK' poolside somewhere within the Bermuda Triangle.
It went something like this:-

MK: Firstly may I say what an excellent fanzine you produce, what's it called again?

KK: It's King of the Kippax

MK: Oh yes, very good - articulate, humorous interesting.... and may I also say what an impressive figure of a man you are, I can see that I won't be able to pull the wool over your eyes....

KK: Thank you, you seem like an honest, genuine and if I may say so likeable person yourself.

MK: Yes I most certainly am!

KK: You said on the radio recently that you were now part of the 'Greatest Club in the World'

MK: Did I? Did I say that, yes, I probably did and that's because WE ARE

KK: On what basis

MK: Pardon?

KK: I mean, is it tongue in cheek?

MK: My dear fellow there's nothing tongue in cheek at my club we are quite definitely the Greatest CLub, it stands to reason and sticks out a mile there's no argueing about it....

KK: Don't you think you could be setting yourselves up to be knocked down and perhaps becoming a laughing stock in the bargain....

MK: No of course not sonny Jim, listen, everybody knows we're the Greatest Club in the World, they all love us and respect us for it, even those Liverpudlians accept it..

KK: But why

MK: It's our support, it's magnificent.....

KK: But clubs like Barcelona, Juventus, Santos etc get twice as much support as you.

MK: Yes but we've a fine fine supermar......... stadium

KK: It's not a patch on Ibrox or Cardiff Arms Park or the Nou Camp or the Bernabeau or

MK: Well, it's based on the times we've won the World Championship...

KK: But you've NEVER won it....

MK: Well it's based on the times we've won the League Championship then...

KK: But you haven't won it since '67 and Liverpool's won it more times since then than you've ever won it - also Forest, Villa Everton, City, Derby, Leeds and Arsenal's won it since you......

MK: Well it's because we've won the European Cup......

KK: So have Forest (twice) Villa, Celtic, and Liverpool's won it four times

MK: Well it's cos we had George Best......

KK: So did lots of women...

MK: Well it's because Bobby Charlton's won more caps than anyone else....

KK::No that's Peter Shilton

MK: Well if it hadn't been for the plane crash...

KK: But Real Madrid were pretty big then and Wolves were racing away with the league championship....

MK: Listen Pal, we've won the F.A.Cup loads of times......

KK: Even Spurs have won it more times than you, and you've never won the UEFA or Cup Winners Cup

MK: Only cos we're banned from Europe. Anyway we've got the England captain, he's wonderful, surely you can see that you four eyed git...

KK: But England have never won anythin' under his captaincy

MK: Now listen you big fat sod you're getting on my nerves, don't think you're too big to go in the pool - Oyston's big, mega big but it didn't stop him going in the pool... have we ever won the Littlewoods Cup, cretin...

KK: No you've never won that either so come, come, there must be a real reason why you claim to be the Greatest Club....

MK: Listen, you big, fat, bald, ugly slobby git, we're the Greatest Club in the whole wide effin world cos I effin well say so and not only that, it's what the fans want to hear, and that's a good enough reason for me, and by the way I've never even read your silly fanzine....

SPLASH!

KING OF THE KIPPAX

Hair.... Apparent

Just how did City win the promotion last season? What did they have that the teams below them didn't?

Was it Mel Munchkin's tactics, Macca's midfield skills or even Paul Moulden's goals? Actually, it was none of these. The real reason for City's success would still be a closeley guarded secret today if it hadn't been for the Evening News' edition of May 8th.

There, on an inside page, was an advert for the SVENSON HAIR CENTRE that revealed all.

"TRICHOLOGICAL HAIR PREPARATIONS and MANCHESTER CITY, a famous combination" "We think Svenson Hair preparations are the greatest ever" say the City playing staff. On it goes - "Personal appearance is important to the football professional and we all use Svenson products regularly to maintain and preserve our hair in peak condition" and to prove it, mugshots of the City squad were shown.

Well, there you have it. The only wonder potion BEN JOHNSON failed to try - the football revelation of 88/89. It is any wonder teams like Portsmouth, Ipswich and Hull crumbled at Maine Road when they saw our boys run out onto the pitch, their heads dripping with trichological hair preparations. When City first used THP's has not been disclosed but the first guinea pigs are thought to have been Big Helen's beehive, George Heslop and John Gidman -the repeated head scratching a bit of a dead giveaway there. Other pointers include Simmo's regular changes of hairstyle Reddo's frequent blond tints and Brian Gayle missing that header at West Brom (he couldn't mess up his THP's, could he?) Also VIDAL SASSOON is believed to have attended a number of games, heavily disguised as a pie seller in Main Stand.

There's no evidence to show that Svenson's trichologist has been active at board level. Swalesy still favours his ATKINSON/SCARGILL coconut matting job and a SYRUP has been spotted hibernating on one of the director's domes. Now the secret is out, it's back to the conventional methods of achieving success, i.e., tactics (back passes-Ed!) ball skills etc. This is no bad thing as prolonged use of similar preparations could have serious side effects. Look what happened to Bobby Charlton and Wilf McGuinness!

"Blue Rinse"

(Other Ed's Note)   The Ed has magnaminously agreed to include this rather touchy article - realising that he's too far gone even for a Svenson recovery!

Fergie 'n Robbo were strolling down the Stretford forecourt when they spotted a dog pooh...steaming!

Fergie: Look at that Brian, looks like a dollop of....
Brian : Yeah, sure does Boss

Fergie: Pick it up Brian
Brian : Pick it up Boss?
Fergie: Yeah, pick it up
Brian : O.K., you're the Boss (so far)
Fergie: Sniff it Brian, what's it smell like?
Brian : It sure smells like dog pooh

Fergie: Taste it Brian
Brian : Taste it Boss?
Fergie: Yeah, taste it
Brian : Mmmmmmmm, sure tastes like dog pooh

Fergie: Bloody hell Brian, good job I didn't tread in it!

CRAP! Manchester United is something else. It's a pleasure to be in charge of the best club in the world.

SEX ORGY AT MAINE RD.
"ATTENBOROUGH" REVEALS ALL!

SHOCK! HORROR! DISGUST!

The football world reeled at the end of last season with the revelations of a wild sex orgy at a Reserve game against Coventry City

Picture the scene: May Day (and it was for one of the participants!). The Blues cruising along nicely, two up thanks to a first-minute Wayne Clarke penalty and an own goal, thrashed in by Coventry's No.6 from an Ian Thompstone cross 10 minutes later.

Nothing to get excited about. Snatches of coversation throughout the Main Stand -"Where yer goin' this year? Rhyl again?" and "D'jer see that film on Channel 4 last night? Alright them Swedish birds ..." Then it happened.

A titter bubbled up in one area; a giggle burst from another; the City groupies shrieked And people looked round, wondering why the tranquillity was suddenly shattered.

Gradually eyes focussed on the rampant orgy taking place on the touchline. Three ducks from Platt Fields lake had decided that a spot of congress would liven things up for the spectators.

Male No.1 fluttered and shifted about, finding a comfy position; the female shuffled and wriggled, eager to accommodate his every desire.

Male No.2 stood to one side, awaiting his tern (sorry, turn) licking his beak in anticipation ....

Off they went, cheered on by a vast crowd of around 600. Never mind the thrust of the Blues' forwards; male no.1 provided plenty of his own as he pursued his role of increasing the Platt Fields duck population. By now the game was forgotten as the al fresco humpty-dumpty became the total centre of attention.

Players started to look puzzled at the spasmodic bursts of applause for nothing more than a safe back pass. The ref wondered whether his shorts had split, so concentrated became the furore.

End of Act One. Male No.1 fell off, preened himself, then together with his mate and Male No.2 waddled towards the edge of the penalty area. Clearly encouraged by the fans' appreciation, Male No.2 then climbed aboard and proceeded to try to affect the parts other ducks cannot reach.

The ball went out of play. The ref, obviously worried by the lax moral standards on display ran across and together with a linesman and the Coventry 'keeper tried to shoo the insatiable fowl away.

A most unwise decision, one that might have inflamed the crowd to heights of mob rule to defend the rights of copulating wildlife; a storm of booing broke around the heads of the interfering trio, ending with an outraged cry from the top of the stand: "Leave 'em alone, you b*****s! 'Ow'd you like it if you 'adn't finished?"

Any official worth his whistle would've fished out a red card (but he was saving that for Jason Beckford later on, having already dished out 6 bookings). For what reason, one wondered? "Fowl and abusive language?" "Persistent misconducked?"

He contented himself with timing the birds with his stop watch and soon Male No.2 climbed off and smirked at the still-recovering Male No.1 Somehow, all 3 found the energy to swagger towards the half-way line, urged on by the embarrassed trio who had observed proceedings from close range, then, as one, they took off in perfect formation, banked, and headed back to Platt Fields over the Kippax Roof to bursts of applause from the audience.

Footnote: at the Reserve game the following Friday against Leicester, a long lull in the proceedings in the second half provoked a mysterious message onto the electronic scoreboard - "BRING ON THE DUCKS."

Ed's note: If we'd have been playing Notts Forest or County, would their players have shouted "C'mon me ducks!?"

John Maddocks

King of the Kippax

CITY DESK

Hello!

Hello culture buffs, Peter Allotment-Holder here. I'm afraid that due to circumstances beyond my control, you'll have to make do with a truncated despatch this month. The truth is that just lately my articles on City for the Evening Blues have not gone down too well at Maine Road. In particular, my use of the phrase 'mind numbing mediocrity ' when describing recent City performances has upset Howard and his imported Scouser Nostra. Also thanks to P.C. of Moston who pointed out that I gave Reddo 9 marks in the Derby, thus breaking my current tradition of giving a City player the customary 5.

I've therefore been banned from travelling on the team bus to away matches and am no longer privy to all the inside stories. Still, if you can't get at the truth, pad out your articles with dirge that's always been my motto.

What's happened?

Well what's been happening? On the transfer scene it's been a case of if he's ex-Everton buy him. Harper, Reid, Ward, Clarke have all been signed. Heaton's in as assistant manager. Adrian Heath's been mentioned and rumour has it that roving scout Jimmy Frizzell has been talking to Dixie Dean through a medium. Back episodes of Bread, the Liver Birds and Brookside are also available from the Souvenir Shop. Playing wise, the coma inducing tactics Howard has introduced are having the desired effect and we're slowly grinding out the points which should help us pull clear of the relegation zone. Hopefully these tactics are just a short term measure and once we're safe we'll open out a bit more. If there's any more performances like Everton and Sheffield Wednesday away or the brutal home game with Wimbledon (club sponsors the Kray twins?) the Manchester branch of the Samaritans will have to take on more staff. Incidentally the video of the Everton match is being used by various organisations to bring about political reform and promote world peace. After its showing on East German TV people were throwing themselves at the Berlin Wall like lemmings. The Americans used it successfully to prise General Noriega out of hiding and Nelson Mandela's last words to the prison governor were "I warned you buggerlugs I'd be off if you showed that tape in here"

Expect developments in Beirut, Terry Waite's captors have been sent a copy and the British Army are to trial it at several trouble spots in Northern Ireland.

The players

Individually some of the players are having a better time of it than others. Andy Dibble has made some brilliant reflex saves but his tendency to dash off his line and punch the back of Colin Hendry's head is a bit worrying. The defence looks more sound and it's not just through weight of numbers. Hendry, Redmond and Harper have all made valuable contributions and Hinchcliffe is pressing forward more. In midfield Peter Reid chugs nicely up and down field like Thomas the Tank Engine and it's good to see Paul Lake having an injury free run (somebody must be hiding the England call-up letters) Gary Megson the bionic carrot has also re-appeared.

Up front, we're struggling. White looks out of place in the centre and Ward so far has been a bit of a disappointment. Allen's been injured and Clarke seems to have inherited Neil McNab's shooting boots. The only one getting regular shots on the goal is Tony Book in the pre-match kick about. Howard is aware of the problem though and another striker appears to be a priority. German Thomas Stickroth was a possibility, however, his limited knowledge of English, (he only knew two phrases "Bobby Charlton" and "For you British Tommy, the war is over") was a bit of a drawback. In addition Stickroth got a bit nervous when Howard told him he wanted to see him on trial in the Isle of Man. The poor lad thought he was to be had up for war crimes.

Away Jinx

The away jinx should have been buried by now, namely at Spurs and Stretford. Both games were there for the taking - especially the return derby. The match itself is well covered elsewhere in this issue but some of the off pitch highlights are worth recording, eg. the puzzled looks on the Reds' faces as the City fans cheered each United player's name as it came up on the scoreboard, the gaps in the Stretford end and the sight of James Anderton's prize chopper. There it was hovering over the stadium , was it for our protection or are they still looking for Glen Miller?

At the final whistle I usually dart straight to the bar for a post-match sherbert, purely medicinal of course, but at the derby I was having trouble with my osmiroids and was still sat in the press box finishing my report.. I couldn't help but notice that for the first time I can recall the City fans, the true Manchester residents, were kept back. What a disgrace, some of them only lived minutes away and most of the United fans had already left well before full time not wishing to be too late for their cream teas back home in Devon.

Having got that off my chest, I must sign off now, I've got an invite to a housewarming party from an old chum in Barnsley.

        Yours in sport,

                Peter.

Ed's note:

Sometimes you can be a silly sod, Allotment-Holder! At least keeping us in prevented us from mingling with THEM and it meant that lots of City fans could go out that night without taking an extra shower ......

MEMBERSHIP and IDENTITY CARDS

WHAT NEXT?

IT'S UP TO THE 'LORDS' TO THROW THE BILL OUT
IT'S UP TO THE 'COMMONS' TO THROW THE BILL OUT
IT'S UP TO THE LEAGUE AND F.A. ADMINISTRATION
TO REFUSE TO IMPLEMENT IT
IT'S UP TO THE CLUB CHAIRMEN TO REFUSE TO IMPLEMENT IT
~ AND IF THEY ALL FAIL?
           IT'S UP TO US ....!

EURO CONFESSIONS OF A BLUE VICAR

PART ONE

EUROPE, here we come!

With the return of English clubs to Europe STEVE PARISH, the Blue Vicar, recalled his earlier career following City.

Fenerbahce? Who? There I was, just started working for British Rail, cheap continental travel in prospect and City in the European Cup and who do we play? Some crummy Turkish team no-one's heard of.

Blow that, I thought, I'll wait for the next round and go to Munich or Madrid or Lisbon. A year later...

17th September 1969. Atletico Bilbao v. City.

Different competition, the Cup-Winners Cup, but free travel to Bilbao. Beat Spurs 3-0 in London, overnight to Paris, French rail strike threatening further progress, but make it to the Spanish border for Monday night. Try and find youth hostel. Eventually find it, no-one around, but lots of bunk beds. Wander round inside the place until suddenly confronted by owner who's bought the hostel and it's now his private home. Directed to new hostel rather than Spanish jail. Natives rather aloof. I've had 14 days to learn Spanish - not too hard if you've done French: just add 'a' to words instead of 'e'. 'Tengo una camisa roja y negra.' (I have a red and black shirt). Stupid thing to learn - everyone can see I'm wearing it. (Funny how the red & black stripes caught on - the first time City appeared in them was at Goodison Park. All the City fans were expecting the all-maroon strip and out come this strange team in red and black. Stunned silence from Blues fans, then a chorus of 'We don't like red..we don't like red!')

Spanish Railways route to Bilbao goes long way round, so decide to hitch the 80 miles from the border. 5 hours to get half-way, so catch the local narrow-gauge train the rest of the way. Find out the fare for all 80 miles would only have been eight shillings. (Gosh, is it that long ago?)

Find boarding house. Book beds for B.R. colleagues coming next day. No tickets yet - only a letter from Maine Road saying I can get tickets at the ground before the match. This was in the days before hooliganism had been exported.

Wander downtown to San Mames stadium. No-one around. Suddenly hear English voices. Ascend stairs and interrupt press conference by Ronnie Allen, Atletico's English manager - paving the way for Kendall and El Tel. 'How do you cope with the language?' ask the press boys. 'Well,' he says, 'you say "What's this?" and nut the ball and they tell you the Spanish for a header.'

They look at me. 'Sorry to interrupt, but how do I get tickets for the match?' Sent off to City team's hotel on the hill over the town. Get three tickets for me and two mates arriving later. Spend evening at hotel. Rumour had it Joe Corrigan punched a bloke who'd offered one criticism too many. This in Joe's shaky days after the early brilliance when they had to stop him giving away corners by touching over shots that were already going a foot over the bar.

Three more BR workers arrive on day of match without tickets. They don't seem too bothered. Try the hotel. Team already out for day. So an hour before the match we're wandering round trying to find someone to get tickets off.

I'm brandishing my letter on MCFC headed paper complete with my own Spanish translation on the back. Sudden excitement from Spanish official as I'm directed down a tunnel under the stand. They open this door for me, and I'm in the City dressing room. It's the shirt and the letter! They think I'm one of the players got lost in the crowd! Surely the glasses gave it away.

Malcolm Alison not fooled. He knows I'm not the sub. Explain why I'm in the dressing room, 30 minutes before kick-off. 'Any tickets, lads?' he asks. Half a dozen comps in hand, I beat a hasty retreat. Three spare tickets given away to local urchins.

CITY FIGHT-BACK ROCKS BASQUES

Tickets not together, but Spaniards in stand are friendly, sharing half-time wine from porro. Football the only winner. Bilbao are two up after 11 minutes but a Neil Young special brightens half-time even before the wine. Thank God for a common language. Gol! Cornair! Foul! (Phrase book said it was falta - obviously written for tennis players.) Guy with porro still friendly even after Bilbao lose 3-1 lead to Tommy Booth and a late own goal. 'Manchester City,' he says, 'bueno equipo mas poco duro'. City, I thought, duro? Neil Young and Ian Bowyer? You should see Nobby Stiles, duro as nails and twice as daft.

Journey home not helped by allergic reaction to something in the paella. But if this is Europe, I'm all for it. Seal tie with 3-0 home win - Oakes, Bell, Bowyer. Into draw for next round. We get Lierse S.K. Who? Where? Belgium? Blowed if I'm going to learn Flemish; I haven't even learned how to spit.

EUROPEAN CUP WINNERS' CUP

U.E.F.A. CUP

EUROPEAN CUP

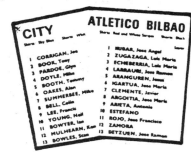

CITY Shirts Sky Blue Shorts White

1 CORRIGAN, Joe
2 BOOK, Tony
3 PARDOE, Glyn
4 DOYLE, Mike
5 BOOTH, Tommy
6 OAKES, Alan
7 SUMMERBEE, Mike
8 BELL, Colin
9 LEE, Francis
10 YOUNG, Neil
11 BOWYER, Ian
12 MULHEARN, Ken
13 BOWLES, Stan

ATLETICO BILBAO Shirts Red and White Stripes Shorts Black

1 RUBAR, Jose Angel
2 ZUGAZAGA, Luis Maria
3 ECHEBERRIA, Luis Maria
4 LARRAURI, Jose Ramon
5 ARANGUREN, Jesus
6 IGARTUA, Jose Maria
7 CLEMENTE, Javier
8 ARGOITIA, Jose Maria
9 ARIETA, Antonio
10 ESTEFANO
11 ROJO, Jose Francisco
12 ZAMORA
13 BETZUEN, Jose Ramon

PART TWO K.K.13

HILLSBOROUGH

When clubs and the police place restrictions on the number of fans in order to herd them into tightly packed enclosures, with little way of escape, there are questions to be asked beyond the particular circumstances of Hillsborough.

One woman caller to the Nick Ross phone-in on Radio 4 said supporters should never have put up with being caged in. But what are we supposed to do? Tear them down before we're actually being crushed or burnt to death? Go equipped with our own boltcutters? What can ordinary law-abiding people do when authority listens to nothing except violence or money?

Yet this know nothing, hear nothing, care nothing government - as impossible to reason with as any hooligan - says it will carry on with the I.D. card scheme. It will be a criminal offence to try to get in a match without one. Brilliant. I.D. cards wouldn't provide the thousand more tickets Liverpool could have sold for the semi-final. How many coppers does it take to arrest a thousand people all wanting to get in without I.D. cards or tickets? What if they won't go quietly?

People are aware of the dangers of crowds in tube stations being crushed when the automatic ticket barriers go wrong, so how can anyone think that a failure of the I.D. card computers would not cause immense and dangerous congestion outside the ground? But cabinet ministers don't use the tubes either.

And how will the I.D. scheme get rid of the hooligan? It may keep out the hooligan who's convicted of a football-related offence, but will do nothing for the hooligans who never seem to get arrested. This society breeds them faster than they can be refused I.D. cards.

All-seater stadia too. Brilliant. A solution to overcrowding that means you can get 15,000 fewer people into a match that's a 55,000 sell-out. Far better to cut back terracing to make room for the 'dry moat' or at least an area which is accessible in an emergency between the terracing wall and a perimeter fence. That would have enabled fans at Hillsborough to get round into the adjacent sections where there was room.

Maybe the days are gone where once inside the ground you could walk around the track to where you wanted to be; maybe we can't go back to when fans of opposing clubs mingled on the terraces with rivalry but no menace, and hearing another view of the game actually calmed the aggressive partisan approach that segregation has only encouraged. Maybe, with a government that takes pride in not listening to other people's views and advice, aggressive answers to aggression are all we can expect.

But Rogan Taylor, of the Football Supporters Association, has it right. There are measures to control violence which spiral up the violence and some that spiral it down. Every football fan knows that matches now could be chaos without the coppers, but we know too of the ways of policing that cause even the mildest of upright citizens to cite police attitudes as part of the upward spiral, with token arrests

of people unconnected with any violence, dogs set loose among fans on the terraces, and careless or callous or just plain rude responses to problems.

This was a year when the fans themselves had begun to bring fun back into football, carrying giant inflatables and attending matches in fancy dress. If the Hillsborough aftermath leaves the supporters without a voice again, insult will be added to injury, and disrespect added to death.

STEVE PARISH

T.V. TIMES
(OR HOW 'LIVE' FOOTBALL WAS KILLED STONE DEAD)

The scene is White Hart Lane in 1990/91 where ITV cameras are covering Spurs v Man. Utd. for the third consecutive season.

BRIAN M: This is turning into a real classic, isn't it Trevor?
TREVOR F: Yes, it's really hotting up. I'd say it's turning into a real classic.
BRIAN M: Yes it's end to end stuff and they'll be talking about that incident which almost led to a corner for a good while, you can bet on that. Let's look at that intervention from Bryan Robson from the angle of the camera we've inserted in Robson's shorts...... yes, a beautiful backpass.
TREVOR F: A really great backpass.
BRIAN M: Bryan Robson really has everything, hasn't he Trevor? Strong, purposeful, committed, still leading England despite our not qualifying for the World Cup in Italy last June.... but that was no fault of his..... This league is still the most competitive in the world.
TREVOR F: Yes, he's got everything and this league's got everything.
BRIAN M: Only 55 minutes gone, but already you'll probably be thinking about who's going to be man of the match..... my money's on Robson, but you never know in a game like this. It's end to end stuff, and all we need is a goal.
TREVOR F: This is turning into a classic.
BRIAN M: Yes, ITV has really got a winner this week No goals in our last three matches, the three recent meetings between Arsenal and Liverpool, but surely one today, and Elton will be speaking to the lady who washes the Spurs kit at the end of the game, we'll be seeing that from a camera positioned in the Spurs toilets..... marvellous competitive midfield game at the moment, don't you think it's competitive Trevor?
TREVOR F: Yes, when these two clubs meet it's always comp.....
BRIAN M: Sorry to cut you off there Trevor just as you were about to make an important point, but Gascoigne just tangled with Robson there.... and Robson's injured.... his shoulder again..... he's having to be helped off.... Let's look at him coming off the field from the camera we have positioned in the helicopter above White Hart Lane.......

(N.B. Any resemblance between the commentators and the average football fan is purely coincidental).

Tony Greyson

I WAS (nearly) THERE – HEYSEL '85

Introductiuon

In May 1985, I was scheduled to go on a business expediting visit to a Belgium company who were supplying equipment for a current project.

The non regular football types in our "party" wanted to go the week of the game, but I managed to dissuade them, as I feared the worst based on "underground reports" of:-

1.   The Manchester clubs playing in Italy in the 70's.
2.   Juventus supporters' performance after the Villa game.
3.   Roma supporters allegedly ambushing the Liverpool fans after the game the previous year.

Apart from that, I didn't really fancy us struggling to find accommodation, plane seats and a quiet bar for the odd drink or two. I was pleased, therefore, that we arranged to go the week before the match.

Discussions

During the visit, I recall a couple of discussions.

One was in the Hotel bar, with a couple of suitably armed Belgian cops. When I suggested that they would have their work cut out the following week with the Scousers and Itis, they laughed and said they'd have no trouble, having just helped the Dutch police sort out the Everton supporters. When I pointed out that the game in Holland had been a completely different situation, particularly as it involved an Iron Curtain country with little travelling fans. they just shrugged their shoulders.

Secondly, and more significantly perhaps, I asked the Technical Manager of the Belgian firm if he'd be going to the match with one of their fitters, who hailed from Liverpool and his young son. No, he said, it won't be safe and reeled off the following:-

1.   It's the oldest stadium in Belgium and crumbling.
2.   There's 5,000 forged tickets.
3.   The neutral area is in the compound, next to the Liverpool supporters and all these tickets have been snapped up by the large Italian community in Belgium.

No Cover Up

Now, I'm not one to cover up for Liverpool fans, the media has perpetuated their "good boy" image myth for years. Ask anyone who's coach has been showered with bricks from that grave yard or had a stanley knife flashed at them when giving out the time in a non Scouse accent, and as for Joe Corrigan hitting himself on the head with a bottle ....!!

But, if blokes like myself and the Technical Manager smelt a rat, then surely better preparations should have been made for the game.

Incidently, I wonder what happended to the 50 Scouse policemen who were reported to be travelling with the Liverpool supporters.

Now, there is no excuse for the behaviour of those fans at Heysel, but the facts are that the deaths were caused by mass panic and a collapsing wall, which probably would not have met the least stringent safety controls in this country. A parallel could possibly be drawn with the Bolton disaster of '46, when the gates were stormed and subsequently collapsed causing the deaths of 33 people.

Sure, the offenders should be arrested, tried and if found guilty, jailed for the appropriate period, but Italian fans were also involved and should be meted the same treatment.

After all this time it must again be stated that no-one has yet got to the bottom of why those Liverpool fans reacted in such a way - the pontificators, who appear on T.V.'s, Question Time and the like, all have some half baked theory of course, but, it is my firm belief that something, other than drink, must have sparked off the frenzied behaviour of those fans.

Outcome

Finally, the outcome of Heysel was that on video camera evidence, approximately 40 Liverpool supporters were arrested and brought to trial. The relative administrative failures brought down the Belgian Government and caused severe recriminations of the police force, the Chief of Police being sacked, and gave widespread condemnation of some Juventus fans, who, despite video camera evidence of hooliganism in the extreme, have never been arrested and brought to trial.

English clubs were banned from Europe for an indefinite period, with Liverpool being banned for an additional period.

Conclusion

In my opinion, the blanket ban on English clubs was vindictive and immoral and yet another example of the incompetence of those who run the game at this level.

It is now left to the F.S.A. to plan and campaign vigorously for a return to Europe for our clubs, for the start of the '89/'90 season, or at the very least 1992, when the European Community Market is opened up further.

I would urge all members, and non members, therefore to back the F.S.A. in this campaign.

chapter 3

E-I-E-I-E-I-O UP THE FOOTBALL LEAGUE WE GO

INSIDE - Profit and loss.Away Daze.Vinnie Vindicated.Tony Currie interviewed.Bremner, the rebel who found a cause and much much more....Altogether now, "If you're off to Old Trafford"...Front cover story - Let's just say that the phone is already off the hook!!

WE ARE THE CHAMPIONS WE ARE THE CHAMPIONS SGT WILKO'S KING!!!

WHEN WE WIN PROMOTION THIS IS WHAT WE'LL SING

leeds united

Supporting Leeds United at the present time should be an enjoyable experience and for the most part it is. But there's always the issue of the behaviour of our fans and the team's so called style of play or lack of it as the press would have it, lurking in the background.

Another issue which directly affects all Leeds fans is racism, and while it's true that racism does exist on the terraces (and in the stands), I think it's fair to say that the atmosphere at Elland Road now isn't a patch on what it used to be, a great deal of credit for this can be laid at the feet of the Leeds fans themselves and the fanzine 'Marching Altogether', which has campaigned against racist abuse and behaviour for a couple of years now.

For many people the picture of Leeds supporters that they hold in their minds are those which were very much in evidence at Bournemouth in May. I can sympathise with them to a certain extent but I do feel the press have done their best to create a larger than life stereotype Leeds Fan, whose idea of a good day out is to raze a town centre to the ground.

All pretty negative stuff so far but it is important to raise these issues over and over again because otherwise the fans and the Club would disappear under a mountain of nonsense which to be honest gets rather tedious. Leeds as a club have tried their hardest to weed out the hooligan element through various membership schemes and they have reduced the incidents of violence to almost nothing. Out of all those arrested at Bournemouth only 9% were official club members, so how many of the others were true Leeds United fans?

The Club's fans have responded as best they can through the pages of the half dozen fanzines that are now available, something that is surely testimony to the fact that there are a great number of true United fans out there. Convincing people outside the club might be a very difficult task (maybe even an impossible one), but the true supporters of Leeds will continue to try as long as there is a club to support.

The Hanging Sheep was born over two years ago and has no real purpose other than to let fans air their views and share their experiences with each other. Hopefully through our pages we've managed to change a few people's views about Leeds supporters in general. If I may quote from the 'Independent' - "The Hanging Sheep dispels the notion that all Leeds fans are fascist psychopaths". It's comments like that which make everything seem worthwhile, along with the belief that one day Leeds fans will be looked upon as fair minded people rather than the hooligans the popular press would like to have us labelled.

Finally, I hope you enjoy this compilation of articles from 'The Hanging Sheep' which should give you a good insight into what we're about. Any comments are of course always welcome and even if you write something nasty about us don't worry, we won't send the boys round!!!

CHRIS STRINGER

Leeds fans in sonic hat smear !

EXCLUSIVE

In this issue of THS we can exclusively reveal that Leeds fans
are under suspicion of RIGGING last season's promotion race,
whilst pocketing over £1.5 Million in winning bets. These are
the ASTONISHING claims made by Commander George free-mason Smith
head of Scotland Yard.

"There is evidence to suggest that Leeds supporter's were using
sophisticated devices to render visiting teams' better players
useless at Elland Road."When we asked just how this was possible
Comm Smith gave us the CHILLING details, "Well, it would appear
that the very popular bobble and baseball type hats are at the
bottom of all this." said the worried officer.

."But how do these harmless football accesories become almost
DEADLY tools of EVIL?"- "It would appear that these hats are fitted with a very sensitive microchip which reacts with the sweaty
atmosphere of the average terrace section within a football gro-
und." "Why then does it only affect the better players?""Well it
somehow works in the same way as the sonic binoculars did in the
racing scandal last year, turning the favourites into carthorses.
This is perhaps the reason why Barnsley were the only team to win
at Leeds in the league all season, basically because they are a
team of donkeys."

That must obviously be good news for Arsenal supporter's as it
appears that their captain Tony Adams will
be able to turn in his 'Blackpool beach'
type performances just the same.
(Adams right- Unaffected by anything, anywhere, ever.)

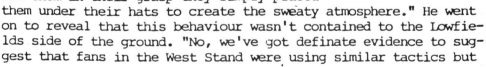

"How then did these criminals get round
the sweaty terrace technique in winter?"
"Quite simply really" said Comm Smith,"It's
a case of observing the behaviour of the
crowd. For instance in the Lowfields large
numbers were seen to send 'couriers' to
buy the warm pies on sale, but once they
had them in their grasp they simply placed
them under their hats to create the sweaty atmosphere." He went
on to reveal that this behaviour wasn't contained to the Lowfields side of the ground. "No, we've got definate evidence to suggest that fans in the West Stand were using similar tactics but
with Bovril in plastic cups, but the South Stand was perhaps the
most disturbing with fans buying upto ten programmes at a time
and placing them under their microchipped hats and simply setting
fire to them." We asked how the Police were going to deal with
this disturbing revelation.

"Well I've already explained these devices effect player's nerves
in a similar way to the sonic binoculars and the only thing we
can do is to remove the sweaty atmosphere catalyst by fitting
all our officer's helmets (!) with fans but failing that we've already looked at the possibility of flying our police helicopter,
which cost £1 million by the way upside down above the affected
areas." The Hanging Sheep will keep you posted on this matter......

THE HANGING SHEEP
the independent leeds
fanzine.

YOU ARE THE REF
THE ᵁᴺOFFICIAL F.A. QUESTIONNAIRE

Do you reckon that you could make a decent ref? Try our ref's test and see how you score.

A An opposing centre forward breaks clear - Upon reaching the penalty area he's brought down by a Mel Sterland tackle which resembles a combine harvester running over a Mini, do you?
(a) Book Sterland and give a penalty
(b) Book the centre forward for being soft
(c) Piss yourself laughing

B In an away game with 2 minutes left Leeds are drawing 0-0. The game is a vital promotion match and Gordon Strachan picks up the ball and throws it into the net (NB The 5,000 visiting Leeds fans know your address) Do you?
(a) Give a free kick for handball
(b) consult your linesman (then blame him for the riot)
(c) Give a goal, shake Gordon's hand and wink slyly at him

C Leeds give away a free kick 20 yards out. Just as the kick is about to be taken you notice Mervyn Day and Vinny Jones picking the goalposts up and moving them 3 yards to the left,do you?
(a) Send them both off (whilst keeping tight hold of your wedding tackle)
(b) Give a goal kick when the ball flies inches wide
(c) Give them a hand to lift the heavy posts out of the way

D During a local derby game David Batty acts completely out of character by elbowing an opposing player in the face,do you?
(a) Send Batty off because it's the 7th time he's done it in the first ten minutes
(b) Book the opponent for 'nosing' Batty's elbow
(c) Ask David how his elbow is

E During the second half of a game you notice that Leeds have sneaked five extra players onto the pitch and are playing two of them in goals beside Mervyn Day,do you?
(a) Abandon the match and report Leeds to the F.A.
(b) Tell Mervyn Day to remove his goalkeeping shirt
(c) Immediately send two of the opposing team off to even things up a bit

F A shot by John Hendrie enters the goal via a large hole in the side netting which has been cut open by Leeds fans behind the goal,do you?
(a) Disallow the effort and demand that new netting be placed on the goals
(b) Book the keeper for swearing at the Leeds fans
(c) Give a goal and collect all the ten pound notes that are fluttering down from the Leeds terrace

<u>SCORING</u>   Well how did you score? Count up all your answers then put them against our master scoring list to see if you are good enough to take your place on the official ref's list

THE HANGING SHEEP REFEREE'S SCORING CHART.

MOSTLY A's: WHat are you some kind of sadist? Your parents must really hate you, stick to shopping with the wife on a Saturday if she hasn't already left you.

MOSTLY B's: Well you're getting there but are prone to making the odd balls up now and then - Keep taking the tablets.

MOSTLY C's: Where the hell have you been for the entire history of the football league? Send off for your ref's badge now you're a natural.

to serve & Protect?

Through this magazine we've tried to bring you the more enjoyable and humourous side to football, and upto now we don't think
we've done a bad job.

So it is with regret that we have to print the following article.
Let's take up the story......Walsall v Leeds, Dec 3rd 1988- It's
half-time and Leeds are leading 1-0. The Leeds fans in the covered side of the terracing are celebrating that fact. A 5 minute
rendition of,"SGT WILKO'S BARMY ARMY" laid testimony that Leeds
fans were once again enjoying an away match, what followed can
only be described as a disgrace. Around 20 police officers wad-
ed from the back of the terracing, pushing and shoving anyone
and everyone out of the way until they reached the middle of the
terracing.

Once there they proceeded to eject/arrest anyone who happened to
be stood in that particular area. One guy around 35 with glasses
on and smoking a cigar (An obvious soccer thug?-ED) was told to
move and when he proved that he wasn't as quick as Ben Johnson
off the mark, he was thrown head first towards a crush barrier by
an understandibly irate constable.

It was at this time that we inquired(politely & calmly) who was
in charge of the police that day. The reply from PC 1996 was something to the effect,"Why? I don't know." We then suggested that
as police officers they were supposed to be acting in the best
interests and on behalf of the general public. (A fair point by
anyone's standards?) The same officer's reply? "I'm not talking
to you, I'm doing something else." More ejections followed, infact a lot of Leeds fans missed the second goal because of all the
nonsense that was going on- But that doesn't matter does it?

Letters of complaint may or maynot have been sent to the West Midlands police, but may we through this mag once again ask this
question: Why did the police jump in and bundle innocent fans out
of the ground?

Maybe it's a criminal offence to sing the word 'SGT' IN Walsall.
So let's just recap; Leeds are winning 1-0, the travelling fans
are singing and dancing to 'SGT WILKO'S BARMY ARMY'. The police
give us their own version of the storming of the Bastille and
anyone asking just what the hell is going is given the same brick
wall reply. Maybe the coppers were instructed to stop any offences
being committed- Fair point, but there weren't any Walsall fans
being jumped on or bottles flying around or even the odd 'burger
being thrown- So one can only assume that the people in charge of
the policing that day were novices.

It's a real eye opener to see policemen acting like they were at
Walsall that day, especially as we've seen numerous chief constables

calling for unity and co-operation from everybody concerned with
football. What would have happened if the Leeds fans had reacted
angrily to the police behaviour that day? Well it's pretty obvious isn't it- Sunday papers would say it all; 'LEEDS FANS RIOT.'
'LUNATIC THUGS ATTACK POLICE.' etc etc etc. No I'm afraid the
only printable comment that we can come up with is the same one
that we used on the way home from Walsall-The behaviour of some
of the police on duty that day was a disgrace, a bloody disgrace.

THE HANGING SHEEP

the independent leeds
fanzine.

a lesson still to be learnt

The events of December the 9th 1989 showed everybody present just what has and has not been learned since Hillsborough. The ineffective actions of most of the people in charge of crowd safety that day were clearly evident for all to see.

The whole issue that the police based their press releases on was the fact that the south east corner of the ground was not full any time during the afternoon which as we know is nothing short of complete rubbish.

From the word go it was quite apparent that the visitors pen was full, because if it wasn't why were the steps and gangways in the south east corner full with fans? Why were late arrivals being brought in via the gates at the side of the section? And most importantly why did the police not see that there was a problem in the section long before they tried to cram extra fans into the away section of terracing?

All these issues were cleverly side stepped by the police officer who conducted the press conference in the days following the match. The same police officer was nearly falling overhimself to show the whole nation the 'official' video which shows some Leeds fans surging down the terrace. This it was claimed caused the injuries to fans and not overcrowding. But why did the video showings never reveal the fact that whilst young children were being lifted over the fence the police were still putting more fans into the section via one of the gates in the fencing?

About the only thing that really came out of those press conferences was the fact that the police and to a certain extent Middlesbrough FC were going to absolve themselves from any blame whatsoever. Never more clearly highlighted than when we were told that there would be an inquiry into the incident (Monday night after the game) then by Tuesday night we had the statements which said that M'boro were quite happy with their safety arrangements and that the police were happy with everything as well, which obviously makes things alright doesn't it?

Another factor that Cleveland police's PR section continually harped on about was the fact that the section we were in was not up to it's full capacity. Infact they stated that there were 2,000 people in a section that holds 2,108 when full - Nothing wrong with that you might think, but it was the next sentence that must have had Leeds fans everywhere choking on their meals as they

watched the drivel pour out of their TV sets. It was claimed that no more than 70 Leeds fans were brought out from the Middlesbro' end of the ground - From way before the match kicked off groups of Leeds fans were being brought into the Leeds section of the ground. So maybe the police kept the number of people in the away end of the ground 100 or so below it's capacity to allow for Leeds fans in the home end. But to try and tell people who were there that they didn't put more people in the section than it holds really is to say the least a crude slur on our intelligence.

During the first twenty minutes of the game Leeds fans were being herded into the empty terracing in the North East corner of the ground, which is where they should have stopped but some intellectual decided to put them into the away section in groups of 15 to 20 despite the fact that people in the away end were screaming and swearing at the police telling them that there was no room in the section.

But it seems a policy of police forces (at football matches) to do as they feel and wait and see if a potentially dangerous incident occurs before using their heads to do what they should have done in the first place. This is clearly the case when the afore mentioned Leeds fans were taken back out of the South East corner (along with a lot more fans) and put back into the North East corner where they were in the first place!

The lack of exits in that section were also a big factor in this whole episode - There were two gates, both in the side but were hardly adequate as one of the gates was being used to put the extra Leeds fans in and the other gate (which was in the bottom corner of the terrace) led into an even smaller fenced off section which is used for segregation.

At the end of the day this whole incident must leave many people with a bitter taste in their mouths and a feeling that the police (or at least Cleveland police force) haven't learnt much or at least not enough to ensure that incidents such as this are a thing of the past and until they do more serious injuries will occur up and down the country.

On a final note on this subject we would like as a fanzine to put on record our utter contempt for those people who said that what happened at 'Boro "was never going to be another Hillsborough". We think statements like that stink - Let's face it before Hillsborough happened nobody would have believed it could happen . You cannot control a disaster but you should be looking to prevent it at least.

THE HANGING SHEEP

the independent leeds fanzine.

7·2 DOWN BUT, (next goalwins!)

No prizes for guessing which match we are remembering today!
"I won't let six in this season." Said Mervyn- Oh how right he
was. Our particular coach trip that day was a nightmare-or was
it?
We arrived at nearly half time, and jumping off the coach we ended up ankle deep in something resmbling a farm yard. "What's the
score mate?" Asked one of our party to a lone copper,"4-0 so far"
said plod."You're f***ing joking aren't you?" And he was, because
no sooner had we got through the turnstiles it was 5-0.
All that action in the first half too! But perhaps the most
encouraging thing from this match was the Leeds fans themselves.
NEVER sour in defeat, as a few intellectual chaps at half-time
pointed out to us all,"Sporny Stoke bastards, broke away five
times and scored a fluke every time!"
The second half started much the same as the first, Stoke doing
exactly what they wanted- Though it must be said that the pitch
was very muddy that day and a few of the Leeds players were obviously upset about the state of their kits.
6-1 before we knew. it, but who gave a toss,by now the lads on
the terracing were having a right old party. I Suppose that by
then we'd resigned ourselves to the fact that we were only going
to get a draw anyway (eternal optimists-ED) The Leeds fans were
really pulling out the stops now. Chants of,"Next goal wins"and
"First to ten" echoed round Stoke's ground. Yes and when John
'Shez' questioned how the Stoke keeper enjoyed sex after he had
scored a penalty the day seemed complete.
7-2 in the end, but if ever I've had a good time in defeat this
was it. As we got back onto our coach everybody was smiling and
joking- Except the lad who had first asked the copper what score
it was. All we could get out of him was, "7-2, Imean 7-2, why
not 5 or even 6 but 7? Oh no 7 fucking2, 7-2." Oh well I suppose
you can't please everybody.

THE HANGING SHEEP

the independent leeds
fanzine.

"Table Top Triumphs"
{tales of strange subbuteo games}

FEBRUARY 10TH 1980.... Leeds Utd 5 Liverpool/Childrens character 0
The greatest Subbuteo match ever to be played was spoilt by the
milkman on the morning of the game when he carelessly stood on the
Liverpool team box breaking half the team. The decision to make up
the Liverpool team with childrens characters resulted in the following table top game v Leeds.

The game started badly for the Reds when Emlyn Hughes tried a Pele
special straight from the kick off. Unfortunately an over flexed
index finger up Hughes's backside saw him sail majestically over
Leeds' back four and straight into the newly reglued camera stand.

A sending off for ungentlemanly conduct was the least of his worries as he trooped back to the team box. The game was only a couple
of minutes old when Peter Barnes tore (literally) down the wing. A
quick cotton and thread job and we were back in business. Lorimer
was on the end of the perfect cross...1-0 to Leeds.

Immediately from the kick off and another Barnes surge (looked like a double flick to some) brought another Leeds goal. Lorimer again on the end of another inch perfect cross. Some debate followed
as to whether or not Lorimer (strangely wearing the No. 14 shirt)
Had actually returned to the Leeds half of the pitch following the
opening goal, but 2-0 to Leeds and things were looking good!

Liverpool's 'guest' star midfielder - Rupert the "Chopper" Bear, a
dirty bastard if ever table football had seen one was becoming
more and more evident in the middle of the park with some telling
passes. Andy Pandy on the Red's left flank was in the process of
skipping merrily down the wing from a perfect Bear pass when a typically well timed Kenny Burns lunge sent him into row F of the
Grandstand and out of table football forever!

The referee's view (a Leeds fan) was conveniently obstructed by
the Leeds flickers left shoulder and despite Liverpool's protests
no booking followed. Half time arrives with Steve Heighway repla-

Rupert the Bear -
'A bit of a kicker.'

cing Andy Pandy.
The second half is only three minutes old
and Leeds have settled things. A Frank
Gray corner is cleared only as far as the
shooting line and up steps Norman Hunter
(out of retirement to 'see to' Jimmy Case)
to smash the finest effort of the season.
From then on Liverpool toiled hard with
Kennedy performing heroics in the middle
without getting any reward.

A Lorimer penalty made it 4-0 after Dougal (of magic roundabout fame)
had chopped Peter Barnes the ever eager winger (well we had to
make some of it up!) Infact Liverpool's best performer that day was
Ray Clemence who made some superb saves throughout the game - Some
would say Nelly the Elephant was in goals, but that would be cruel
wouldn't it?

A minute before time and Eddie Gray who had slipped quietly off the
bench did a Burnley special to make it 5-0. So the whitewash of
the Liverpool/Childrens XI was complete. The only thing that marred
the victory was the fact that on close inspection the Leeds team
box did infact read SWANSEA CITY, still never mind they did at least play in all white

THE HANGING SHEEP

the independent leeds
fanzine.

chapter 4

No 7   November 1988   50p

Voice of The Valley
The INDEPENDENT Charlton mag

Sports Minister
Visits Selhurst

charlton athletic

In January 1988, Voice of The Valley magazine appeared for the very first time, and its front cover ensured the attention of everyone connected with Charlton Athletic F.C. The headline "Let's Go Home" referred to the plan to boycott a selected fixture at Selhurst Park, and go instead to The Valley in protest at the club's continuing tenancy of Crystal Palace's ground.

Fortunately, the boycott was never needed, as the club announced plans to purchase the ground only five weeks after that first issue was printed, but since then VOTV has been the supporters' standard bearer in the fight to return to The Valley, a battle which now appears to have been won.

Throughout its existence, the magazine has maintained its campaigning approach towards Charlton's affairs, and not just in the hope of persuading Charlton's board of directors to reverse the catastrophic decision to leave The Valley for Selhurst over five years ago.

In the spring of 1988, the club purchased the 10 acre Valley site, but planned initially to develop it, in order to raise money for a new stadium nearby. VOTV was at the forefront of the campaign to convince them otherwise, and a year later, in front of a packed Town Hall in Woolwich, both the tears and the champagne flowed freely as chairman Roger Alwen announced that The Valley would once again become home.

But nothing involving Charlton is ever that simple, and following the decision of Greenwich Council to reject the football club's plans to rebuild the ground, Voice joined forces with the Charlton supporters club to form the Valley Party, a brand new political body that would eventually shake the Council out of their lethargic and negative attitude.

At first, the formation of the Valley Party was greeted with derision by Labour and Conservative politicians alike, but Charlton fans are made of stern stuff, and set about their task with enthusiasm.

The first shock to the established political parties came with the announcement that the Valley Party would contest every single ward, with a total of 60 candidates, just two short of the maximum allowed. The Charlton fans could have fielded two more candidates, but decided not to run against the only two men on the council to vote in favour of the original application to return. Still, the politicians failed to take the Valley Party seriously, until campaigning began in earnest. Unbeknown to the Council, one of the largest advertising agencies in the country, BMP, has a director who is a Charlton fan, and together with two colleagues (who incidentally follow Man. Utd.) worked voluntarily on an advertising campaign for the Valley Party.

The result was a 30 site, borough wide poster campaign, depicting five different designs, each encouraging people to 'Vote Valley'. The effect of the posters was twofold. Not only did they increase local awareness about the issue, which at the same time caused the Council a great deal of discomfort, but they also attracted the interest of the nation's media. Valley Party items were broadcast on BBC, Thames, BSB and Cable television, as well as on radio stations, LBC, GLR, Capital FM, Capital Gold and RTM. Column inches on the campaign appeared on a national level in the Guardian, the Telegraph, the Mail, the Sunday Times, the Sunday Express, 90 Minutes and Football Weekly, as well as the Evening Standard, Time Out, and all the local papers.

Politicians at both local and national level were bombarded with letters and the streets of the Borough were awash with determined teams of volunteers delivering leaflets, giving out balloons, badges and posters, knocking on doors, and just generally drumming up support.

The club's relegation meant that a return to The Valley was more important than ever before, and the campaign reached fever pitch a fortnight after Wimbledon had condemned the club to the Second Division, just two days before the election. Literally hundreds of people descended upon the Valley Club to find out how they could help, and were given the rallying call 'to go back to their constituencies and prepare for government!'

The next few days were a blur for those most heavily involved, culminating in a last, desperate push on polling day, with the Charlton fans out in selected wards, ferrying people to polling stations, and pleading with those who hadn't voted already to do so.

Even as the count began, officials of all major parties, but the Labour Party in particular, continued to pour scorn on the efforts of the Charlton fans. Their election agent even went so far as to predict a derisory vote of less than 500 in total, which, in his opinion, would have demonstrated just how unimportant people conceived the Valley issue to be.

Indeed, the initial results seemed to back up that claim as the Valley Party scored a mere 66 votes in one ward and 88 in another. But the Charlton supporters who packed into the Town Hall that evening need not have worried, because those early setbacks were overcome and the Valley Party's total vote steadily increased. In one ward 992 votes were polled by one candidate, who came within 350 of unseating the actual leader of the council, but the biggest prize of all was yet to come.

At around 4 a.m. on the morning of Friday May 4th the returning officer attempted to announce the result of the Eynsham ward in London SE2, but he was drowned out by the delirious cheers of the Charlton fans, as it became clear that the Chair of the planning committee that had rejected the plans in the first place, and the No.1 opponent to Charlton playing at the Valley, had paid with his seat.

The so-called no-hopers of the Valley Party had claimed a famous victory, and the final total of 14,838 votes (compared to 6,381 for the Liberal Democrats and 4,372 for the Greens) captured a healthy 11% of the total votes cast.

Once the dust had settled on that memorable evening, the Council's attitude towards Charlton underwent a dramatic change, and suddenly they were available for meetings and receptive to ideas. At the time of writing the formal rubber stamping of a revised application is all that is needed to signal the long awaited homecoming.

No-one can deny that the fans have played their part, and equally, no-one could deny the role played by the Supporters Club, and Voice of The Valley. People power can work, you know.

Let's Parler Chairmanspeak!

with Ron Noadesamoney

1. It's a great opportunity for this club.
Meaning: We're going to crucify another club.

2. There's money available to strengthen the squad.
Meaning: Charlton have had a couple of good attendances lately.

3. I'm sure all Palace fans realise the benefits of Lifeline.
Meaning: Hand over your money, suckers.

4. Everybody will be doing it in two years time.
Meaning: Nobody will be doing it in two years time, because I'll have proved it doesn't work.

5. We're the best of friends with Charlton.
Meaning: We're the best of friends - as long as they're paying their way.

6. I'm totally opposed to the Super League.
Meaning: I'm opposed because Palace weren't invited.

7. We've had no contact with the player.
Meaning: He won't sign for us because the terms are so bad.

8. We've drawn up extensive plans to improve the ground.
Meaning: I'm going to build another supermarket.

9. Charlton fans will come to appreciate the advantages of groundsharing.
Meaning: They'll eventually work out the advantages are all ours.

10. We'll be equal partners at Selhurst.
Meaning: I'm in charge and you'll do as you're told.

VOTV 7 Nov. 88

Voice of The Valley
The INDEPENDENT Charlton mag

Why I Used To Hate Tommy Hutchison........

Richard Wiseman on the resurrection of a dream.

Tommy Hutchison isn't a player for whom Charlton supporters will have a great deal of affection. Starved as we are of notable records (e.g. which club had two players sent off for fighting each other?), we were rightly proud of Bert Turner's unique 1946 achievement of scoring for both sides in the FA Cup Final.

I for one had often produced it in pub football conversations as an exasperated counter to the tedious trophy counting of more successful supporters. So, when Hutchison repeated the feat at Wembley in 1981, I took a strong dislike to him for ruining a Charlton conversation piece.

I was forced, however, to reassess my evaluation of the man the other week when he was reported, at the age of 41, to have scored for Swansea in a League match. To my immense relief this proved the existence of at least one player still in the Football League who is actually older than I am.

In case you haven't experienced it, let me tell you that the knowledge that every single one of the 900 or so players running out all over the country at five to three is younger than yourself brings with it an unforgettably cold shiver of fear and regret. It is an omen of middle age; a sign that boyhood is really over at last. For me, however, it was a particularly traumatic discovery because it brought with it the realisation that maybe, after all, I wasn't going to fulfil my lifelong ambition of scoring the winning goal for Charlton in the last minute of a Wembley Cup Final.

This is a goal I rehearsed countless times during my paper round in the late 1960's. A perfect throw from Charlie Wright had sent Bob Curtis down the right wing. He ran sixty yards before releasing a deep, swirling cross and I, timing my run perfectly, leapt at the far lamppost to power the ball past a stranded keeper.

Over the years I carried on perfecting this goal, directing bullet headers past bus stops and parking metres from a variety of centres, provided by Phil Warman, Harry Cripps, Terry Naylor and, on one memorable occasion, I even managed to get on the end of a mishit Ray Tumbridge shot and squeezed the winner between the pinch points outside Charlton station.

As I've grown older inhibition has made me more discreet, but even the other day discerning observers would have noticed the most subtle of neck movements with which I dispatched a low John Humphrey cross past two flat-footed ticket collectors at Charing Cross. The roar of the crowd was as loud as ever, but I disdained the histrionics of the modern goalscorer and continued modestly up The Strand.

But with the news that Billy Bonds has really retired this time, I have to admit that I've been standing forlornly on the terraces this season unable to escape the lamentable fact that I am leaving my breakthrough into the professional ranks breathtakingly late.

So you can no doubt imagine my elation on hearing the age-defying news from The Vetch Field. My confidence is back; all the old sharpness is there and I have a killer instinct that makes Derek Hales look like Larry The Lamb. Now, thanks to Tommy Hutchison, if we can just make it through the five previous rounds, you can rely on me to be in the right place at the right time at Wembley in May.

VOTV 8 Jan. 89

Voice of The Valley
The INDEPENDENT Charlton mag

Something CompletelyDifferent

THE SCENE: *The Club Shop. An assistant stands behind the counter reading a copy of Charlton News. The door opens and a tall, grey-haired man in a long raincoat comes in carrying a birdcage. A pause. At length the assistant looks up.*

Attendant: *Good afternoon, sir.*

Customer: *Good afternoon.*

The assistant resumes reading his Charlton News.

Customer (sharply): *I wish to register a complaint.*

The assistant looks up.

Assistant: *Really, sir, I'm sorry to hear that. Don't tell me - your Crystal Palace bath towel has run in the wash and turned all your clothes a horrible colour?*

Customer (impatiently): *My names is Noades. You may remember that I came in here a few years ago and bought this 'ere eagle.*

Assistant: *Ah, yes, sir. The lesser spotted red and blue striped eagle. The bird of the eighties, if I might be so bold.*

Ron Noades (for it is he): *The bird of the eighties? And on what ground do you base that assumption, my man?*

Assistant: *Why Selhurst Park, sir. It's the only ground left in the country. You've closed all the others down.*

This bird's a magnificent specimen, such fine colouring . I'm sure you agree, sir.

Ron Noades: *Well, actually, no. I don't agree.*

Assistant: *But surely, sir, you can see how Bright the bird is. It's the Wright one for you, I'm certain.*

Ron Noades: *It's dead.*

Assistant: *Come again, sir?*

Ron Noades: *This eagle is dead.*

Assistant: *I don't quite follow you, sir.*

Ron Noades: *It's DEAD. Look!*

He opens the cage, removes the bird and bangs it repeatedly on the counter.

Assistant: *Oh, no, sir, it's only sleeping. Big birds like this one tend to sleep most of their life. It's something of a sleeping giant, in fact.*

Ron Noades: *Sleeping giant? I'd call it a dead duck, myself. It's been like that since 1981.*

Assistant: *Surely not, sir. This bird is capable of pulling 30,000 crowds.*

Ron Noades: *Absolute rubbish. Especially now that it is dead.*

Assistant: *It's not dead, sir, it's missing its natural habitat. It's pining for the Fourth.*

Ron Noades: *Pining for the Fourth? What kind of talk is that?*

This eagle is dead. It has ceased to fulfil its fixtures. It has kicked the trainer's bucket. It has done a Stanley. Its lifeline has been cut. If you hadn't nailed it to the perch it would be pushing up the penalty spot.

IT IS AN EX-EAGLE!

Assistant: *Am I to take it, sir, that you no longer want this bird?*

Ron Noades: *That is correct. I would like something with a little more life in it. Something that will survive in the rarified atmosphere of the First Division for more than five minutes.*

What about that bob bob bobbin' little robin over there?

Assistant: *That, sir, is our pride and joy. Extremely rare in these parts. The red, red robin, a plucky little bird guaranteed to last a good deal longer in top class company than your eagle.*

What's more, sir, when he goes it'll be in his own, brand new, cage.

Ron Noades: *I'll take it. Valley Gold Card?*

Assistant consults list beside till.

Assistant: *I'm sorry, sir. I don't believe that card belongs to you. Perhaps you'd be happier with something you can pay for in small change. We have a very nice little pair of wings, not very sophisticated, but an amusing little diversion just the same. They're looking for a decent home................*

(By Steve Dixon and Rick Everitt, with apologies to John Cleese for the comparison.)

Voice of The Valley
The INDEPENDENT Charlton mag

Chelsea Blues

Charlton 3 Chelsea 0

STEVE DIXON reporting from the gutter

First Division leaders Chelsea, many people's early evening tip for the back-page lead, were sensationally beaten last night at The Valley.

The shock defeat came at the hands of those perennial strugglers, Cheltenham Athletic, who are bound to be down at the bottom of the inside back page again for most of the season.

Chelsea, roared on by a magnificent following of top football writers, totally dominated most match reports from start to finish, but somehow conceded three goals.

drunks

After a blistering opening paragraph of intense hyperbole, in which many readers felt the visitors could have taken a four-goal lead, the headline-making Blues fell behind when a hopeful upfield punt found one of those little red chaps in an offside position.

Astonishingly, the Saint and Greavsie editor kept his flag down and a sudden gust of wind took **WILLIAMS'** freak shot over the bravely-advancing Peasant and into the goal.

banal

Despite this setback, the Bridge boys blazed back in the next paragraph, very nearly winning a crosshead, after international full-back Tony Dingo's shot canoned off a corner flag. Then the injured Pheasant went close with a long goalkick.

A picture of a Chelsea player scoring appeared

inevitable, and indeed a goal did arrive, but to the utter confusion of many sub-editors, it was the Blues who fell further behind.

The giant Preasant showed just why he has been called up for regular interviews with the tabloids by picking the ball out of the net with considerable aplomb.

claptrap

The second half was a familiar story, with anyone still interested sentenced to endless Chelsea attacks, eventually punctuated by an outrageous 20-yard miskick from **MORTIMORE** which gave the unfortunate Pleasant no chance.

Chelsea boss Nobby Campbell was in typically eloquent mood after the game, filling what space remained with a string of very meaningful and important words of wisdom.

The attendance of 5,500 was lower than four matches in the Vauxhall Opel Premier Thatcher League Division One last night.

Another world class save from Preasant during last night's match with Crystal Palace

VOTV 14 Oct. 89

Voice of The Valley
The INDEPENDENT Charlton mag

People In Glass Houses

Steve Dixon on the peril of Palace actually achieving something for the first time in their entire history.

Whisper it quietly, but I know a bloke who supports Crystal Palace. Worse still, I actually work with him.

As you can imagine, his life was hell for a month or so following THAT match at Anfield. I had some fun, but he just smiled and kept silent, as if he somehow knew that he'd have the last laugh. I hate to admit it, but he was right.

Our performance in the League game was a disgrace, while the ZDS Cup tie could not have come at a worse time. Even we couldn't help laughing at the dig in the latest Eagle Eye: "The FA have informed us," they wrote, "that even if we beat Charlton for a third time this season, we will not be allowed to keep them.

But they might as well, for all the success we've had against them. And of course, there's still that game in April to consider. What's the betting that defeat that day will be the result that sends us down?

It's going to be hard enough to take as it is, but to be relegated by Palace doesn't even bear thinking about. However, they've beaten us twice already and must be favourites to do so again. They also look likely to stay in the First Division, while we're already planning trips to Port Vale and Barnsley.

This catalogue of disasters would be enough to try the patience of any good Charlton supporter, but it doesn't end there because, by the most improbable sequence of events since Jeffrey Archer's last novel, Palace have crept into the semi-finals of the FA Cup.

While we slithered out at The Hawthorns, courtesy of a cunningly-positioned puddle, Palace sailed serenely on. Admittedly, they have the toughest possible semi-final, against Liverpool, but that is only because there were no Fourth Division teams left in the competition.

Do you realise that the toughest opposition they have so far faced are Portsmouth, from the lower reaches of Division Two? And even then they struggled, trailing 1-0 and having to rely on a last-minute penalty from Andy Gray that was probably awarded by Kelvin Morton's brother.

Clearly feeling that this had overtaxed our feathered friends, the gods of fortune next offered them the seemingly insurmountable challenge of a home draw with Huddersfield Town. Surprisingly, the Terriers were unable to breach the Palace rearguard and went home thrashed 4-0.

And who came next? Rochdale! Bloody Rochdale, one of only two Fourth Division sides left in. Thanks very much, Bert. They had already disposed of mighty Whitley Bay, so we consoled ourselves with the thought that it was now one Mickey Mouse club against another.

Could the minnows triumph this time? Unfortunately, the answer was yes, largely due to an astonishing last-minute miss by the visiting centre forward, who shot straight at Martyn in front of a packed Sainsbury's/Allder's/Members' Terrace.

So eight balls duly went into the little velvet bag for the Sixth Round draw. Liverpool were in there, as were Manchester United and Aston Villa, but it made little difference. Even the comatose old men of the FA knew that Palace would get Cambridge.

There was a slight technical hitch, resulting in them becoming the away team, but that was the only surprise. Come on, admit it. You were all saying: "I bet the stripey bastards get Cambridge?" And lo and behold they did.

It wouldn't have been so bad, however, if they'd gone down to the Abbey and pulverised the last Fourth Division team in the competition. Instead of which they had to rely on a distinctly dodgy late goal from a Crewe Alexandra reject.

Thus, the nightmare is fast becoming reality and now only Liverpool stand in the way of a tide of red and blue Wembley 90 souvenirs washing down Wembley Way and the mass suicide of thousands of Charlton fans. We understand that if they do stumble through, plans are in hand to eliminate both the other semi-finalists and reinstate Halifax Town to meet them on May 12.

A potentially ghastly side-effect of their progress is that they'll also be on public display on the big day. Of course, it might yet turn out for the best - Liverpool may feel that they let them off lightly back at Anfield and go for double figures. But if Alan Pardew pops up for a late winner......

The way I see it, we are left with two options. Either we all go down to The Valley on semi-final day and pray, or we get along to Villa Park and join the Red Army. Anyone fancy running a coach?

VOTV 19 Apr. 90

WINNER

Judged Man of the Match for the recent game against Watford at Selhurst Park was Ted Rivers of Floyd Road, Charlton. Ted had to get up at 6am to be at the ground for noon, clawing his way through the Bank Holiday traffic on the South Circular and walking the remaining mile and a half to the ground after having to park near Norbury. Then he had to pay over twenty pounds for himself and his two sons to watch the game from the Arthur Waite Stand. A deserved winner, although there are thousands of others like Ted, just as deserving. Well done all of you, and keep smiling. Only fifteen months to go.

ADAM PETERS

VOTV 3 Apr. 88

Voice of The Valley
The INDEPENDENT Charlton mag

Th..Th..Th..That's All, Folks

A philosophical Rick Everitt reflects on the last four years and wonders what the future might hold

So it's over, at least for the time being. Even Houdini failed in the end, and we shouldn't blame Lennie Lawrence for the fact that he has finally fallen off the First Division tightrope.

There are at least fifteen thousand Charlton managers out there in Kentish suburbia and we'd probably all have done things differently given the opportunity. However, Lennie's record over the last five years - promotion and three successful escapes - speaks for itself.

But how, with the benefit of hindsight, will we come to regard these last five seasons? And perhaps more important, where do we go from here?

A disinterested (and some might say uninterested) party, Mick Dennis of the Evening Standard, told us back in December that our Selhurst sojourn will come to represent a golden age.

I commented last month that his argument in that article was patently ludicrous, and in terms of his ridiculous analogy with Arsenal fans campaigning for a return to Woolwich, so it was. But might he have a point in narrow playing terms?

There can be no real dispute that the players who have worn the Charlton shirt since the summer of 1985 have been immeasurably superior to their immediate predecessors.

Indeed, we can go further and say that not only have we been watching our best teams since the 1950s, but that they continued to improve as the eighties moved their conclusion. And it is deeply ironic that we will be relegated with what many regard as the best Charlton side they have ever seen.

For example, which right back of recent memory compares with the athleticism of John Humphrey? Who could match the intelligence and creativity on the ball of Colin Walsh? And what Charlton captain ever demonstrated the leadership qualities of the sadly departed Peter Shirtliff?

Nor can we dispute the rich harvest of cherished memories that we will take back to the Second Division. The closing week of the promotion campaign was the first landmark, with the incredulous celebrations at the Fulham and Carlisle games.

No-one who was at Old Trafford for our first Division One victory since 1957 will easily forget it, nor the play-offs with Leeds, or the brutish confrontation at Stamford Bridge.

Even this season, the quality of Charlton's passing and finishing in the game with Chelsea stands out, while the breathtaking raw talent of Scott Minto, Paul Mortimer, Paul Williams and, last year, Mickey Bennett seemed to offer real hope.

And there are other, less glorious, folk memories. The waterlogged cup tie at West Brom will earn a place in most mental scrapbooks, as will last year's apparently pointless trip to Nottingham Forest. We'll also cherish the four defeats at Anfield; a brave performance and a penalty against us in every one.

No-one could really dispute the relative quality of the football we have seen. But was it as exciting, say, as watching the swashbucking, unpredictable antics of the Nelson years? The players and opposition then might not have been as good, but the entertainment value was unmatched.

And we played at The Valley. Mr Dennis won't appreciate the point, but the truth is you can't isolate one aspect of the experience of watching football from another. That's the real reason why his view that the last few years will come to represent a golden age is a load of rubbish.

For me, everything that has happened to Charlton since September 21, 1985 has been flawed by the fact that it has taken place away from The Valley. I've had a good deal of enjoyment out of the last few seasons, but I'd swap it all never to have left Floyd Road.

I'm very sorry if that doesn't suit Mr Noades or the Fleet Street hacks, but it remains the case. What's more, I know the majority of Charlton fans reading this will agree with me.

And there is one more good reason why you cannot isolate the venue from the football. Had we been playing in the proper place, gates would have been that much higher, resources that much greater and transfers like that of Colin Pates and Mickey Bennett unnecessary.

We cannot change the past. But hopefully we can influence the future and that is where a return to The Valley comes in.

More immediately, it is imperative that we retain enough of the present team to once again climb out of the Second Division. The example of Leeds and Sheffield United, coupled with our own experience of some 29 years, should be enough to convince us that this will not be easy.

Next season we will also have the handicap of very little income at the gate. It would be nice to think that the hard core six thousand will continue to trek across to Selhurst, but the harsh reality of visits from Port Vale and Barnsley suggests otherwise.

The playing success of our years at Selhurst Park has so far concealed the real vulnerability of the club's position. Promised a return, most came reluctantly, but offer them mid-table Second Division fare, with a sprinkling of the traditional free transfer signings in the side, and you could be talking about 2,500 or less.

There is just one glimmer of hope, and that is that relegation could provide the springboard for another promotion campaign, this time coupled with a triumphant return home. It is a romantic scenario, and one that would require great courage and determination by the board of directors.

But it is not quite impossible. It would be the happiest of endings to the most extraordinary of sagas. And then we might have a real golden age.

EDITORIAL

Three Cheers For Democracy

In many ways, the fact that three months have necessarily intervened between the local elections and this issue of VOTV is no bad thing.

For perspective, in the hours and days that followed May 3, was in desperately short supply.

Even with the benefit of many weeks hindsight, however, it is clear that something remarkable happened.

Only an elementary knowledge of voting behaviour is necessary to be aware that single-issue parties do not easily command electoral support. If they did, then the present duopoly would not persist.

People take electoral choice very seriously, in some cases absurdly so, given the dominance of one party or the other in their locality.

And yet in May a great swathe of the Greenwich electorate voted for a party that was not only new, but one which had no ideology and no programme for office.

Nothing to offer, in fact, but a commitment to return Charlton Athletic to The Valley.

What it did have, of course, was roots. The generations that have watched our football club are represented in every ward and on every street corner.

And as we have said before, those roots were what this argument has always been about. Not convenience or profitability, relevant considerations though they may be, but identity and validity.

Some points do need to be made. For a start, 14,838 votes do not equal 14,838 voters. Many wards have dual representation.

By aggregating the higher of the two totals in such places and adding it to the tally in single-member wards you get a minimum figure of around 9,250.

Allow for those who supported the second Valley candidate,(in almost all cases the one lower on the ballot paper,) but not the first, and a final total of around 10,000 appears reasonable.

It would also be stretching credibility to argue that all were Charlton supporters. Doubtless there were hundreds of Millwall fans, dozens of Arsenal and Spurs followers, even the odd Palace fan, who gave us their support. We thank them all.

But we should remember too that the great majority of our fans were disenfranchised. We should note the rumours of hundreds of spoilt ballot papers in Bexley, Bromley, Lewisham and even Croydon.

And we should take the greatest possible pride in the fact that nowhere did we do better than in Charlton itself.

The Valley Party was a huge gamble and one that might easily have backfired. Had we failed to gain respectable support, it could easily have destroyed all our hopes.

Instead, it was a success of hugely improbable and glorious proportions, an achievement that will be remembered for as long as Charlton Athletic itself.

It was the clearest possible evidence that football fans can mobilise and organise effectively. That the game retains its unrivalled place in the fabric of the community.

More than that, it will mean that we shall, after all, return to The Valley.

VOTV 21 Sep. 90

MATCH REFEREE

Kelvin Morton

(Bury St Edmunds)

Began refereeing in Cambridgeshire when 16. progressed through to the Football League Referees List via the Eastern Counties League and Football Combination.

Married with two children, Kelvin is a complete and utter lunatic.

20 over-used facts about Millwall

1. Millwall are in the East End of London.

2. Every game at The Den is a right old Cockney knees-up.

3. Tony Cascarino was once transferred for a set of tracksuits and some corrigated iron. (Boring)

4. This is their first season in the First Divison after 103 years. (Even more boring).

5. Millwall always beat Charlton.

6. Millwall believe they are the biggest club in SE London.

7. This is not true.

8. We are.

9. Terry Hurlock is mean and fearsome.

10. Every time Millwall are mentioned in the papers, the words "Old Kent Road" are sure to follow.

11. Every one of the 20,000 fans who went to the Liverpool match has been a regular for forty years.

12. The Den is a well-appointed and spacious ground with a particularly inviting visitors' enclosure.

13. It is also extremely easy to find.

14. John Docherty is a dour Scotsman.

15. All Millwall fans eat jellied eels and say "Cor blimey, Guvnor!"

16. When they were televised live on two successive Sundays recently they were stuffed out of sight. (We are rather fond of this one.)

17. Harry Cripps and Barry Kitchener were "loyal servants" of the club.

18. Referees and visiting fans always get a good reception at The Den.

19. Millwall have a creche on matchdays.

20. They sing "no-one likes us", but it is not true any more. The South London Press thinks they are wonderful.

Steve Dixon

Every Father's Nightmare

Voice of The Valley
The INDEPENDENT Charlton mag

"So what do you REALLY want to do then?" This is the very loaded question that the Job Centre lady is asking me in June 1989, and I am stuck for a meaningful answer. Two years before I'd given up working in offices to write a play that was so boring and so inept, I couldn't even kid myself. As a fan of WHEN SUNDAY COMES (and a contributor) I had toyed with the idea of starting my own. After months of navel contemplation, it was my turn to show up at the DHSS.

Did you notice how government schemes have really cool names? Dynamic stuff like ENTER-PRISE INITIATIVE or RESTART; well, something like the "We've put up with you for half a year you scrounging swine, do you think we're gonna support you for ever, scum" scheme just doesn't capture the imagination as much, does it? It looked like it was back to the office for me, until I dropped a hint that I wouldn't mind having a go at doing a fanzine. This could have been the biggest mistake of my life, and given the chance I'd certainly have chickened out. However I was put into the sink or swim situation that either produces something worthwhile or a load of old tat. 18 months on, I'm still not sure which it is.

Is 'Through The Wind & Rain' the only government sponsored fanzine in Britain? Maybe so, but I would recommend this method of starting. £40 a week combined with my first year's proceeds kept me afloat; content was not tampered with (they couldn't have cared less if the truth be known); more importantly I could work full time on the fanzine. Even though the year's allowance ran out some time ago it still isn't necessary for me to supplement my income by means of the w-word. When new-issue-time comes along, with worries about the printers, sending parcels all round the country and standing outside Anfield in all weathers etc. etc., I cheer myself up by reminding myself that it beats working. To paraphrase Stevie Smith the poetess, Through The Wind And Rain is not waving...... but it's not drowning either.

A Liverpool fanzine has advantages and disadvantages. There is a huge potential in sales of course, but time and again I come across the retort "What have you got to complain about?", which not only fosters the Anfield myth of perfection, but pigeonholes fanzines as moan-sheets pure and simple.

The Anfield myth often reminds me of the line in the Watergate film 'All The Presidents Men', when Robert Redford's secret source sneers "Forget what the press say about the White House. Truth is, they're not very bright guys". They must be doing something right, of course, but it remains a paradox that The Family Club puts up such a forbidding front that even its own sup-porters can sometimes feel like intruders. They never felt like that in Shankly's time; a change has come over the club, and it isn't for the better in my humble opinion. Links are beginning to come though, in particular the local FSA branch is getting its feet under the table. Even the fanzines are 'appreciated' - the club's word, not mine. One small step for man.....

As for the question of what IS a fanzine, to give any rigid definition would simply impose un-wanted restrictions. 'Alternative' is usually a key word, which means less sycophantic drivel, open criticism of players (yes, some Liverpool players DO have faults) and officials, taking great care to include standard fanzine fare like racism, sexism, facilities, policing and so on. And hu-mour, which is so peculiarly individual as to be indefinable. Watch a standard sitcom; those people genuinely believe the word 'willy' to be hysterical, they're not pretending. It takes all sorts....

The Liverpool fanzines will always be haunted and affected by the events of 15th April 1989. Several traps lie in wait for the editor, especially someone with as sick a sense of humour as mine. The Liverpool expression 'dead' (replacing 'very') is out; a bad back pass is not a catastrophe; if there's a tight squeeze in the away end you are not being 'crushed', and if you use the word 'disaster' you'd better have a damn good excuse. Add these to the usual fanzine outs; expressions like 'poofter' and 'tart' (when contributors don't have your ethical stance), and the LFC mag can be a minefield of cock-up possibilities.

That might be why there are only two of them; fortunately we have an excellent relationship with WHEN SUNDAY COMES (Ian Tilley is a personal friend) but if there were more I would welcome them and encourage them. That advantage I talked about - the level of Liverpool support - is slowly but surely coming round to the idea that the fanzine is a Good Thing. Issue 1's print run of 2000 did not sell out; I'm fairly confident of selling all Issue 7 - about 4000. Nothing magnificent, but it's getting there.

The reaction of other supporters to Liverpool F.C. is bizarre to say the least. Most tie in with the "I don't like them, but you've got to admire them" stance. The rest despise us. Forget silly old Millwall; no-one likes US, yet we do care actually. It falls in with a general decline in opinions about Merseyside as a whole. The fanzine deals with this too; people can simply put it alongside what they consider to be Scouse self-pity, but we simply shake our heads with the sad knowledge of a true paranoiac who just KNOWS everybody's out to get him.

You can't play this hand too much though, as over 50% of the Anfield faithful now come from all over the country. This has meant a general increase in animosity towards Manchester United; non-Merseyside Reds understand the Everton rivalry, but don't really FEEL it. Now the important fixture is United, and the fanzine duly reflects this. In a sense this can involve a certain amount of pandering to your readership; as long as we keep winning trophies, I personally find the media's unjustifiable obsession with Old Trafford comical. It is still something that can anger the average Liverpudlian, and we take great care to make sure the pre-Hillsborough sickness does not return - at least not in TTW&R's pages. Perhaps now the Babes can rest in peace.

The Liverpool supporter is a bizarre beast; it is safe to say that nothing like him/her has ever existed before. They follow a team which has almost made the Hardest Championship In The World To Win (thank you, John Motson) their own personal property. There is now a generation of fans who can't spell 'struggle', a generation who blink uncomprehendingly at the word 'defeat'. And yet Anfield is one of the few places where an opponent's skill will be applauded. Confused? Liverpool supporters may not have anything to complain about, but do you think that stops them? We have some of the biggest moaners in football - it's a miracle we're not all like that, but we're not. Honest!

Through The Wind And Rain's primary objective, then, is to amuse, enlighten and entertain, (Pretentious? Moi?) but if the team falls below their usual high standard, the fanzine will be ready. Supporters are not treated with the respect they deserve, and TTW&R highlights this. I've no illusions about our current status in the scheme of all things Red, but I'm optimistic about the future. Because of the fanzine and the FSA, I feel I can stand up to the people who want to destroy football; if John Barnes does go to Italy, I may have to prove this against the racists who disgraced us before 1987, for instance.

Because of the fanzine I count myself lucky to have found new friends - Billy, Barry, Mark, Dylan, Ian of course - some I've never even met; Dave from King of the Kippax, Tony from Eagle Eye, Dave from The Italian Job, and my most faithful reader, Karl from Treherbert, who I mention only because Treherbert has never been listed in a football book before! Thanks a lot, folks. I've applied for an extention to our 15 minutes of infamy. I'm confident we'll get it.

WALKING ALONE

In June, I received my renewal form for my Anfield Road season ticket. Another tenner up- that made 25.00 in two years, less one match. A 25% rise over two years- go and ask your boss for that, and he/she'd kick you down the stairs, after they stop laughing. Grumbling, the cheque went in the post. What the hell else was I going to do? Early July, I was told by letter that the seat I had occupied for seven seasons was no longer mine, the away fans were getting it. Slightly stunned, I called the club to find out just what was going on.

After 10 minutes talking to LFC's ticket lady, I knew I wasn't the only one who was disgusted- she sounded like she'd been through a mangle, and actually thanked me for not threatening her. "Someone's coming round to kick my teeth in," she moaned. I know how he feels, I thought, but kept it to myself. Three weeks later, I made my way to Anfield, with my friends, to spy out my new seat. It was o.k., but we got back to the office to find out we'd looked at the wrong seats. Did you know 119 comes after 115? It does in the Anny Road end, and put us behind a roof support into the bargain. After three journeys back and forth, we found good seats- in the Main Stand.

So, twelve years of standing and sitting in the Anny Road comes to an end- from the terracing days of the Barmy Army to the seated days of Dad's Army. A tidal wave of classic football and a thousand memories good and bad- hoping Liverpool would one day score at our end, rejoicing if we got the 2nd half. Waving to the Kopites during the 7-0 against Spurs in 78; mingling with the Albion fans in 79; worrying about my seat when the Geordies stood on them in 84; getting butted by a Geordie wearing a baby bonnet in 87; being nicknamed Shaggy because of my inadequate facial hair; countless verbal battles with the away fans; the strangers around you turning into good friends; all gone in one, heartless swoop.

****
We are sorry that one or two of them are a little upset, but we think it's a small price to pay considering the overall planning. PETER ROBINSON 7/7/89
****

It didn't take a maths genius to work out the advantages of the all-seater stadium, the panic solution to football's ills that is being touted by every two-bit 'expert', but here goes. (all figures rough) Average gate 40,000. 20,000 sit, 20,000 stand. 3.50 to stand, 6 quid to sit, 20 games a season. 20,000 x 3.50 x 20 = 3,800,000. 40,000 sitting x 6.00 x 20 = 4,800,000, a profit of one million pounds a season. Not to be sneezed at. The creation of a run on Kop season tickets, and sadly Justice Taylor's excellent proposals, have only strengthened the club's hand with regards to putting seats in the only remaining terracing at Anfield. Having wiped 5,000 off its' capacity, there is hardly any rational reason why the Kop cannot be seated, except maybe the wishes of the fans?

****
Football must consider its' supporters because they are our greatest sponsors. Without the fans there would be no game...
PETER ROBINSON 23/2/89
****

Surely the club's Chief Executive himself wouldn't deny he has wanted an all-seater stadium for many years? During any season, barely a month goes by without Mr. Robinson telling the press that the modern trend is for people to sit, and, coincidentally I'm sure, creating the impression that Kopites stood because they had to, not because they want to. It would be very easy to adopt a tabloid mentality to connect the disaster with the club's plans for Anfield. Without using those odious methods of expression, it seems obvious to me that a plan has been in the pipeline for years, for commercial reasons only, and that Hillsborough has become the catalyst to bring it about. Even expressed in such insipid words, the thought is monstrous, but it's more and more typical of the kind of thing I am hearing from more and more Liverpudlians. (Yuppie Club was one expression I heard from a steward) Through the pursuit of money- more recently, our involvement in the ITV money row and new speculation about the so-called Super League, plus the now annual change of team strip- the club is moving further away from its' lifeblood-the fans. Having the manager tell us we are an absolute credit every few months isn't going to be enough.

There was certainly room for improvement for our ground. The old Anny Road terracing, connected to the Kemlyn, must have angered the club many times. It was hardly ever needed, and the sight of empty space at a lock-out annoyed many fans too. To Peter

THROUGH THE WIND & RAIN
A LIVERPOOL FANZINE

Robinson, that potential revenue going to waste was just too much to take. However, pity the poor away fans. True, they now have one of the best views in the ground, but they'll pay for it. No terracing for them either. The claim that the changes were made for safety's sake, and more convenient policing (haven't we heard that somewhere before?), ring incredibly hollow. There is now only one place where empty space may occur- the Kop, and soon the poor old part time supporter (a much maligned breed) will not be able to go there, either. The 'odd match' supporter is now almost literally barred from Anfield, a full year before ID cards. That's some going.

The policing angle is particularly odd, set against all the arguments against I.D. cards ie that trouble takes place outside the ground. If this work was considered of such importance (and, when I swapped my season ticket,I had a first hand view of the administrative chaos these changes caused, never mind the angry fans), why has it taken until now to do it? As for police convenience, this might lead to the kind of complacency so apparent in South Yorkshire. There is a quote in an old Orson Welles film;'a policeman's job is not supposed to be easy..it's only easy in a police state.' Being a policeman in Britain is fast becoming the easiest job in the world.

The silence of the local media immediately after the announcement hardly seemed like a conspiracy-it was more like fear. It was the same as the citizens of a town like Barrow, who tell you how wonderful nuclear power is (radiation?? yum yum give us more) knowing full well that if B.N.F.L. pull out, local unemployment would reach 80% plus.In a football-crazy city like this, good links with the clubs are so vital. A lack of soccer stories, and coverage that lacks depth and inside information, would cause severe problems for a newspaper or radio station in Newcastle or Liverpool or Glasgow.The fact that a few thousand locals were treated shabbily by one of the area's major organisations would have had people in uproar- in normal circumstances. Was the ensuing silence a measure of how Liverpool F.C. are regarded within the community? How many fans stayed silent, fearing an act of vindictiveness by the club?
****
If we could charge 15.00 or 20.00..... it would be a very different situation,but we have always tried to keep our prices as low as possible. PETER ROBINSON 11/8/89
****
Of course, a sense of proportion must be kept.Reading through the local papers for any mention of the anger these changes have caused,you came across the usual daily diet of death, rape, unemployment, and realise that sitting somewhere else in a football ground is no big deal to anyone else. It's a big deal for us,though. Like most things in life, it isn't what was done but how it was done that matters. After Hillsborough and before ID cards, Liverpool treated a fair-sized portion of its' support with utter contempt at a time when they should have been looking after them properly.

It should also be noted that the efforts of Smith and Robinson on the financial side have resulted in Liverpool being amongst the elite. The club's finances have to be spot on to keep the big stars coming here - whether the fans will tolerate continuous price increases to subsidise unnecessary ground changes is a different matter. It only takes a quick flick through 'Betrayal Of A Legend',the scathing attack on the Edwards' running of United, to realise that Liverpool supporters have been very lucky to have had the likes of John Smith and Peter Robinson working for our continued success. Having said that, it cannot be over-emphasised that the majority of the revenue the club has been built on came from the pockets of their loyal and devoted following. In the last five years, great strains have been placed on that loyalty- Heysel and Hillsborough forced many to question their presence on the terraces. Sadly, some have decided not to go the match anymore (Franny, if you read this, please reconsider) and the timing of the Anny Road fiasco could not have been more callous if football's enemies in the government had engineered it.
****
KOPITES ARE....SITTING ?!
It seemed unthinkable, but the Kop may soon be full of those cheap, red plastic efforts we've seen in other parts of the ground.No, not inflatable flamingoes,seats. I was never that sentimental about the Kop; us Anny Roaders used to have a name for the people who stand there.It rhymed, and it wasn't very pleasant. However, the pictures of it after Hillsborough brought a lump to the throat, if it wasn't already there, and I'd prefer to leave it as it is. Converting the Anfield Road End to seats finished off the singing there,and it seems to be a football rule that people in seats don't sing,except. away from home,where they often drown out the terracing. Anfield with no singing,even the minimum we get nowadays,is unthinkable. The club must know we don't just go for the football; we'd stay at home with the rest of the bums otherwise. Maybe I'm being selfish. Kopites- write to T.T.W.&.R. and tell me what YOU want.

THROUGH THE WIND & RAIN
A LIVERPOOL FANZINE

LMC - a tower of jelly

During the summer, was there anything as pathetic as the climbdown by the League Management Committee, in the face of ITV's objections to the new fixture list? (English cricket) Well, apart from that, (the SLD's Euro-election results) oh shut it. The sickly "we don't want to offend television, they bring so much to the game" attitudes of Doug Ellis and others simply re-inforced the Super League propaganda machine, something I thought the Football League strongly opposed. The Big Four and a Half provide 20 league fixtures per season-10 of which were televised last season, with the threat of more this year.

Brian Moore:"Talking about title chases, you get the feeling Utd. will be amongst them...you'd never argue against Forest ...and I know in London many fans feel Spurs could be in with a shout.. and not forgetting my Evertonian friends." This chilling segment from the Liverpool/Arsenal Makita friendly gave a reminder of t.v. priorities for the coming season. Top 10 teams Norwich, Derby, Millwall, Coventry etc weren't even mentioned, and the typical first batch of televised games is only confirmation of continuing t.v. ignorance of the wishes of football fans. Knowing full well that there are 4 million people, like me, who'd even watch blow football, ITV ignores them completely as a guarenteed minimum audience whose feelings don't have to be considered. Big city bias, goals galore promises, showy video technique and sickly presenters are now the norm, in a desperate bid for a mass audience.

There is no worse sight on the small screen than that of Elton Welsby and Jim Rosenthal smirking and grinning, then grinning and smirking through The Match. Sports linkmen are a symbol of televised sport; They're all the same, anyway, aren't they/Big goons running around and sweating a lot/ Use the same face to front it all, no matter how little he knows/Drag out the old stars of the sport to inject the most basic, inane comments/ Cue close-up on a woman in the crowd showing some cleavage, and, here's ANOTHER action replay. Most important of all only show the elite, the lower contestants and clubs DO NOT MATTER.

If you take a look at the facts, big club coverage on the small screen is often a turn-off, in quality terms-the best match last season was Millwall 2 Norwich 3; the year before it was highlights of Blackburn 3 Leicester 3, closely followed I admit by Liverpool 3 United 3- the obvious conclusion to make is that ITV care nothing about quality, just quantity of viewers, and short-term quantity at that. Television is trying to do a job on football, the same one it did on cinema going. Once it's finished, it will move elsewhere, to feed off something else.

Over the last two seasons, t.v. has been the main culprit in screwing up Reds fans' enjoyment of a traditional Saturday afternoon match. 3pm kickoffs-remember them? In 86/87, we had fourteen of the blighters, including GASP! a derby. In 87/88, the Reds once went 7 weeks without such a fixture, and only had ten all season. Last season, we only had eight, although Hillsborough obviously played a part. Liverpool beat the Saints on January 21st-apart from thrashing Wednesday on Grand National day (11.30am start), they did not play a home game on a Saturday for the rest of the season. Enough is enough.

The re-scheduling of Liverpool v United for television was a total disgrace. Football is under the thumb of ITV, and for a portion of the money supporters generate. The two clubs now have to put up with a 21-day gap between league games. Enough is enough. The squalid grabbing of short-term cash by the League, FA and the clubs is a sure-fire step backwards. Small clubs may go to the wall because they haven't a high enough profile to compete with Liverpool or United, even on their own patch. Someone at the top has to finally realise one basic truth- you don't have to sell EVERYTHING. Mind you, that's close to a national philosophy at the moment. Voting for a Chairman like an Ellis or a McKeag is not the answer, not even close. (p.s. Bill Fox -who he?)

NEW T.V. DEAL
----
1. All 20 Big Four and a Half matches to be televised live.
2. Any club deemed 'unfashionable' by ITV to be fined for achieving top spot.
3. Interviewers allowed onto the field of play.
4. Jim Rosenthal takes all the penalties.
5. Any team going 5 points clear is deducted 5 points.
6. All defenders have to play 'statues' when the ball is in the area.
7. Stocks and rotten eggs for referees who don't give three penalties in a game.
8. Top 2 sides play off for the title, no matter how many points between them.
9. In the event of a drawn game, the referee will play injury time until
        someone scores a dramatic, late, viewing-figures boosting goal.
10. I'm Greg Dyke, I don't sign this because I'll do what I like but
11. You have to sign it, so get writing Fatso!

                              SIGNED   DUG EJJIZ
                                        WOT ERA

SONG AND DANCE MAN

Make 'em laugh,make 'em laugh,Doncha know all the world wants to laugh
My Dad said be a Chairman, my son,   But be a fifty-day one
They'll be standing in line for that old 'humble man' monkey-shine
You put on your red kit and hit the back of the net
Then all your backers pull out and you frown and you fret
And everybody finds out you're just one greedy get
Make 'em laugh, Make 'Em Laugh, MAKE 'EM LAUGH!!

Make 'em laugh,make 'em laugh,Doncha know all the world wants to laugh
My Dad said don't despair my son At least you gave the scousers some fun
There were roars, there were screams Everywhere 'cept the theatre of dreams
Now all we get is Doom and Gloom and Fergie's despair
And all we've got to laugh about is Bobby C.'s hair
At least we know the Butcher's Boy is still in the chair
Make 'em laugh, Make 'Em Laugh, MAKE 'EM LAUGH!!

With all reverence to Donald O'Connor and SINGING IN THE RAIN. Just one of
many delights on a new K-tel lp,GET MELLOW WITH MICHAEL,includes I Who Have
Nothing,What Kind Of Fool Am I, The Games People Play,Buddy Can U Spare 20
Million,Simple Shy Man Says,On My Own, Yesterday, Give Me Just A Little
More Time (the Chairman Of The Board classic) and many more. This record
costs 10 million up front (3 months to pay,though?!)

"Vot iz it zat yoo vant me to do?"
"Agent Wilkinson,we are now in the 145th year of
Conservative rule,and we have snuffed out all forms of
proletarian pleasure - except one. Football, damn it! We are
sending you back to a time when it seemed to be on its' last
legs. 1989. Death on the terraces, our own smart card
shambles, greed of all kinds, violence, field-goal kickers
posing as footballers etc etc. Your mission is to go back to
that time and drive in the last nail. You will assemble a
grizzly gang of cut-throats. You will bully. You will bore.
You will cheat. You will stand in a line with your arm in
the air. You will, in short, finish football forever."
"Zen vot?"
"Then the people will take up hockey!"
"Hmmm, piece of cake."

Howard Wilkinson IS The Terminator

THROUGH THE
WIND & RAIN
A LIVERPOOL FANZINE

BOOKWORM

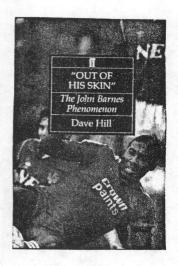

OUT OF HIS SKIN - DAVE HILL (Faber and Faber £4.99)
"The story is bigger than the individual,but without that individual, the story would have been harder to tell." And harder to sell,too,although Dave neglects to mention this. A blistering indictment of British racism-Liverpool in particular- and its' inevitable affect on the national game,wouldn't have had people racing to W.H.Smiths in droves,with their unwanted Xmas book vouchers. A bio, official or otherwise,on the game's most talented player, is an assured best seller. Somehow the book, good as it is, can never really shake off the cynicism of its' origins.

To understand Hill better,it is essential to read his other opus, an excellent book on Prince.His theme soon comes to light -'Blackness', and the varying degrees of it. Prince and J.B., according to Hill,are world stars who have denied this blackness, for the sake of success in the white world. In both books there is a figure on the fringe of the action who directly oppose the star. Hill gives tremendous detail of two careers that are intended to run along side the main subject. In both cases (In A POP LIFE, it is Morris Day of The Time, In OUT OF HIS SKIN it is Howard Gayle) the book is seriously weakened by comparison to an obviously lesser talent.

Hill states,again in the preface,that Barnes "being associated with this book wouldn't be consistent with his diplomatic goal and I have no wish to hinder his pursuit of them any more than,as a white man,I intend to pass judgement on it." How big of him! Hill knows full well THAT's a judgement in itself,and leaves you in no doubt of what he thinks - in case you miss it, though, there are countless snide references to 'The Diplomat's Son'. Besides, when did anyone write a biography without judgement?

The weak link of the whole book is the large portion given to the LFC career of Howie Gayle. Hill's sympathy for the people of Liverpool 8 is clearly sincere, but he does his (and their) arguments no good at all by mentioning Gayle the player in the same breath as Barnes the player. Hill dwells on his excellent display against Munich in 81,yet doesn't even name two players whose rearguard action played just as large a part on that memorable night. Colin Irwin, also Scouse, and Richard Money, both had to move elsewhere because of the lack of 1st team chances;however they were white, and spoil his argument, therefore they are of no interest.

Howie's COMPARATIVE lack of ability, plus his often vile temper, were not the reasons for his Anfield exit but,of course, racism. Never mind that he hasn't been successful since he left (again comparatively), and that he was quite at home with the Psycho brigade at Birmingham (Hopkins, Blake,Harford,Van Den Howsyorfather etc). Never mind the endless list of LFC casualties (including The Great Paul Walsh, who once scored 17 goals in 22 games for Liverpool)- in Hillese, Howie The True Black was pushed out of Anfield because of racism whereas Barnes the Metaphorical Mulatto, the (cue snort) Diplomat's Son was accepted. Lenny Bruce once said Jim Crow was bad,but Crow Jim was the worst; Dave Hill's opinions on blackness are very questionable; as a white man, he has no right to insist on any code of conduct for people whose problems he can only ever guess at. That is just another form of racism. Whatever you think about positive discrim-ination,(I believe in it for what it's worth) you can't give a player so much benefit of the doubt. Gayle was a striker, but Liverpool chose Rush. Can anyone seriously claim LFC did not make the right choice?

And it spoils an otherwise great book; Hill is an excellent writer. The

word journalist has become synonymous with the drunken, lying tit-fiend so beloved of satirists everywhere, but he has the classic reporter's skill of piercing a subject with one telling phrase, instead of the chunk of junk a lesser talent would need. When he calls Bobby Charlton 'the model prole patriot', you know exactly what he means. He dissects the racist remarks of people like Grobbelaar and Tommy Smith, and gives them a rubbishing they really deserve. The pre-Barnes attitude at the club is found to be more than wanting; all the old shite that should not exist in a so-called civilised age. His description of 87/88 is good too, but it left me sad. I longed for that brief, intoxicating moment when we weren't just The Best, we were The Only. Who cared what anyone else was doing? He also, rightly, gives a few namechecks to the other players in that side-it wasn't a one-man achievement. He is extremely flattering re The Supreme Being; some of us knew it all the time, Dave!

His claim to be a Red rings hollow; more likely, he spotted a story and, with true journalistic diligence, slogged around the country like a true supporter. He affords himself a small gloat about Arsenal's title win, and generally the book does Merseyside a disservice. This man is writing about prejudice? Or,as a Scouser, perhaps I should be pleased at being described as having "laughing gas in one hand and a switchblade in the other"? His publicity (e.g. an appearance on Granada Reports and 2 whole pages in When Saturday Comes) painted him as a truth-teller that baddies LFC and Barnes are trying to silence. The truth is less romantic- Hill is more akin to Albert Goldman, only less scurrilous and less entertaining. Could the objections actually be because the book tries to pass itself as biography, which it clearly isn't, or that John Barnes might actually find the thing offensive to himself, and not give a damn about "diplomatic goals." Think of him- on one hand,he gets racist crap from the kind of bonehead still on Janet and John books,then has to put up with others more or less calling him an Uncle Tom? Wherever the abuse comes from it must all hurt.

It's very sad that a gifted player like Barnes is often a spectator in a book which is supposed to be about him. The real sadness is that this book, confused as it is, will sell by the 1,000s, whereas LOOSEN THE SHACKLES- the REAL horror story- will sell in single figures. OUT OF HIS SKIN has even been serialised in the local press, whereas SHACKLES has been villified and given the switchblade treatment- apparently, it can't be true because the police weren't involved! That's life as they say, it's not pleasant. A book dealing with racism in football has been long overdue and OUT OF HIS SKIN deserves to be read.A major book on the subject needed to be beyond reproach itself. It's a pity that someone else hadn't written it. When I read an unattibuted quote-"to them, he's just got a suntan"- I feel angry. Them is me,too. Thanks for throwing me, and 1000s like me,into the same group as Nazis with shit for brains. It hurt to be the victim of an unreasonable prejudice- maybe that was the idea. The problem has always been; Silence is complicity. If John should leave, we mustn't let the same thing happen again.

LIVERPOOL ARE SHITE - it's official! We asked the football experts to evaluate the last 16 seasons, giving a percentage mark to estimate quality of play, strength of the first division, outstanding individuals etc etc. TTWR collated the results and produced the following graph;

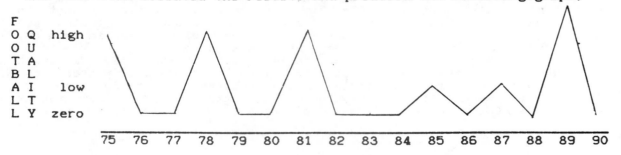

As you can see, a definite pattern began to emerge......

THROUGH THE
WIND & RAIN
A LIVERPOOL FANZINE

REACH FOR THE STARS

Gorritt,gorritt,gorritt - HAVEN'T! Yes, it's there - the last card to complete your 'Wonderful World Of Soccer Stars' collection. For three weeks you've had the whole set except for one, yet your addiction is such that you have continued to buy four packets a day. In desperation, you change your newsagents but your army of swaps just grows and grows. Of course you have read the guarantee in the back of the album which proudly declares "no specific stamps have been withheld or kept in short supply"- but do you really believe this? Perhaps there is a bitter and twisted employee who is systematically sifting out the player you need. You can picture him at his desk, laughing manically whilst stealing a glimpse at 6,000 Dave Wagstaffes in his bottom drawer.

THE ELUSIVE WAGGY

But then, whilst in the advanced stages of paranoia, it happens - you find someone who has just started collecting, and he already has 'Waggy' on swap. You eagerly exchange your 150 swaps for the much treasured sticker of Mister Wagstaffe. On arriving home you seek out the glue and keep to the strict instructions;'Apply adhesive here only', never venturing beyond the dotted line. With Wagstaffe firmly in place you can relax and the album can gather dust on your window ledge. It would surely have been a great deal easier just to send off to the manufactur--ers using the order form in the back of the album, but that was considered cheating. What dickhead decided it was cheating?

Anyway,all the weeks of wheeling and dealing in the nation's soccer players are over and you are left to consider if it was worth all the effort. Was Len Badger really a fair swap for 2 Steve Kembers and a Malcolm Page? Did anyone read the little pen pictures,and,when you were only 11, could you understand them? The following are a selection of my favourites and their real meaning;

DIMINUITIVE STRIKER - short-arsed little nark
COMBATITIVE MIDFIELDER - dirty and tackles evrything that moves
INTELLIGENT SCHEMER - lazy,tackles no-one but gets all the praise
GOAL-HUNGRY FORWARD - greedy and shoots from anywhere
UNCOMPROMISING FULLBACK - gets the man if he can't get the ball
FLAMBOYANT ENTERTAINER - skilful,never gets dirty,won't play if it's cold
LOYAL SERVANT - has a long contract and no other club wants to buy him
OLD FASHIONED CENTRE-HALF - no skill but can head a ball
FOOTBALLING NOMAD - persistent trouble-maker
VERSATILE UTILITY PLAYER- can't get in the first team unless someone else
                       is injured (some of these sound too familiar -ED)

I can particularly remember Terry Hibbitt's portfolio which stated that he had an educated left foot. Did this mean the rest of him never went to school? It's funny how you can recall some of the less famous footballers simply because of the unusual names.For instance,Chelsea's Marvin Hinton, Coventry's Dietmar Bruck and Leicester's John Sjoberg.

The all time classic Soccer Stars series must be the 1970-71 which included not only the first division teams, but also the best players from the 1970 World Cup, a second division 'star gallery' and the European Cup finalists,who were Celtic and Feyenoord. The latter included that famous bespectacled Dutchman Rinus Israel - did he really play in those glasses?

THROUGH THE
WIND & RAIN
A LIVERPOOL FANZINE

Another collector's item was the 1973-74 album which included a double page spread of the Sunderland FA Cup winning team (1-0 against Leeds heh heh - ED). However this was definitely a one-off as second division teams were never included, which explains the absence of Manchester United from the 1974-75 album (nice subtle dig).

I'm sure that the biographies which were to be found 'in the appropriate space in the album' inspired today's beloved T.V. commentators. How else can you explain David Speedie being described as a 'pocket battleship' or Paul Mariner as 'Johnny-on-the-spot'? Most disturbing of all is John Motty Motson's continual description of Gary Stevens as a 'natural athlete'. This might give Bobby Robson ideas about drafting in Linford Christie or Steve Cram to bolster our World Cup chances.

Now we have a whole new breed of TV football presenters in the shape of the Kick Off boys. What a pathetic trio they are- Elton 'Short phrases. No sentences.' Welsby, Clive 'Wild Eyes' Tyldesley (described in KING OF THE KIPPAX as the cabbage patch doll - ED) and Rob 'Big Suit but No Shoulders' McCaffrey. Bring back gulping Gerald 'Party Man' Sinstadt, Paul Doherty and the fuzzy photo. Not forgetting Bob Williamson who sang ridiculous foot-ball songs, wearing a Bolton Wanderers shirt while strumming an acoustic guitar. Now there was a real soccer star!

CHRIS CAREY

Captain Courutches - A New Image?

Why is it that a hero always lets you down? Liver-pudlians have had the money-grabbing Keegan, the squeaking royal jester Thatcherite Hughes, and now, every Tuesday in the Echo, Tommy Smith. Sometimes I wonder if the man even lives on the same planet as the rest of us eg. the sample on the left. On the surface it looks okay, quite liberal even. True, the stress on any stupid aspects of the fight against racism is a very old bigot ploy, but that's nitpicking when you read the justified and harsh slagging he gives Gatting's bloodsuckers.

TAXI !

HARVEY'S VOTE OF CONFIDENCE

MIKE GATTING and his rebel cricketers should finally call it a day in South Africa and salvage a little bit of self respect. At what point does money become totally worthless?

I don't know how Gatting & Co. can sleep at night. The former England cricket captain, rather than say anything constructive about the apartheid issue, has chosen to bury his head in the sand like a madcap ostrich.

It goes without saying that no-one should ignore the importance of the race protests over there. But I can't get quite as passionate about a black and white row going on in our own backyard.

Soccer bosses have been attacked for not including black players in their teams. The fact that we are talking about the game of Subbuteo puts it all into perspective.

Apparently all the European Subbuteo sides have pink faces, upsetting the Commission for Racial Equality. Equally Brazilians and the like have dark skin.

For the life of me, I can't see that it matters. I don't think children even think twice about it. All they are interested in is having fun with a very enjoyable game.

It's adults who plant thoughts of discrimination in their minds by pressing ahead with such petty complaints.

"But wait!" I hear you shout, there must be a Tommy Smith clone, giving bogus interviews to Dave Hill for his Barnes book. Here's a brief extract;

'THE WHITE NIGGER'   91

of his best efforts, words like 'coon' and 'nigger' soon begin to fall from his lips. The possibility that he might have been talking to, say, the husband of a black woman never seemed to cross his mind. 'I'm not prejudiced,' he explained, 'but if a coon moved in next door, I'd move, like most white people would. If me daughter come home with a nigger I'd go mad! But I'm only being truthful and normal.'

It seems to be Smith's understanding that racial tensions occur because people have stopped regarding blacks as second-class citizens. Those 'coloured people' whom he considers his friends have achieved the distinction by learning to, in Smith's own words, 'think like the white man.' He had his own special epithet for them. In time, Howard Gayle was awarded this bizarre, backhanded plaudit too. 'I used to call Howard "the white nigger",' says Smith. 'Now that is a compliment. It was the only way I could find to describe that I thought he was OK.'

Suddenly everything is clear; 'race' protests are important, so long as they take place thousands of miles away and there's no chance of them moving in next door or marrying your daughter. The Everton fanzine has a name for Smith- BILLY TWOFACE. It is not hard to see why.

MANDELA'S GETTING FREE, TOMMY'S GETTING READY

THE LOONY LEFT

Amazing Ablett's special target

AUSSIE RULES

By HARRY MILLER

GARY ABLETT will arrive in North America this week as the man with a mission.

The Born-Again Christian intends to prove he is the undisputed king of Aussie Rules football.

Ablett, an amazing character, kicked a record nine goals when the Geelong Cats lost 144-138 to Hawthorn Hawks in last week's gripping Grand Final in Melbourne.

THIS MIGHT
EXPLAIN THOSE
CLEARANCES...

A LEAN AND MEAN
MACHINE

They say you have to be a bit mad to be a goalkeeper. To be a left back for Liverpool, you have to be pyschosonol--igically active or inisodynamically ordinate. (or if you prefer have a screw loose and be allergic to drivers) In times past Alec Lindsay (enough furniture on the cheek to fill a removal van) used his suave curly hairstyle to fool many wingers into only trying to get round him for a date.

There was Gerry Byrne, capable of self--inflicting bone breakage throughout his whole body but still carrying on. Ronnie Moran played 343 games at left back and now hangs around dug outs with an uncivilised leer, causing distress to visitors by frequently bawling obscenities to no-one in particular. (like those men with Union Jack shopping bags and Brasso on their breath, who hang around railway stations)

As you can see, a precedent had been set very early on. In more recent times Gary Ablett used to like lifting the ball long and high down the line, over it and into the stand, with the forward rushing hopelessly this way and that. Joey Jones would do the same thing, except Joey used to propel the right winger into the stand as well as the ball. His high stepping technique made him a vision at corners. As the ball came over he'd make a mighty dash to meet it, miss it, then turn to watch the ball land at the back post he was originally guarding, where a large swarm of the opposition's forwards were waiting for their early Christmas present.

The striding style of Alan 'I Saw It First' Kennedy was a common sight in the early 80s. Undaunted and unchallenged, he would cross yards of territory and then thunder in a shot, see it smash into the net past an astonished goalkeeper and turn to accept the acclaim for his genius. 1-0 to the opposition.

Back to the present day, Liverpool are blessed with two graduates of the Norman Bates School Of Excellence. Steve Staunton, Young Turkey of the Month; one of the quickest players in the game, always able to tackle back immediately after giving the ball to an opponent. Practice makes perfect. Master of the high cross, a kind of orbital church in a space station.... (Station of the Cross, you illiterate peons), he can deliver this with rare inaccuracy. Sometimes playing in the same team is David Burrows, whose maxim is 'If it's going past me, it's going to the abbbatoir'. Acknowledging his debt to Joey, he spits in lumps, kicks with farming implement legs, and volleys abuse at anyone close enough to listen. He also possesses an ability to give away penalties akin to Britain and her colonies.

It should be noted that although Barry Venison wears no.3 on occasion, he's considered far too sensible to play at left back. (sure about that? -SK) Others who have been tried at left back, and found wanting, are the educated Mark Lawrenson,and the cultured Nigel Spackman. Then there was Jim Beglin, who had begun to show signs of right stuff in the 86 Cup Final,but whose career was cruelly cut short when he lost his place. And his leg. Gary Gillespie never made the grade, Tommy Smith was a miserable failure and Brian Kettle was a hopeless prospect because of his name. And so it can be seen that if you want to find a weakness in the Liverpool line-up, then try somewhere else.

SPARTAK

**

SK   What, no mention of Avi Cohen? A
**   translation of the above can be had
for a small fee (come on, Steve, you know
we're a bit thick up here!)

THE LOONY RIGHT

Most people in England were delighted with UEFA's decision to allow English clubs back into Europe. Most. At times of national importance, there are people in this country whose bigotry and xenophobia is unmatched by any other part of the world.

Football is a pastime, a sport, an entertainment (hopefully), but it also has a tremendous hold over its' followers. It is also capable of bringing people together. Football is popular all over the world - it can cross any divide, be it country, race, religion etc etc - but it can also exacerbate these tensions and rivalries.

There are many right-wing headcases in this country, and many have figured out the divisive potential in football. They feel that Black and White should not mix, and spew forth their uniquely vile brand of filth at football grounds, for instance, but it is their attitude to Europe that holds the possibility of greatest danger for us all.

Let's get it right. We're not just talking about Mr. Average Fascist here - the proles with half-mast kecks, comparing tattoos and brain cells at the back of the bus - we're talking about people in positions of power and influence throughout the land. And it starts at the very top.

Margaret Thatcher has made no secret of her contempt for football, nor can she convincingly disguise her distrust of a United Europe. In 1985, however, a prime minister who would never hear a bad word about Britain was suddenly pressing for a complete withdrawal of English clubs from Europe, and putting the entire blame for Heysel not just on Liverpudlians but on the football fans of the entire country - all British subjects.

Subsequently this has been portrayed as Thatcher's attempt to 'dirty' supporters, to make us perfect guinea-pigs for her national identity card scheme, but was it? Anyone who watched the wonderful scenes at the end of the 1990 World Cup match between Italy and England senses that football can be a tremendous power for

THE ONLY FASCISTS WHO EVER BELIEVED IN EUROPEAN UNITY

----

good, for unity. As 1992 lurks round the corner, ready to expose the PM as the petty shopkeeper she really is, the members of her party have launched into Bigotry Overdrive.

We have all read Mr. Ridley's remarks on the Germans, and are expected to believe that this was none of Maggie's doing. We have taken note of Mr. Tebbitt's Cricket Test for Asians. (who I suspect heard the news that Norman got a gardening fork through his foot with the same sorrow as the rest of us) When it comes to the beautiful game, though, only one Tory is worth mentioning; David Evans, the Right Honourable 'Member' for Transvaal Central.

His hysterical outburst when he heard the news of UEFA's decision in the summer was a classic of its' kind - the pre-dominant theme was "inflicting our thugs on the rest of Europe". Were we expected to believe that Mr. Evans' primary concern was the safety of those poor, quaking Dutch football fans, or the nervous wreck that is an Italian policeman? Of course not. A man who used his chairmanship of Luton FC not only to get into politics but to actively campaign against football does not care about Europe's safety - he cares about closer links with Europe, with loss of sovereignty, with loss of 'Britishness'.

The judiciary is the arm of The State, and the police is its' fist. In both bodies, xenophobia is rampant. Judges are notoriously bigotted; in fact the stranger their decisions, the more people in this country seem to like it. Only in England could we make a celebrity out of a man who jails a young woman for shoplifting, even though she was pregnant. Judge Pickles (for it was he) even suggested she tried to get out of a prison sentence by deliberately getting pregnant - needless to say the girl was black.

To sit in judgement over the guilty or innocent in this country is a license for prejudice. When football is in the dock, it is

THROUGH THE
WIND & RAIN
A LIVERPOOL FANZINE

interesting to note two things. Firstly, have you noticed that of all the players who've committed misdemeanours (and there seems to be a lot of them) the only two who went to jail were a Scouser (Mick Quinn of Newcastle), and a foreign player with a Scouse accent? (Jan The Man) Think Tony Adams will do time? Like hell; he'll get what Captain Flasher got. Nothing!

Secondly, it has been noticeable that a lot of hooligan cases have been thrown out of court for one reason or another, usually technicalities you thought only existed in LA Law. When thugs have been convicted, the appetite to make the punishment fit the crime (and anti-social/violent behaviour seems serious to me) is strangely lacking. Being Irish in the wrong place at the wrong time usually brings that appetite right back, though.

It is not necessary to remind supporters of the bigot tendencies of our wonderful police force. As Liverpool fans, we have confronted it time and time again. You would think they'd appreciate European football's return, even if it was only for the overtime, but they are just servants after all, though maybe not the public's

If you can think back to 1988 and Chelsea v Middlesborough, you will remember that Chelsea's lunatic fringe managed to get from one end of Stamford Bridge to the other (easily 200 yards) without encountering a single policeman. Since London's most 'notorious' club had just been relegated, a minimum of foresight could have prevented this - if, indeed, they wanted to prevent it. I'm sure it was also a total coincidence that Colin Moynihan was on national TV, with a prepared statement, within an hour of the game's end.

In May 1990, we had those upstanding chaps from Elland Road tearing through Bournemouth. The connection? Before both incidents, it was widely reported that UEFA were about to lift the ban on English clubs. Yet another coincidence. Many fans over the years have been the victims of police who seemed to want to create trouble rather than defuse it. Looked at in this context, the Hillsborough tragedy starts to take on sinister overtones. Could it possibly be that policing designed to cause a riot

(Liverpool fans again - what could be better for Jacques George?) went disastrously wrong?

The newspapers are the enemies of football - and European unity; certainly the right-wing papers (about 80%?) are. Racist gibberish abounds, whether supporting Nicholas Ridley, attacking Muslems or Saddam Hussein. (funny; when Reagan went into Grenada that was okay) It is in the area of soccer 'hooliganism', or creating the vision of stadiums on the brink of all-out war, that the press has so willingly supported its' lord and mistress. Sardinia was rife with hacks on a mission; find trouble, make trouble or make up trouble. I feel this went beyond trying to find a story; the media has a startling effect on people's perceptions. Where else can they find out things? Eg I only have to open my mouth down south, and people think I want to mug them, sell them drugs or do my comedy routine, simply because that's all they're told about Merseyside. In the wrong hands, the press is a lethal weapon. The press is in the hands of the Right. ------------------

In 1973, Bill Shankly watched Red Star Belgrade give his beloved Liverpool a football lesson. From that night on, things had to change; from that night on Liverpool had to change. The seeds were sown then that would make us the greatest club side England had ever seen, or is likely to ever see. We are still flourishing from that lesson - a European lesson. England's World Cup progress can be put down to a new formation, similar to that practiced in nearly every European team.

In ordinary life, as well as in football, we can learn from the Europeans. There is so much they can give us, and a lot we can give them - Jeremy Beadle for a start! Unity is the only way forward, yet there are people in this country who will tell you different. They are easy to spot; they use phrases like German Racket, Wogs Out, Hop Off You Frogs etc. They'll watch some thickhead nutter cripple a fellow pro for life and say "We've the hardest league in the world" as if it was something to be proud of. They listen to Gullit being degraded by thousands of people at Wembley and refer to it as "good natured ribbing"! They are scum.

LIVERPOOL'S FANCY DRESS PARTY 1989

THIRD, JOHN BARNES AS A KU KLUX KLAN MAN
SECOND, BRUCE GROBBELAAR IN HIS ARMY GEAR
BUT THE WINNER IS, BAZZA AS AN ENGLAND PLAYER!!

THROUGH THE
WIND & RAIN
A LIVERPOOL FANZINE

CLASS OR CLUB?

Why is it that all football clubs, players and supporters become subject to regional classification by chants eg Cockneys, Geordies, Scousers etc, even though all teams (and most sets of supporters) are comprised of a national, sometimes international, mix? For example, how many Scousers play for Liverpool or Everton?

It appears that this is the path that racism and fascism have chosen to claw their grubby way into the game. If you are of the opinion that this is all rather harmless, take a closer look at the various London rivals of Tottenham, where organisations like the National Front ferment the usual propaganda against the so-called Jewish element, and glory in songs about The Final Solution.

Add this to the continual highlighting of each club's individuality, embodied within ther fans, and the promotion of the 'wolf-pack' gangs by sensationalist press reports, and a deeper, political conspiracy can be seen. By this I mean the Establishment using the tried and trusted method of Divide & Rule to destroy any sign of fraternity within the working class. Thus the highlighting of tribal loyalties by various means prevents a mass movement of young people joining together, simply by an active promotion of the idea of Opposition=Enemy.

As an example of the media's ignorance of the rational, objective views held by most football fans, one only has to look at the comments given in the press and TV by representatives of the FSA. Since Hillsborough, their media exposure has declined, and only cursory comments were allowed over the ID card scheme. Also how many rain forests have been pulped to provide miles of sensationalist newsprint over the Liverpool/ Manchester rivalry?

BUT WHO FIRST STIRRED THE MUDDY WATERS OF THIS CONFLICT? Was it fuelled by a desire to prevent the two largest populations in the North West (the largest area of unemployment post-Thatcher) forging an alliance via sport? Two largely working class areas now view themselves with distrust and suspicion; the continual harping on minor disagreements, blowing personal differences out of all proportion - now the conflict goes beyond football. How many times has this been seen on holidays abroad?

Skillful use of the media has highlighted the minority of morons within our midst out of all proportion to their numbers, and further alienating the general public from football. They not only join the 'hang 'em/flog' em' crusade, but turn a blind eye to legislation which is designed to further curtail the enjoyment of supporters. Legislation that may be turned on them, as this country lurches towards a Conservative inspired police state.

A further example of media manipulation can be seen at Millwall. This club has been carefully cultivated as a breeding ground for mob violence; a place where the nutcases would rather watch Lions v Christians, rather than Lions v Liverpool.However, a closer look at the place itself reveals it to be a largely working class club, retaining its' roots through local support and involvement within the community. Is this why their supporters were always depicted as shaven headed neanderthals? Especially by the extreme right-wing press; it's interesting now to see how the same media attitude to the 'Millwall bashers' is softening, for one reason only - money! Just look at all the prestigious development being carried out in the area. The monied minority cannot afford to have property

Once upon a time, there was this Millwall supporter....

values lowered simply because they live in the proximity of 'that club'. Have you seen so-called press releases emphasising the yuppiefication of Millwall, stressing the positive side of the club and promoting another image for a change eg matchday creches. The club is shown to have rapidly undergone a Cinderella-like change; "you shall go to The Den"! Keep an eye out to see who the new whipping-boys will be, because football fans have to be discreditted.

Leading on from this, we come to the Identity Card scheme, now hopefully consigned to the dustbin of history, because it was designed to restrict the mobility of Joe Public. It would serve us well to remain vigilant, however, as it still lies on the statute book, ready to change shape but not intent. No doubt another form of restrictive practise will emerge to take its' place. Favourite one at the moment is taking away our passports. It can be recalled that denying people the basic right to freedom of move--ment was successfully employed during the miners' strike. Used to temper 'flying pickets' ie confining strikers to their own community, thereby isolating them from national support, this has led to the persecution of the travelling football fan, with regular stop and search, restrictions on coach routes and times of arrival/departure etc, hoping you eventually jack it in as too much of an inconvenience.

Stereotyping has been used throughout history by political bigots of all kinds, and now football fans are the victims. The underlying Fascism in such terms as Irish bastard,black bastard, sometimes even just one word eg Jew, was encouraged and has inevitably kept the working class uneducated and bigotted. How many intelligent people read the Sun? Prejudice is encouraged against those people classified by it, whether it be colour of skin, nationality, religion and now, incredibly, by region. To give a person the characteristics of an animal means that treating them as such is no big deal. Each draconian measure used against the football fan - ID card, restricted travel, fences) becomes acceptable as we are portrayed as 'social undesirables', even though 99% of us obey the law.

This will probably be seen by some as another Red sounding off with yet another half-baked theory. A few years ago this was the same reaction to those who spoke of a conspiracy to eliminate trade union and Labour party involvement in Liverpool by destroying it's industrial base and creating a fear of unemployment. And look what happened - no more Metal Box, Birds Eye, B.A.T., Tate & Lyle, Tillotsons etc etc TO NAME JUST A FEW, while elected councillors are surcharged for 'militancy'.

I rest my case - any arguments against?

JAKE PARKER

Luddite Legionnaire

GET READY FOR LEEDS NO. 4

GUCK OGG!

Excuse me, is that your hand up my arse?

THE ULTIMATE DETERRENT

THROUGH THE WIND & RAIN
A LIVERPOOL FANZINE

You'll Believe A Man Can Cry!!!

THE TERROR CONTINUES!

IN EXCITING WHINEE-AROUND

SHARP xxxx

NO THRILLS

NO ACTION

COMING TO A FOOTBALL GROUND NEAR YOU
(unless it's Wembley)

BRYAN ROBSONS ARSE

TEN OUT OT TEN
TABLOID OWNERS SAID
THEIR HACKS PREFERRED IT

THROUGH THE
WIND & RAIN
A LIVERPOOL FANZINE

Advertisement

If we said that I.D. cards
were a good idea

That wouldn't be very
truthful would it ?

If we said Tony Adams
was a true sportsman

That would be
slightly exagerating

If we said Paul Gascoinge
was now very slim

You wouldn't really
believe us

If we said England
will win the World Cup

That would be taking
optimism a bit too far

If we said Everton
will win the League

We'd be to truth what David
Burrows is to beauty(remote)

If we said Liverpool will win
the League, it'd be the truth

Well, probably

If we said United
will win the League

It'd be another
Mirror exclusive

Liverpool: Probably the best team in the world

chapter 6

OUT OF COURT

European Special. No. 13

February/March 1990

40P

AFCB ANNOUNCE A PROFIT!

FOUR EXTRA PAGES!!!

FREE!!!

Perhaps the club will buy us a drink?

Yeah. One glass of water and eleven straws!

INSIDE!!!!

Red and Black -- On the way back?

D. Showers solicitors

Boscombe St. Johns

Awayday Wolves

Your say at last?

Redknappolis Restaurant

A S**********n fan complains (well, wouldn't you?)

And millions of sentences ending with a full stop.

An Independent AFC Bournemouth fanzine

No doubt like many football fans, the inspiration for starting 'Out Of Court' came from the birth of 'When Saturday Comes'. At last, here was an outlet for those of us who felt angry and frustrated at being cast as hooligans, baby snatchers or whatever.

The first issue appeared way back in September 1987, making us the first fanzine dedicated to AFC Bournemouth. But why did it appear? Well, it wasn't because the team was playing badly. In fact we'd just been promoted to the Second Division for the first time in our history. Nope, it was the same old reasons: incompetent directors, over zealous policing and the introduction of a 100% membership scheme for the home fans terracing.

And three years later have things changed? We're back in the third division, having lost quality players such as Ian Bishop and Paul Moulden. The membership scheme has at last been scrapped, only to be replaced by the ridiculous threat of all seat stadia. (How irrelevant to most clubs that is! There will always be some grounds where standing won't be a crime). Our directors have remained as incompetent as ever, coming up with various new stadia, all scrapped at the 'dream' stage, and their treatment of fans who aren't local councillors and top business people remains as shabby as ever.

That is why 'Out Of Court' exists. To monitor these people. To ask how a profit of £115,000 at the end of one financial year can be turned into a loss of £10,000 per week! For yes, these people are truly business people! Oh yes, and we want to make people laugh aswell.

What follows is a personal selection of favourite articles written by our regular and irregular staff. So if AFC Bournemouth are a club you've never given a moment's thought, it's about time you did!

And now here, for the first time, are the exciting details of Chairman Jim Nolan's Plan of a brand new stadium for AFC Bournemouth. This new sporting arena will house several features unique in this sort of conception. Club supremo, Brian Filer told our reporter that the capacity will be reduced to 2,500 plus 30 high class Executive Boxes plus the Directors Stand, which will cater for 1,000 exclusive non paying club guests. Mr Filer said that this should ensure that if the team ever reaches the 1st Division then it should be playing to a full house at every home game. The whole complex would be built on Council owned land close to Dean Court. Meanwhile Dean Court itself would be sold off to a local developer who, it is hoped, would then build up market quality residences in a tree lined executive estate. The new stadium is to be called "No Court".

Jim Nolan's Division 1 Superbowl - AFC Bournemouth's new yuppie stadium

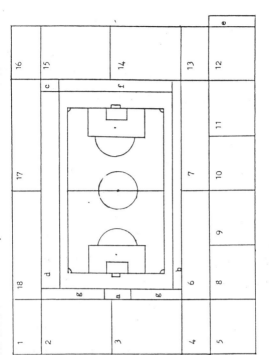

Key:-

a Home Supporters Terracing
b Home Supporters Seating Area
c Away Supporters Terracing
d Directors Stand & Guest Bars
e Disabled Enclosure - unfortunately you can't see the pitch, but everyone keeps dry
f I D card Computer Control Room
g High Class Executive Boxes

1 Casino
2 Operatic Theatre
3 Overseas Properties Estate Agency
4 Swiss Bank
5 American Express Office
6 Real Tennis Court
7 Dry Ski Slope
8 Stock Brokers
9 Luxury Cruise Booking Agents
10 Porsche Showrooms
11 Rent a Jag - Limousine Rental
12 Helicopter Pad
13 Wine Bar
14 Game Bird Breeding Aviary
15 Indoor Clay Pigeon Shooting
16 Licensed Restaurant
17 Yachting Showroom
18 Racehorse Stud Farm

Three of a kind

First we had the Walker Stand. AFC Bournemouth was to have been the first club to turn its ground into a sports facility for people of the town. At the start of the 1972/73 season an artists impression first appeared in the official match day programme. This project was the first phase of the proposed redevelopement of Dean Court.

Next came Rodney Barton's plan for a new home to take the Cherries into the 21st century. Former transatlantic yachtsman Mr Barton wanted a new stadium, new sports hall and an all weather pitch with seating for 5,000, new to give them a new home", he said.
"The English Hockey Association are looking for new headquarters and we would love to give them a new home", he said.
The football part of the scheme was scheduled to be ready for the start of the 1989/90 football season.

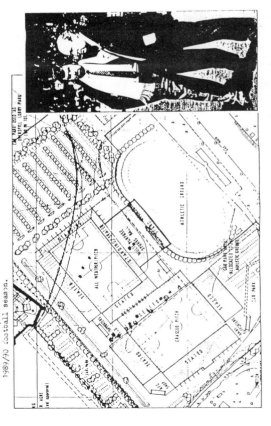

HOOLIGANS AT CHELSEA

It was rather a surprise on entering Stamford Bridge for the recent Chelsea game to see a stream of Cherries supporters heading in the opposite direction, accompanied by a steady stream of uniforms.

I must admit that getting into the ground was also somewhat dodgy, I often wear a blue Glasgow Rangers shirt to games and unfortunately the local police can't tell the difference! Despite having a cherries hat (the only id I had was a capitalcard) things looked desperate until my mate piped up "I'll vouch for him, I'm from Clapton". The copper looked convinced (obviously he failed his geography exams) and let me in.

Unfortunately most Cherries fans spent the game trying to avoid getting nicked for: nothing, which was extremely difficult, rather than supporting the lads. I personally witnessed at least 30 arrests for various misdemeanours, or for nothing. Quite what the final tally of arrests was I would be interested to hear, or the number of charges made, but at this rate its easy to see how Moynihan gets his figures.

Two people I know were arrested, both for foul and abusive language, like 'Oh bl**dy hell' and 'you're a load of c**p ref'. One was charged and the other wasn't, showing that even this absurd policy wasn't consistent. One lad entered the terrace, 10 seconds late 'you're rubbish Chelsea' and up comes the police officer; "Right, that's it, you're out", "What for?", "provoking the Chelsea fans". Another lad I know is disabled and cannot move freely, he was physically grabbed by an officer who accused him of trying to trip him up! During the second half I managed to work out what was actually happening. A Superintendent positioned at the top of the terrace was sending in snatch squads of three or four into different areas, once at least one arrest had been made they would withdraw and move elsewhere.

It must be stressed that there was no hint of any kind of trouble throughout the game, though these actions went on until 5 minutes from time when hostility began to be expressed by a number of supporters. At this point the snatch squads disappeared, though it was their provocation that brought about the hostility.

Unfortunately (or not), I'm not the kind of person to stand and accept such unwarranted actions and yes, I complained about the policy to the officer in charge. This was met with the immortal phrase "you obviously don't come here often, do you?". Of course I don't I'm a Bournemouth supporter you idiot.

I and the other lad who complained were informed that should we wish to make a written complaint we could spend two hours doing so at the local police station. With better things to do, I thought otherwise, but I have since written

a letter of complaint to the Fulham Police, and hope that others similarly appalled, will do likewise.

To conclude I found the police actions totally unwarranted, deplorable and unacceptable. The policy has obviously been designed to put supporters off travelling to Chelsea. Though a distorted press has given Chelsea fans a hooligan reputation, there was only set of people that Bournemouth fans felt any threat from, and sadly that was the police..

Ian Barnes

A recent article from Postman Pat provided the final straw that led me to make this appeal.

To summarize the article, for the sake of those who didn't catch the last edition, his trip to Plymouth was spoilt by the pathetic behaviour of the Devon and Cornwall Constabulary. Pulled over on the A38 the fans in his minibus were 'kidnapped' by the Police and held up until near kick-off. In contrast to me however, they did see the match.

At the end of last season, you may recall, our friend Tommy Tynan told us, via the Echo, how he was going to send us back to the footballing wastelands which is Division Three. In protest to this statement, and as a tribute to Tommys footballing ability, a small crowd of us went to last seasons game with a supply of carrots to wave at the aforementioned number nine. They may not help you see in the dark but they did stop Tommy netting against us for the first time in living memory.

Would it work again this year I wondered? On the way to the ground I purchased a pound. At about twenty past three Tommy hooted a shot high in the away end - whilst some of the away fans shook loosely clenched fists I shook my carrot and joined in the loud chorus of 'eeee-oorr'.

For this 'Provocative gesture at the home fans' I was to spend the rest of the afternoon in a Police cell - about six foot square with no window and the light turned out.

My father, who was at the game, was appalled, and wrote to the Superintendant. The reply was two pages of garbage and lies.

Seeing similar letters and talking to other regular supporters it seems that everyone has a story. For this reason I would like to coordinate a campaign on the rights of supporters. If I could accumulate enough stories I would be willing to write to the national media and to MP's to bring this situation to the general public. We would only need to convince a reporter that he need only attend a few games, as a normal supporter, to see the injustice that occurs on many grounds every Saturday.

So, if you have any stories please write to me at the above address with as many details as possible. I would also be keen to hear peoples opinions on where they have found the worst and the best policing. I say 'best' because I have met many good coppers on my travels who are a credit to their uniform.

These good policemen do seem to be becoming more and more a minority however. So if you care for your rights then please drop me a line. If 'OOC' will give me the column space I will print an update on the situation in an issue or two.

Craig Grant.

P.S. - It would seem that aliases are the 'in thing' in 'OOC', how about Jasper!

Ed - Out of Court urge as many people to 'assist Craig with his enquiries' as they say. Why should the majority of fans be victimised for a few! Get writing.

ODE TO IAN BISHOP

Wayne Hopkins looks back on the all too short Dean Court career of 'The Bish'.

The departure of Ian Bishop will come as no surprise to Cherries fans, as he is a class player, and the money received for him has further strengthened our forward line. Like Colin Clarke, one short season was all we got to see of him. I saw him play in every game bar one last season & although he only scored a couple of goals his passing and vision were brilliant. He had a good game on his home league debut against Chelsea, but the away match at Swindon was where he really shone. We went two goals down until Kevin Bond pulled a goal back just before half time. For the whole of the second half Bish put on a performance I've never seen before by a player wearing the red shirt of Bournemouth.

He got everywhere that night, creating space and putting inch perfect passes accross the pitch for 45 minutes. Sadly we didn't have Luther then to put away the glut of chances and Swindon stole a third goal on the break in the last minute.

Without doubt that was Bish's best performance for us, but several others came along during the season. Away games at Bradford and Leicester were steady if unspectacular performances where Bish controlled the game & always used his knack of looking before passing to good effect.

The game against Man. Utd at Dean Court bought Bish to the attention of the nation and his passing to Cookey on the wing was amazing, only luck stopped Utd. falling to a great performance by The Maestro.

Bish put in his second best performance at his new club, away at Manchester City. Three goals down by half time, he supplied the passes for the first two Bournemouth goals and put the willies up City enough to make them fall apart and give us an equaliser.

It's sad that Ian had to leave, but we wish him luck. The desire to play for a 'big' club in the first division is understandable. In a way I'm glad he chose to go to City, rather than one of the "Big Five", where his talents would possibly only come to light on a few occasions. If teams other than the big five are to have a chance of success they must entice players to them. I'm sure players are starting to realise that you must be exceptional to get into a big clubs first team (How comes Tony Adams gets in then? · Ed). Unless you are a world class player already, the chance of developing further will be

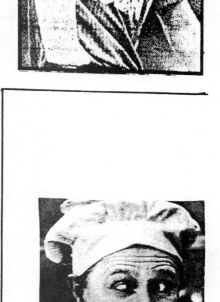

limited at Old Trafford and the like.

I think the move to City was the best all round. It's annoying that Carlisle get such a slice, but there we are. Ian had the potential, but no one knew whether it could be fulfilled. It would have been a gamble to pay the £150,00 straight up for him, so maybe the best thing to do was to agree a future profit deal. Something tells me that it was more to do with a lack of cash rather than the risk that swayed the decision. Getting players to come here is difficult, although if we dropped our membership scheme we could get gates to match clubs like Ipswich and Leicester. Lets hope that signing a player with the potential of Paul Moulden has is the first step to making the club a big club. The money from Colin Clarke built our last promotion team and I think the monet from Bish will build the next one. Lets hope the board are as keen, the team looks promising.

The class of Bish will be missed, but the likes of Holmes, Shearer and O'Connor will fill the gap. Lets hope Ian gets the recognition he deserves in the first division, I'm sure he will. From mere mortals come great men, in this case from a great player could come a great team. Farewell oh great one, you will be missed.

Wayne Hopkins

DR.PSYCHO'S PROBLEM SPOT - Our resident psychiatrist gives the answers to all your little problems.

This months problem comes from James of Boscombe

Dear Dr Psycho,

My problem is this. I am a well off chairman of a football club. My manager made a profit on transfers of over £500,000 last year. Despite this I have very little cash to give him for team strengthening. My second problem is that nobody believes me.
James.

Dr. Psycho replies:-

"Are you telling porky pies again James?"

Remember, I am here to help you. Out of Court and I want to hear from you so send in your questions or tell us your problems - we have the answers.

OUT OF COURT

rot

According to the Pocket Oxford Dictionary, the definition of rot can be 'nonsense, absurdity, foolish course'. (It is also a sheep disease, so Mint Sauce of Not The 8502 had better be careful -Ed).

For the benefit of this article, R.O.T. also means "racism on the terraces", but both definitions are really the same.

What a good idea that A F C Bournemouth have decided to make a stand on this matter by indicating that 'supporters' will be kicked out for racial abuse.

Unfortunately it seems that this trend has not changed dramatically over the past two or three seasons. Racist taunts are nothing new and certain groups of so called supporters have a certain reputation that precedes them. However through the work of the FSA and fanzines these problems are now being tackled.

It does seem that some of the political views of the National Front have found a foothold on the terraces. If you follow AFC Bournemouth around the country, I am sure I need not tell you where the problems of racism are evident.

Whether we like it or not, England is a muti racial society. I accept that certain areas are more prone to ethnic difficulties but why should football be prone to such action. The main problem would definitely appear to be anti black, rather than anti Scot for example. A lot of black players have great skills and this cannot be denied.

What really is stupid though is the selective racism frequently found at grounds. This is where (for example) the home 'fans' taunt a black player on the opposing side whilst having a black player on their own side. What idiots they are anyway.

I feel that the policy of banning racist fans from Dean Court can only be for the good of the game, BUT will it apply to ALL who attend, regardless of who they "support", and regardless of where they sit or stand?

Arthur Price

Left to Right. Luther, Peter and George. All 'victims' of quite pathetic and hostile barracking at Crewe.

Desperate to come up with a new angle on the seasons fixture list, we commissioned Arch-Consumer of Most Things Alcoholic, Peter Wicks, to give 'OOC' readers a guide to the tastiest breweries on this seasons travels. He advised us that most places don't have breweries now, so being a purist, he wasn't sure if the idea was practicable, but anyway, he sent us the following, and now the drinking is up to you!

August 25 1990
Brentford - Fullers Chiswick, London Pride, ESB!

September 8
Wigan - Burtonwood MILD!, Bitter
September 22
Exeter - Exmoor Ale, Dark, GOLD!

October 2
Reading - Brakspear's Mild, Bitter, SPECIAL!, Old
October 6
Southend - Crouch Vale Woodham Bitter, Essex Porter, WILLIE WARMER!
October 23
Huddersfield - Linfit OLD ELI!, LEADBOILER!, ENOCHS HAMMER!
October 27
Preston - Thwaites Mild, BEST MILD!, Bitter

November 24
Birmingham - Ansells MILD!, Bitter

December ?
Chester - Oak Best!, Old Oak Ale, DOUBLE DAGGER!, Porter, WOBBLY BOB!
December 22
Grimsby - Darley MILD!, (actually part of Wards, itself a Vaux subsidiary)

January 1 1991
Bolton - Thwaites Mild, BEST MILD!, Bitter
January 12
Bury - See Bolton
January 26
Stoke - Titanic PREMIUM!

February 2
Bradford City - Timothy Taylors Golden Best, LANDLORD!, Ram Tam
February 12
Cambridge - Greene King XX Mild, IPA, ABBOTT!
February 23
Rotherham - Stones

March 9
Swansea - Felinfoel Mild, Bitter, DOUBLE DRAGON!
March 16
Fulham - Young's Bitter, Special, WINTER WARMER!
March 18
Tranmere - BoddisHigsTwitbread I suppose
March 30
Mansfield - Mansfield RIDING! & Old Bailey

April 6
Leyton Orient - Charrington IPA
April 20
Crewe - Greenalls Mild, Bitter, Original

May 11
Shrewsbury - Banks's MILD!, Bitter

Peter Wicks - with additional research from, & much thanks to, Brian Byles - Halifax Town Supporters Club, London Branch

THE BATTLE OF BOURNEMOUTH (part 785)

The ambitious £6 million project to move Bournemouth pier to a new site, five hundred yards from its present position is running into more problems following the recent Bank Holiday riots. Now a local Member of Parliament has put forward what he claims is the ideal solution. The Right Honourable David Prattkinson, Conservative Member for Bournemouth North North West, said, in an exclusive interview with Out of Court, "It seems to me that the pier causes more trouble than it is worth. The time has come to move it inland to an out of town site." The diminutive Tory, who assured us that he never drank lager, continued, "I live quite close to the pier and the idea of constructing a new one five hundred yards away fills many local residents with horror. The pier should be rebuilt at a site out of town. Hurn would seem to suit all the requirements of relocation. I shall shortly be addressing the House on this matter." Supporters of Bournemouth Pier are bound to ask, "Is this another occasion where a publicity seeking local politician hopes to gain credibility from a situation that he neither understands nor gives a damn about ?" Mr Prattkinson is 14½.

M.P. DAVID PRATTKINSON

BOURNEMOUTH   PIER

PRODIGAL SONS

In the twenty years I've supported Bournemouth there have been quite a few players who decided the grass and the plastic pitches are greener elsewhere, and yet have come back to Bournemouth to play out the twighlight of their careers · although a few hardy souls have continued with other clubs afterwards, because with very few exceptions the return of the 'Prodigal Son' firstly does not last long, and secondly is not usually a success, or at best does not compare favourably with the first spell.

Kevin Bond is one of those rare successes · he was an apprentice in the early seventies and never played for the

before joining Bournemouth reserves · I mean Seattle Sounders!

Colin Clarke made a great return (will he make another? · ed) and maintained his goal in every two game ratio last season in his brief comeback.

Howard Goddard was a regular goalscorer at various clubs and followed 18 goals in 62 games with 2 in a brief spell of 6 games.

The player so many of us hoped would return was Supermac himself, Ted MacDougall. Of course he could never repeat the 103 goals in 146 League games that had gone before. I was one of the amazing 6005 League gate to watch a Fourth Division game V

Brian O'Donnell never really achieved much as an apprentice or when he returned to play nine games in the 81/82 promotion team.

Harry Redknapp has of course made a brilliant return · as a manager, but as a player only the one league game!

John 'The Bear' Smeulders has made more returns than most of us have had indegestion free meat pies at football matches. Mr. Dependable himself · thanks John · probably the only player to have played for Bournemouth in both the 4th and 2nd Divisions, apart from Tom Heffernan.

Heffernan was a whole hearted player who was our nearest answer to

first team, but is now team captain, and has played over 50 League games. He played more than 100 games for Norwich, Manchester City and S**********n and looks like joining Alan Ball, Peter Shilton and not many other players in getting the 'ton·up' at 4 different clubs.

Frank Barton had two spells in the late seventies · 13 goals in 66 games was followed by 2 goals in 22 before he trod the familiar road to Seattle Sounders.

Least said about John Benson the better · Incredibly he managed three League clubs · the J**n B**d left overs. He certainly played better for Norwich (1 goal) than he did for Bournemouth when he could pick himself!

David Bests career was almost over when he returned aged over 30. He managed only 2 games compared to over 230 previously.

The sadly missed Micky Cave was never the same when he returned from York and managed only 3 goals in 42 games

Darlington and Teds return to Dean Court. It took him 8 games to open his league account and with Norwich and S**********n he had achieved tremendous success including heading the Division 1 scoring charts and scoring in Europe and for Scotland. He'd even had a column in the Daily Mirror · if that's a measure of success!? I saw Teds last game too · when he came off injured in a goalless draw in front of 3201. Still, he achieved his 500th League match and 250th League goal before joining Blackpool.

Trevor Morgan went and returned in the same season and achieved a better goal ratio: he followed 13 goals in 53 games with 33 in 88 games.

Mark Nightingale seemed to have lost his silky skills when he returned via Norwich (!). However, he gave good service and left just before the championship season of 86/87. Although his goals were usually penalties it took him 100 more games to score the same number of four.

Liverpools Chris Lawler. He never really re·established himself on his return.

I didn't see Jimmy White when he was first with the club but his solid work as a half back which ended after J**n B**d became manager was more consistent than some of B**dys signings · remember Ian Davies and Jim De Garis?

Finally Roger Brown. A great defender who was probably John Bensons best signing. He went briefly to Norwich · Who didn't? · then Fulham but came back to provide some outstanding displays in the heart of the defence. Like his contemporary John Beck, Roger went into management.

In conclusion most of the returns were unsuccessful, but who cares? It mae life interesting. I always hoped Phil Boyer would return · but no joy. Now I hope Nigel Spackman, Colin Clarke or Paul Moulden become prodigal sons!!

Mike Williams

DISASTER ON THE CARDS

AFC Bournemouth 3 V 1 Middlesbro'. What a fantastic night that was! Just under 14,000 people (officially) packed into Dean Court to witness a superb game, and most of those fans were following Bournemouth.

The popularity of professional football has been improving nationwide for the past four seasons, to such an extent that this year an estimated 20m people will pass through the turnstiles. The second division is currently boasting a 25% increase.

One club where the picture is oh so different of course is our very own Dean Court. Here, we've had FA Cup games against Manchester United, arguably the most popular club in the country, that unforgettable local derby in the Littlewoods Cup, and even Second Division matches against Pompey.

The West Ham game is a perect example. It should have been a complete sell-out, but only attracted some 7,000 'home' fans. The club were eventually forced into abandoning their high-minded principles on all ticket matches by touting them around ON THE DAY OF THE MATCH!

In the West Ham programme Brian Tiler criticised fans for using the 'Echo' to air their grievances. This followed the criticism from Harry concerning the admittedly poor attendance for the Oldham Athletic fixture. It's a bit rich really, seeing as the club used the media themselves to have a go at the stay aways.

Why the club should still be mystified about low crowds is rather baffling. You know the reason. I know the reason. In fact, judging by recent letters in the Echo (which closed the subject coincidentally on the day BT said he was getting fed up of reading them!), all Bournemouth fans know the reason. Yet AFC Bournemouth still need to be told. It's that bloody membership scheme.

At the FSA meeting mentioned in the last issue, Brian Tiler pledged that the club would listen to the fans. AFC Bournemouth advertise in the FSA National newspaper as "the club that cares about it's fans". Well, perhaps he also should try listening to those who are staying away. Yes, the club needs them, but it must come up with a way of winning people over, as slagging off the very people you want to attract has never been a very successful marketing policy.

So what has our membership scheme acheived? Sadly very little. What on earth is the point of closing the membership scheme temporarily AND making games all ticket? Ask those who turned up for the Portsmouth match. They were given a voucher and told to turn up on a non-match day for tickets for the West Ham game. The barriers set out on the Sunday for the expected thousands must have looked pretty pathetic when only 700 tickets were sold. This wasn't the first time the club have pulled that stunt, and for those like the Exiles, who travel miles just

for HOME games, its a pretty insulting way of rewarding their loyalty.

Competition for fans has never been more crucial. If I went to buy a car from a garage and they told me to come back at midnight, and then charged three quid just to look around the showroom, I'd soon find a garage that offered more reasonable terms. Football isn't quite like that, but some people have pointed out that they can visit another club only 25 miles away, watch First Division football (thats the division where 19 teams battle it out for second place), get in without any hassle, and, believe it or not, there aren't riots every week.

Colchester United were another club who introduced a 100% membership scheme, but they, unlike Luton, didn't get the publicity that came from having David 'Pinocchio' Evans as Chairman. A few months later they were forced to abandon their scheme as fans stayed away in their tens.

Luton Town supporters attempted to let fans from Norwich in for a game as an experiment, because the Carrow Road fans aren't notorious for their troublemakers. The police would have none of it. One is left to wonder who exactly runs the game, and what, if any, external influences are placed on AFC Bournemouth to keep their scheme, against the wishes of the majority of its supporters.

On the subject of the police, it was very re-assuring to see that AFC Bournemouth were amongst the top ten when it came to police bills, yet our crowds are probably the smallest. The club pulls the wool over no-ones eyes when it suggests that this is was it takes to make the ground trouble free. The membership scheme was supposed to do this, and if a reduction in policing costs cannot be acheived (as we predicted right at the start), then it is no good whatsoever.

And lets not forget the new stadium. If AFC Bournemouth do eventually move to Hurn, they will have to work even harder at persuading fans to turn up. Fans are traditionalists at heart, and once prised away from that favourite spot in the new stand, or that splinter in the main stand, they will need convincing that the extra travel will be worth it. Maybe its time they started practising for that day.

What this club desperately needs, as we enter a new decade, is a board both willing and able to cope with the rising demand for live professional football. We must become a club that WANTS 17,000 people at Dean Court for every home game, and not one that continually manages to deter both loyal and casual supporters. If they are frightened of that challenge, perhaps they should do the decent thing...

'Son of Frank Barton'

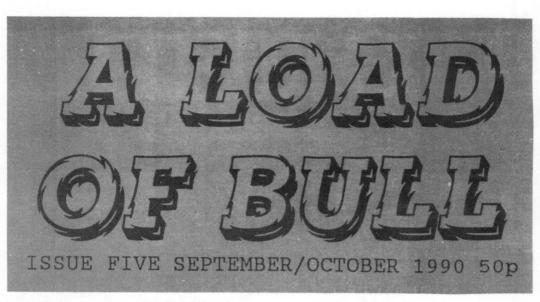

The 1980's can only be described as 'eventful' as far as Wolverhampton Wanderers were concerned. We could be forgiven for thinking that we were watching the footballing equivalent of a yo-yo at times, as the famous Old Gold changed divisions with alarming regularity. After pinching the League Cup at the start of the decade, no-one could have forseen the collapse that lead to the club languishing in the bottom half of the fourth division, having been dumped out of the F.A. Cup by the mighty Chorley. Disillusionment and anger set in as we twice fought off the Official Receiver. Times were so hard that the club couldn't even afford to pay the milkman. Then came 'The Revival' instigated by Graham Turner and his players, and the yo-yo was on its way back up the League.

Against this background 'A Load Of Bull' spluttered into life at the start of the 89/90 season. The events of the past years meant we were never short of things to write about; whether it be past players (the good, the bad and the bloody awful), the woeful neglect of Molineux (two sides are closed and have been since the Bradford fire) or our experience at the 92 League grounds (yes - some people have done them with Wolves if you conveniently forget about Maidstone!) Then of course there's a bloke called Bull, who enjoys the status of GOD in this Black Country town.

If we learned anything at all from the last decade, it is not to take our football club for granted. Whatever the next few seasons hold, the one certainty is that they won't be boring. We'll be there battling it it out at one end of the table or the other.

DAVE WORTON/RUPERT/CHARLOTTE RHODES

Dear ALOB,
Did you know it takes 527 reruns of Bully's goal against the Albion to wear out a Scotch Video tape?

BOB ADAMS, NUNEATON.

WHAT DO WE DO WHEN
WOLVES HAVEN'T A GAME?

On Wednesday 17th January, a group of Hatherton Wolves Supporters Club
members made for the Crem to see Wolves reserves play the Shit. During
half-time a discussion started about what we would do on Saturday 27th
January when Wolves have no game. I had already checked out Maidstone but
found out that they were away to Stockport on that day, otherwise it
would have been the ideal opportunity to complete the 92 grounds.

Some bright spark mentioned that Hartlepool were playing away at
Gillingham, a comment that was received with boos and laughter. But when
he explained that Hartlepool fans came to Molineux when we were bottom of
the 3rd Division and looking to go out of business we began to think more
seriously about it. Steve Plant and Monty took up the idea and a quick
concensus revealed that we could probably fill a coach. Contact was made
with Hartlepool Supporters Club who thought it was a wind-up at first but
when they realised we were serious they thought it was a great idea.

The trip was agreed by the committee of Hatherton Wolves and travel
arrangements made to take a coach departing at 8:30am.

The day before the match we realised that only about 30 people would be
making the trip so Dave Quarrell contacted Happy Days to find out if we
could have a smaller coach. 'Sorry' came the reply 'all smaller coaches
are hired out but, as Wolves don't have a game, would you like the Wolves
team coach at no extra cost?' Not 'alf !!!

8:30am, thirty Wolves fans sat comfortably on the team coach thinking
they were superstars - half a dozen videos at the ready. By the time we
got to Willenhall, we'd knackered the video. I don't think it was ever
working to tell the truth but I hope it's repaired before Bully and Co
have to use it again.

So it had to be card schools and music from the radio instead. Dave told
us a fascinating story of the monkey hanging episode in Hartlepool a long
while ago when locals found a monkey on the beach and hung him when they
thought he was a French spy. Apparently Hartlepool folk don't think the
story is very funny and we warned Roy Tansley not to mention the story at
the match. That was a mistake! We all knew what the first thing Roy would
mention would be.

As usual, Roy did his best to get us lost but we eventually made our own
way to Priestfield and the Gills Social Club. We asked the Police where
we should park the coach and he got on his radio. 'The Wolves coach has
arrived, where should they park?' 'But we're not even playing Wolves'
came the reply. After a brief explanation we got off the coach and joined
the Gillingham and Hartlepool fans for a pre-match drink.

We were welcomed by both sets of supporters, exchanged pennants and
addresses and discussed the performance of our respective teams. One lad
from the Hartlepool Supporters Club apologised in advance for comments
made by their Supporters Club Chairman in the local press who had
apparently stated that he wasn't in favour of Wolves fans turning up to
support their team. He stated that the Chairman was from their Official
Club, that his views were not the views of the everyday fan and that the
Chairman was out of touch with the real fan and very rarely, if at all,
travelled to away matches.   He told us that as far as
he and his colleagues were concerned this was a tremendous gesture by the
Wolves fans which was greatly appreciated.

A LOAD
OF BULL

Fortunately, I'd had the foresight to take along 50 copies of 'A Load of Bull' which were sold in about 2 minutes and had both sets of supporters begging for more. I also took the opportunity to purchase the Gills fanzine 'Brian Moore's Head' which I found to be good value and interesting reading.

Into the away end of the ground - Wolves fans, Hartlepool fans and Gillingham fans who wanted to come in for the 'atmosphere'. Before the match it was cries of 'Ooh Bully Bully', during the match we did our best to encourage the 'pool' and at half time we had a chorus of 'two little boys'. Final result 0-0; enough to lift Hartlepool off the bottom of the league and we played our part. Nobody seemed to notice that Roy had been shouting 'Come on you monkey hangers' throughout the game. Wolves fans find it hard to work out what he's saying at the best of times so the lads from Hartlepool had no chance.

Handshakes all round after the match. A great day was had by all, just a pity that this sort of adventure gets very little publicity whereas any hooliganism or trouble making could be sure to make the headlines.

Also good luck to Hartlepool, our adopted second team.

Phil Murphy
Chairman
Hatherton Wolves Supporters Club

Hartlepool Mail

'Hartlewolves' fans help put the smile back on Pool faces

THE SMILE returned to Hartlepool football on Saturday when a fine defensive performance gave a goalless draw -at Gillingham.

The game may not have been a thriller but it gave Pool their third away point of the season and took them above Wrexham at the bottom of the league.

It was only the second point Pool have taken from Priestfield in eleven visits but what gave them most satisfaction was a second successive clean sheet.

Pool's throughly professional performance was cheered on by their faithful fans augmented by about fifty supporters from Wolverhampton Wanderers.

Appreciated

"When we were struggling in the third division," organiser Steve Plant explained, "a load of Hartlepool fans came down to support us."

"We appreciated that and said we would do the same one day and as we haven't got a cup match this afternoon, this is it.

The combined choir of Black Country and North East voices chanting "Hartlewolves!" should have been recorded and sent to Mrs Thatcher and anyone else who thinks that all football fans are morons who only want to fight each other.

'Monkey Business'

BULLY BOYS

Have you ever watched Wolves away ??? Judging from our experiences at Gillingham recently it must be a hell of an experience. Apparently a bus load of Poolies went to watch Wolves a few years ago when they were struggling. Some of their fans promised to return the compliment and so, at Gillingham, our usual travelling support in the south, about 150 people, was reinforced by a bus load from the Black Country. They were brilliant !! They gave the lads so much encouragement, I couldn't believe it. At the end of the match we all stood round applauding each other, and some Poolies later joined them for a pint, or two. Cheers lads !!!

As usual the southern beer was disgusting. The only highlight of the pre-match drink was £10,000 Russell Doig pushing past me in the Livingstone Arms, to get to the bar. For trivia fans, he drank orange juice.

The match, although crap, was nerve-wracking stuff. We were kept in it by the saves of England's No.1 Jason Priestley. It can't be long before Bobby Robson gives him the nod. The only thing keeping him out of the squad must be his haircut. It's weird !!

'Pools played the sort of grimly defensive game that has failed them every time since Sir Cyril took over. This time they got it right, and were we relieved or what ? You would never have guessed that there were 3,500 Gillingham fans in the ground, they were quieter than Salman Rushdie. Pehaps they were as stunned as we were by the half-naked Wolves fan clinging to the fence shouting his head off at the lino!'

THE CARING FACE OF FOOTBALL

Dear ALOB,

First of all let's welcome you to Wolvo, and my sympathy goes out to you for where you live. Still, it could be worse - you could be nearer the Al... ground. This is a Wanderers typewriter, and is programmed to not type the letters boinla in a certain order.

To my point. Who do you think are the toughest and hardiest Wolves fans?

It is not the 16 stone inhabitant of the South Bank with W.W.F.C. tattooed across his or her (yes her, have you ever had a drink in Darlaston on a Saturday night?) forehead and chest. Nor the Vivian (Young Ones) lookalike with Love and 'Ate on his knuckles. It's 'ate by the way, because he bit his own finger off in temper and frustration when we played Torquay last year and blew the chance of a Wembley return.

No. To my way of thinking, it's the lads and lasses who week in week out sit on the sidelines, or wherever it is convenient for the Molineux (bar) stewards to put them in their wheelchairs.

Rain or shine they are there. No cover, no anything. And they sit there season after season, while the Gallaghers and the Wolverhampton leisure services argue in the warm about who is going to look after them. And whilst this happens, freeze on boys and girls. Perhaps some facilities may appear when you become too ill to take advantage of them, as opposed to the other way around.

Before anyone questions my credibility to raise this issue, I have been in a wheelchair since 1980 due to an accident sustained on the way to the Wolves/Forest Cup Final. The right result for the lads, but not for me.

Keep going ALOB - I think we need you to put the true feelings of the fans across.

Steve McCormack, Blakeley.

P.S. Who is the only player to acknowledge the delight of the disabled Wolves fans when he scores down the North Bank end? You guessed it, the people's champ himself. Nice one Steve.

"Now don't get cold will you, and if you want anything just wave at box 31 and we'll see you if we are paying attention."

GREAT MOMENTS IN MOLINEUX HISTORY

NO.1 - GEORGE THREATENS THE BALL BOYS

A LOAD OF BULL

THE USES OF IAN ORMONDROYD

NO.1 - VILLA INSTALL   £650,000
WORTH OF FLOODLIGHTS

VILLA AND MEB HAVE A LOT IN COMMON

Like the Villa, MEB work as a team. We put our individual abilities together
so that you can make the most of electricity - at home and at work

LOOKALIKES

Tesco carrier bag, Brighton player

A LOAD OF BULL

WELCOME TO 'THE MATCH'

AN ARTICLE CONCERNING ITV'S WISH TO POSTPONE THE ARSENAL/LIVERPOOL GAME UNTIL THE END OF THE SEASON.....

SATURDAY MAY 12 1990, 3PM.

WELTON SMARMSBY: Well, here we are today at Highbury for what promises to be a great match. Arsenal, the Champions, against Liverpool, in what has now been billed the "Championship Decider". My guest today, Jimmy Greaves. Hello Jimmy, quite a match in prospect, hey?

JIMMY: Hello Welton, yes. All the better since Liverpool were yesterday docked five points, which has now made the two teams level at the top.

WELTON: Yes. Unfortunate for Liverpool, but lucky for us and the viewers....and the ratings.

JIMMY: The reason for the loss of points was a little unfortunate too. Taking five points off because "Kenny Dalglish doesn't smile enough whilst being interviewed on TV" seems a little harsh.

WELTON: Yes....well...anyway on to match commentator Brian Bore.

BRIAN: Hello Welton. Today we have a special guest, the Minister Against Sport, Colin Moanihan. Hello Colin.

COLIN (speaks): Hello Brian. Nice to be sitting here next to you rather than on those horrible terrace things.

BRIAN: Ah...Colin. I wonder, could you tell me if there is any truth in the rumour that you want to introduce all-seater stadium because you can't actually see from the terraces?

COLIN: No, of course not, I don't like going to football matches anyway.

BRIAN: Oh, right. Anyway, on to today's teams. Arsenal, in goal Lukic...etc...and Liverpool are unchanged from their previous four games which were all on TV anyway, so you should know them by now. And here we go, Rush to Beardsley, back to McMahon,back to Hansen, back to....By the way, we had some letters asking why we scheduled today's game for this date, when the F.A.Cup Final is on the other side. The official reply from higher up is that "we honestly did not know it was on, and it is purely a coincidence.....
A little while later.....

BRIAN: ....and there it goes, Ian Rush, one-nil Liverpool.
COLIN: Look at that, it's terrible.
BRIAN: Sorry? What's wrong Colin?
COLIN: All those people on those terrace things, jumping up and down, and waving their arms. It's disgusting. They should be kicked out, or arrested or something.
WEST MIDLANDS POLICE RECRUITMENT OFFICER (who happens to be sitting there): Ah sir, have you ever considered a career in the Police Force, especially in the West Midlands area?
COLIN: And look at this! One of those spectators has run on the pitch and is hugging the players. He should be shot or...or....
JIMMY: Er....didn't you do that in Seoul, Colin?
COLIN (high-pitched): Aaaaah! What's he doing here? Go away. You haven't got an I.D. card....
JIMMY: Neither have you.
BRIAN (whispers): They're not in yet, Colin.
COLIN: But I'm a Minister and.....
JIMMY: Oh stick it up your....
COLIN (really squealing now): It's not fair! I'm not staying if he is. I mean it! I'm going to scream and scream and scream and them I'm going to be sick and then you'll be sorry.
BRIAN: Alright Colin, alright, look he's going, nasty man. There, there.

Later still.....

BRIAN: Well half time folks, and it's still one-nil to Liverpool. What do you think of it, Colin?
COLIN: I think it's really unfair that no one passes to that man in the black. I mean he's even got a whistle to attract their attention and everything.
BRIAN: Yes Colin, anyway back to Welton.
WELTON: Thank you Brian. Well we have a treat for you second half, folks. A new innovation which we hope to keep going next season. The two goalkeepers will be carrying hand-held cameras to give you a more realistic view of the game from the keeper's point of view. Just part of our continuing effort to bring you the best football coverage on TV at the moment. What do you think, Jimmy?
JIMMY: I think it's a load of......

SWITCH OVER TO BBC1

JIMMY HILL: Well here we are at half-time in the Cup Final, brought to you exclusively here on the good old Beeb. Next season, we here at the Beeb have decided on a few changes, to make the F.A.Cup Match Of The Day Programme even better. There will be no offside allowed, the goalkeepers will only be allowed to use one hand and, in any match, the team from the higher division will have to wear Mickey Mouse or Donald Duck costumes to give the other team a better chance. More entertainment and more goals, and of course when one team wants to play a joker.....
DES CARDIGAN: That's the wrong one....that's another programme.
JIMMY: Oh yes....well it is at the moment anyway. On to our studio guest, Mr Bobby.Robson. Bobby, what do you think of it so far?
BOBBY: I blame the pitch.
JIMMY: Pardon?
BOBBY: And the heat.
JIMMY: Yes, well, back to the game.....

SAINT WOLFGANG.

"I blame the weather..."

THEY SAID IT

"What a beautiful attempt that was from Zavarov. He's got lovely feet" (Jimmy Hill - Holland/Russia 1988).

"West Ham, wearing white tonight, defending the cock-end in the first half" (John Motson - Arsenal/West Ham. Yes he really did say it, I've got the evidence on video!)

"Four First Division teams and Bristol City through" (Nick Owen on the Littlewoods Cup Semi-Finalists).

"We understand from the dressing room that he's got a calf muscle" (Brian Moore on an injury to Gordon Strachan).

"You indeed feel that the first goal in this game will be important" (Brian Moore again - Newcastle/Man Utd).

"Peter Reid is hobbling and I've a feeling that's going to slow him down" (John Motson classic).

A LOAD
OF BULL

SCOUSE INVASION

Tuesday 4th May 1976

Liverpool travelled to Molineux needing just a point to clinch the League Championship from under the noses of QPR. Wolves, on the other hand, needed a victory to avoid relegation, providing eternal strugglers Birmingham lost at Sheffield United on the same night.

Millions of TV viewers sat down in eager anticipation of seeing a game to remember. Well, not quite. It wasn't on the TV, not even edited highlights later on. All we had were the goals on the news, despite the feeling amongst people that this game was as important as the F.A. Cup Final itself. Add to this the fact that the match was not all-ticket and, yes you guessed it, we had a recipe for absolute chaos. Not that tickets would have made much difference anyway, half of Liverpool (the red half) must have been in Wolvo that night.

Rush

It was the only time I can ever recall my dad rushing home from work in order to get to the match early. IT WAS THAT IMPORTANT. In fact, we arrived at the back of the South Bank at around 6.15 to find a massive crowd of people waiting to gain admission already. Being only eleven at the time, I split off from my dad to gain admission through the Juniors turnstiles. As kick-off time drew near, the crowd pressure intensified, and so did people's frustrations. There was no way out of the crush even if I had wanted one. For what seemed like ages, I was wedged tight, only able to move whichever way the crowd took me. All I could see were grown-ups midriffs and a small patch of night sky above. Police control was non-existant. Yet I had my size to thank for getting me in, from out of the free-for-all at the turnstiles. On seeing my pale, worried, breathless expression, there were still enough kindly souls in such a panic-stricken situation to shelter and make way for me. I lost count of the number of times I heard "Watch out, there's a kid down here!" All these years later I can still remember the engulfing sense of helplessness.

Incredible

In! Gasping for air, I struggled through the crowd to take my usual place, standing on the girders at the Molineux alley side of the South Bank. This was the section where away supporters used to congregate in the days of massed battles across the police no-mans land before the segregating fence was erected and the away fans moved to the other side. I don't know what I had expected, but this was not it. From my lofty vantage point over-looking everybody else's heads, the sight was incredible. No no-mans land, no mass of chanting Wolves supporters, just a vast sea of red and white. I can safely say I've stood on the Kop without ever visiting Anfield. The official attendance that day was given as 46,097, but there were thousands more inside. I'd like to know who fiddled the tax man, and how many had scaled walls into the ground or run in through the gates. The real attendance must have been well into the fifties. People were scaling the floodlights, stands, walls and fences, trees, buildings over looking the ground, anything that afforded even half a view of the game. The aisles down the South Bank were non-existant. Some supporters climbed as high as the rafters in the roof - including one who fell off! Molineux was just one heaving mass of people.

My dad turned up just after kickoff, pleased to see that I was alright - we'd both misjudged the crowd. He'd been right by the turnstiles as they had been closed with thousands still outside. The large exit gates had been forced open in the ensuing panic and desparation and, thinking of me inside, he'd run through with masses of other people before the police sealed the gap. Really though, he'd had no choice - there's no arguing with a surging crowd especially in the confined, walled-in space behind the South Bank. Luckily, the terraces were large enough to deal with such a surge.

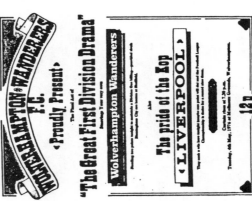

As for the game itself, Steve Kindon stormed through (if you ever saw Steve you'll know what I mean) after thirteen (!) minutes to crash us into a 1-0 lead in front of 'The Kop'. We were in the midst of a pocket of Wolves supporters and proceeded to go mental. I still don't know how we remained in one piece! Would West Midlands Police have ejected us in these days I wonder?

Despite a brave rear-guard action from our players, it seemed only a matter of time to a Liverpool goal, although they didn't manage it until the 76th minute. 20,000 plus Scousers went crazy and it took some while to clear the pitch. The over-powering strength of that red machine then buried our shaken, weary heroes with two more goals in the dying minutes. Both were followed by massed pitch invasions.

Down

We were down, and Liverpool in exile celebrated. The news that Birmingham had gained their required point at Bramall Lane didn't soften the disappointment of losing the lead. Why was it that the Brummies always used to survive by the skin of their teeth? At least we came back with a vengeance the season after - a season which gave me a lot of happy memories.

I became quite a hero at school because I was the only one there who managed to get in - a fact which I have become quite proud of since! However, my everlasting memory of Tuesday 4th May 1976 will always be the crowd scenes inside and outside the ground, tempered now by the thought of what could easily have happened 13 years before Hillsborough.

DAVID WORTON.

	P	W	D	L	F	A	P
Q.P.R.	42	24	11	7	67	33	59
Liverpool	41	22	14	5	63	30	58
Man. Utd.	41	22	11	10	66	42	54
Derby	42	21	11	10	75	58	53
Leeds	42	21	9	12	65	46	51
Ipswich	42	16	14	12	54	48	46
Leicester	42	13	19	10	48	51	45
Man. City.	41	16	11	14	64	44	43
Tottenham.	42	14	15	13	63	63	43
Norwich	42	16	10	16	58	58	42
Stoke	42	15	10	17	48	50	41
Middlesbro	42	15	10	17	46	45	40
Coventry	42	13	14	15	61	66	40
Everton	42	15	12	15	60	66	40
Newcastle	42	15	9	18	71	62	39
Villa	42	11	17	14	51	59	39
Arsenal	42	13	10	19	47	53	36
West Ham	42	13	10	19	48	71	36
Blues	41	13	6	22	56	74	32
WOLVES	41	10	10	21	50	65	30
Burnley	42	9	10	23	41	66	28
Sheff. Utd.	41	6	9	26	32	81	21

(Up to and including April 24)

SAINT PETER?

Ever felt like slamming the door in the face of a Jehovah's Witness and shouting "That one's for Peter! No? Well THE CULTURED LEFT FOOT has, and who are we to argue?

Anybody got the BBC's "Match of The Day - The Sixties" video? No? Well slip a tenner in the old lady's purse and add said item to the next shopping list.

Apart from some of the most wicked 25 yard screamers that you'll ever see from that bald bloke who used to captain Manchester United, some brilliant ball skills from Best, Law, Young and Rogers, and Alan Clarke Playing for Leicester in some of the worst-fitting shorts I've ever seen, there are also a few noteworthy Wolves bits. Now the Sixties, in my opinion, have always been a bit of a grey area where the Wolves are concerned, as if the demise of the great Fifties' side had been almost sinisterly hushed up. However the brief clips contained in the video shed a little light on the mystery.

Birth Of A Hero

There's a Dougan hat-trick against Hull on his home debut in 1967. The third goal defies description. It's a sort of reverse bicycle flick, knocking the ball which had gone behind him back over his head with his heel, followed by a thunderous volley as it dropped which almost tore the net from its moorings - and all in the six-yard area too! Okay, so the marking was a bit slack, but who gives a toss. The North Bank went up and a hero was born.

There are the goals from a 2-2 draw at Sheffield Wednesday, apparently shown, if Motson is to be believed, merely to compare the trendy haircuts of Peter Knowles and Alun Evans. In any event, Knowles scores a blinder early on (followed by shots of Wolves fans dancing on the terraces right next to home fans who were not). Wednesday go 2-1 up with two crap goals, and an 18 year old Evans scores a last minute beauty to equalise after a rumbustuous run down the wing from Mike Bailey before he became a barrel. Great stuff.

Then there's a lengthy piece of film of an interview with Peter Knowles, and we all know what about. Now, I never saw Knowles play but, like all the rest, I had heard about his undoubted potential. I've got a book somewhere that says he was on an undisclosed shortlist of players to go to Mexico in 1970. He must have been a pretty decent footballer.

As it turns out, he reveals himself to be a complete pillock: "And I know the person that I am, the flair I've got, that I could one day break someone's leg... and I'd hate this on my mind." For pete's sake, Pete, you COULD break somebody's leg if you spent 90 minutes showing twelve studs to every knee cap you came into contact with, but you'd soon be out of the team and out of a job too. The lengths he goes to to qualify this pile of shite is extraordinary.: "... it's the thought that that person could be a cripple for the rest of his life, and when you're a cripple you come down in wages... and you're hanging about the house and you get niggly with your wife and this could easily break up a marriage." I've heard about an apple for the teacher, but this bloke seems to have his tongue permanently thrust down the back of God's underpants. Go to the top of the class, Knowles, spake He.

Witness This

What more could he say to please Jesus H? Ah yes: "... I found the nearer it got to Saturday I was dragging myself away from my wife and my religion... I was thinking about how I was going to play, and what I'd do if somebody kicked me..." Yes, he said it. Well Pete, I'd hazard a guess that you'd probably kick him back, apologise to his missus, and sell your house and all its belongings to make the remainder of his life as comfortable as possible. All in all, he was the epitome of the sickly antiseptic Jehovah's Sales Executive and, thus sanitised, he was able to give his only real bit of foresight: "... sport's gone out of the game now. It's big business... people are getting smashed over the head with bottles and people are getting stabbed... I can see that it's going to come to a big climax in one game."

Why, oh why did you have to answer the door that morning Peter? Why did you let them in? Why didn't you just tell them to p**s off like the rest of us?

"... the dying seconds of this UEFA Cup Final at White Hart Lane... Knowles, shrugs off Coates, wrong foots Chivers, through to Richards... it's there!!"

THE CULTURED LEFT FOOT.

A LOAD OF BULL

IGNORANCE AND BLISS

Attendance at the England-Czechoslovakia international was made doubly satisfying by the certain knowledge that a breakfast of humble-pie and muesli partaken by the media the following morning would certainly lead to belated acknowledgement that here indeed was a hero fit to receive the accolade, "England's Number Nine."

Switching on the video in Thursday's early hours, the pictures provided testimony for the fulsome praise that should have been Steve's by right, but the commentary did more than hint that preconceived notions need more than a virtually flawless performance to be swept away: Obviously a certain humility, even a sense of justice, was required by our sporting media-men to admit that a player, who does not fit their image of an international, could be the key to England returning from their Mediterranean sojourn with something more than unfulfilled hopes and the duty-free.

The tone was set in the opening few minutes by Barry Davies assuring us that Steve Bull's endeavour could not be questioned, before raising the issue of his suitability to perform on the stage of the World Cup; or his ability to stomach the plastic extrusion of bonhomie that fits hand in sleeve with a Sporting Triangles' jumper, he might just as well have added, for there is something about this reluctance to praise him which has less to do with his merits as a footballer than his suitability to be deemed a "personality" or indeed even, the ultimate accolade, a "character".

Paul Gascoigne is a character. We know this because he can be referred to as "Gazza", has appeared on a Question of Sport and appears overly-familiar in Bryan Robson's presence. Steve Bull, however, has an image like his surname, haircut and accent: parochial and proletarian. But the sheer lack of pretentiousness allied to the goals and aircraft impressions make him the embodiment of Renaissance Man in this book.

Incidentally, it was Gascoigne who provided the through-ball for Bull to score his first goal. But then you probably knew that already, for the TV commentary seemed to suggest that Steve's angled chest-down and waist-high volley, the trajectory of which approximated roughly with the base line of a protractor so that the ball flew to the back, and not into the roof, of the net, was overshadowed somewhat by the brilliance of a ball played with, wait for it, the OUTSIDE of Gascoigne's foot!

To denigrate the latter's performance would be churlish; he had an excellent game in England's midfield and could indeed be the man to "give the ball to Stevie Bull" needed by our national team but, since self-deprecation does not appear to be his strong point, let others extoll his merits.

The commentary for Steve's second goal disabused me from the notion that I had seen yet another example of the man's ability to lose a marker and clinically despatch a hopeful cross so that the Czechs were reduced to the tired histrionics of men eager not to appear too personally culpable for the meeting of laminated plastic and nylon netting.

Barry Davies, again, "It was a lovely cross, curling away from the goalkeeper, and Bull, well, it was a gift for him, absolutely right on his forehead. All he had to do was to get a little bit of meat and it's three for England."

A LOAD
OF BULL

Trevor Brooking tempered the theme, "Stevie Bull, as you say, unmarked, a free header, but you've still got to put them in." (I think, given Trevor's relative lack of experience at this level, we can forgive his lapse into hyperbole at the end there.)

So, there you are: Reaching the byeline is apparently football's equivalent to crossing the Rubicon, whilst Steve's goal is no more laudable than a trip to the butchers. But you thought it was goals that count? How crass.

"One of those occasions when he might have hoped his hair was a bit longer" chuckled Trevor Brooking, as another Bull header zipped across the face of the goal. All good hearted stuff but a quip that has lost its humorous edge in inverse proportion to its familiarity at Molineux, where a star is shorn is merely an axiom, albeit a fine example of pretentious word-play.

To be fair, Jimmy Hill did start his after match analysis by humming his praises, even more creditworthy as this was in response to yet another enquiry as to what he thought of Paul Gascoigne's performance, but then followed the most wasteful abuse of video-tape as we were treated to a show of "Gazza's" response to England's first goal - scored by somebody or other, I'm not sure who - as he didn't see fit to congratulate the man who had turned his good through ball into something the Czechs should worry about. The Coe-like celebrations were all heartily endorsed by a commentary as obsequious as it was banal. Meanwhile I suppose there wasn't time to hear Bobby Robson's comments about Bull, presuming of course he was asked.

Not that much solace may have lain there as the next day's press conference given by the England supremo witnessed the scarcely credible assertion that there was a chance Bull might not go to Italy if involved in play-offs with Wolves. Chris Waddle was, of course, in a similar situation with Marseilles but had "less to prove". For Robson to describe Steve's situation as a "dilemma" was little more than an open invitation to rock the boat at his club in order to catch the plane to the World Cup Finals - come on Steve, wise-up and travel in style with "team-mates" whose congratulations for your goals can be most generously termed muted, and more accurately as perfunctory, where they exist at all.

"Severely limited technique" exposed by international defender's assured touch

A LOAD
OF BULL

All Our Yesteryears

After two years of uninterrupted success (Torquay) proved us to be human afterall) the dark days of the Bhatti era seem an eternity away. However, how many of you cut there remember those mega-talents who graced Molineux in that period? Certainly there were the good (rarely), the bad (all the time) and the ugly (Ray Hankin).

The main things looked for by club management at the time were no talent, no ambition, own boots, and most important of all cheap! The players detailed in this article fitted the bill.

The opening game of the 1982-83 season heralded the beginning of the Bhatti era and was played in a blaze of publicity and emotion. A 2-1 victory over Blackburn Rovers was the result.

Due to a series of injuries, DAVID WINTERSGILL became the youngest player ever to play for the first team at sixteen years of age, and was regarded as the new Jimmy Mullen. After his debut, Mullen went on to play for another twenty-plus years for Wolves and was capped by England - Wintersgill played two more games for Wolves and has never been heard of since.

Another Bhatti youngster that made his debut in front of the T.V. cameras was DALE RUDGE. A string of cultured passes (three) against then table-topping QPR and an interview with Jimmy "The Chin" Hill led Wolves fans to believe that another superstar was born. Eight crap appearances, a free transfer to Preston North End and a one way ticket to obscurity proved us wrong.

The major signing of that season was BILLY KELLOCK from Luton, described on his arrival as one of soccer's nomads. This term basically means that the player is crap and cheap, so clubs are willing to take a chance on him. Nine appearances and three goals later, the nomad got on his bike.

By a miracle 82/83 ended in promotion, as the 83/84 First Division season approached, Wolves fans awaited big name signings. They became inquisitive, worried, then shocked as all the stars left to be replaced by Mike BENNETT, JOE JACKSON and MARK BUCKLAND. Buckland was signed from A.F. Leamington for £27.50 and the promise of a railway ticket to Lower Gornal. He proved beyond doubt that a Mars a day helps you work, rest and run around like a headless chicken for ninety minutes without getting near the ball. All heart but no talent.

Another signing was STEVE MARDENBOROUGH, best remembered for his off-the-shoulder creation of a goal versus Liverpool. He ran like a greyhound and unfortunately played like one. Since leaving Wolves he has done a tour of South Wales.

Greyhound racing at Anfield

Five Minute Hero

A hero for five minutes, DANNY CRAINIE signed from Celtic and scored two goals versus the crew, but did very little else. All the talent in the world, but no application. He had a liking for

wine, women and song, unfortunately this usually happened on the night before a game.

A loan signing that season was SCOTT McGARVEY, a well-known shirt lifter - similar to Crainie but less talent.

It is not fair to say that all the new players from 83/84 were a talentless pile of donkey droppings. One player stood out, SANDY TROUGHTON brought over from Northern Ireland, a very determined and skilful player who made nineteen appearances. Another appearance would have meant giving more money to Glentoran as part of the transfer deal, so he never played again. Just the enterprise you would expect from the soccer-mad, fun-loving Bhatti's!

Relegation inevitably followed and in the 84/85 season a new manager was hired, TOMMY "Never mind the result, listen to the joke" DOCHERTY...

In the next issue of ALOB the Bhatti class of 84/85 will be explored. Read about the stars RAY HANKIN, MIKE COADY, NICKY SINCLAIR and more

In the next issue of ALOB the Bhatti class of 84/85 will be explored.

ERIC .CODDARD - AUGUST 85:
"We are in the Third Division following two successive seasons of little achievement or merit. The club is being rebuilt from top to bottom. It takes time to get things right. I am confident that we are now on the right lines."

"We weren't. Eight months later we were again bankrupt. He was a liar.

TOMMY DOCHERTY - AUGUST 84:
"Don't expect miracles. I promise you only that as long as I am around we will always be competitive and always give good value for money. I believe in battling. I believe in my players never giving up."
Observations on this crap:-

We were never competitive.
We never gave good value for money.
We never battled.
We always gave up.
He was a Bhatti!

Rupert

GROUNDS WE HAVE VISITED
no.2-Blackpool

....singing in the rain, just singing in the rain....

GROUNDS WE HAVE VISITED

NORMID

NO.1. BOLTON WANDERERS

A GEORDIE LAMENT

This is an old North East love song, usually sung by swarthy mining folk during times of great personal tragedy, last orders, a favoured whippet dying, Newcastle being humiliated at home... It goes to the tune of the Blaydon races, as does every other song from that area.

"WHEN THE BOOT COMES IN"
O-h-h-h the lads, you should ha' seen us c-r-y-ing,
Just as Newcastle's defence had given up t-r-y-ing,
All the lads and lasses couldn't stand no m-o-r-e.
As the men from Molin-o-o-o-o,
Just made it number four....

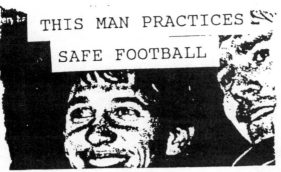

THIS MAN PRACTICES SAFE FOOTBALL

"I always make sure I look good on the pitch, even at the expense of any newcomer. As we know, it doesn't do to have too many partners. Mine is called Peter, that's all I want to say."

GALxxx

Left margin (vertical text):

THE K/FORD SKIN

Q. What is the difference between Colin Moynihan lying in the road and a rabbit lying in the road ?
A. There are skidmarks in front of the rabbit !

GIVE A GAME TO STEVIE BULL ♫

?

ENG-ER-LAND ♫

POOR LITTLE PETER BEARDSLEY IS LOST IN MIDFIELD. CAN YOU HELP HIM FIND HIS WAY TO GOAL?

MEMORIES FROM LAST SEASON

CARDIFF CITY (AWAY).

Being a clever sod, I decided to sit down for this one (I got soaked there a few years earlier). Best decision I've ever made I thought, as I watched the Wolves fans on the terrace being battered by a snow storm.

The game ended in a totally forgettable draw with the usual polite 'request' for the visiting supporters to stay in their places for five minutes. I noticed that the Cardiff fans and police alongside us had nearly all departed, leaving just a 4ft wooden partition between myself and Monty (the only Chelsea fan to watch every Wolves game last season!) and the warmth of the double decker parked just over the road. Thinking my luck was in after my earlier decision, I soon cleared the fence and headed down the stairs, already smiling at the thought at being first back on the coach.

How wrong could I be! I was quickly surrounded by a few hundred Cardiff fans waiting to wish the visiting fans a good journey home. While I was being totally surrounded, Monty walked unmolested across the road. At this point I realised why I had been surrounded, and Monty hadn't. The Wolves ski jacket didn't help, but I think the England hat put the icing on the cake. For the first time in my life, I was glad to see a solitary policeman, complete with alsatian dog.

We reached the coach totally unscathed. Perhaps it was my lucky night afterall!

NEXT ISSUE: Bristol City - three points, £8.50 in loose change and a firework display.

THE K/FORD SKIN.

TALES FROM THE TAP ROOM

A mythical conversation not overheard in a non-existant Wolverhampton pub.

Bully - O.K. lads, as I'm the best paid I'll get the drinks. Shout 'em up.

Floyd - Mine's a large one.

Bully - I know that, but do you wanna drink?

Floyd - Oh sorry, I'll have a babycham then.

Shane - I'll have a pint of that as well.

Psycho - As I'm driving I'll just have a snakebite please.

Veno - (sulking) I don't feel like drinking. I'm fed up 'cos nobody sings songs about me.

Bully - As I'm feeling generous, you can borrow one of mine.

Veno - Great! Can I have the one that goes 'Ooh Bully Bully' ?

Bully - Course you can. Now drink up. It's only half an hour to kick-off..

RORY L. BELTEK.

A LOAD OF BULL

chapter 8

THE LAD done brilliant

ONE MAN TEAM

WITH MOTORISED SPIT

with

THE **Ruud Gullit** STORY

ALSO

MOYNIHAN SPEAKS
FSA secretary RAPS
THE POPE THAT CHEERS
ACTION From BIRMINGHAM

acid
exploitation
scandal

16 15 pages of (and a crap cover)

FOOTIE FUN

35p

17/10/90

DEAR MARTIN,

Here are some "Highlights" of The Lad for your forthcoming compilation — I have included eleven pages to represent the best and worst, I hope you agree with the format.

I looked at "El Tel Was a Space Alien" and thought a bit of history would be appropriate — you don't want to hear about my luxury yacht, and the race horse.

I also noticed your questionnaire and was disappointed that I didn't get one, so here are my answers.

ADRIAN BROWN ; 27 ; THIS SORT OF THING ;
GEORGIE BEST NO SORRY MANCHESTER UNITED ;
I SCORED FOUR GOALS ONCE ;
THIS ONE ; FRANK WORTHINGTON ;
I DON'T DRIVE ; R.E.M., KLF, (ANYTHING WITH THREE LETTERS) ;
HORROR/GORE/DISNEY ;
THE EMPEROR'S NEW ONES ;
GREEN LAPSED SOCIALIST ;
SIMON STURRIDGE AND PAUL TAIT IN 5 YEARS TIME .

And this is me.

Thanks again for asking me to contribute, I will of course be troubling you soon with the Xmas edition of the LAD Done Brilliant.

Cheers Ade.

THE LAD done brilliant

WITH MOTORISED SPIT

A COMPLETE RECORD : 1988 / 1990. by ADRIAN BROWN

Roundabout November 1988, I got talking about football fanzines with Andy and Dave and I said that I wanted to do a "comic fanzine" along the lines of Shoot, Roy of the Rovers and Viz. I imagined that it would be called "Dribble!" but someone beat me to it. Luckily, Andy came up with the name "THE LAD DONE BRILLIANT" and after various experiments with different adjectives, the name stuck.(Shortened to the affectionate title "THE LAD".)

I did a hundred copies of the first one, by hand, on a photocopier. This was enough to persuade me to get them printed in future.
The print run is now 500, and having flirted with the idea of major, world wide distribution, I think I'll keep it that way. Although, if anyone can spread the word, they are welcome to steal,plagiarise, or otherwise use for broadcasting purposes the contents of the LAD.
FANX are due to The LAD's DAD, Spartak, John Mulcreevy (who has since gone on to appear in more fanzines than Colin Moynihan (probably)), Andy Dodd, least but by no means last The Executive Glassmen everywhere, and Andy C. for that inspired bit of cliche-mongering.
   BUT MOST OF ALL TO KAREN, FOR GIVING UP SOVEREIGNTY OF THE KITCHEN TABLE.

Moynihan's ID CARD arrogance

"destroying the game as family entertainment"

COLIN MOYNIHAN has plans to require all football supporters to carry identity cards. The move is an attempt to head off the threat of ☛ opponents of **the Government's** anti-terrorist legislation, in particular the Prevention of **Football** Act and the abolition of the right to silence for Walsall, **Supporters'** ● **Moynihan's** whole policy is based on fiction. Attending a football match is not a criminal ☛ activity or even, in grounds; they should be a means of trapping criminals rather than an inconvenience or deterrent to ordinary people. "In any case," Moynihan told MPs:

"The genuine supporter, his wife and family will no longer be able to attend football matches."

His point is supported by a rising graph of arrests for violence against the person in Luton,

"The Prime Minister believes".

Many football supporters would, swim through a moat full of sharks to get to a football match."

Officials were anxious not to involve Mrs Thatcher too closely with the proposals.

Moynihan is reported to have promised:

There will be a national membership scheme, and that is non-negotiable.

The football authorities and assorted allies intend to fight the scheme with every weapon at their disposal, which

will more than anything else separate the true football fan from the thug." particularly the football authorities, should "stop bleating" and get down to infiltrate opposing "ends",

This would require at least 60 hard-line Conservative rebels, Most Conservative MPs with knowledge of football, and some casual supporters,

Hooligans, at first supported ID cards, "but we had not seen what the scheme would entail."

● Allowing casual supporters to register as temporary members as late as noon on the day of a match.

PLUS turnstile congestion,

At Luton, the local scheme has around 90 members,

"Pink relaxes the muscles," she explained. But an FA spokesman reacted: "It's a better idea than ID cards, but what effect would it have on players?"

● AGGRO at soccer grounds could be minimised...if floodlights were tinted pink, claims colour therapist Marie Lacy, a teacher at the London Institute of Complementary Medicine.

THE MIRROR – 27/1/89 .

Colin Moynihan, is a civil servant who, one presumes, believes that he is right and almost everyone in football is wrong, and costly and unnecessary as the hooligan problem has largely been eliminated inside football grounds thanks to closed circuit surveillance. Only the reporting of hooliganism has boomed. The media have become the message, with a vengeance.

The Government **are staggering from one disaster to another.**

Moynihan advocated that it should not be an ID card, but

● **A magnificent member's badge.**

He said the scheme was a chance to give the 450.000 spectators who went to League matches each Saturday **less than free access for casual supporters** and error if computer-held data on spectators is sold, an unnecessary financial burden, and actually cause trouble outside grounds. **The Conservatives' plan to computerise football hooliganism with a slice of**

banana

6,147 arrests were made last season, representing 0.03 per cent of the total attendance. In society as a whole, according to Home Office figures, 3.7 per cent of the adult population were arrested

Yet what has happened at Luton, the Government's pet club?

ASTONISHED Marion Vincent scooped up handfuls of £20 notes after her Luton identity **card triggered a hole-in-the-wall jackpot.**

She only wanted £100, but the electronic machine coughed up £2,560.

Marion stuffed the bundles of crisp notes into her shopping bag and made a run for it — straight into the manager's office. (TO BUY MICK HARFORD?)

Lutonise football, cut the crowds, discourage away supporters, and have peace at a price"

"The soccer fan has to foot the substantial bill for the extra police presence out-

football supporters:

Should

● **BOMBARD** their local MPs with protests.

TO MAKE THIS ITEM SEEM NEW, REPLACE THE NAME MOYNIHAN WITH "ANNIE BASSETT".

Moynihan lists what he describes as major incidents of hooliganism so far this season.

These include:

stone-throwing

The casual supporter "beaten up on the terraces".

"Luton Town's scheme The club chairman, David Evans, a Conservative MP,

Other rabid fans of Margaret Thatcher

Margaret Thatcher's reaction to the 1985 Heysel Stadium disaster.

every 'major incident' of football hooliganism this season.

And Sports Minister Colin Moynihan

Moynihan is expected to tell them that the Government is examining ways of ensuring that supporters are driven away from football.

If they cannot go there, they will go somewhere else."

Mrs Thatcher, shows no sign of expertise.

Maggie card scheme will kill football

Nor were the Government. going to be deflected by facts.

hooliganism takes place, in the main, away from grounds; that the police, aware of computers' fallibility, fear a spate of claims for unlawful arrest;

+++ YOU'RE BETTER OFF TALKING TO

YOU ARE THE LAW

IT'S TIME TO MEET THE MANINBLACK AGAIN. THIS ISSUE WE SEE WHAT YOU KNOW ABOUT THE OFFSIDE RULE.

1 IT IS 0-0 5 MINUTES FROM THE END OF AN F.A. CUP TIE. THE AWAY SIDE BREAK THROUGH (RIGHT) WHAT IS YOUR DECISION?

2 IN THE SAME FA CUP TIE THE HOME SIDE STAGE A SWIFT COUNTER-ATTACK (BELOW), WHICHEVER SIDE YOU DECIDED AGAINST IN SITUATION **1** ARGUED FIERCELY WITH YOU, BEARING THIS IN MIND, WHAT DO YOU DO?

3 IN A LEAGUE MATCH THE AWAY TEAM IS EFFICIENTLY USING THE OFFSIDE TRAP. THE GAME IS BEING SHOWN LIVE ON TV. WHAT IS YOUR DECISION? (LEFT)

4 (BELOW) PLAYER A PASSES THE BALL BACK IS THIS OFFSIDE?

5 A "WELL-KNOWN" DEFENDER PLAYS THE FORWARD ONSIDE. IF PLAY CONTINUES, THE FORWARD MAY BE AT RISK OF INJURY FROM A "SO-CALLED" PROFESSIONAL FOUL. DO YOU (a) GIVE OFFSIDE (b) RELISH THE CHANCE OF A SENDING-OFF or (c) KEEP AN OPEN MIND?

DON'T FORGET TO ALLOW FOR THE ANGLE! NOW TURN THE PAGE UPSIDE DOWN FOR THE ANSWERS.

ANSWERS. ① IT DEPENDS IF YOU FANCY WORKING MID-WEEK FOR THE REPLAY. ② AS THIS IS AN IDENTICAL SITUATION BUT ONE TEAM ARGUED BEFORE, YOU GIVE THE OPPOSITE DECISION. ③ YOUR DECISION IS CONTROVERSIAL. THIS ENABLES THE TV COMPANY TO USE THE 18-YARD LINE CAMERA. ④ YES BECAUSE HE WAS OFFSIDE WHEN HE RECEIVED THE BALL. ⑤ (a) or (b). YOU SHOULD NEVER KEEP AN OPEN MIND, THAT SIGNIFIES WEAKNESS.

BOB
THE
BALL

BILLY AND BOB HAVE BEEN KIDNAPPED BY A GANG OF SMUGGLERS

Young William had been left in an old shed...

IF I CAN JUST KICK BOB THROUGH THAT OPEN WINDOW.

Bob made a break for freedom!

out of the window.

The clever ball bounced down the hill. But then disaster struck!

But along came a footballing sheep and Bob's rescue mission continued.

Plucky Bob found his way to the main road and rolled into town.

And into Bill's Uncle Jack's Garden.

mmm! it's Billy's ball!

I'll put a knife through it. That'll teach the little bugger!

MUCH LATER

NEXT: The return of the footballing sheep!

FROM THE LAD # 5

ONCE UPON A TIME IN A FAR OFF FIELD, LIVED A SPECIAL SHEEP.

MM! THAT ONE SHOWS SOME NICE TOUCHES ON THE BALL.

THE SHEPHERD WAS ALSO A SCOUT, AND SOON...

BIG CITY
COPA CABANA
PLAYERS CONTRACT
SIGNED M. SHEEP
BRITA LITE NITE SPOT
GO-GO

... THE SHEEP FOUND HIMSELF PLAYING FOR BIG CITY IN THE FIRST DIVISION.

GOAL!

BEING NATURALLY TALENTED, HE WAS ABLE TO DISPLAY HIS PROWESS AT ALL LEVELS...

COMING TO THE DISCO, SHEEP?

BUT, WITH ADULATION, CAME BAD INFLUENCES AND HANGERS ON ...

AGA DOO! DOO! DOO! PUSH PINEAPPLES, SHAKE THE TREE!

... AND THE SHEEP WAS LED ASTRAY.

BEFORE LONG, THE STRAIN OF THE HIGH LIFE SHOWED

ZZZZ!!

EMPTY WALLET

OH DEAR! OH DEAR! HE'S JUST ANOTHER BAAA FLY!

NEWS

EXTRY! EXTRY! READ ALL ABAHT IT!

SOCCER SHEEP SHOCK
THE FOOTBALLING SHEEP S BEEN SENSATIONALLY ACKED BY BIG CITY ING A DISCO SGRACE

YEARS LATER.

YES, I WAS ONCE THE TOP SCORING SHEEP IN THE 1ST DIVISION.

MUNCH! MUNCH!

COME AWAY RODNEY! THIS SHEEP IS AN OLD HAS-BEEN!

THE MORAL OF THIS TALE IS: "LIVERPOOL ARE ALWAYS AT THEIR MOST DANGEROUS WHEN THEY ARE LOSING". AEDSOP.

Great Football Characters NO. 2

FROM THE LAD #2

Willy Weedo & his very small ego...

Fanzine Writer.

Er,excuse me.Have you got the latest issue of 'The BOY did GREAT'.Erm,it's an alternative view of football,er,non-sexist,non-violent,er,non-racist,er...Yes,um,with ID cards and executive boxes its the fans who suffer.Erm,what does Thatch...um,Mrs THATCHER,know about football.I bet she doesn't even know who's in the team, ha! ha!ha!er!...oh!You're a Tory oh,well it's a free country....er...Yes there's a good articleabout non-league grounds with cantilever stands,er and a profile of117 players who's names sound like South American dictators.There's a guide to disarming hooligans with a meat pie,er... Oh,and there's a very funny item, I think,about how First division players' eyebrows have evolved throughout the years,hahaha...oh...you're not interested. Oh well, never mind ...enjoy the game. Er,excuse me.Have yougot the latest...

THERE HAS BEEN AN INCREASE IN FOOTBALL-RELATED CARTOON STRIPS (AS IN FOOTBALL-RELATED VIOLENCE) IN THE TABLOIDS RECENTLY. HERE IS MY VERSION OF ONE OF THEM.

THE CAPTAIN ENGLAND STORY

* DURING THE 1986 WORLD CUP CAPTAIN ENGLAND'S ARM FELL OFF.

* DURING THE 1990 WORLD CUP CAPTAIN ENGLAND WAS INJURED.

AND SO OUR TALE ENDS WITH THAT BRAVE SON OF EMPIRE HAVING DRAWN UPON THE COURAGE OF JERUSALEM TO HOIST ALOFT

OH SHUT UP! :EDITOR.

MEET THE **NEW** CAPTAIN ENGLAND IN THE LAD DONE BRILLIANT # 6.

From THE LAD #1 — THE EXECUTIVE GLASSMAN HAS A SHOCK IN STORE IN #6 !

THE EXECUTIVE GLASSMAN.

" I AM JUST A FAN WHO HAPPENS TO OWN A CLUB. "

" I HAVE GREAT PLANS FOR THE STADIUM. "

" I HAVE FULL CONFIDENCE IN THE MANAGER. "

" I KNOW WHAT THE MAN ON THE TERRACES WANTS. "

OUT OF SIGHT OF THE PITCH

" YES, I HAVE ALWAYS GOT THE BEST INTERESTS OF FOOTBALL IN MIND. "

£££ £££
£££
£

c/o GAAARGH!

INCREDIBLE HULL

Here in the sumptuous countryside bordering the Wolds of England, lying amids
the choral symphonies of Handel's water, music to the eyes, that mystical fusion
of half-rotting human bodies, chemical effluent, never once affluent and dead fi
live the happy, gay, simple and sometimes sexually deviant folk of Hull.

Here where the sun doesn't shine any more, where it never in fact did, ever,
here lies the centre of the universe for four weeks only, here at the three
grounds where will be played a certain tournament, the three main sporting arena
of Hull, Craven Street, Boothferry Park and The Boulevard St Michel.

Here, where infrastructure - not a bit of it - the homely accomodation knocke
up by Alf Jones(Builders), several wooden slats will partition the living,
training and changing conditions of the twenty three visiting nations. Here they
will attempt to last out the period of confinement in the inhumane, cramped,
disease-ridden, yet charming, traditional and undefiled by tourism, ideally
situate adjacent to the glue factory.

Far to the left is the Nutrition Complex, where the players and supporters
mix in a malacological miasma of thick chip oil and full throated pastries,
the cafe. Run by that extraordinary breed of Kingston femalespawn, the landlady,
Mel Ignant, "Can sir eat another?" Her homely catchphrase, much copied throughou
the known cafes of the Wold, echoes as she prepares the meals for over 528 playe
based as ever on her own secret recipe involving, yes, dead fish.

Whilst the officials, doctors, physios, trainers, coaches, managers, director
presidents, secretaries and referees are drip-fed a daily solution of micturate
gin, Belanov caviar and assorted sweetmeats from the magnificent cellars of
Ben Ine, "Can sir drink more?"

Well, we must leave the wine-soaked gullets of the upper classes, the junk-
filled stomachs of the peasants and move to the city centre, an architect's dream,
a visitor's smelly bottom, a sense of imperial power and a repulsively overwritten
commentary. These are just some of the accolades poured upon the magnificent
epicentre of cultural brouillard, displayed ipso facto, upon this most fantastic
of facile facades facing four finely rounded frontages fragrantly festooned from
forecourt, from foyer, finally finding fine figments fractured for fresh fruit,
fast food and dead fish.

After dark, Hull is a night city, the orange and purple skies at sunset turn to
a laser red glow of activity which must be experienced close up to be believed.
The heady pink lipstick of the once great names of football, now forced to play a
different game on the streets of this fair city. See the eerie starlit sky become
burnished with darting yellows and crimson flashes as yet another building goes up
in flames, for arson is the citizen of Hull's favourite pastime.

"Going to the match?" has always been a saying to bring a smile to the mouth of
the people of Hull, epitomised in this famous Ken Wagstaffe poem,

THIS PICTURE
HAS BEEN REMOVED
ON THE ORDERS
OF THE EXECUTIVE
GLASSMAN

A MAP OF HUMBERSIDE   No.1

'We seek to lighten, the load of the torch,
We go to Brighton, the sand to scorch,
We show the spark, to burn the thatch,
The visitors come to Boothferry Park,
And there they meet their match!'

Hull, where there are no Germans, Hull the first city of the free world, Hull
where you can buy almost anything, including more of those fucking dead fish.

Hull, where I went once, by mistake, yes, Hull is the Mundial 90, the Wembley
1966, the Humbialito, hosting the finals of the cup of the world of the fourteen
tournament of nations of the association of the associations of football of the
countries involved or 'Not bloody Uruguay again' as we say in the bizz.

Yes, Hull, here where the almighty forgot to exorcise his right, here where
there are more fucking dead fish than anywhere, here will glory find a home, and
I might well be put in one, Hull, gateway to the supermarkets of humanity, eye o
the kingdom, I...I...I can't go on...

BLOW the WHISTLE

THE ULTIMATE SPACE FILLER IN ANY FANZINE IS TO USE CUTTINGS AND OTHER PEOPLES' JOKES. THIS SECTION OF THE LAD WAS FIRST CALLED GREAVSIE ON THE BOX (BECAUSE HE COULDN'T "HEAR US") BUT I DECIDED TO USE THE FANS' PLEA FOR THE END INSTEAD. HERE, I SHALL "BLOW THE WHISTLE" ON SOME TIMES WHEN THE LAD DONE NOT SO BRILLIANT.

AND! AND! AND! IT'S A GOAL! BECAUSE BEER™ REFRESHES THE PARTS OTHER BEERS CANNOT REACH!

The HISTORY of FOOTBALL No.1

Early Caveman Watching "Match of the Day"

Roy Racist

OKAY! YOU CAN PLAY FOR THE ROVERS, BUT YOU'RE NOT ALLOWED TO SCORE ANY GOALS!

WE'RE OFF TO SEE THE WIZARD! FROM THE LAD #4

OFF THE BOIL

I FIRST ENCOUNTERED JOHN MULCREEVY IN THE PAGES OF BOIL, WHICH IS A SELF-PUBLISHED COMIC WITHOUT SO MUCH FOOTBALL IN IT. I WROTE TO HIM AND SOON HE WAS DOING IT FOR THE LAD. SADLY, I WAS TO FIND OUT THAT HE WAS A VILLA FAN, BUT LET THAT NOT SPOIL YOUR FUN. YOU CAN FIND HIS WORK IN THE PAGES OF SICK OVER A PARROT, BUT LOOK FOR BOIL IF YOU WANT THE BEST.

AAAAAARGH! ...CLIVE THOMAS HAS COME OUT OF RETIREMENT!!!

HELLO FRIEND! I HOPE YOU'RE READY FOR A BUSY AFTERNOON!

MMM! THE FACILITIES AND FOOD AT FOOTBALL STADIA ARE INDEED WONDROUS!

WHY! SOME FANS ARE EVEN OFFERING ME MEAT PIES AS A KIND GESTURE OF FRIENDSHIP!

RELAX! YOU WERE NERVOUS THATS ALL

MAYBE! BUT IT'S NO EXCUSE FOR MISSING A PENALTY

ANOTHER STRIKER SPECIAL

SOMETIMES, THE REAL STRIKER OUT-DID MY BIZARRE VERSION!

WHEN IT COMES TO SOCCER, AS IT OFTEN DOES, I AM A BIRMINGHAM CITY FAN. THIS MAY NOT BE CLEAR FROM THE PAGES OF THE LAD, SO LET ME SAY IT HERE...

THE LAD HAS MISTAKENLY BEEN CALLED A "VIZ-TYPE" COMIC, HOWEVER TRIBUTES TO BILLY THE FISH DO NOT HELP MY CLAIMS OTHERWISE.

THIS AWAY CUP TIE TO THE LEAGUE LEADERS WILL CERTAINLY TEST THE LADS' ABILITY

YES AND WITH THE SAD DEMISE OF OUR FISH HERO, TOO!

THEY SAID THAT NO ONE COULD REPLACE HIM

SURE ENOUGH, FULCHESTER PLAYING WITHOUT A KEEPER!

UNFORTUNATELY, THE BIG MATCH ATMOSPHERE HAD RATTLED THE YOUNG FULL BACK...

PENALTY!

TABS BREAK BEER

THE LAD'S DAD IS A REAL PERSON. HE ONCE WENT TO THE TOILET AT SAINT ANDREWS, 5 MINUTES BEFORE HALF-TIME, BECAUSE HE DID NOT WANT TO MISS THE BREAK. CHEERS DAD.

WITH AN OPEN GOAL THIS SPOT KICK WILL BE A MERE FORMALITY

BUT...

SAVED!

FANS SAY NO ID CARDS

ACTION REPLAY

TOTALLY AGAINST THE RUN OF PLAY!

READ VIZ COMIC

IT'S BILLY the TIN OF CAT FOOD!

KATTO with FISH

9 OUT 10 CATS PREFER IT.

MEMBERS ONLY

It's alright officer, I'm in the Conservative Club Here's my affiliation card. I think you'll find it's all in order.

TEN THINGS YOU DIDN'T KNOW ABOUT
albania   OR   FOREIGNERS ON ALBANIA

The figure of Enver Hoxha is all-sided, giving his work and life the dimensions of an epoch — the most brilliant epoch of our ancient people. He was born and molded as a revolutionary at a time when the country and the people needed a far-sighted leader, loyal to the interests of the nation. Enver

Rod

the

Plod

Once upon a time there was a band called Half Man Half Biscuit. One day they wrote a song called 'Dickie Davies Eyes', contained within this song was the immortal line "Brian Moore's Head Looks Uncannily like London Planetarium". Little did they know that they had thus played a part in the birth of a football fanzine. For one day, a group of sallow youths were sitting around in the front room of the house that was to become one of the major publishing centres of the Western World, debating what the title for their embryonic publication would be. Uninspired ideas such as 'A Sixth of a Pint' (a gill - Gills, think about it), 'A Footballing Backwater' and 'Priestfield Progress' were dismissed as being crap. Then one of the group spake 'Why don't we call it after the line in the Half Man Half Biscuit song 'Dickie Davies Eyes'?' The others were confused, for they had never heard of Half Man Half Biscuit, and knew not the line in question. 'What line?' they asked in unison. "Brian Moore's Head Looks Uncannily Like London Planetarium". And the others saw that it was good, and lo, Brian Moore's Head was born, and there was much rejoicing throughout the land (Well, maybe not...)

AROUND BRITAIN

BMH can claim to be a truly national fanzine. I hear you scoff at this bold statement, but lets consider the facts. When BMH was launched (August 88) I was living in Thatchem (Berkshire), so the fanzine began by shuttling back and forth between there and Gillingham, before being sent to West Norwood for printing (and then back to Gillingham for sale).

But stranger things were to happen. After a brief spell back in Medway I moved to North Shields (that's near Newcastle for all you bloody southerners - a fabulous place where Newcy Brown could be obtained at the local shop for 82p a bottle). Now the fanzine was typed in Rochester, posted to North Shields to be put together, then sent to Sheffield for printing before ending back in Gillingham for sale. A few problems resulted - editorials were sometimes written two weeks before publication (we purchased a crystal ball from funds to ensure that we wouldn't be embarassed). The erratic nature of the postal system meant more than one extremely late night with the Pritt and dry transfer lettering to meet the deadline. Still, you probably don't give a damn, do you?

I went into a pub in Gillingham the other day and was charged £1.50 for a bottle of Newcy....Life can be cruel.

ROBIN HALLS

PSST, WANNA BUY A FANZINE?

Selling fanzines can be quite enjoyable. I mean, how can you not derive pleasure from ending up with pocketfulls of money just for standing at the entrance to a football terrace for half an hour before a match, waving a few copies of Brian Moore's Head around?!

However, there are negative aspects involved. There are the long periods when there is hardly anyone coming through the turnstiles and sales are few and far between, when you suddenly feel the cold, and get so bored that you find yourself listening to the pre-match musical entertainment coming out of the tannoy. This is usually fairly dire stuff, although, to his credit, the DJ did play 'Two Little Boys' by Rolf Harris before a home game last season. Then there are the times when kick-off is approaching and you're just about to stop selling and make your way to your favoured position on the terrace before the game starts, and you're suddenly besieged by a dozen or so late arrivals , all wanting a copy of BMH and all waving fivers and tenners at you (in fact anything apart from the correct money) and you're desperately short of change. Then there is the problem that every fanzine seller up and down the country can identify with. Yes, it's the idiot who comes up and asks if it's the programme. After he's been told that it's a fanzine, not a programme, and this point has been heavily emphasized to him, he then buys a copy and walks off, only to return half a minute later and demand a refund as he thought it was the programme.

Selling before the game is usually quite easy, you stand in one place and people come up to you and cross your palm with silver, gold, or those stupid little fivers in return for 40 fun packed pages known as a copy of BMH (he says modestly). At half time us sellers have to make a bit more of an effort and go on a 'Rolf's Walkabout' around the Rainham End seeking out any potential customers we may have missed before the game.

Unfortunately, I don't get involved in the best part of selling fanzines, the counting of the proceeds at the end of the day (Brian). This is left to the BMH treasurer who, having collected up the booty from us sellers, nips off pretty sharpish to tot up the takings and fill a few of those nice green money bags in the privacy of his own home.

As well as selling BMH on matchdays I also have the task of taking 200 copies up to Sportspages bookshop in London. This is a fairly arduous task (they're pretty heavy for a start!) and it's one I've got as I'm the only BMH editor who works in London. So once every four weeks or so, when the other commuters on the 7-24 Gillingham to Cannon Street train have got their briefcases, I've got a box advertising the Springwell Lock Bakery full of fanzines. I usually stick out like a sore thumb on the train anyway, reading fanzines while everyone else has broadsheet newspapers, but on the day I take the box up I get more than a few funny looks. The quizzical looks continue when I reach London, from the girl at Smiths at Cannon Street when I buy a paper, the security staff at work, my work colleagues, and finally the people who see me struggling up Charing Cross Road to deliver the box to Sportspages during my lunch hour. However, the job does have one compensation, the moment when I swap the fanzines for a Sportspages cheque is a very satisfying one indeed.

ANDY FORD

BEHIND EVERY FANZINE THERE'S A FOOTBALL CLUB

The emergence of Brian Moore's Head has somewhat unfortunately coincided with a disappointing period in the history of Gillingham F.C. The fanzine boom arrived too late to see us revel in the glory of the mid-eighties Gills side of Sir Keith Peacock, and instead we have been around to reflect on a largely uninspiring spell.

We made our debut at the start of the 88-89 season when, although things were not looking entirely rosy, they were not looking entirely doomladen either. It is probably true to say that all footie fanzines need a target to take the piss out of, and then Gills chairman Roy Wood was a sitting duck. He was not a popular fellow, having sacked probably the club's most popular manager, the aforementioned Sir Keith, largely on the strength of one disastrous defeat. His attitude towards the supporters was not exactly calculated to win our undying devotion, as we were treated with the sort of respect usually accorded to a cow in an abbatoir. Add to this the fact that he shared his name with the bearded ex-pop star and that he bore an uncanny resemblance to Harold Bishop from Neighbours and Roy never stood a chance. He was always good for a cheap laugh, especially when he came out with what was to become his catchphrase, 'I've put a lot of money into the club without any thought of monetary gain'. Roy saw himself as the club's saviour (it is true that the club was facing a winding-up order when he took over, thanks to the activities of the previous chairman Charles 'Wide Boy' Cox, who was later found guilty of stealing from the club lottery - and is now chairman of Ashford Town!) and he seemed to get most upset when the fans refused to view him in this light.

As it turned out , 88-89 was a disastrous season, a run of 12 consecutive defeats dooming us to relegation from an early stage. Manager Paul Taylor (who also had a catchphrase , 'I saw some good things out there today and was impressed by our approach play', invariably wheeled out after another dismal home defeat) was dismissed after the tenth of these. Taylor was a man with rare comic timing. Interviewed after the ninth defeat he said 'I honestly believe that we can beat anyone in the division, that sounds stupid doesn't it'. One 5-0 defeat at Preston later and it certainly did! Taylor drove away from Priestfield with a gusto he rarely exhibited as manager, mounting the pavement and narrowly missing a TV cameraman, earning himself an appearance on 'Saint and Greavesie' in the process.

Taylor's successor was Keith Burkinshaw. Well, it seemed like a good idea at the time. In hindsight, employing a man who had been out of the country, and out of touch for a number of years, not to mention paying him £50,000 a year with the club's debts rumoured to be over £1M, was an act of sheer folly. Burkinshaw bottled out after five months and Roy Wood soon followed.

The last couple of seasons have seen the damage inflicted by the previous regimes gradually repaired. A quiet revolution took place in the boardroom, with a completely new set of directors taking over without the sort of in-fighting that usually characterises such activities. And, shock, horror, gasp, - the new men are actually interested in talking and listening to the ordinary supporters.

The loss of Roy Wood as official BMH target has been compensated for by the sudden appearance of Maidstone Utd. in the Football League. To add a bit of spice, the squatters from Watling Street have a team packed with Gills rejects and managed by the man himself, Sir Keith Peacock. Finally, after all these years as Kent's only League club, we have a proper local derby. In true Gillingham style we lost at home to them in the first such game in front of our biggest League crowd for years, and this season we repeated the trick. Some measure of revenge was gained with last season's win at Watling Street, and revenge has never tasted so sweet.

However, this season so far has been an immense disappointment, and it leads me to wonder whether BMH is a jinx, will Gills ever achieve anything while we are around? And how much money do you think the board would give us to stop publishing it right now?

SIMON BAKER

FOUR-EYED GIT!

Amongst the insults commonly hurled at the
referee is the polite suggestion that he
should see an optician because his eyesight
may be slightly less than perfect. Now I'm
not exactly a shrinking violet when it
comes to letting my feelings be known, especially when it comes to incompetent refereeing, but I've always felt a bit silly
shouting that particular insult because,
basically, I'm shortsighted myself (perhaps I should become a ref!?)

Anyway, apart from being a blow to the
personal vanity of any individual, wearing
glasses can be an occupational hazard when
attending games. However, I'm too lazy to
get contact lenses, so for the forseeable
future (I wish I could bloody see!) I'll
be prone to the problems that I first encountered in 1983....

Although I could see okay, by 83 I felt
that a certain sharpness in identifying
players was missing, so by the start of
83-4 with the arrival of Cochrane to join
Mehmet and Cascarino I felt it was time to
pay the optician a visit.

The last game I saw without glasses was
Charlton v Man City. The most important
point on that day was that it pissed down
whilst I stood on the open terrace. At the
time it didn't cross my mind, but standing on an open terrace in heavy rain would
never be the same again!

The first game with my new glasses was
a midweek game at home to Exeter. We scored
twice in the first six minutes and from
then on the whole game was a joy to watch
(we won 3-1). Once christened with a win
my glasses went on to 'see' every home
game for three years until I lost them on
the way home from a game in 85-6.

Anyway, for those smug bastards with
20:20 vision, I'll now let you in on some
of the problems.....

Firstly is the problem of open terraces
and rain. No-one likes getting wet but for
me it became a new hazard. Basically, trying to watch football with hundreds of
droplets of water on your lenses is bloody
tricky. Especially when the floodlights
are on, because the lights glare off all
the droplets! It is not always easy to
wipe them off either, because either I've
got nothing dry, or I'll smear them, thus
risking the possibility of missing a goal!

During our memorable 85-6 win at Reading
it rained (just like usual), in fact it
really pissed down, so although the match
was brilliant some of my memories are more
blurred than others. David Byrne's goal
after 2 minutes, and Reading's equaliser
(15 minutes) were fairly clear, but by the
time Elsey's rocket had found the net, I
must say it was a bit blurry. It certainly

made hanging on to our lead all the more
exciting because I didn't always know what
was going on down the other end!

Sometimes however, it rains so hard
(Port Vale 85-6 and at a neutral game at
Scarborough last year) that no more droplets can fit on the lenses and I give up
worrying about it.

The Cup game at Ipswich in 84-5 ill-
ustrated another problem which occurs
when the Gills score at away games. Basically everyone goes apeshit - however, I
have to try and avoid getting my glasses
knocked off and smashed, and so have had
to perfect a way of celebrating a goal
whilst minimizing the risk. At Ipswich,
when we equalised the celebrations were
so err...exhuberant that my glasses were
nearly shoved up my nose. We were so
jammed in that I couldn't move my arms to
do anything about it and so had to wait
for them to slip back down.

One particular problem I had, was when
one of the little screws became loose. I
was standing on the Shelf at Spurs (it
was raining!) when suddenly my view became
pretty weird as one lense dropped out
onto the ground. Once my brain had registered the fact panic set in. Watching
through only one lense was very strange.
Fortunately I found the lense (plastic
and so unbroken) and then had the task of
screwing it all back together using a
biro!

One very rare problem that I once saw
befall a fellow sufferer occurred during
a pre-match warm-up at a Rotherham v
Scunthorpe game. We were standing behind
the goal when one of the Rotherham forwards got a bit excited whilst warming
up and smashed a shot over the bar. It hit
a bloke square in the face because he turned round just as is arrived, it must have
hurt because it cut the bridge of his
nose badly and redesigned his glasses!

At least non-spec wearers don't get
cut and have their abilty to watch the
subsequent match threatened by enthusiast-
ic shots.

For any reader who is not yet feeling
more sympathetic towards the plight of
the 'four-eyed git', I suggest they take
their minds back to an away game at Lincoln in 84-5. It was so foggy that at the
far-end we could only hear the corners
being taken (thud) until they emerged
from the gloom. Being able to see all the
action is more important than looking like
Tom Cruise or Tim O'Shea! Even Elton Welsby
has got some glasses now (all he needs now
is a brain to go with them -Ed) so it must
be okay!

- Elton Welsby's Agent

Nostradamus
— Mystical football pundit or senile French git ?

Four hundred years ago, Michel de Nostredame sat alone in a dark secret room studying the forbidden books on the occult. By his side stood a brass tripod and placed on that was a simple bowl of water. But the water shimmered and grew cloudy and from within its depths came visions of the future .... visions which told of the Great Fire of London, the second world war, air travel, the assassinations of John and Robert Kennedy, the deposition of the Shah of Iran and the rise to power of Ayatollah Khomeini. Occasionally, after a visit to the pub, or when his mum was out, things got really weird.

So, (initially at least), runs the blurb on the back of a book entitled 'The Prophecies of Nostradamus'. Most people will have heard of Nostradamus and some will be familiar with his more successful predictions; however hundreds of his quatrains, (as his four line french ramblings are known), remain indecipherable, not least because they are, for the most part incredibly vague and waffling. Most commentators on his works claim he disguised his predictions deliberately so as to prevent the church from nailing him to a post and setting fire to him, as was their wont in 16th century France.

Despite the fact that he died over 300 years before the establishment of the football league, when viewed by an astute footballing mind some of his writings have an important message for the future of the game.

Unfortunately, I cannot find any references to the fortunes of a club whose emblem is a white horse, but here is a sample of three genuine quatrains from the man, which in this light may be considered the Saint and Greavsie of his day. (Well OK, not both of them, but you know what I mean).

9

Pendant que l'aigle & le coq à Savone Seront unis Mer Levant & On-grie, L'armee à Naples, Palerne, Mar-que d'Ancone Rome, Venise par Barb'¹ horrible crie.	While the eagle is united with the cock at Savona, the Eastern Sea and Hungary. The army at Naples, Palermo, the marches of Ancona, Rome and Venice a great outcry by the Barbarian.

The Eagle united with the Cock seems to imply a ground sharing scheme between Crystal Palace (The Eagles) and Spurs (emblem, the Cock) at Savona, which is on the Italian coast west of Genoa. This seems likely to be a move which will further displease Spurs fans already unhappy by the rebuilding work on the shelf at White Hart Lane, while Ron Noades at Palace is such a dickhead that you cannot rule out such a hair-brained scheme if there is the slightest whiff of any money for him in it. Perhaps Selhurst Park will be demolished for an extension to Sainsbury's; maybe a new 'Homebase' department. Where this leaves Charlton is anyone's guess, but my personal favourite is ground sharing with Erith and Belvedere. Mention of the Eastern Sea possibly forecasts a joint pre-season tour of the far east, maybe Japan. The two clubs, it seems will also have Hungarian connections, between them perhaps, they will supply the entire Hungarian national team. It cannot be ruled out with Spurs unorthodox sources of new signings in recent years.

The rest of the quatraine seems to imply that Italian fans at the places mentioned are not pleased with this move. 'A great outcry by the Barbarian', may refer to the Rugby Union team the Barbarians, who are currently without a permanent ground, normally playing at Twickenham. Perhaps they are upset as they were already planning a similar move to the same part of the Mediterranean coast.

BRIAN MOORE'S HEAD LOOKS UNCANNILY LIKE LONDON PLANETARIUM

Alternative possibilities arose however, when I consulted my London A-Z. I notice there is a Savona Close in Wimbledon off Worple Road; but seeing the current level of apathy for Wimbledon, I do not envisage SW19 being able to support three first division clubs. Alternatively, there is a Savona Street in Battersea near the power station on the approaches to Victoria, which would be very handy for rail travellers but does not explain the opposition to the scheme in cities as far apart as Sardinia and northern Italy.

59

A la Ferté prendra la Vidame· *Nicol tenu rouge qu'avoit produit* *la vie.* *La grand Loisne naistra que ferà* *claine.* *Donnant Bourgongne à Bretons* *par envie.*	At the Ferté Vidame he will take, Nicol the red who had produced life; to the great Louise who acts secretly one will be born, who gives Burgundy to the Bretons through envy.

Nicol the red can only be Steve Nicol of Liverpool, who sometimes puts a bit of life into the team , which probably means that the great Louise is Jan Molby, who does act rather secretly but has been found out on several notable occasions. Ferte Vidame is a small town to the west of Paris, with no obvious footballing connections. However, as followers of Nostradamus will be aware, he sometimes uses anagrams to disguise names or places. Perhaps to throw the church off his scent, when they had actually got to the 'polishing the thumbscrews stage', or alternatively because the bowl of water was even more cloudy than normal or more likely, he just didn't know what he was on about. In this light then, it is interesting to note that Ferte Vidame is in fact an anagram of 'Die Trev Fame', and so perhaps foretells of the early demise of a famous Trev, maybe Brooking or Francis?

Back to the quatraine in question, I don't feel that the next part, that Steve Nicol and Jan Molby will have a baby can be taken too literally, perhaps it refers to an important goal or run of success for the team for which they are responsible, maybe even leading to a cup (the baby?). What ever it is, seems to involve Burgundy. Big Jan is known to enjoy a drink or two, but whether or not red wine is up his street, I do not know. Why the Bretons also get some remains a mystery.

86

Comme un griphon viendra le roi *d'Europe* *Accompaigné de ceux d'Aquilon,* *De rouges & blancz conduira* *grand troppe* *Et iront contre le roi de Babilon.*	The king of Europe will come like a griffon, accompanied by those of the North; he will lead a great troop of red and white, they will go against the king of Babylon.

Here we see Nostradamus getting really quite precise. The Griffon clearly refers to Brentford, who play at Griffin Park, particularly as he leads a great troop of red and white, which of course are Brentfords colours. 'The king of Europe will come like a griffon', can only predict great European success for Brentford, 'accompanied by those of the north', perhaps referring to disgruntled fans of Spurs and Arsenal who, possibly, will see lean times coinciding with Brentfords rise to eminence. The Spurs fans are probably fed up at having to travel to Italy for their home games.

Babylon is near present day Tehran and so this could foretell of a deciding match is some great Euro-asian competition yet to come, against some crack Iranian side. Certainly exciting times ahead for Brentford fans.

— <u>Ian Hancock</u>

Next week: If Gillingham were formed in May 1893, that makes them a Taurus. What do the stars foretell for the future of the club ? Russel Grant, the rotund astrological shirtlifter writes.

how to make a FooTbAL' REcoRD

Regular readers of this organ will doubt-lessly be familiar with the 'Flair' comp-ilation album, wh .h collects together some 46 songs produced over the last de-cade or so by clubs up, down and outside of the Football League. In my youth I had more than an interest in avant garde music and would be often found listening to rec-ords such as those produced by a group known as 'Whitehouse' (who I believe are still together) which consist largely of electronic noise and screaming. 'White-house' publicity boasted that 'the list-ener will always enjoy the most extreme reaction of all because these are the most violently repulsive records ever made' and it occurred to me, during my first hearing of 'Flair', that this maxim is also applicable to most songs produced by football teams. So why make them? What blasphemous intent lurks in the disordered minds of the perp-etrators of this most virulently repellant art? A few months ago I learnt the answer to these questions when I assisted Radford Social United in the creation of their stunning waxing 'Come on Radford Social United'. So now, speaking from experience, I can allow our readers an insight into why and, perhaps more importantly, how a football record is made.

First of all you will need;
1/ Friends, as many as possible. You will probably be getting through them at quite a rate, so it would be prudent to place an advertisement in the classified section of your local newspaper.
2/ A recording studio.
3/ Some instruments.
4/ Musicians (of whom at least two should own 'The Greatest Hits Of Boxcar Willie').
5/ A dungeon complete with manacles.
6/ A cassette tape player with continuous play facility.
7/ A football team (one only, records by more than one team are notoriously diff-icult to sell; Of the 2,000 copies press-ed of Everton and Waterlooville's 'There's only one Everton or Waterlooville' only 3 were ever sold).

• STAGE 1 - The Tune

As is the case with most of the creative arts, the first step is the most important. The tune has to be exactly right. It's really no good just making do with the first jolly little melody that comes into your head. Sit and hum to yourself with your eyes closed, making it up as you go along, developing and elaborating upon any memorable refrain that you come across. When you find that your foot has started to tap uncontrollably you are getting some-where, but do not stop yet. Continue until

you can almost feel the presence of Reg Varney, Tommy Trinder and Max Miller there in the room with you. When you open your eyes and are surprised that the aforement-ioned are not there your tune is ready.

• STAGE 2 - Demo Recording

First hum the tune to the musicians and get them to record it in the studio. Make a copy of this music on cassette and load it into the cassette tape player. The play-er should then be put onto continuous play (so that the section of music is played, rewound, played, rewound again and so on ad infinitum). Place the cassette tape player in the dungeon and secure one of your friends in the manacles (see fig.1). Your friend should NOT be able to reach the player to turn it off. Then leave the dungeon, returning every other hour to check upon your friend's progress, which you can compare with the chart below to ascertain the success of the music.

a/ <u>Your friend eventually dies of star-vation</u> - the song needs more work. Repeat stage 2 until you meet with success.

b/ <u>Your friend chews through his or her arms and legs in order to reach the cass-ette tape player and turn it off</u> - You are nearly there, but will probably need to re-mix the music or add some further in-strumentation. Repeat stage 2 using the new recording of the music on cassette.

c/ <u>Your friend is driven incurably in-sane or kills him or herself by strang-ulation with the chains</u> - Excellent! You may now proceed to the next stage.

• STAGE 3 - Writing the lyrics

You are on your own here. There is no tried and tested system for setting words to a piece of music as artistic genius must come from within. However, the words shoul , where possible, be relevant to the team for whom the song is being made, also they should rhyme. One of the golden rules of writing a hit is to remember to make the lyrics rhyme, so to help I have incl-uded a listing of words which may be of use, along with some which rhyme with them;

<u>GOAL</u> SOUL/DOLE/HOLE/BOWL/REMOTE CONTROL/VOLE

<u>SCORE</u> SINGAPORE/SORE/JAW/DOOR/MORE/SEASHORE

<u>MATCH</u> BATCH/TONY HATCH/SNATCH/EYE-PATCH/SCRATCH

<u>F.A. CUP</u> 7-UP/PICK-ME-UP/BALLS UP/ WISE UP/GALLUP*

<u>REFEREE</u> BY THE SEA/LOOK AT ME/CERTAINLY/JAMBOREE

<u>BALL</u> FALL/WALL/WALSALL/MAUL/ASTERIX THE GAUL

<u>SOCCER</u> DOOR KNOCKER/DAVY JONES LOCKER/FOKKER*

BRIANMOORE'S HEAD LOOKS UNCANNILY LIKE LONDON PLANETARIUM

*1 = AS IN POLL
*2 = GERMAN AIRCRAFT CIRCA WORLD WAR II

•STAGE 4 - Adding the vocal track

Once you have your lyrics you can assemble your football team in the studio. It
is wise to record each players vocal contribution seperately. The reason for this
is that a single player with even a modic-
um of singing ability can ruin the entire
song. Individually recording each voice
eliminates the possibility of the 'Bernard
Bresslaw factor', as it is known, as should
a player be found to be singing in tune
his voice can then be isolated and dropped
a semi-tone by digital harmoniser. This
should ensure that the finished vocals possess that richly dischordant quality which
can be found on all the best football
songs.

• STAGE 5 - The final touches

No football record is complete without
sound effects. You should be sparing with

your song, b/ a number of dead bodies to
dispose of, and unless you are extremely
wealthy, c/ a hefty studio bill. Human
meat fetches an extremely high price on
the black market these days so, providing
you have the contacts, points b/ and c/
should cancel each other out. If you don't
have the contacts even the smallest towns
tend to have stretches of wasteland where
bodies can be conveniently disposed of.
Unfortunately this still leaves you with
the cost of the studio time you will have
used, not to mention the further expense
of pressing your record. One method of
raising capital often overlooked by football record producers is without doubt the
simplest method: Blackmail. All that is
required is to play a cassette of the song
to selected individuals and then ask them
to pay you NOT to release it. When you
have raised enough cash press the record,
print a sleeve and hire a distributor for
your product.

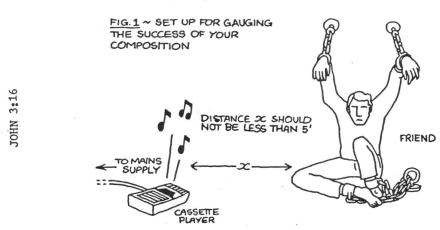

FIG.1 ~ SET UP FOR GAUGING
THE SUCCESS OF YOUR
COMPOSITION

JOHN 3:16

DISTANCE x SHOULD
NOT BE LESS THAN 5'

TO MAINS
SUPPLY

x

FRIEND

CASSETTE
PLAYER

these as the middle 8 instrumental break
will of course contain the sound of a roar-
ing crowd, which lessens the necessity for
sound effects elsewhere. However, the odd
rattle or whistle here and there is quite
permissable providing restraint is excer-
cised: You don't want to drown out the
words or the music with the sound of 1,000
bananas being inflated. With your special
effects added you are ready to do the final
mix of the song. A cassette of the completed song should be tested in the manner
described in stage 2 (see fig.1), however,
as this is the version of the song which
will be released only suicide can be taken
as a confirmation of the success of your
final mix. Should your friend merely go
mad or gnaw through his or her limbs you
should start again from stage 3.

•STAGE 6 - Releasing the record and raising the capital to do so

By the time you reach this stage you
should have a/ a completed master tape of

•Final Points

Do not be discouraged at any stage by
the rate at which corpses are piling up
during your search for musical perfection.
The timeless classic 'Look out first division, here we come!' by Yeovil F.C. was
only completed after the deaths of some
'75 plus people and this is peanuts compared to the massive body count which results from larger clubs like Arsenal or
Spurs' musical excursions.
    The cover artwork should ideally be
rendered by a player's kid sister. Failing
this Prestigious Designs of Surrey (whose
work you may have seen adorning most Jive
Bunny releases) usually turn in a good
job at a fair price.
    Finally, good luck, happy recording and
I'll see you in the charts.

- Pete Waterman

P.S. Be sure to buy Sonia's new interpret-
ation of 'I had too much to dream last
night'. Out now!

BRIANMOORE'S HEAD
LOOKS UNCANNILY LIKE
LONDON ☆ PLANETARIUM

Typical Awayday ?

- HARTLEPOOL 1 GILLS 2
- 9TH SEPTEMBER '89

What is the worst nightmare that could be envisaged on our return to the Fourth Division? A defeat at Halifax on a wet Friday night? Or how about losing at somewhere even further and grottier, to a team who are bottom of the League and has yet to score a goal? Well, here goes.....

It's 7.30am, and we've just stumbled along Strood High Street to wait for the coach to Hartlepool. I had drunk too much the previous evening, so a poor night's sleep had left me rather unsociable at that unearthly hour. This, we agreed, was dedication of the highest order. After all, we could have had a lie in and gone to watch Maidstone lose, instead of paying a fortune to travel to the other end of the Country to watch the only two League teams without a goal to their credit. The coach duly arrived, and having muttered a few pleasantries to fellow sleepy idiots, I crashed out.

By about 10.30am, we were stuck in traffic on the M1, so someone decided that it would be a good idea to transfer to the A1. This meant we lost more time as we crawled through Bedford. The A1 was at a standstill due to an accident and it became apparent that we would not arrive on time. At 2.30pm, after <u>NINE</u> sets of road-works (most with contra-flows and all with lengthy tail-backs) we had got no further

dy move, Hillyard!', came a shout from the back seat. At this point, another car nearly hit us - how a 60 seater coach can be in a car's blind spot beats me.

After the alarm of nearly being in a crash eased, we tuned into the local radio station, and mass panic broke out as the first reports filtered through. Newcastle were winning at Bournemouth, but Barnsley had scored against 'Boro'. Our game was 0-0. We got to Darlington, but were still miles from Hartlepool and no-one knew where the ground was. The coach (or the driver) did not seem willing to go above 50mph, and things became a bit heated as another set of road-works were reached. The driver was given all sorts of abuse for giving way at roundabouts and refusing to use the hard shoulder for over-taking.

We were just enjoying a tour of Middlesbrough when the smug radio reporter announced that Gills were now the only team in the League not to have scored a goal, and by all accounts nothing looked like changing. It was party time at the Victoria Ground, he gasped, although he did add that the travelling fans in the ground probably did not agree. The ones who had just spotted the first sign to Hartlepool (10 miles) were hardly ecstatic either, although we did have the consolation of a good view of some railway sidings. Half-time came and went, and our frustration

- APESHIT 1 - LEE PALMER CRASHES HOME GILLS FIRST LEAGUE GOAL OF THE SEASON. IT ONLY TOOK US 5¾ HOURS TO GET IT!

WHAT'S HAPPENED TO THE MIDFIELD ACE FROM LAST SATURDAY'S GAME ?

than Leeds. It was decided that we should press on for Hartlepool even though we would miss the first half-hour, the alternative being Leeds v Ipswich. We were still miles from Scotch Corner at 2.58pm when someone remarked that the Gills must be coming out. A round of applause rang around the coach, along with a few chants of 'Ronnie, Ronnie Hillyard'. Someone started commentating. Hartlepool were attacking and flashed a shot just wide, 'Bloo-

increased. I had lost all faith in coach travel (even though it was the first time I had missed the start in over 100 trips) and I vowed that I would be going nowhere near Carlisle in a fortnight's time. Finally, at 4.10pm, we pulled up outside the ground, and sixty people scrambled to get out the door all at once. The Police smiled sympathetically and let us through a side gate without paying. We ran along a corridor, up some steps and emerged be-

BRIAN MOORE'S HEAD LOOKS UNCANNILY LIKE LONDON PLANETARIUM

tween a portakabin and some temporary seats, to receive a standing ovation from the 100 or so Gills fans already in the ground, and bemused looks from the rest of the rather sparse crowd.

First things first - the latecomers split into two groups. Eight hours on a coach without stopping meant a toss-up between the loo and the food hut. Then we regrouped on the terrace determined to make the most of the last half-hour. Inevitably, it started to rain.

One coach had arrived barely two minutes late, mainly because their driver watches the football, so made sure they got there as quickly as possible. I can quite believe the stories of cutting up juggernauts at roadworks and elderly drivers being grabbed by their startled passengers as the coach sped by on the inside. The Travel Club coach was only a quarter of an hour late.

is based in North Shields so had got up at noon and faced a mere half-hour journey to the ground).

I had shouted myself hoarse in the space of twenty minutes - it was all too much to take in. The Hartlepool supporters were very subdued, except for a few obnoxious kids. Rob got annoyed that the Police refused to do anything, but as he is on a teacher-training course, he was understandably concerned at the lack of discipline. The Police were considerably more tolerant than those at Orient.

Ironically, having missed the first hour, we stood frantically whistling for time with five minutes remaining. From what I saw, Hartlepool were pretty crap and posed few problems (their 'keeper looked particularly suspect). Nevertheless, in the last minute we got careless in the box again, conceding our fourth penalty in

● APESHIT 2 - PETER HERITAGE CHOOSES THE PERFECT MOMENT TO OPEN HIS ACCOUNT IN LEAGUE FOOTBALL.

YES...SOME TEAMS ARE BETTER THAN OTHERS...BUT NO TEAM IS UNBEATABLE.!

What followed was unbelievable. I have never known so much frustration be relieved simply by entering the ground, and by the end we were all happy shoppers. Still trailing to the first-half goal, we seemed to be on top. Lovell went close, and Gavin fluffed a sitter and was soon substituted by Peter Heritage. With 17 minutes left, Lee Palmer crashed home a Haylock cross amid scenes of total delirium in the away pen. Within two minutes he scored again, but it was ruled out. I suppose two goals would be too much to ask. Anyway I was still celebrating the equaliser, while the groundhoppers amongst us argued whether the 92 club would accept half an hour at Hartlepool. With 7 minutes to go, Heritage sent a superb header into the top corner, and it was apeshit time again. Robin fell over celebrating the goal (deservedly so, in my opinion, as he

three games. Only one of the previous three had gone in, but none of us thought we could survive again. The bloke taking it did not look confident, and the God Hillyard dived to save his 19th penalty for Gillingham. People clattered about hysterically in the away pen. It was too good to be true. The final whistle went. Billy Manuel jumped on the heroic 'keeper, we gave the team a standing ovation and then filed out of the ground and back on to the bloody coach. The general consensus of opinion was that, as we hadn't paid AND we missed the first hour, we were the lucky ones. Meanwhile, on the way home, everyone booked up for Carlisle.

. - C.L.

(The man with the party piece that's got to be seen to be believed -Ed)

THAT LITTLE SOUVENIR OF **A TERRIBLE YEAR**

It's an odd and vaguely interesting fact that there are numerous fashions associated with the wondrous game of footie that instantly identify a certain era. Look at a photograph of a pre-First World War crowd and you will see packed terraces populated almost exclusively by old men in flat caps (with the odd youngster being passed down to the front of course!). Between the Wars the flat caps were gradually replaced by trilbies (a symptom of greater wealth?). Post-War and the hats have begun to disappear entirely. As the years rolled by the newly uncovered bonces started to be populated by ever greater amounts of hair, reaching a peak of quite extraordinary hairiness in the mid 70's.

But it's not just the mode of cranial decoration that changes. There are a miriad of objects and articles of clothing that seem to characterise a certain point in history. For instance, if you see a photograph of a crowd in possession of a number of oversized inflatable objects it is obvious that it dates from the late 80's. In years to come football historians will be able to date the same photo as precisely as we can now, whether they will be able to ascertain the precise reason why a large number of fans chose to watch their football in the company of a five foot blow-up banana is another question.

It is also a fact that the nature of certain objects appear to mirror the era to which they belong. Chunky wooden rattles, thick woolly bar scarves and large rosettes conjure up images of a bygone era, when Britain was great, there were no hooligans (honest it's true, my Granny said so), and you could go t'match, have a slap up fish supper, a couple of pints, and still have change from half a crown. An era when packed crowds watched great players stride across the hallowed turf of St James Park and Molineux like giants striding the Earth. All total bollocks of course, but it is an image which still endures today.

In contrast to all this greatness, I first cut my footballing teeth in the early 70's, and what was the 'in' footie accessory, the required article that marked you out as a true fan, the object of desire without which your life was incomplete, the object which summed up the era? - The plastic peak cap... Seemingly all young fans had a plastic peak cap in their team's colours (I had a Chelsea one, but we won't go into that). If ever there was an article to prove the theory this was it. The early 70's, a time when an unending stream of naffness was engulfing the nation, the vaguely hip bell-bottoms of the late 60's were turning into the utterly ludicrous flares of the mid 70's. The exciting newness of late 60's music was degenerating into a tide of dross that would not abate until the arrival of punk in the late 70's. And industry was discovering ever more stupid things to do with plastic. Homes were disappearing under mountains of cheap and nasty plastic rubbish. The plastic peak cap was a symptom of the age. Why did we wear them? They looked terrible and had only one apparent function - to make you sweat profusely.

It wasn't only the terraces that saw the rise of horrendous plastic fashion accessories. Events on the pitch were not immune - who remembers the disturbing sight of Leeds United's plastic number tags. Worn as ties around the tops of the socks, these were items of quite outstanding naffness. Despite all the monstrosities since imposed upon us by the strip manufacturers they have yet to come up with an equally stupid or more pointless idea. From an aesthetic point of view, the Leeds number tags were the equivalent of hanging bright yellow plastic bunting around Nelson's Column.

As the 70's progressed (a decade so completely useless that it makes the 80's look reasonable) faceless men in dark rooms were formulating devious plans. When Admiral unveiled their new England kit little did we suspect the horror that was about to be unleashed. This was the era when shirt design began to go badly wrong. Great chunky stripes crept surrepticiously down sleeves, nasty collars spread throughout the land, and multi-coloured sock's pernicious influence was felt across the football fields of Britain.

There is no doubt that the 80's were the 'designer' decade. Just as the 70's had seen an endless production line of cheapo plastic crap, so the 80's gave birth to a similar market of 'designer' garbage. The difference being that, in a 'consumer' society, the products, though still nasty, were no longer cheap. We were expected to pay good money for things we neither really wanted or needed, and had

no discernible use.

The 80's version of the plastic peak cap was undoubtedly the half and half ski hat. Thousands of fashion conscious hipsters could be seen wandering around with Arsenal/Celtic, Chelsea/Rangers or other such combinations stretched over their designer haircuts. Quite why I've never been able to entirely work out, although there was a disturbingly sectarian motivation behind some people's choice of teams. There was actually a company offering a choice of any combination of English First or Second Division club and any Scottish Premier Division club. In a season where Gills missed promotion by 11 minutes, and Meadowbank were only denied promotion to the Premier thanks to a blatant stitch-up by the Scottish League I could well have become the proud owner of the world's only Gillingham/Meadowbank hat, unfortunately it was not to be.

■Nigel de Gruchy: unreasonable workload.

The 'designer' phenomenon is neatly summed up by the case of Tottenham Hotspur PLC. The range of goods produced by this once great <u>football</u> club is quite awesome. It is not uncommon for their programme to contain a 24 page catalogue of 'leisure goods' containing such necessary accoutrements to your enjoyment of supporting a football team as a baseball cap with the word HUMMEL emblazoned across it, an obviously vital possession for any self-respecting Spurs fan to own, and a Tottenham Hotspur soap dish, without which no person can consider themselves a true supporter of the club. Complete and utter crap all of it. Any self-respecting 70's marketing man (if there is such a thing as a self-respecting marketing man) wouldn't have dreamed it was possible to con people into buying such complete and utter rubbish.

Where is this all leading? What new terrors await us as we skip gaily towards the brave new world of Radion automatic (can't you sometimes smell a sweaty smell when you're ironing?) and lead-free perrier. Can we expect to be able to purchase bits

of the Berlin Wall painted in club colours? Will the programme be printed on recycled paper?(it bloody well should be). Will you be able to get ozone-friendly bovril at the tea hut? We can but await our fate, one thing is sure though, we'll still be able to buy tons of useless crap!

- Gordon Roadstand

─ SOME ── interesting ── FACTS ─

I wonder how many of you, our wonderful readers have spotted any of these strange coincidences/happenings during the first half of the season. Not many I should say? This is probably because they are really pretty boring. If any of you are aware of similar occurrences then I strongly advise you to keep them to yourselves. We at BMH are simply not interested.

1/ Saturday 8th September - Sheffield Wednesday played Arsenal, and followed this up with a Littlewoods match against Aldershot before returning to league action against Aston Villa. Thus they played the three A's in successive matches (well, well, its a funny old etc. -Ed).

2/ The referee at the Tranmere v Tottenham Littlewoods tie was one L.Shapter (you mean there's another one? -Ed) who any self-respecting football fan knows hails from sunny Torquay. This meant all three places with teams beginning with T were represented in the same match (quite remarkable - Ed).

3/ Lincoln followed up their home defeat against Gillingham with a cup tie against Billingham Synthonia (avec Monsieurs Shearer & Cochrane). Thus they hed successive opponents who rhymed (Lummy! -Ed).

4/ On Saturday 2nd December, Gillingham fans set off for York while Maidstone supporters prepared for a home game against Exeter. On Saturday 9th December, Gillingham supporters set off for York while Maidstone supporters prepared themselves for a home game against Exeter (in the cup) (meanwhile, back on the planet earth..-Ed).

- Ernest Chalk

...WHEN MOORE HAD HAIR

Half past twelve on a Saturday lunchtime. On London Weekend Television the 'Bucket of water song' had just been sung and Sally James, Chris Tarrant and co. had just flung their last custard pies of the morning. Another 'Tiswas' was over and it was time for 'The World of Sport'. Presenter Dickie Davies, with the grey streak in his hair even in those days, would run down the afternoon's sporting events to be featured in the show before handing over to Brian Moore for his 25 minute lunchtime football preview 'On the Ball'.

Meanwhile, over on BBC1, Noel Edmonds had uttered those immortal words 'Who's on line 6 to the Swap Shop?' one last time, and Cheggers had finished swapping 'Stretch Armstrong' for 'Ker-plunk'. Another 'Multi-Coloured Swap Shop' had finished (thankfully). After the weather it was time for 'Grandstand' presented by Frank Bough. In those days the only lines Frank took were off his autocue so he wasn't floating around the 'Grandstand' studio high as a kite on cocaine. Frank would introduce 'Football Focus' with Bob Wilson, who was not accompanied in those days by that useless squeaky so-called expert Emlyn 'come on team, we'll go away please Dave' Hughes, as Hughes was still playing football under the misapprehension that he had some skill.

With both football programmes on at the same time, a choice had to be made (no video recorders in those days to enable you to watch one and tape the other). I always watched 'On the Ball', one reason being that I thought Wilson was boring and tedious (no doubt due to his association with Arsenal) (And nothing at all to do with the fact that the author ia a closet Spurs fan -Ed).

At three o'clock if I wasn't at Priestfield, it was 'Grandstand' or 'World of Sport' for the early scores. Dickie Davies usually gave out the scores at about 3.10pm after the 'ITV Seven' had finished, whilst on the other side a few minutes later, Frank 'Coke is it' Bough usually read out the scores to the watching millions just prior to the rugby. Between 3.15pm and half-time it was best to stick with the rugby on BBC1 (with the volume turned down so you didn't have to endure Eddie 'Up and under' Waring's grating commentary) as the latest scores were flashed up on the screen. ITV was a no-go area at this time as they usually featured sports like ice-skating or rallying and there was never a hint of any latest scores. At half-time both sides would give out the scores. I usually watched ITV as Brian Moore would report on the game to be featured the following day on 'The Big Match'.

As for the second-half ITV and BBC were both shunned. I couldn't sit through 45 minutes of Kent Walton being over-enthusiastic about Big Daddy and Giant Haystacks wrestling, in the faint hope that Dickie would interupt every so often with the latest scores. BBC was no good either as by this time I'd be sick of the rugby (even with the sound turned down), so I usually listened to Radio 2 for the second-half commentary or Radio Medway (as it was in those days) for the Gills scores.

At 4.40pm it was back to BBC1 for the teleprinter. This was in the days before David 'Bill Beaumont, quite amazing, what happened next?' Coleman read out the results from the teleprinter and interspersed them with the sort of trivial information now used on News at Ten by Sir Alistair 'crawl, crawl' Burnett and Sandy Gall bladder. You know the sort of thing, 'Burnley - three games without a win 0, Gillingham - deep in relegation trouble 8!. After the teleprinter it was time for the classified results read by Len Martin, who dreaded for years the scoreline of 'East Fife 4 Forfar 5' cropping up. On both channels the results were followed by match reports. Then 'Grandstand' would finish and on would come a show like 'The Pink Panther' on BBC, whilst on ITV it was usually 'Metal Mickey' or 'Worzel Gummidge' after 'World of Sport' had finished.

Then the countdown to 10.00pm and 'Match of the Day' began. The evening was usually wiled away watching BBC1, 'Jim'll Fix It', 'Larry Grayson's Generation Game' etc.. The football was usually preceded by a detective series like 'Kojak', 'Starsky and Hutch' or 'Shoestring' followed by the News. The worst Saturday night of the year was when BBC1 televised the 'Last Night of the Proms' as it invariably overran and

delayed the football quite considerably.

Jimmy Hill, in those days without glasses but with beard, presented 'Match of the Day' and introduced highlights of two matches with commentaries by Barry Davies and John 'surely chin of the season Jimmy' Motson. Bob 'Autocue' Wilson provided a round-up of other games. After an hour of 'Match of the Day', on came the best cure for insomnia ever, Michael Parkinson.

Sunday mornings were usually spent reading the match reports in the papers. The television wouldn't be switched on until the religious programmes and 'Weekend World' had finished. At this stage there was about an hour until the start of 'The Big Match', this hour was usually taken up with programmes like 'Randall and Hopkirk (Deceased)', 'Thunderbirds', 'Stingray' and 'University Challenge' (Your starter for ten , no conferring -Ed). 'The Big Match', introduced by Brian Moore, who in those days had a few more hairs scraped over his Planetarium shaped head, usually came on at about 2.15pm, although at one stage it used to start at 2.45pm to allow the Sunday lunchtime pub-goers to get home for the start (Disgusting -Ed). Mr. Moore himself would commentate on the main featured game, involving a London club. Then there were brief highlights from two games from other regions which allowed us to savour the commentaries of, amongst others, Martin Tyler, Kenneth Wolstenholme (Sheer delightful commentaries -Ed) and Hugh 'Francis - pause - Shoots - pause - Goal! One nothing Birmingham City!' Johns. After the regional

highlights that was it for another weekend of football.

Of course, it's all changed now, We had a few seasons of swapping programmes around, 'The Big Match' on Saturdays, 'Match of the Day' on Sundays, but it's got even worse since then. 'World of Sport' and 'On the Ball' are no more, and all ITV offer us is Ian 'You kill me Greavsie' St.John and Jimmy 'Wish someone would Saint' Greaves. I suppose we should be thankful that this is quite entertaining (Is it? -Ed). 'The Big Match' has also gone (Shame! -Ed), now we get 'The Match' (Shame! -Ed) live , where we have to suffer the inane comments of Ron 'I'm a great manager and expert although my club is always bottom of the League' Atkinson and David 'Mind the kerb' Pleat. As for BBC, well we only get 'Match of the Day' on F.A. Cup days, Frank Bough went high in the Sky via 'Breakfast Time', and Bob Wilson doesn't do a regular football slot on 'Grandstand', as since ITV did a deal with the League for exclusive rights to League action, BBC are about as interested in League football as Princess Anne is in Mark Phillips.

For a while during the seventies, football coverage was just about right. Why did they have to mess around with it?

- Bernard Bresslaw.

(There's no future in nostalgia, I say -Ed)

GREAT BORES OF TODAY (1) THE terrace moaner

66 .... come on Gillingham, you're useless get that ball out to the wings I've seen better football in the Medway Sunday League get into him pass the ball I don't know why I bother coming get that ball down take him on Smith what's the matter with you ref foul offside penalty bring back Gerry Summers I say you're nowhere near as good as the 58/9 team I remember those days we played firm but fair none of this offside rubbish a quick handshake after a goal not this kissing and hugging lark oh come on Gills move it BLAH BLAH BLAH 99

BRIAN MOORE'S HEAD LOOKS UNCANNILY LIKE LONDON PLANETARIUM

Democratic Party elects Afro- American leader

'Brian Moore's Head', the fanzine that's NOT afraid to SPILL THE BEANS can now EXCLUSIVELY reveal the BOLD new plan currently under discussion at Gillingham F.C. to SOLVE the current financial crisis and give the club a BRIGHT new start at the dawn of their EXCITING Division 4 era.

By POSTPORT REPORTER

PERVERT

Through extensive bribing of a club employee - both with money and in return for perverted sexual favours with a BMH staff member (also involving an alsation and several yards of goal netting), we can now reveal that the club intends to:

* SELL Priestfield Stadium

* BUILD a new ground locally

* CHANGE the club name following a MASSIVE new sponsorship deal

SO(L)D OFF

Priestfield Stadium, scene of many club triumphs (ie Division 4 championship 1963/4), is to be sold off to make way for a new furniture superstore/haulage firm complex we can EXCLUSIVELY reveal.

ORGY

A new multi-thousand pound stadium is to be constructed at GILLINGHAM STRAND on the site of the soon to be closed open air swimming pool. The new 3,000 capacity all seater ground will be known as the STRAND STADIUM. The home end will be known as the 'PITCH & PUTT END' while the away end will become the 'BOATING POOL END'.

RAMPANT

It is also anticipated that the Strand miniature railway will be EXTENDED to the main station to allow away fans to be transported directly into the ground. Its capacity of 18 people is judged to be sufficient for Division 4 away support (although an extra carriage will be laid on for "local" derbies such as Stockport).

WHIPPED

In a remarkable gesture designed to retrain some of the traditions of Priestfield, we can EXCLUSIVELY reveal that the Gordon Road Stand will be taken apart plank by rotten plank and relocated in the new stadium. However, in line with the Safety at Sports Ground Act 1985, it will remain closed. It will be renamed the Moynihan Stand. The good old Strand helter-skelter WILL be retained, converted into new multi-level executive boxes.

THE NEW EXECUTIVE BOXES (PRIOR TO REDEVELOPMENT)

'Massive protest' at pool closure

'ADSCENE' W/E 10/2/89

FONDLE

The new sponsorship deal will extend the role of Gillingham F.C. into the community by linking up with the Borough Council. The team, we can EXCLUSIVELY reveal, will be renamed, "Gillingham Borough Council and Municipal Related Services F.C.".

Players will become employees of the Council and when not training will be involved in community activities such as youth training sessions, school liaison, personal appearances, road sweeping, clearing the leaves from Gillingham Park and promoting Poop-Scoopers (only 99p for 10). In return the Council will offer the services of the Municipal Majorettes for half-time entertainment. The deal may also involve some MONEY.

GROPE

On being approached with our EXCLUSIVE revelations, Manager Mr 'Burky' Burkinshaw was reported to have said "Bugger off, you Southern woofter". We phoned Mr 'Carpets and Bedding' Lukehurst for his comments but he was out shopping. I approached a typical Gills fan for his comments but he couldn't understand what I was saying.

A GILLS FAN (ARTISTS IMPRESSION)

RUBBER

I'm sure that all Gills fans will look forward to these far-reaching changes, which mark the start of a new era at Kent's FOREMOST league club. So come on, you moaning minnies, get on your bikes and let's head for Dartford.

Mr Peacock is 38 years old.

NEXT WEEK: how to fit a self-bore water valve

THE (wait for it) KELVIN MORTON MASTERCLASS

Following his vintage performance in the
Bristol Rovers game near the end of last
season BMH decided to contact referee
Kelvin Morton and ask him what it takes
to be a top referee. He didn't know, he
did, however, send us this article:

If you desire fame, if you want millions
of people to constantly have your name on
their lips, what do you do? There are many
ways to achieve the desired notoriety, unfortunately most of them seem to require
talent of some kind. So what do you do if
you are a talentless jerk (as I like to
think I am). Football refereeing is an
absolute God send for those of us who
do not have this talent - we may not be
able to make wonder saves like Neville
Southall or tackle like Des Walker or even
appeal for offside like Tony Adams, but
this is not going to stop the more determined among us becoming as famous as our
beloved Minister for sport Colin Thingy,
you know the one, that shortarse git, you
know who I mean, whatsisname....
    Anyway, if you want to achieve immort-
ality through a career in football but you
haven't got the necessary skills you are
faced with three options:- 1/ give it up
as a bad idea, 2/ sign for Wimbledon or
3/ become a referee.

STARTING OUT

    Once you have chosen refereeing as your
means to an end you have to decide what
sort of referee you wish to be. This will
almost entirely depend on the aptitude you
show for the job. It became clear to me
at an early stage that i was a short sight-
ed incompetent git. This may have decided
a lot of peoples minds against continuing,
but I am made of sterner stuff, I decided
to make a career out of being a short sight-
ed incompetent git.
    Before you begin this wondrous journey
into self-discovery there is one thing
that is vital, you must make sure that
your life outside of football is extremely
dull:

Referee: Kelvin Morton

Mr Morton is an accountant. He is married
with three children and lives in Great
Barton, Suffolk. Mr Morton commenced
refereeing when he was sixteen and progressed through the Eastern Counties and
Football Combination to the Football
League. He is heavily involved with his
local Referees' Association, along with
being assessors' secretary for the Eastern Counties League and secretary of his
local Tennis Club.

The reason for this is plain, the more
frustrating and tedious your life the more
you will enjoy letting off steam on a Saturday afternoon. It is for this reason I
recently moved from Bury St. Edmunds, a
town I found much too wild and exciting,
to a total non-event of a place called
Great Barton. My job as an accountant is
ideal, as it allows me to become so wound
up and angry during the week that I can
really give my all during the match. Another important thing to remember is that you
need to be something of a sadist to really
get the most out of it, the ability to wind
supporters up until they are fit to explode
is a delicate art but, when done well, it
makes for an extremely satisfying hobby.

EQUIPMENT

There are two pieces of equipment which are
of the utmost importance, the whistle and
the red card. All other pieces of refereeing regalia are almost entirely incidental,
with the exception of the notebook and
yellow card, which can be useful when you
feel you have awarded enough penalties (I
usually limit myself to a maximum of five
per game) and ordered your full quota of
players off (not wise to exceed four per
game if you want to remain on the League
list).

ARRIVING AT THE GROUND

When you arrive at the Ground it is important to examine its layout. find out where
the dug-outs are situated, this enables you
to lurk in their vicinity and book or send
off (depending on your mood) any manager/
coach/physio/substitute who steps out of
line (another good move to remember is to
deliberately lecture the wrong person, this
can get them so annoyed that they end up
being charged with bringing the game into
disrepute). Try and find out where the most
vociferous supporters stand, this is the
ideal spot to make your most controversial
decisions. Make sure you talk to the Police
Officer in charge to book your Police esc-
ort at the final whistle. Make sure your
dressing room has a sturdy lock to keep
out enraged fans (it is also a good idea
to bring a book to read after the game
while the Police are clearing the lynch
mob).

THE GAME

It is a good idea to let the first fifteen
minutes or so drift by uneventfully, this
will lull the crowd into a false sense of
security and will make your later decisions
seem all the more infuriating. Try a couple
of pointless free-kicks in the centre-circle just to let everyone know who they're
dealing with. The most important thing to
remember is to make all your decisions in-

stantly, if you allow yourself even a split second to think you may begin to doubt whether you are making a correct decision and an opportunity to annoy people will have been wasted. If you see even a half-chance to give a penalty/send someone off/ disappear down the tunnel for no apparant reason then you must take it, you may not get a better chance later in the game.

PENALTIES

Remember - the more confusing a penalty award the more it will anger people. My only criterion for awarding a penalty is that the ball must be in the area when I point to the spot (you would look silly if you pointed to the spot with the ball bobbling about in midfield, besides which the crowd would be following the ball and would not be looking at you - which is, of course, your main aim). Once you have awarded a penalty don't just limit yourself to upsetting the side you have awarded it against, once it has been converted let the celebrations go on for a few seconds and then order it to be retaken. Don't allow one team too much of an advantage, award one to the other side later on. You can annoy both sides still further after they have both been awarded penalties by refusing to point to the spot again, no matter how blatent the foul.

RED AND YELLOW CARDS

I make it a rule only to book people for offences they can not possibly be sent off for(i.e. attempted murder) and save the red card for more serious offences (looking at me in a funny way, playing for Portsmouth or being Gary West). It is a good idea to practice pulling your red card out of your pocket in front of a mirror at home, with patience you should be able to pull it out and brandish it at your chosen target before he knows what's hit him.

OBSCURE RULES

A sound knowledge of all the little known and seldom rules is essential, in fact I would say more important than such trivialities as offside or corners. It allows you to make decisions that absolutely no-one in the ground understands with the confidence of knowing that if anyone argues with you they can be shown the relevant paragraph/sub-section/special note. This makes them feel very small and makes it seem as though you have a sound knowledge of the rules of the game, thus showing that you are a good referee after all.

THE PRESS

Your ultimate aim is to get your name in the Sunday papers. My success in achieving thi can be gauged by my scrapbook, which is bulging with my press cuttings. I like to think I have succeeded in my aim to become the most controversial referee since Clive Thomas. I have, however, only achieved this at League level. It is my wish to succeed in becoming a FIFA referee, this will allow me to achieve the same Worldwide notoriety as Clive after his brilliant disallowing of a last minute Brazilian goal in a World Cup match , a moment of style and panache which I hope to one day emulate.

- Kelvin Morton (honest)

HILLSBOROUGH, APRIL 15, 1989

Remember Hillsborough? Did something happen there once? Something about 95 people being crushed to death in a confined space. Ah, yes, I remember now. There was an inquiry going on. I read about it on page five of my newspaper next to something about restored Georgian houses in Toxteth. It may seem trivial and insignificant now, but it must have been important once. It held the attention of Fleet Street for three whole weeks.

At the time it introduced a new sense of perspective. Everyone could see promotion and relegation for the empty prizes they surely were. Whisper who dares, but even money seemed unimportant. Yes, at the time it sent shock waves all over Europe.

It took a massacre of several thousand people in Beijing to remind me that the Hillsborough incident was only a minor event at the downmarket end of the leisure industry (sic) on a small island anchored just off the west coast of Europe. "It must never be forgotten", we all said in a rare show of unison. But who remembers the last time something similar happened, at Ibrox Park in 1972? Events in China are clearly going to reverberate around the world for years, decades, maybe centuries to come. Hillsborough might just about rate a brief mention in the BBC review of 1989. "It must never be forgotten". But it already is.

- David Hagerty.

THE FOOD X1

Yes, we've thought of another one, I'm sure you're all really bored with XI's now aren't you? Well tough, 'cos we've got an infinite supply of them.

This one is really scraping the bottom of the barrel, I would suggest that it contains the highest number of fruit and vegetable jokes ever published in one article.

1/ RON BEAN - As he was a goalkeeper and not a winger, Ron, who played three times for Gills in 1951, probably wasn't a 'runner' bean (Oh God -Ed), and at 6ft1in. in height, his weight of less than twelve stone would indicate that he wasn't a 'broad' bean either (BANG! -sound of Editor shooting himself).

2/ LES BERRY - As Les is still playing at the age of 33, an elderberry would seem appropriate for him. Maidstone are currently enjoying the 'fruits of his labour'.

3/ DAVID PEACH - No doubt scored 'a peach of a goal' on a few occasions for the Gills. His contribution of 30 goals in 186 games certainly 'bore fruit' for Gillingham many times.

4/ STEVE JACOBS - Steve didn't manage to score for Gillingham, so there are no 'Jacobs crackers' to remember him by. As he only played 6 times, there was little chance for the Evening Post to use the headline 'Jacobs takes the biscuit', which rivals 'Proud as a Peacock' as a classic headline.

5/ VIC NIBLETT - How to make your dinner last longer, don't bolt it, just nibble it. (KERSPLATT! -typist suffers fatal brain haemorrhage)Vic played 154 games for the Gills and suffered a severe goal-famine. He didn't manage to score at all.

6/ JOHN CRABBE - Scored 13 goals in 4 years of scuttling around in the Gillingham midfield, which suggests forward movement into attack as opposed to the usual sideways motion of the crab, as perfected by Ray Wilkins.

7/ RON BACON - Winger Ron made some streaky runs down the flanks between 1958-61. His 15 goals show that he 'bought home the bacon' for the Gills on more than one occasion.

8/TONY EELES - This slippery character manages to squirm his way past opposing defences who never manage to catch him. Currently having a 'whale of a time' for the Gills, and he certainly doesn't look like 'a fish out of water' in the first team.

9/ HAROLD GREEN -
10/MIKE GREEN - 'Eat your greens and you'll grow up big and strong'. This statement has been used countless times by parents trying to get their offspring to eat platefuls of cabbage and brussel sprouts. As greens are an intregal part of most meals, they cannot be left out of a food XI, so here are two that played for the Gills. Harold was at Priestfield fro m 1964-5, and scored 17 times in 33 games, Mike netted 24 times in 131 games between 1968-71.

11/ REX CHERRY - Cherry was signed by Gillingham at the ripe old age of 20, and was picked for the first team on 10 occasions before moving to Hastings. His 4 goals for the Gills prove that his stay at Priestfield was not a fruitless one.

- HATTIE JAQUES

𝐟antastic 𝐟acts

Next time you go to a boring match, don't be miserable afterwards and complain about how many pints you could have bought instead. I adopted this attitude after the Reading v Wigan match at Elm Park in 1989. Wigan won 3-0 and it was crap (apart from Elsey scoring an own goal). However, while glancing at the programme the other day I discovered all these amazing facts which changed my feelings towards the game completely:

1/ Both teams fielded someone called Senior! They wore the number 2 and number 9 shirts. If you add these numbers together you get 11 - the number of players each side used during the game! (Yes, that's right, despite getting shat on by a team in the bottom four, Reading did not use a sub).

2/ The surnames of Wigan's numbers 9 and 10 rhymed! They were Page and Ramage (well it depends how you pronounce Ramage, but it's interesting all the same).

3/ Wigan fielded two England cricketers - Atherton and Russell! (Hemmings, a squad player, sadly did not make the line-up).

4/ Reading almost fielded two famous cricketers too - (Viv) Richardson and (Graeme) Hicks!

5/ Reading's number 11 (Payne) spells a famous pop-star backwards - Enya! (if you leave out the P).

6/ Two of Wigan's players are associated with referees - Entwhistle and Page (in the notebook)!

7/ The linesman with the yellow flag was Mr T. Rogers. The attendance was 3,821, which is the TV show Mr T. Rogers presents (if you miss out the 8)!

Fab, huh?

- Professor Yaffel

I HAVE A dream!

It is often said that listening to people talk about their dreams is mindnumbingly boring. Unconcerned about what our readers may think, and under pressure from the rest of the BMH mob who think I am mad, I am going to tell you about a number of vivid dreams I have had about the Gills. Not just vivid either, but realistic too, as we keep getting stuffed. The exception is the most recent dream I've had, where we won 7-0 at Mansfield in the first leg of a Littlewoods Cup tie. The only noteworthy feature was when I got back on the coach afterwards, Alan Liptrott made a bid to be included in 'Moore Quotes' by saying that he thought we would be okay in the second leg as long as Mansfield did not score an early goal.

Prior to that, another restless night's sleep found me at Priestfield, standing in my usual spot, for a game with Wolves. Wolves fans even had half the Town End (like last season's fixture) but the Rainham End was sparsely populated. At half-time we were 0-3 down, but Steve Lovell pulled back a goal early in the second period, putting in a rebound after a ball had hit the post in a scramble. Strangely, the Wolves fans behind the goal celebrated. We decided that this must be because they wanted to see a close game, but this didn't explain their chants of 'Ooh Bully Bully'. Anyway, Wolves went on to win 6-3 and even missed two penalties, both going wide (I'm sure Ronnie had them covered). I ran onto the pitch to protest about the second penalty, but I suddenly changed my mind having run a few yards, and I sheepishly scampered back onto the terraces.

Eddie, however, had not been so lucky when he invaded the pitch in a previous dream. We were playing Notts County at home in the last game of the season. The ground was packed so I presume it was last season and we needed to win to stay up. We scored early on, but our celebrations were cut short by the linesman's flag. Eddie was in the centre-circle remonstrating with the referee, and was soon being frogmarched behind the Rainham End goal by two Coppers, although he still looked unreasonably cheerful. We lost 0-4 and so I'suppose we were relegated (Phew! what a nightmare that must have been -Ed),

At the time of the Spurs Milk Cup tie, I dreamt that I was refereeing the match. It was played on a very sunny Thursday afternoon, and the game finished goalless, mainly due to my disallowing a Gillingham goal because the crowd didn't cheer enough! Curiosly, the pitch had a tremendous slope on it that afternoon, and the houses in Gordon Road appeared to almost be encroaching on the touchline.

Another 'big match' dream concerned the West Brom cup game. I started off watching from the terraces, but soon I was actually playing. we lost 1-7 and the last goal was my fault, as I fell over in the six yard box. From my position on all fours in the mud, I peered apologetically through the netting to the crowd at the Town End where I spotted Suggs out of Madness. He muttered something about fishmen and I promptly woke up in a cold sweat.

What does it all mean? Does the 7-0 victory at Mansfield signify a forthcoming change around in Gills fortunes? while some dream analysts would probably see it this way, most BMH readers would no doubt not give a toss, simply hoping that I am locked up in a suitable mental home.

- C.L.

—ORIENT 1 GILLINGHAM 2
—SPRING, 1970

School in North London was a tough place for me. Though I nicked the odd goal for the school and gained some kudos thereby my life was, as a rule, blighted by endless taunts, threats and, infrequently, violence; the exclusive source of this unpleasantness was my well publicised support for Gillingham. The aggro, naturally, came from Spurs and Arsenal fans (the majority), with a few from Chelsea, West Ham and Palace. The nearest I came to equality was with the single Fulham supporter, who I could beat up anyway.

So it came to pass that the season we began by losing the first six league matches was due to end at Orient, the champions, with the issues cut and dried. Gills, fourth from bottom, were two points behind Bournemouth, fifth from bottom, but had a better goal average, as it was. Bournemouth had finished their matches. Nothing less than a win therefore would keep Gills in Division Three. It had also come to pass that, in the preceding days, my young self had bet a frightening number of pounds on the out-

come; this with my charming peers. These honest lads, harbingers of Thatcherism, no doubt felt that even-money on Gills failing to beat the champions away was as shrewd a piece of private enterprise as could be imagined. My heart however ruled my head, as it has to do when one follows a team managed by Basil Hayward.

Orient missed a penalty on the half hour but scored a minute before half-time. Gills needed two goals and they pressed but it was not until fifteen minutes from time that Mike Green stabbed in after a scramble. Gills were fighting and going down, we thought, with honour. It didn't seem right that there would be two divisions between the teams next year. The lights came on in the stand behind us; always a bad sign if you need a goal. Derek Woodley set off down the right wing - desperate last moments - he cut inside, shot - time stood still - the ball hit the base of the left hand post and came out. My grandad punched the terrace and left a dent. Brian Yeo was following up. Control it, I thought, but he hit it first time; a defender lunged and it went in. Three more dreadful minutes were played before the end. Basil Hayward was quoted 'we will never get into this position again'.

The journey home was as if on a cloud. There has never been a better football feeling. I had jam on it the next morning, establishing a personal debt collecting agency, impervious to the half hearted taunts of 'fix'. For one day then, out of about a thousand, my Spurs and Arsenal dominated school was one in which a Gillingham fan was king. Basil saw to it that the next season my Monday morning routine of being greeted with hysterical laughter was resumed.

- Paul Caister

MESSINGHAM HORSE & FOAL SHOW SOCIETY

Show Date : June 7th, 1982

Dear Sir,

I read with considerable interest the letter published in the last issue of 'Brian Moore's Head...' written by Mr. Hancock from Canterbury referring to the 'mystery' Gillingham player appearing on the cigarette cards at the beginning of 'Match of the Day'.

I am sorry to dissapoint Mr. Hancock, and therefore presumably deprive him of his prize, but the player depicted is most certainly not myself. As you will see from the enclosed photograph I looked nothing like the player depicted (I'm the one second from the left). This picture shows me shortly after my discharge from hospital in September 1939, and is therefore a fairly accurate representation of how I looked in my playing days.

The injury I sustained at Worcester which finished my Gillingham career was sufficiently severe to necessitate a nine month period incarcerated in St. Mauds Infirmary in Droit-witch, and when I was finally able to leave hostilities with Germany had already broken out. My desire to have a crack at the enemy received a nasty setback when I was declared medically unfit for active service with His Majesty's armed forces, my injury still leav-ing me too incapacitated for the rigours of military life.

However after a bit of discreet string-pulling, and no doubt helped by the Spiffs' distinguished military history back as far as the siege of Corunna during the Peninsular War, I managed to get myself a post at Fishguard in West Wales as Second in Command of a coastal defence battery of 6" guns. I spent my entire war service there, and during that time I regularly played football for the local side. The team was made up mainly of fish-ermen, dock-workers and servicemen, and our other duties meant we seldom fielded the same side in successive games, so we never did terribly well in the various competitions in which we played. Probably our most notable feat was to take quite a strong Swansea Town side to a replay in the League Cup in 1943.

However the most memorable match in which I played was in early 1942 against a team from the gunnery range at Aberporth. Going into the second half we were 2-0 up and the chaps were really playing terrifically well in awful weather and on a quagmire of a pitch. Suddenly, quite without warning, over the brow of a nearby hill there appeared a German FW109 fighter, belching smoke and losing height rapidly. As he shot towards us we all dived for cover, shedding bits of wreckage he passed low over our prone figures, narrowly missed the goal-posts at the far end of the pitch, and crashed in a huge explosion in the field beyond.

We stood and watched for a bit, and then, feeling that we shouldn't let this distract-ion divert us from our game, we prepared to resume play. It was then we discovered that George, our venerable goalkeeper, had been hit by a piece of debris as the plane passed overhead and knocked unconcious. The Aberporth captain rather uncharitably suggested that this wouldn't significantly effect his game, and while I felt that there was a certain element of truth in this observation (I was later proved right, during a match at Lampeter, but that's another story) I couldn't let him get away with this sleight so I squared up to him ready to give him a demonstration of the 'Spiff Tickle'.

The situation looked quite ugly for a moment, but then things were saved by the arriv-al of the German pilot who had parachuted from his plane shortly before it crashed. Feel-ing that he was somewhat to blame for our keeper-less predicament he sportingly offered to take George's place for the remainder of the game. This he duly did, and in fact he played so well, even saving a penalty, that afterwards we took him for a couple of drinks before handing him over to the military police.

Imagine my horror the next day when I discovered that, as soon as we'd driven off in the truck, the police, apparently not believing that this mud-covered gentleman dressed in goalkeepers jersey and gloves and smelling of beer was a captured German pilot, had let him go!

Many years later, after the war, he turned up at one of our battery re-unions, and I learned the rest of his tale. He'd lived rough for about a fortnight, surviving on six pots of apricot jam stolen from a farm window, before managing to steal a boat and rowing to Ireland. He'd fetched up in a fishing village in Cork where the locals didn't find anything odd about a German speaking goalkeeper rowing into the harbour and had accepted him happily into the community. He married a local girl and so far as I am aware he lives there to this day.

Returning to the identity of the mystery Gillingham player on the cigarette cards I am afraid I cannot really help you as to who it <u>really</u> is. However there are a couple of players from my time who, if memory serves me, it could have been. One was Jack Hoggins, a Scot, a man of few words (which was quite a good thing, since no-one understood him anyway) but a fine defender, and the other Hamilton Pickett who was studying to be a doctor but played a fair bit during the university holidays. Perhaps on of your other readers may be able to shed some more light on this matter.

Give the Gills a cheer from me,
Yours faithfully,

Taragon Spiff D.S.C. , M.C.

chapter 10

The CROOKED SPIREITE

no. 9
Dec.'88
40p.

Easier to read than a Steve Baines back-pass!

Another sensational "CS" scoop!

NEW PLAN TO BOOST OUR GATES

"So we'll have it ready for the Mansfield game", says I. At that moment a brick came through the window of the pub where we had met to finalise the publishing of "The Crooked Spireite". "Who wants to do the bit about crowd trouble?"

We had first talked of setting up a Chesterfield fanzine a few months before it hit the streets on January 1st 1988. A disaffected group of former programme contributors, we were appalled at the way the club was going down the hill so quickly, with seemingly no-one prepared to (or aware of how to) pull on the brakes. Our board consisted of a solicitor, a builder and a tax exile; they would be our first targets.

A week before Issue 1 went to the printer, the board resigned, making way for a popular consortium of ex-directors. 'So what?' thought I, 'We'll break new ground by being the first fanzine to be *content* with our directors!' Our policy of trying to avoid slagging off people at the club was thus formed and it has led to us being accepted by the club, albeit sometimes grudgingly at boardroom level. Sure, we could probably sell more than our current 800 a month by being harder, or having a go at the team when they're crap, but it wouldn't make them win more often. As more and more fanzines are banned, sued and forced off the streets by clubs, I'm quite pleased that ours seems to be tolerated, at least.

STUART BASSON

The CROOKED SPIREITE
No.12 Apl. '89 40p.

LOOK WHAT WE'VE FOUND!

Months of dilligent research by the CS team has led to the discovery of something once thought impossible:

a card that is even more useless than a football ID one.

Here it is:

Donor Card

When I die,
I'd like someone else
to have my brain.

Signed *Colin Moynihan.*

STILL 28 PAGES! (Against my better judgement.)

INSIDE:
The JAMIE HEWITT interview
They AGREED to play for Wednesday!!
a JOKE about the Dee-dahs
ID Conference report
(does that fill up enough space at the bottom?)

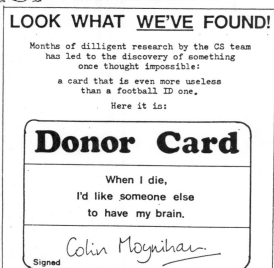

Number 1 : Jan. '88
The CROOKED SPIREITE
30p.
Such Good Value!

COX IN NEW DERBY JOB SHOCKER

Buy a scarf, pal?

SUNDERLAND:
Rules k.o'd p.6
EXCLUSIVE —
No Directors set to quit this week...

STOKE CITY FOOTBALL CLUB LIMITED
Victoria Ground, Stoke-on-Trent, Staffs. ST4 4EG

PORT VALE FOOTBALL CLUB COMPANY LIMITED
Vale Park, Burslem, Stoke-on-Trent, Staffs. ST6 1AW

EJECTION NOTICE

NAME:
DATE OF BIRTH:
ADDRESS:

You have been ejected from

Football Ground for a breach of Ground Regulations.

Stoke City Football Club and Port Vale Football Club
have authorised Staffordshire Police to warn you that should you
be ejected from a football match on a future occasion involving
either of the two Clubs, you will be banned from attending matches
at The Victoria Ground, Stoke, and at Vale Park, Burslem.

Yours faithfully,

Secretary
Stoke City F.C. Limited

Secretary
Port Vale F.C. Co. Limited

Ejection Night Special

As usual it was gresley weather in Burslem as the "Town took their first step on another cup trail. Our hopes were floundering after only ninety seconds, but when Bruno levelled the scores we thought it worth rejoicing. Unfortunately, not everyone in the visitors' end thought so, and it was not long before the usual 'pitza-faced' police officer in probationary pampers came and asked, "OK, lads - don't get excited, calm it down, can you?" Only it wasn't so much a request, more of an 'or else...' By the end of the first half we were at a loss as to how to cheer on the Blues without actually raising our voices.

Come the second half: "Town 2-1 down and under pressure from 'Vale's attack, while the 'Town supporters were under pressure from that bloody awful electronic scoreboard. How I hate electric scoreboards! They are fine when they stick to the score and scorers: it's when they start all this "Corner!" "Penalty!" "Saved!" that I get angry. I KNOW what's happening; I paid four pounds for the privelege. So, in utter desperation, I turned and gave the scoreboard a "Harvey Smith". Within seconds I was dragged away by pimple-face and a more senior constable who whispered into my shell-like, "Now then. I'm ejecting you from the ground for sticking your fingers up at the scoreboard and flicking a wank at the Vale fans." "I did what?" I asked, and the officer repeated word-for-word. I then asked what exactly flicking a w*nk involved: he obliged me with a demonstration, flicking one at me.

I admitted the first sign but, as for flicking the w*nk, "You've got the wrong man, guv" I explained, "It won't stand up in court, but I bet you don't give a toss, do you?" I hoped my attempts at humour might diffuse the situation, but the blank looks told me that all was not well.

Still pleading my innocence I was hauled away to see the Desk Sergeant who snarled, bit a piece from his truncheon and opened the evening's account. I was the first in the book for that night! I was asked to spell out my name and address; I managed to lose him on the 'r' in Chesterfield, forcing him to ask for a re-cap.

Having ushered me into a corner the sergeant took two photographs of me with a polaroid. "I bet you have to do this a lot, don't you?" I asked.

"Yes," he replied.

"I'm not surprised, if you go around treating supporters like this," was my parting shot as he showed me the door.

I watched the rest of the game from a wall high above the ground, where I chatted with a young 'Vale fan that had been ejected for fighting. This lad was simply slung out - no ejection notice or photographs, clearly a case of double standards, with one rule for the home fans and another for the travelling cattle. My night was ruined - for the first time in twenty years of Spireite supporting I had received my first premature ejaculation from a ground, for supposedly 'flicking a w*nk'.

No doubt many will think me guilty, but after the match I had had enough. If this was the way that football supporters were to be treated in future, then I wanted no part of it. Fortunately, three pints of Pedigree and the insistence of my travelling companions persuaded me to give football a second chance - after all, it was not football's fault.

"The Flicker"

Of course we don't condone any behaviour that DESERVEDLY leads to anyone getting chucked out of a ground. Judging by this chap's letter and article, though, I feel that he is not yer average bladder-brained "Invasion of Burslem" merchant. Which is, perhaps, more than can be said for the person that filled out his ejection notice for him; he clearly had terrible trouble remembering exactly which ground he was in! The crucial part of the article indicates that fans can get on with eachother when withdrawn from provocative policing. The Staffordshire Constabulary used to be well-respected, but went down in my estimation when Pompey played at Stoke two years ago: they insisted I join all the other Pompey fans on a London-bound train, despite my having a ticket marked "Chesterfield via Derby." I missed the train and was forced to wait for more than an hour for another one. Can anyone find any sense in that?

S.B.

MANAGER'S NOTES

December 31st, 1999
Chesterfield vs. Nottingham F.
Maxwell League, Elite Division.

May I take this opportunity to welcome the players, officials and supporters of Nottingham Forest to the Wheeldon Mill Stadium. Forest are enjoying a good season under Nigel Clough following their return to the higher reaches of the Maxwell League. It was commendable that they should have won the Second Division title in his first season after taking over from Sir Brian.

May I remind you that in a fortnight we will play our first Sony FA Cup tie of the new century, against Mansfield. Although the Stags are at present in Division Five they will be looking to put one over on their illustrious neighbours so I want as big a crowd as possible here at the Old Greyhound Track to cheer the team on.

It is apposite that on the last Saturday of 1999 I take a look at the world of football. At the highest level Germany seem unbeatable and must be favourites for the Pepsi-cola World Cup in 2002, in Seoul. If there is a second-favourite, excepting the erratic USA, it must be Great Britain. Sir Paul Hart is well on the way to defending the trophy we won in Romania two years ago. The recent 1-1 draw in Estonia was disappointing but, as Sir Paul says, there are no easy games in the international arena anymore.

It is a pity that the government insists on the introduction of ID cards before allowing domestic clubs back into Europe. Last year we missed out on the chance of playing such crack Euro opposition as FC Basle and Dynamo Gorbachov. The return of the White Horse Anglo-Scottish Cup is no compensation, although our win over Glasgow English brought back happy memories of games against their predecessors.

We all know that the Tories' idea for membership is unworkable. I was part of a working party that met with Mrs. Thatcher's hologram and her Home Secretary, Sebastian Coe, at New Downing Street. It seems that Sports Minister Eddie Edwards will attempt further trials at Fourth Division Luton next season. It is beyond belief that it should still be thought necessary for such a scheme when 37 million fans attended League matches last season, with only twenty-seven arrests. I can only point out that there were more arrests in the Commons last year when the King came to open Parliament.

I will end by wishing you all the best for the new century. Keep filling the seats here at Wheeldon Mill and cheer Chesterfield on to another title!

Ernie Moss MBE.
(aka Peter Whiteley)

5

OLYMPIC SYMBOLS EXPLAINED

 Association Football.

 Argentinian Football.

 Freestyle Crowd Control.

 Equestrian Crowd Control.

 Synchronised visiting the Football Ground Toilet.

 Men's Individual Celebrating the Hugo Sanchez Goal.

The 5 kilometre run for the last train after some idiot has kept you in for half an hour at Port Vale.

The Men's team dope test - Positive.

Issue 8: Nov. '88

It's your line to...

the RADIO SHEFFIELD

GRUMBLE & PRAISE spot!

Bob: Hello? Who's our first caller on the 'Grumble and Praise' spot? Hello? It's Dave on line 4....

Line 4: Brrrrrrrrr.....

Bob: Right, then; Dan on line 2:

Dan: Hello, Bob....

Bob: Hello, Dan, from where?

Dan: Parson Cross, Bob...

Bob: Parson Cross, Dan... and is it a praise or a grumble?

Dan: It's a praise, Bob...

Bob: Who for, Dan?

Dan: I'm coming to that, Bob... it's a praise for Dave Bassett. He's doing a great job at Bramall Lane...

Bob: Aye, another fine win today, 4-0, at home to Portsmouth... Did you go, Dan?

Dan: No... well, it's a bit too far to go, isn't it? Especially to watch all that long-ball rubbish...

Bob: Right! That was Dan from Parson Cross... next it's Sheila, from Mosborough...

Sheila: Hello, Bob...

Bob: Hello. Is it a praise or a grumble?

Sheila: It's a grumble, Bob...

Bob: Oh, dear, Sheila... who at?

Sheila: Rotherham United, Bob...

Bob: But they won to-day, Sheila, 5-1!! How can you grumble about that?

Sheila: Oh, it's nowt to do with to-day's game, Bob, it was the other night... my young son had to queue for fifteen minutes to get in, and when he got there he couldn't stand in his favourite place...

Bob: Yes, but it was the Cup, Sheila, they were playing Norwich, you know, they're a good side... there were fifteen thousand there...

Sheila: Well, it's put my lad off ever going again...

Bob: That was Sheila, grumbling about Rotherham... Now Alan, on line 7... Alan from where?

Alan: Thar what?

Bob: Where are you from, Alan?

Alan: Er... it's a praise, Bob...

Bob: Alright, then... who are you praising, Alan?

Alan: Ron Atkinson, Bob... He's doin' a reet good job up a' 'Tillsborough...

Bob: It's good to hear someone say that, Alan... Are you a regular at Wednesday?

Alan: Me? Nar, Amma Blades fan! Woaaah ha ha ha...

Bob: Someone with a sense of humour, there... now Tony, on line five... hello, Tony, where are you from?

Tony: I'm from Heeley Bottom, Bob, but I'm on my way back from Chelsea...

Bob: You've been to see Wednesday and you're in a car, then?

Tony: Aye, that's right (sounds of others in car singing 'Jackson is a w*nk*r)

Bob: Is it a grumble or a praise, Tony?

Tony: A praise, very definitely...

Bob: So, although they lost six-nil, they didn't play too badly?

Tony: Oh, Wednesday were rubbish. I'm ringing to praise the people who make these car phones. They're great! It means I can ring you up and let everyone know how rich I am...

Bob: Fine, so that was Tony, praising car phones... next it's Doctor Hill... hello again, doctor!

Dr. Hill: Hello, Robert.

Bob: Where have you been today, doctor Hill?

Dr. Hill: I've been along to Bramall Lane, and it was very good.

Bob: How about Booker, Stancliffe and Deane? They were all sent off, weren't they?

Dr. Hill: Yes, but they didn't deserve it, really. They were very good.

Bob: So it was the referee, then? was he a bit whistle-happy?

Dr. Hill: No, he was very good.

Bob: So they were all very good?

Dr. Hill: Oh, yes, Bob, very good. Except Cannon. He was f*cking garbage...

Bob: Er, Doctor Hill, there. Next it's George from Attercliffe. Hello, George: is it a grumble or a praise?

George: Well, it's a grumble AND a praise, Bob...

Bob: Ah, you know I don't allow that, anymore...

George: It won't take long...

Bob: ...because, you see, if I allow everyone to do that, then we wouldn't have time for more than about two or three callers...

George: Well...

Bob: ...No, George, I have to be strict... I can allow you a grumble or a praise, George, but I cannot allow you one of each, otherwise everyone would want to do it, and we only have twenty minutes for the 'grumble and praise' spot, so I have to gat as many callers in as possible, and I won't do that if I allow everyone to have as many grumbles and praises as they like. So, George, is it a praise or a grumble?

George: It's...

Bob: Well, that's all we have time for on the 'grumble and praise spot. Now it's over to Brian Bradley for the non-League round-up:

Brian: Zzzzzz........

SB

Issue 16: Nov. '89

JUST ANOTHER SUNDAY

(Diary of A Sunday League Manager: part 3)

Another Sunday morning, a search through the airing cupboard for the kit ends in the usual frantic skirmish with my brother as we battle it out for the best pair of socks. This resolved and another search reveals damp boots, which I'd promised myself I'd clean over the Christmas period, now surrounded with a fluffy covering of mouldy mud.

At the ground a cold January wind enforces the feeling that getting out of bed could prove to be a huge mistake; but all to soon it is to late as the opposition arrive - looking for all the world like the zombies we feel - they cough and wheeze their way across the car-park and into the changing rooms leaving us, the poor unfortunate home team, to put the nets up.

Once this ghastly task is finished it is back to the changing rooms; carefully we push open the door and hold up the club canary, the poor bird falls from its perch - knocked over by the rancid smell of rubbing oils and over ripe farts - a deadly combination lethal enough to turn the strongest of stomachs. With the poor bird laid to rest we grasp noses and charge to the clean air end of the room where we brew our own evil cocktail.

A little more awake now and laughter ripples around the room, in a rather loud whisper, about last nights sexual chauvinism as certain players boast, in a rather loud whisper, about last nights sexual conquests; what they did, where they did it, and how they made it physically possible. "Bullshit!" is the cry from those of us who spent Saturday night with a bag of crisps, a bottle of beer and the late film. "You're only jealous!" comes the return cry; and of course they are right, - the sods.

Little yellow balls of feather are sent skidding across the floor as players head for the great outdoors - "These bloody canaries!" The door is opened and the toxic gas escapes. Fueled by methane, it jets into the atmosphere, ruptures the ozone layer and is carried away to fall as a shower of shit over Finland around Wednesday tea-time.

Legs that an hour ago had difficulty in walking break into a trot, we pass two of the visiting team , hands on knees, leaving us a side salad on the car-park, while a third member is doing his bit for pollution by seeing how far across the river he can peee.

The warm up, for us, consists of thrashing our only ball everywhere and anywhere, while the visitors stand in shivering groups of 3 or 4, thin wisps of pale blue smoke escape above their heads and disappear.

The referee calls the captains to the middle. The opposition captain shuffles up, knocks a fag out on his hand and places the un-smoked remnant behind his ear for later. The kick off brings end to end football at break neck speed - (is this really the 22 zombies who collected an hour ago?). A visiting player goes down injured and the trainer makes an appearance; but what does this miracle worker bring with him to tend his wounded warrior, - magic sponge? - pain relieving spray? - Boots first aid kit? - Red Cross parcel? - no, nothing so grand. He quickly lights a fag and places it between the lips of the stricken player, and with comforting words encourages the victim to smoke. The player takes two deep pulls on the magic weed, rubs his ankle, and sprints back into action.

Half time brings that much needed break, and the opposition smash land speed records as they head for the side where girlfriends and wives are already lighting them a fag. Having probably the only non-smoking squad in the league enables us to play the ace up our sleeve. We wait till the opposition are well engrossed in their smoking, and smartly walk back out on to the pitch. "I've only half finished me fag!" comes the fraught whisper as panic takes hold of the visitors bench. Quickly they drag on their cigarette - short sharp pulls without releasing any smoke. Like demented steam trains they chuff their way through three-quarters of a fag before finishing in a breathless frenzy. Then, coughing and choking, their purple faces splutter back into position, more tired now than they could ever imagine. With the wind gone from their sails we coast the 2nd half and win easily. The opposition trudge back to the changing rooms with familiar wisps of pale blue smoke drifting away above their heads.

By the time we've taken the nets down the visitors have gone - our back up canary lies cold at the door to the changing rooms, and another shower of shit is forecast over Finland about Thursday lunch, and by the time we have changed they could be expecting another sometime on Friday. So much for the sweet smell of success.

Dave Radford

Issue 11: March, '89

(Diary of a Sunday footballer part 5)

Right then, last month I had a damn good whinge about how the Saltergate Club had cheated themselves out of the cup; well I can honestly say now that what that they did was sod all compared to the antics of a certain Middle Pocket F.C. player.

I turned up to watch the game, and to show there was no hard feelings I offered to run the line. The first half was pretty even, Ian Ashton had a goal disallowed, but 0-0 seemed a fair reflection. I'd taken the usual load of "cheating linesman" rubbish from their centre forward - but basically it had been a good sporting half of football. Richard Bonson had marshalled the defence well; the midfield had worked hard, and the forwards had chased everything, I couldn't have wished for more.

I was looking forward to the second half and that started especially well - Mark Jones chased a through ◆ ball, and just as I was about to curse him for pushing the ball too far, he stuck out a leg and cracked in a smashing opener. The second was not far behind; their keeper did a brilliant impression of a Scottish goalie and dropped a harmless shot at the feet of Pete Bentford who gratefully trundled it over the line. With Jim Brown's Sunday league career being cruelly ended a few weeks ago the 2 goal cushion was much needed.

I was still getting mouth from their centre forward, but at 2-0 up I couldn't even be bothered to answer him back.

Then big Ian breaks free and calmly whacks the ball in from 18 yards, the ball skidded in the net, through a hole in the back and finished on the road. Who cared, 3-0 - the ref knew it was a goal, we knew it was a goal, and even they knew it was a goal . . well, all except one who thought Ian had actually missed. Of course as soon as he started complaining they could all see the chance of getting a goal ruled out and the score back to 2-0. However, the ref was not a silly bugger, he simply took them to the back of the nets and showed them the hole, (it was as big as a house side, you could have pushed Ian Ashton through it let alone a ball.)

That was when hell broke loose; their centre forward marched up to the ref and said something to the tune of, "If you allow that goal there is going to be a blood bath," - nice lad! He carried on walking towards the ref and calling him a cheat, well, what could the poor bloke do, he had to book him - at least. This turned out to be a difficult task, for the player concerned decided to take the law - and the ref - into his own hands. He pushed the ref, took a couple of punches at him, (which the ref managed to weave away from very nicely) Should I protect my referee? this honest linesman thought . . and thought . . and thought . - it was only when I saw the stupid prat wheel around and put my brother on the floor that I decided I ought to help. Super linesman to the rescue (ho bloody ho).

When I reached the scene there was a lot of shouting and a lot of swearing but no one was particularly interested in quietening this youth down - I think if you had said hello to him it would have got you decked. I had just realised that our Chris had gone down with nothing more than a shove, when this youth turned round, took one look at me, called me a cheat and grabbed me by the ears!!! Jesus wept it hurt. At one point I thought he was going to rip me lugs away from the side of my head. Fortunately I had the presence of mind not to bring my knee into his groin - he would have ripped me apart if I had. No, like the true hero I am I wrenched his hands away and called him names from a very safe distance indeed.

Eventually he was sent off. the game was ruined, Saltergate ran out 4-2 winners, but no one was interested. The rest of the Middle Pocket lads were ok, a nice bunch who seemed genuinely sorry; apart from the centre forward the game was very sportingly played.

As for the centre forward; well I hope he gets banned for life - idiots like that don't deserve to be on a football pitch; they don't deserve to be anywhere; mind you I can think of a few places for him. The youth is nothing but a nuisance, if only he knew what a complete plonker he made of himself.

Foot note, Dave Radfords ears are currently recovering in the Royal Hospitals ear,nose, and throat ward. - Dave Radford is recovering from shock, and his mother is still trying desperately to get the brown out of his underpants.

Issue 20: March, '90

Hearts were three up before United took the game seriously, fosaking the poncey stuff and pulling two goals back to set up a rousing finish that had the crowd on the edges of their seats and the blokes in the cinema seats on their feet, exhorting the ref to "BLOW YA F***IN' WHISTLE, YA F***IN' F***AH!!!" Other Hearts fans were more restrained, none more so than the two who were dressed in club shirts and wooly scarves, watching the game from an overlooking tenement window! If Hearts ever play badly, I wonder if they sit in their front room and say "I'm not going to watch them this week"?

On the whole, then, a fun time, and Ken was quite cheerful, despite the result. As soon as the fixtures come out for next season I shall look to see who Hearts are playing on third round FA Cup day and plan another trip. My second visit to Edinburgh was far more pleasant than my first - three weeks in the city ten years ago, working on the Fringe Festival with the place full of posers and 'Darling luvvie' actors, and no money to spend on beer! Scotland is, on the whole, a far more civilised place than England - witness the fact that a grown man stood on Edinburgh station in an Albion Rovers bobble hat and scarf, completely unmolested. It couldn't happen at Euston.

Stuart.

Issue 19: Feb. '90

Issue 1: Jan. '88

FRUSTRATED by poor referees?

Would YOU have sent off Reuben Agboola?

Now "CS" offers you, the fan, the chance to have your say with our super cut-out and paste referee's whistle! Simply cut along the solid lines, fold along the broken ones and cut out the hatched areas. Screw up the bits you cut out to form the pea and put this inside before glueing up, and you too will have a whistle that is every bit as effective as Mr. Robinson's!

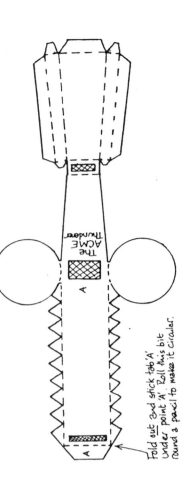

The ACME Thunderer

Fold out and stick tab 'A' under point 'A'. Roll this bit round a pencil to make it circular.

GORGIE BEST

"Where shall we go on Fourth Round day?" was the question on everyone's lips as we sat around the luncheon table at our stopping-off point on the way to Colchester. Several pints later Ken suggested Edinburgh; "Yesh, hic, alright then!" came our beery reply.

Ken has always been something of a Dundee United fan: he writes for their programme and is a good mate of Pete Rundo, CS's sole agent for the east coast of Scotland and United's programme editor. Whenever 'own aren't playing he usually goes up to Haggisland to see them and usually tries to drag a few of us with him. Having been taken along for my first Scottish game I would recommend the experience to anyone.

Here's how to do it. Depending on your destination you start either from Manchester Piccadilly for the west coast or from Doncaster for the East. From Donny you can get an 'Edinburgh Shopper' ticket for £21.50 which delighted us, as we were expecting to have to pay about thirteen quid more. The 9.20 from Donny gets you in at about 12.30, giving you plenty of time to practise how to say "Three pints of heavy and a britvic orange' in Scottish before trying it out on the bar staff of Edinburgh. Get out at Waverley for lunch; hop on a train to Haymarket at about two and it is only a fifteen minute walk down the road to Tynecastle, home of the Heart of Midlothian Football Club.

I haven't told Ken yet, but I've had a soft spot for Hearts since I was (all too briefly) sexually acquainted with a woman from that part of the city who was herself and avid Tart, of the Jam variety.

For some reason, the intimidatory, confrontational atmosphere that often plagues big games in England is no longer present in Scotland. This manifests itself in the large number of people, men, women and children, that you see sporting their team's colours.

Terrace songs are generally restricted to chants of support for your own team, little ditties like 'You're gonna get your effin' 'Ead kicked in', having long slipped out of the Scottish hit parade. The people I spoke to were friendly and continued to speak to me long after they found out that I was English. We were not fed on a diet of reprocessed sheep brains: the pies had meat in them but, for every ounce of meat, they contained a similar amount of pepper.

Inside the ground I was intrigued to see that a small section of the stand was filled with old tip-up cinema seats. "Probably for some executives or other," suggested my Scottish host. As the teams came out the dozen or so "executives" took their places, stamping their feet in time to Hearts' crappy club song: they were, to a man, completely pissed out of their minds! Membership of this exclusive, well-seated club must be restricted to the most outrageously foul-mouthed, drunken people amongst Hearts' support, for they spent the whole game abusing either Dundee United players ("GET OFF THE PITCH, YA DIRTY F***AHS!!!") or their more moderate fellows in the stand ("COME ON, SING, YA MISERABLE F***AHS!!!") or the ref (NO WAY WAS THAT A PENALTY, YA F***IN' USELESS F***AH!!!), providing nothing but amusement for the more sober-minded people around me. After the final whistle they left chanting "WE WANNA BEVVY!!!" I should be surprised if anything stopped them: it obviously hadn't up to then!

United were content to start with a 'look at us, we're so good' performance. As the eager Hearts went at United's casual defence they were a goal up in minutes, and what a goal! it was a goal that every Englishman dreams of seeing a Scottish goalie concede: the ball is whacked in from the wing, the keeper comes to the near post and chests it in to his own net! Classic 'Saint & Greavsie' stuff! Hearts have some great players, none more so than the winger Colquhoun (I've probably spelt it wrongly) for whom Everton would probably pay two million which, on reflection, isn't much of a compliment.

BRYN GUNN- A JEWEL IN THE CROWN.

The Bryn Gunn Story- for there is one- is really quite remarkable. A 21 year old European Cup winner becomes a 27 year old bricklayer drifting out of the game; it's not the sort of riches to rags story which makes the tabloids but it's incredible enough for any of us brought up on the notion that to be a first division footballer is more or less to have the world at your feet.

The story begins with our hero a budding goalkeeper(!) being tried out at Forest at the age of 12-not for the first team I hasten to add-"... but I was too small; I was getting lobbed from three yards." Somewhat by chance he signed for the then second division outfit three years later and six months or so before the arrival of one Brian Clough. "I was playing in a youth team that was winning 10-0 every week and I was just standing there in goal getting cold. So I asked to come out for a change and after a couple of games I was noticed by a Notts Forest scout who happened to turn up one sunday morning." The answer to the mysterious question of how he got to sink so low in 1986 is probably to be found in Bryn's recounting of his origins into the professional game. "I was very lucky," he says, "within a year I'd had a bad game that morning. There is such a thing as modesty but...I used to think there were far better players than me in my hometown. I just got a good break. "At this I was sitting there stunned. Is he saying that professional judges with years and years of experience in the game picked him by mistake? That he was the only young defender they could find at the time. To listen to Bryn you'd think he only got to play 11 first team games at 17 and 120 in division 1 later on because of a case of mistaken identity!

The picture further develops as he assesses his failure to nail down a regular place in Clough's first team:"At the end of the day I couldn't have been good enough to be in the first team or I would have been. I was a good stop gap. I could come in and 'do a job' but..I wasn't tall enough; he likes big boys who can head it." Now this is quite commendably frank and who knows, maybe an accurate analysis of the situation in retrospect but the way Gunn tells it you wonder if would rate himself highly enough to have played 37 league games in the big league in '81-2 season, and 33 in the one following. I can offer you and Bryn an alternative view"..he should have played more at Forest." P.Hart.

By the end of our Championship season, 1984-5 he'd finally decided he'd had enough of plugging holes like a lump of Polycell and decided to get away at last. There were three loan deals that season and the first was the one which seemed to mark a watershed in his career. He went to Shrewsbury, then in division 2, played 9 games there and 'loved it. I played well, they were a good set of lads and the crowd seemed to take to me.' He very much wanted to sign the contract that the Shrews were offering him but the £60 000 asking fee demanded by Clough was beyond Gay Meadow's resources so no deal. He then went on to Walsall for a brief spell of 6 games where his form was patch and up to Mansfield Town."I hated it."-for five. Of both these latter two loan spells he says "I had no enthusiasm for it at all. I wasn't bothered-which is wrong. I know. I suppose I was still flat from not signing for Shrewsbury."At the end of the season Clough put Bryn up for grabs-for free! He was "absolutely gutted", not because the great enigma hadn't rated him worth a fee but because the same 'valuation' a few months earlier would have seen him playing second division football and there is little doubt that he would have been a contented man on it. From there, things then got even worse.

"There's a pink form that goes round to all the clubs in the league telling them that a player's available on a free," This is a scheme organised by the PFA to help the glut of professionals on the market every June find a new job. The PFA rep at Forest didn't seem to have things organised and Gunn's pink form didn't do the rounds. Consequently no-one knew he was available and no-one came in for him."I was working as a bricklayer two weeks before the season started. Then one of my mates wrote to Peterborough and told them I was available and they rang me up, asked me to go along for a trial and I said, 'Yeah'. "Why didn't he write to league clubs, put himself about a bit?" "It's just not in me to do it. It's not pride, but....,no answer. It is quite astonishing that a footballer as talented as this could be prepared to just let himself drift out of the game. You could argue that he didn't have enough push, enough determination, character, and you might be right. An alternative analysis centres around his apparent refusal to believe in his footballing talent; a quality in abundance and obvious to all but the most dim. Perhaps he simply lacked the self-confidence to actually consider the fact that there may well have been at least several managers in the game

who would have snapped him up, as Peterborough did, in minutes had they known that Forest were letting him loose for nowt. He admits to being "too laid back" and "too easy going." In retrospect he says he should have left Forest much sooner-he was there eleven years-but the wages were good, my wife came from there and every time I thought about going I'd come in for a few games, get a sniff of it." His apparently natural tendency to chronically underrate himself then, nearly caused him to be lost to the game and to Chesterfield, would Paul Hart have found anyone as good and as cheap and as versatile at the end of the season if there'd been no Bryn Gunn on the market?

He spent 3 seasons at his new club, one which is "geared for higher things" according to Gunn, but in his time not able to climb out of the fourth. His manager, Noel Cantwell was practically invisible while Mick Jones, assistant to the ex-Manchester United Cup Final captain(1963) turned manager after Gunn's first season "worked his balls off for the club" whilst going un-loved and ill-regarded by the fans. So would he have been happy to have plodded along in division 4 for season after season unless the Posh had been able to get their act together? "If there's nothing else you've got to do it." In three years he played 131 league games-he was ever-present for two of them-and in that time became the excellent penalty taker we all know and love. So how did that come about? "In my first season there I was brought down in a game in the box and when I got up to throw it to someone they were all standing on the line. They might as well have been standing on the half-way line 'cause none of them were going to take it,"and that's how it started. I'd never thought about it before, "In his first and third seasons at London Road he notched seven goals, practically all pens, and though the yearbooks give him 0 for the middle one, he swears it's wrong and that he put away "about 5" until he missed just one and gave the job to Mick Gooding until he signed for Wolves at the beginning of last season.

And so to the art of notching from the spot."I always used to put it to the goal-keeper's left but this season I've swapped sides a lot. It all depends on how you feel at the time."Is it essential to make your mind up where you're going to put it before you step up as I'd heard from various sources over the years? "Yeah. Against Southend-it's no excuse-but it was really windy, and I've gone to place it and then I've thought 'Oh, shit. I'll smash it' at the last second. It was a bad one and I changed my mind and that's what did me." You're very cool about them, I said and he agreed. "There was just one where I did feel it and that was against Halifax. It was a good one but I was like this." Bryn pats his chest rapidly with his hand."For some reason I'd got it into my head that I wasn't sure where I was going to put it. It was the only one though."

From Peterborough to Chesterfield then at the start of this season. This, obviously, was directly Paul Hart's doing. Rumour has it that the gaffer was after B.G. last season but Posh would have wanted Dosh at a time when we didn't have any. Come last summer and the sale of Darren Wood to Reading, Hart swooped-'I knew exactly who I wanted' Hart has said of the signing, 'to fill the right back berth.' "I played left back mainly at Peterborough. In fact I hadn't played there for three years but he said, 'Can you do the job?' and you're not going to say 'No'." Gunn says it's "More relaxed here. There's discipline but it's more relaxed which helps a bit." At his first two clubs there was a tendency for players to view the managers in the same way as schoolkids view Headmasters, with fear and a 'lookout! Hide he's coming!' At Saltergate the management team involve themselves more personally and is appreciated. The atmosphere according to Gunn is exceptionally harmonious; "Much better than at a lot of clubs."

Paul Hart recently described Bryn Gunn's switch from right back to centre back as the main turning point of the season so far. He fitted in there "Like Beckenbaur," he said after the Gillingham game. He's also described Gunn as 'an absolute gem'. And yet Bryn is surprised that he kept the centre back spot, his favourite position by the way, when Tony Brien came back into the side after suspension. Typical of the man, it's not modesty. It's a man who doesn't seem to realise his worth. Surely it's this which explains why his talents were left to gather dust on the top shelf at the back of the shop before Hart came along to polish up this jewel in our crown.

(CT)

POLICE RELEASE ME...

What aspect of football is probably the most controversial? that's right - the police. They turn up at Saltergate, get in for nothing, walk round a bit, wait until the depressed away fans go home and then go and have a cup of tea, don't they? Well, no, not really. How do I know? Make yourselves comfortable and read on.

When we played Donny on New Year's Day I stood on the Pop Side and the bloke behind me came out with a load of racist abuse aimed at their black players. This, together with what Calvin and Bruno had to endure at Hartlepool got me thinking, 'What can we, as fans, do to stop it?'

I contacted the police to find out about their policy on the subject and an officer called at my house to arrange a meeting between myself and Inspector Burrows, the officer in charge of policing at football matches. One week later we met in an interview room at the Chesterfield police station.

Insp. Burrows detests racism and would like to see it stopped but, strictly as far as the law is concerned, there appears to be little that can be done. At present the law caters only for inciting racial hatred and a prosecution brought for shouting 'You black bastard' could easily be defended, as some incitement of racial hatred has to be proved. Taylor, of course, has called for a new offence of using racial abuse to hit the statute books but we'll have to wait for Parliament to get their act together on that one.

Hold hard, though. As soon as you set foot inside a football ground you become subject to the ground regulations set down by clubs, which give clubs and the police extra powers. Often inconsistently drawn up and applied across the country, these give the police and stewards the right to chuck you out for anything from invading the pitch to using cameras or radios. There is plenty of scope here for nobbling the racists under exisiting regulations, simply by adding 'racial abuse' to the list of proscribed offences under the ground regulations.

From here, the discussion broadened. I was interested about the police's policy regarding swearing: I sometimes indulge in this myself, usually aiming it at the ref, especially when he gives penalties to Gillingham. I might also save a few choice words for someone like Steve Lovell, when he misses said penalty. Well, effing and blinding are out. Fair enough, you might say something like 'Bloody 'Ell, Ref, that wasn't a throw', but expect to be warned to watch your lip. Similarly, players are not allowed to do it, but it seems that the heat and passion of a particular situation will be taken into account. Before each game the Inspector will have a chat with the ref about players' conduct. If a player stands in the middle and bellows out a string of obscenities he will most likely be cautioned but if, say, Jamie was to use a more vigourous version of "Ouch!" when hitting the adverts on the bounce after a Scarborough tackle, allowance might be made for the unusual circumstances.

I asked about the five or so Lincoln fans that were involved in a fight on the Kop last year. I said that it seems frustrating to decent fans that troublemakers are only usually taken round to the Cross Street end and allowed to continue watching the game. I was assured that anyone causing a fight in the ground will be arrested as, it seems, some Lincoln fans were. If an away fan is found on the Kop he will usually be ejected but fans who realise that they're in the wrong end and and approach a policeman will usually be escorted to the other end. Anyone ejected who then attemted to get back in elsewhere will be arrested. Police are stationed at the turnstiles to stop away fans getting onto the Kop but this policy is rendered difficult to enforce as few away fans are ever so obliging as to wear their team's colours while doing so.

A Burnley fan was attacked in West Street after our game last year. Do the police have a policy about keeping away fans in? It depends, quite sensibly, on their numbers. If there's a lot they may be kept in, but for as short a time as possible. Cross Street is usually closed for a while after the final whistle; coaches park right outside the exits and away fans' cars can be parked inside the school opposite the exits, so there is usually little need to deprive anyone of their liberty at the end of the game.

There is hardly any trouble at Town's home games, although as the team has been successful and attendances have picked up, the police have noticed known troublemakers returning. It seems that most of the trouble is caused by drink, although the officers on the gates will deny entry to anyone who is obviously the worse for a lunchtime session.

Apart from a fortnightly trip to Saltergate Inspector Burrows has to deal with safety committees and speaks almost daily to Bob Pepper, the Club Secretary. Before seeing me he had been on the phone to Burnley, to liase with their police about the number of Town fans that they should expect to receive the next day. Again, our success has brought more travelling idiots out from under the compost heap; eight were arrested at Halifax, all for drunkenness. On the other hand, I was interested to find out from 'The Peterborough Effect' of how well-behaved our fans were, there.

If you are nicked the police automatically apply for an exclusion order as part of your bail, with details and photographs being forwarded to Town's forthcoming opponents: this has led to at least one Town 'fan' being arrested at an away match. The system works, and without I.D. cards!

We spoke about an incident that will have upset every true Town fan, the vicious attack on Hugh Craven, the Maidstone fan. The police are looking for a lad of about 18 or19 years of age, with short ginger hair, possibly shaved at the sides, with an earring in his left ear. Not a lot to go on, but if you know who did it then TELL THE POLICE.

If we are going to rid football of hooligans and racists then responsible fans and the police must work together. YOU could be beaten up because a hooligan is free to roam about so, if you know of anyone going to a match to cause trouble, let the police know. Likewise, if you are troubled by racism and obscene language approach a police officer and politely let him or her know of your feelings, so that they can sort it out when it happens again.

We finished with a brief chat about the Taylor report. Inspector Burrows feels that the recommendations about swearing and racism will make his job easier. The all-seater proposal will cut our capacity by 10% per season for the next ten years: it seems that the only way that the Government will see sense on this is if their is another Hillsborough in somebody's main stand. That is not on.

Reflecting on my hour with the Inspector I wished I'd asked more about matchday arrangements, and so on: I was left with the feeling of being lucky to have someone in charge who does it in such a low-key manner. He was pleased to answer my questions and suggested that anyone who wanted to know more could put questions through the Support-ers' Club, a representative of which he sees at most matches.

Ironically, Inspector Burrows moves on at the end of the season. His last match will be our last in the Fourth and he is already showing the ropes to his replacement: I hope his successor has his ideas, attitude and approach.

BILLY WHEATCROFT.

The Yorkshire Ghost

Unlike some of the Crooked Spireite's other contributors, I'm not being very successful in my attempt to join the '92 Club'. If there were a '46 Club' I'd just about qualify for membership: on the other hand, I have managed to visit a couple of ex-League grounds, or rather pieces of land where once Third Division football was played. I came across New Brighton's Tower Ground in the early 'eighties just before it became a housing estate, and trekked along to Accrington's Peel Park last year (as described in CS 14). This summer, a sunny Saturday trip into Yorkshire brought up an unmissable opportunity to chalk up another visit to a piece of Northern football history and so, after checking inside Simon Inglis's "Football Grounds of England and Wales", the travelling fan's Bible, I turned the family car in the direction of Bradford in order to seek out the district of Little Horton, wherein lies the former home of Bradford Park Avenue.

Anyone who has driven through West Yorkshire will know that helpful road signs are not abundant in the old wollen towns. It was only after a long detour around the city's south-western suburbs that the first signs of former football life appeared. Travelling downhill back towards the city centre we found on our left a long black wall with barbed wire atop, and an old painted message: "Private car park. Home directors only. Driving round the block, however, all I could see was an ugly corrugated red building, like a mini B&Q, a patch of overgrown waste ground and the odd glimpse of what looked like derelict terracing. Upon closer inspection, through a crack in the wall, I saw that a cricket match was taking place and all the decaying terraces seemed to face the square. Worryingly, I came across a new supermarket behind the top wall: had Park Avenue come to this?

Entering through the one working gate, to the left was the cricket ground with the fenced-off banking at the far side, the supermarket beyond and, to the right, the nasty red construction. Still seeing nothing that resembled a football ground I approached a bloke in a deck chair and asked if he knew where the ground had stood. For a moment I thought he meant that the bloody thing had actually been put up on the pitch: I was right. I was lucky to have come across this bloke. He was very friendly and informative and turned out to be an old fan of the Avenue. Having seen his favourite football team disappear he was left to watch second-class cricket on a pitch abandoned by the Yorkshire County Cricket Club. The pavilion has gone and half the banking left to rot: instead, Yorkshire have built an indoor cricket school, the hideous red building, leaving Bradford without first-class cricket and ensuring that the reconstituted Park Avenue FC will never play on the old club's pitch.

Ex-Avenue man Ron Greenwood surveys the work of the demolition men, 1980

I was glad to see him point away from the supermarket but puzzled when he indicated the red monstrosity. There's still some good terracing on both sides and if Yorkshire CCC have lost interest, then there is no reason why the place should not be turned into a pretty good non-League ground. It seems strange for a team named Bradford Park Avenue to be playing somewhere else. I saw the Avenue play only once, at Saltergate, where they lost 4-0 in a game remembered by the man in the deck chair as Bradford's penultimate League game. For his sake, and for the other residents of the area who have lost first-class football and cricket, I hope the Avenue can come home soon to bring the cheering back to Little Horton. And for God's sake let's hope our beloved Saltergate never ends up in such a state.

My informant told me that he'd seen crowds of over 30,000 at the ground, when the stadium had its own railway halt and a much higher capacity than Bradford City's ground. He reckoned Park Avenue to be the better of the two and, having visited Valley Parade in 1975, two years after the Avenue left their stadium, I can well believe it. Now, of course, V.P. is greatly improved, with a new stand and Kop, but the state of what remains of Park Avenue has to be seen to be believed. Beyond the cricket school, that patch of waste ground earlier mentioned turned out to be the stadium. Unlike Accrington, where the sadness at the team's demise has long since passed and the old ground is a neat school playing field, Park Avenue is a tragic

---

PARK AVENUE NEEDS YOUR SUPPORT

To present and past supporters, we appeal to you and your friends — Help to keep Park Avenue alive.

We may not be the best but our team have given 100% effort in the last two games. With your support and encouragement the present form could be maintained.

HELP PARK AVENUE

---

sight. The remaining half of the pitch is knee-deep in grass, the slopes at both sides are unrecognisable as stands or terracing and, saddest of all, is the huge open Kop end. The solid perimeter wall still stands; the bases of crush barriers are still there, there's a pile of rubble where once there was a floodlight pylon but the terrace is gradually disappearing under nettles, thistles and other assorted shrubbery. When my small son Gregory followed me on to the banking and nettled his legs he became surely only the latest to stand on that end and shed tears. he was barely visible among the weeds which have obliterated both sides and will soon claim the end, too.

It is strange that Park Avenue should have followed another team with a distinctive name, Accrington Stanley, into oblivion. Bradford's demise is more chilling for fans of teams like our own because they were a club with solid support, a better-than-average ground and a history rooted in the First and Second Divisions. When they were relegated to Division 4 for the first time in 1963, their total of 40 points was at the time, the highest ever recorded by a club suffering relegation from the Third. Bradford City finished 91st. in the League that season. It's hard to get rid of the feeling that if Bradford could die, it could happen to almost any other club, just as easily. Fans of Halifax, six or seven miles away, must have nightmares every time they pass Park Avenue's ground - one end of The Shay already seems to be falling into the kind of decay that has befallen Bradford's Kop.

The revived Park Avenue FC don't play in the city at all, having found a temporary home at Bramley's rugby league ground in Leeds. Before my visit I thought that the team might one day use the old pitch, but that is no longer possible. However, the cricket ground, within the same walls is, whilst currently being left to die, still capable of being rescued.

Chris Hall.

RELATIVELY UNSUNG HEROES

Number Five – Ray McHale

Ray Mchale had a good start to his Saltergate career, being a member of the successful 1968-69 Northern Intermediate Cup-winning side; a team which included Alan Stevenson, Ken Tiler and Ernie Moss.

In those days Ray was a winger but in his league career he became known as a dominant midfield dynamo with a ferocious right foot shot. Despite his prominence in the juniors side he had to wait until September 1971 for his debut, away at Bournemouth. His first goal followed 3 days later after only 106 minutes of league football, the goal earning a 1-1 draw at Fellows Park.

His most impressive period for the team was probably in the 1973-4 season when his 8 goals and those he made for Ernie Moss almost had the Town pushing for promotion to the Second Division. Lack of quality in other areas prevented the climb, as we all know, however. The contributions which most stand out in the memory from that season are 2 pinpoint crosses for Ernie to head in against Watford in a 3-0 win and 2 winning goals in the space of 3 days at Christmas. The first was the only goal against a dismal Rochdale side, who won only 2 games all season, when Ray struck a hard and low free kick into the Cross Street goal, and the second was a piledriver at the Kop end against Bournemouth to clinch a 2-1 victory 3 days later. The sheer ferocity of that shot still lives in the memory.

Another McHale speciality was the penalty kick; in Ray's time with the Town he scored eleven and missed just once, against Colchester, when the howling gale at his back upset his poise and he ballooned the ball over the bar and into Newbold Road, if my warped memory serves me correctly. At the time this was a sad blow to me since Ray was a big favourite of mine and these failures hit naive young lads hard. In similar vein, his transfer from Saltergate was a bitter blow in September 1974 when he went to the perceived obscurity of Halifax Town along with Albert Phelan in a deal that saw another penalty king, Terry Shanahan, coming in the opposite direction. This deal was not one of manager Joe Shaw's master strokes since McHale went on to better things, becoming a big hero at the Shay and an even bigger one at Swindon. Whilst at the County Ground he even got to appear on telly against Spurs when his Spireite origins got a mention. This was fame indeed for an ex-Town player.

All this super-hero stuff soon diminished, however, when Ray started to go downhill with swift moves to Brighton, Barnsley, Sheffield United, Bury, Swansea, Rochdale and Scarborough. His goalscoring exploits at these places were almost non-existant. This story does, in fact, end unhappily since as a world weary Spireite of some 30 years old I saw Ray playing for Scarborough against Newport along with Ernie Moss. Ernie had a good game and was running about like a 16 year old. Sadly, Ray looked overweight, unenthusiastic and, quite frankly, crap. How easily are boyhood heroes made to become mere mortals.

Statistical Summary

Debut – v Bournemouth (a) 25.9.71 0-1
Last match – v Hereford United (a) 28.9.74 0-5
Total – 123(+1) games – 27 goals (League)
        18 games – 3 goals (FA and FL cups)

First goal – v Walsall (a) 28.9.71 1-1
Last goal – v Grimsby Town (h) 21.9.74 2-0

John Taylor

HARTLEPOOL UNITED: An apology.

In recent years we, in common with a number of other football fanzines, may have inadvertently given the impression that the Hartlepool United Football Club were a no-hope outfit, full of Darlo rejects and had, for the last seventy years, merely taken up a space in the League that might more productively be occupied by a progressive non-League club.

We may further, from time to time have indicated, by citing the example of his brother, that their Manager came from a family of loonies; that their Assistant Manager built a career on the strength of scoring only one decent goal on the Big Match, and that their supporters were so stupid as to be unable to tell the difference between a monkey and a Frenchman. We may also have alleged that the majority of their supporters only go to the Victoria Ground in the mistaken belief that someone has built a supermarket on it.

We now realise that Hartlepool United are, in fact, a skillful, well-balanced side, with many fine players who will surely, in the fullness of time, elevate their team to a place in the First Division. We also accept that Mr. Cyril Knowles is a master of football tactics and that their stadium, far from being a tip, has a warm, homely appeal much beloved of such architectural experts as Simon Inglis.

We would like to offer our heartfelt, profound apologies to Hartlepool United, their players, officials and fans, for any distress caused by our previous articles and express the hope that, by stuffing Tottenham in the next round of the cup, they can bring an end to the sickening cult of Gazzamania.

Issue 23: Sept. '90
(Hartlepool beat us twice in four days)

chapter 11

AN ALTERNATIVE LOOK AT
QUEENS PARK RANGERS F.C.

ISSUE 8

EXCLUSIVE!

WHY FRANCIS HAD TO GO...

SIXTY PAGES...................£1

Those people who make it their business to find out about such things say the average man thinks about sex every fifteen minutes during his waking hours, and as someone who could be described as fairly average (*"Dave"*, I often hear, *"that was really average..."*) I'm not about to argue.

The thing is, though, if I'm clocking up four erotic thoughts an hour, does this not disprove conclusively the accusation often levelled at me that I think of nothing in life other than Queens Park Rangers Football Club? Maybe it does, maybe it doesn't. One thing's for sure though, I wouldn't want to have to provide evidence come the day they make supporting QPR a criminal offence.

After all, the prosecution would have an open and shut case. Exhibit A would be the milometer from my trusty old banger showing a clock up of some 16000 miles between late August and early May, m'Lord - this despite a near-libellous comment about its roadworthiness from a certain Dave Wallace, who lives somewhere in Manchester and believes himself to be King of the Kippax, whatever or whoever they may be. Only the fact that I'm such an all-round good egg and he has a wife and children to support stops me sueing the ass off him (as they say) for defamation of charabanc.

Witnesses would testify to my uncanny ability to turn any conversation around to QPR, while others would swear that despite overwhelming evidence to the contrary, I have never in my life conceded that QPR are not really the finest football team the world has ever seen.

A succession of past employers would provide damning evidence that my periods of sickness over the years have been uncannily linked to the fixture list. Mind you, with a smart lawyer I could probably use that one in my defence. Watching QPR can do that to you.

But the prosecutions *coup de grace* would be my wife, Sue, extracting revenge for years of my spending our last measly few quid on midweek trips to Southampton or Luton, where victory would be guaranteed to lift us to fifteenth place in the table or defeat would confirm that for the 114th year in succession our name was not on the cup.

Her evidence against me, detailing the lonely Saturdays, the bad moods when QPR more often than not get beat, the excessive alcoholic celebrations when they win, the tantrums on the very occasional matches I can't get to for one reason or another, the huge phone bills when that quick call to John in Birmingham or Martin and Liz in Warrington to confirm next Saturday's arrangements turns into an hour and a half's inquest into last Saturday's defeat, the number of calls which always interrupt any programme she has settled down to watch and, most damning of all, the countless hours I spend locked away upstairs in the company of my equally trusty typewriter, as I put together, swear at and panic over the latest edition of *A KICK UP THE R's* - all this would have the jury baying for blood and the judge dishing out the kind of sentence which would make the one passed on Tony Adams look like a pat on the head and told there, there try not to do it again.

Mind you, what they wouldn't be able to show is this rather interesting tattoo on a certain part of my anatomy, which reads *QPR*, but every quarter of an hour actually says... *QPR*. Well, we're not all as well-blessed as others.

So you see appearances can be deceptive. It may look as if I spend all my time thinking about QPR, but in reality nothing could be further from the truth. The evidence would point conclusively to the charge, and yet the evidence would be wrong. I don't know quite how I would prove my innocence, however. I would have to give that one a lot more thought. But not right at this moment if you don't mind. You see, I've just noticed the time and I've got a much more interesting thought coming on....

DAVE THOMAS

RING, RING

QPR Clubcall Any Day W/C 28.11.89

Interview with Don Howe, Subject: The Bleedin' Obvious

CLUBCALL: Welcome .... to Queens Park Rangers Clubcall .... with all the
news from your favourite Club ....
12p   Well .... what a week it's turning out to be at the Club.
There's so much happening, I hardly know what day it is ....
But never fear .... because here at QPR Clubcall we promise to
24p   keep you right up to date with all the latest news from your
favourite Club ....
Later on we'll be talking to Don Howe about his new role in the
36p   Club .... or is it? .... All will be revealed in just a few
moments .... here on Queens Park Rangers Clubcall .... But first
here's the fifth part of our interview with Tony Roberts ....
48p   and listen out for the new heckler of the Reserve team in the
background .... Yes it's Robbie Herrerra .... What a guy ....

£1.20p later

180p   Well what a great bunch of lads .... and they say there's a
problem with morale in the Club .... What a load of nonsense ....
and now before that interview we promised with Don Howe, we
thought you'd like to hear what the players have for breakfast on
192p   match days ....

£0.60p later

252p   And now here's that interview we promised with Don Howe ....
First we asked Don how he sees his new role in the Club in the
264p   light of the departure of Trevor Francis.

DON HOWE: Well you know it's a funny thing is football. Trevor Francis has
gone sure, but Queens Park Rangers Football Club carries on,
276p   Trevor Francis or no Trevor Francis. That's the great thing
about football. We've got a match on Saturday when Queens Park
288p   Rangers Football Club will be playing against Crystal Palace
Football Club and that's what I'm interested in between now and
300p   3 o'clock on Saturday when the match kicks off.

CLUBCALL: But Don, how do you see your role now?

DON HOWE: Well let me put it like this. I'm the coach of Queens Park
312p   Rangers Football Club. I was the coach of Queens Park Rangers
yesterday and I expect I'll be the coach of Queens Park Rangers
324p   Football Club tomorrow.

CLUBCALL: But Don, do you see your role changing at all?

DON HOWE: Well, I'm still the coach, but now I expect I'll have to pick
the team as well.
336p
CLUBCALL: I suppose what the Club needs now is a period of stability?

DON HOWE: Well yes, that's right. Of course stability is important but
348p   the most important thing at the present time for Queens Park
Rangers Football Club is the next game against Crystal Palace on
Saturday afternoon.

CLUBCALL: Does your football philosophy differ from Trevor's in any way?
360p
DON HOWE: The game of football is bigger than any individual's philosophy
in my opinion. Football is about getting possession of the
ball, scoring goals and stopping the opposition from scoring
372p   goals against you. I believe firmly that if you can score one
more goal than you concede, you'll win football games. I just
like to take each game as it comes and try to instill in my
384p   players that football is a game of two halves and that the game
is never over until the final whistle goes.
396p
CLUBCALL: Our thanks to Don Howe for that revealing insight into the
happenings at QPR this week .... Coming up on Queens Park Rangers
408p   Clubcall later this week, we'll be talking to Simon Barker about
his new role as a ball winner .... We'll be finding out what the
420p   first team have for lunch on Wednesdays .... There will be parts
six and seven of our interview with Tony Roberts .... and a very
special interview with David Seaman who'll be talking us through
his tonsils operation.
432p

Keep calling on 0898 121162

QPR LISTS

"I say, I say, I say..." – 10 things you never hear at Rangers Stadium

1) "Rangers Stadium"
2) "It's always nice to welcome Clive Allen/Terry Fenwick back..."
3) "Ooh look, there's Michael Wale..."
4) "The programme's good today..."
5) " A KICK UP THE R's – new edition out today..."
6) "Get off the pitch Parker, you're useless..."
7) "Oh no, not the bloody television cameras again..."
8) "Well played Wimbledon..."
9) "It's a brilliant view from the Loft, isn't it..."
10) "If there's one team I don't mind losing to it's Chelsea..."

QPR LISTS

"Put that in 'store'!" – 10 QPR match report cliches

1. "Despite enjoying most of the play, Rangers were unfortunate to fall behind to..."
2. "McDonald was booked in the..."
3. "Rangers had never previously won at Old Trafford and that record never looked..."
4. "...but Parker's shot was well wide."
5. "A mix-up in the Rangers' defence led to..."
6. "Maddix's challenge looked a good yard outside the box, but referee Hackett..."
7. "As the Fourth Division side suddenly scented victory, Rangers' 1-0 first leg..."
8. "Wegerle's jinking run took him past several opponents, but he was dispossessed..."
9. "In a typical end of season game, QPR recorded only their second away win of..."
10. " Clarke was again caught offside..." (delete)

A KICK UP THE R's

Daily Wail

April 1st 1990. Printed in Manchester and therefore never, ever reports QPR matches.

The Daily Wail - because good fish and chip wrapping always shows

SHOCK HORROR
SOCCER THUGS
GANGS BOVVER
HOOLIGAN MOB
VIOLENT SCUM
TERROR SHAME

EXCLUSIVE by DAILY WAIL CORRESPONDENT IAN FLUENCE

The soccer world was reeling last night after dawn raids by police investigating soccer violence netted Britain's most wanted hooligan. 24 year old Matt Clark, self-styled leader of QPR's notorious "East Paddock 49ers", was arrested at his Clapham home and taken to Streatham police station for questioning, along with "several" members of his gang.

Undercover officers were yesterday celebrating the success of the operation - codenamed "Got any Cans or Bottles?" - as the full story of the gang's two years of terror emerged. A high-ranking source told the Daily Wail how the trouble often started miles from the ground, usually on the number 49 bus taking them to Shepherds Bush. He told how the gang:

*Failed to queue up in an orderly manner
*Often paid only as far as Battersea, but travelled the whole route instead
*Deliberately occupied the seats reserved for the old and disabled (continued page 2)

Behind bars: one of the gang members

(continued from page 1)

The reign of terror continued on the terraces of the Loftus Stadium, home of the gang's supported team, Queen's Park Ranger's. Our source told us: "The East Paddock 49ers conducted a two year sustained orgy of soccer violence." This included:

*Jostling other fans as they fought to get the best position on the terrace
*Pushing youngsters and older people out of their path
*Treading on people's toes - deliberately the police now believe

The gang also indulged in singing, chanting and clapping and could often be heard subjecting linesmen to torrents of abuse as they:

*Disputed offside decisions
*Questioned his eyesight
*Shouted for a Rangers' throw-in, despite knowing full well that the ball had come off a Rangers' player

Terror at the sea-side: Fans flee in panic as the East Paddock 49ers go on the rampage at last season's Wolves v QPR match.

But it was at away games that the gang caused most bovver. Our source told us: "Each away game was planned with military precision. They would always travel by rail, posing as ordinary passengers but once they were on the train they would:

*Use the toilet only when the train was stationary in the platform
*Put their feet up on the seats when the guard wasn't looking
*Annoy other passengers by playing personal stereos at full volume

They would often meet up with the "opposition" to confront each other, with only the police standing between them and a full scale riot. We managed to infiltrate the gang and discovered that they took photographs of their victims, kept a scrapbook of their "action" and even had their own calling cards which said: 'Congratulations on your new baby girl', only the last four words had been crossed out and replaced with the words 'meeting the famous East Paddock 49ers'. The card would be left behind them when they got off the train."

It is now believed that the gang's capture will lead to the Government abandoning their controversial I.D. Card scheme, a measure originally initiated by the demands of millions of law-abiding football fans who were being prevented from attending football matches due to "the unacceptable level of violence".

Clark was in hiding last night after being released on bail. A police spokesman said that charges were unlikely to be brought.

STRING THE BASTARDS UP! says the Daily Wail - see comment on page 17

A KICK UP THE R's

EJECTED, REJECTED AND DEJECTED

* It is vital that police discipline and self-control be of the highest standard and that friendly relations with supporters are cultivated. I know that this is achieved at some grounds but there are reports that, at some grounds, some police treat supporters, especially away supporters, with a measure of contempt. When this happens it unfortunately sours the attitude of the supporters towards all police" - Lord Justice Taylor, Hillsborough Report.

" Some police officers unfortunately use Saturday as the day they are let off the leash" - John Stalker, Former Deputy Chief Constable of Greater Manchester.

The problem with printing anything which is critical of the policing of football matches is that it can imply an anti-police attitude. It is worth stating, therefore, that A KICK UP THE R'S recognizes the important role that the police play in ensuring the safety and comfort of the vast majority of law-abiding citizens who attend football matches. At the same time we endorse the Club's aims to "promote sportsmanship" and a "family atmosphere" with our "co-operation and traditional support" by enforcing the ground rules with regard to violence, swearing, indecent gestures and dangerous pushing. However, it would be wrong not to respond to the increasing number of complaints we have been receiving with regard to the policing of the Loftus Road members terrace ie the Loft and, in the interests of balanced journalism, invite both Superintendent Johnson of Shepherds Bush Police and Fred Luff, Head of Safety, Security and Supporters Liaison to respond to the criticisms levelled not only by Simon Thomas in this article but by QPR supporters in general.

Writing in critical fashion about a beloved football club, with which one has enjoyed and suffered an extreme love affair for fourteen years, is a tearful business. However, following the events of Monday 26th February when, during the F.A. Cup 5th Round 2nd Replay v Blackpool, Shepherds Bush police officers stormed the home terrace and removed at whim a number of R's supporters, myself included, speaking out becomes a duty commensurate with resentment towards unsympathetic, authoritarian and ignorant policing of standing spectators at football matches. In case of doubt, I should point out unambiguously that I abhor hooliganism and violence in football grounds and, in unity with most of us, loudly applaud its diminishing incidence amongst crowds. I have been watching Rangers since 1976 (when I was eight) home and away, have held a season ticket and supporters club membership and in that time have been involved in no violent disturbances of any kind. On the evening in question, I noticed a gentleman to my immediate left being harassed by one of the infiltrating officers. I had been standing in close proximity to this gentleman for much of the game and at no time had I observed him indulging in violent or dangerous behaviour liable to warrant ejection. Neighbouring supporters may recall the loud chorus of hissing and booing that accompanied this gentleman's forcible arrest as the officer ignored his repeated protestations of innocence. When I immediately objected to another officer in loud, though non-abusive tones on his behalf, I was astonished and outraged to discover this officer suddenly grasping my arm and dragging me towards the back of the terrace. When I demanded an explanation, I received the ignorant reply: "Ground rules." I reminded him that the principal ground rules at Q.P.R. encompassed prohibitions on violent pushing, obscene gesturing and swearing and I had contravened none of these regulations. I was then informed that it was owing to my being "over-excited". This latter comment evoked the image of a judge dismissing the defence counsel for remonstrating too vigorously with the jury on behalf of his client. I was subsequently marched around to the police shed and received the hospitable treatment for which our force is so renowned. Moments later, the other, victimised gentleman was dragged in surrounded by about ten officers, the perceptive reader might regard this show of strength a touch excessive to restrain a single individual. I have recently learned that he is to appear in court on an obstruction charge in three weeks. (This basically means that if the police don't like your face, arrest you for a made-up reason and you understandably resist arrest, they can charge you merely with the fact of your resistance). At such times, justice clearly goes on holiday.

Shaking with rage as I heard Kenny Sansom's goal greeted with roars of approval to put us 2-0 up from my position on the South Africa Road pavement, I marched round to the Directors entrance to see Fred Luff, Head of Security. This man's complacency makes me think there is a position awaiting him as Chancellor of the Exchequer. In brief, he washed his hands of the entire incident with the cynical indifference of a latter-day Pontius Pilate. I, meanwhile, was now feeling like a young Jesus Christ heaving his cross up to Calgary as I trudged around to Shepherds Bush Police Station with a hurricane blowing my face in and the heavy heart of one who realizes with personal justification that the police really are allowed to abuse their powers these days and get away with it. Interestingly, Inspector Goodwin's remarks at his nick made a striking contrast with Luff's earlier comments: his constabulary enjoyed "very close liaisons" with the security/stewarding personnel at Q.P.R. Mr Luff, I concluded, was a "jobsworth" or Inspector Goodwin was being economical with the truth. Possibly both, I don't know. Having my experiences published in the club programme would be like the Daily Express printing the Communist Manifesto. Nevertheless, I have circulated a lengthy letter among the club directors and am taking the matter through the Police Complaints Authority.

We must stand up and be counted. Solidarity is the only weapon we have against such virulent minority dictatorship on the terraces. So next time you notice a fellow supporter being unduly hassled, do what I did and get the officer's number and register a complaint against him. Write to the club and the supporters' fanzines. Make a fuss. Sing up and sing strong.

* I have subsequently discovered that, contrary to my earlier fears, the police will not be transferring my personal details to the club and so my club membership will not be jeopardised. This begs the most serious question :- if "miscreants" supposed offences are not considered serious enough to warrant communication to the club by the constabulary, why are they thought serious enough to warrant ejection at all?

SIMON THOMAS

A KICK UP THE R's

ITALIA '90 ....FROM THE BAR STOOL

THE HEROES — ROGER MILLA AND THE INDOMINATABLE LIONS OF CAMEROON PERFORMED THE 'YAOUNDE BUTTOCK-BOUNCE' AFTER EACH GOAL!

BLIMEY AN ARSENAL PLAYER — DAVID O'LEARY'S PENALTY DECIDER AGAINST RUMANIA WAS JOYFUL ALTHOUGH JACK CHARLTON WAS MORE INTERESTED IN FISHING....

SCHILLACI - TOPSCORER AND NON-PERMED ITALIAN.....

GOD SAVE ETC. — GASCOIGNE WAS SUPERB, HIS CHAMELEON TONGUE ANTICS AMUSED, WHILST SOME F.A. OFFICIALS PREFER TO USE THEIRS AS A WAY OF FURTHERING A CAREER

THE MIGHTY **PAUL PARKER** 'YOU KNOW THE REST...' — NOT FOR SALE

THE VILLAINS — CARLOS VALDERRAMA CAME BACK FROM THE DEAD VERSUS W. GERMANY....OR DID COLOMBIA JUST SEND SHIRLEY BASSEY ON AS A SUB?

YES HIM! SUCH TALENT CANCELLED OUT BY EVERY CON IN THE BOOK! — FRANK 'THE FLOBBER' RIJKAARD MADE SURE THAT RUDI VOELLER BECAME THE LATEST MEMBER OF THE GREEN PARTY

JURGEN KLINSMANN SPENT MORE TIME IN THE AIR THAN A LONDON TO SYDNEY JUMBO AND PRODUCED MORE ROLLS THAN THE ENTIRE MILAN BAKERIES!

THE MUSIC — NEW ORDER'S 'WORLD IN MOTION' WAS THE TRENDIEST WORLD CUP SONG, GOING HIGHER IN THE GERMAN CHARTS THAN THEIR OWN SONG, ALTHOUGH THE JOHN BARNES RAP WAS FULL OF CRAP. CATCH ME IF YOU CAN 'COS I'M AN ENGLAND MAN. ALRIGHT THEN JOHN!

THE *§☺*--ERS — MR. SELF-IMPORTANCE WAFFLED HIS USUAL DRIVEL.... WELL I THINK THAT THE TEAM WITH THE MOST SOCKS PULLED UP AT THE END OF EXTRA TIME SHOULD WIN

AND HIM...! SCREECH! GIGGLE! LIVERPOOL PLAYERS SQUEEK! HEE! HEE! INANE BANTER! SPORTING TRIANGLES. PISS OFF EMLYN

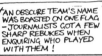

THE FLAG — BOLLOCKS. AN OBSCURE TEAM'S NAME WAS BOASTED ON ONE FLAG – JOURNALISTS GOT A FEW SHARP REBUKES WHEN ENQUIRING WHO PLAYED WITH THEM!

THE FANS — 'BRAZILIAN FANS PROVIDED THE ITALIAN PRESS WITH AMPLE PHOTO OPPORTUNITIES WHILST THE SCOTS COULD ONLY REFLECT THEIR TEAM'S MIGHTY PERFORMANCES!'

THE WINNERS — MOST PEOPLE'S CHOICE WEST GERMANY, ALTHOUGH ENG-GER-LAND ENTERTAINED + THE FANS GOT US BACK INTO EUROPE. ROLL ON 1994 AND THE U.S.A. CHEERLEADER PRACTICE AT GENERAL SMUTS PUBLIC BAR TUESDAYS AT SEVEN.
© FLOOHÄST PRODUCTIONS 1990

Life With the R's #4
by Sledge Hammersmith

HEY BOSS, CAN I HAVE SOME TIME OFF?

WELL KNOWN BEATLE LOOK-A-LIKE MARTIN ALLEN ASKS FOR TIME OFF WITH HIS WIFE

THE MAESTRO SAYS... FINE

MRS. ALLEN GIVES BIRTH TO A £1508 BABY. TRIBUNAL TO DECIDE NAME.

AND A FINE IT WAS!

ANOTHER FINISHED DRAWING. GOING TO COVENTRY. PRODUCTION ©

TRICKLE POP

2 MILLION ON TRANSFERS & CLARKEY SCORES A BELTER...

CRUNCH SPLAT

ONE DEFEAT IN TEN GAMES. THE USUAL QUIET GAME VERSUS WIMBLEDONKEY & ITS TALK OF A CHAMPIONSHIP CHALLENGE TEAM FOR NEXT SEASON. HA HA HA HA

A KICK UP THE R's

A KICK UP THE R's

UNITED IN PIRACY

And so the Kingdom of Manu mourned, it fretted, it wept and blew its nose on the embarrassing checkered handkerchief its aunty had given it for Christmas. Its princess, 'Points-In-The-Bag' had been kidnapped and no-one knew how to get her back. At least this was the case until Manu's king decreed that the person who rescued his daughter would receive riches and trophies beyond their wildest dreams (the sort of dreams they had after watching a Jane Fonda workout video.) For it was this incentive that prompted one of the king's subjects, a pirate captain named Ferguson, to declare that he would round-up his crew and set-off in search of 'Points-In-The-Bag' without delay.

So, once the pirate ship 'United' had weighed anchor, Captain Ferguson hoisted the 'Quite Chuffed Thank-you Roger' and set sail with his Motley Crue. However, the United had not travelled far before Captain Ferguson realised that 'Motley Crue' were far too loud for his taste and he returned to port and took 'Curiosity Killed The Cat' instead.

Hours soon turned into days, days into weeks, weeks into months, and then, finally, Leslie Judd turned months into a Mothers Day card with the aid of some sticky back plastic. And after all this time the pirate ship United still had no 'Points-In-The-Bag'.

It was at this juncture that Captain Ferguson wondered whether the problem may lie with his crew and he soon concluded that he would have to put into port again and send his 'scouts' into the press-gang market to 'pick up' a replacement or two.

Once ashore the Captain's scouts found that the press-gang market had gone through the thatched roof whilst they had been away and that you now had to administer several blows to the head to get even the most mediocre of crew members.

Not having brought enough 'currency' with them (in other words they only had one baseball bat between them) the scouts decided that they would have to use their brains instead of their brawn. Thus, when they discovered a man called Webb in the Kingdom of Nottingham, instead of issuing their invitation of employment in the form of a well aimed blow to the back of the head they cunningly lured him into a trap with the aid of some carrots (for it was thought that he bore a remarkable resemblance to Bugs Bunny.) They then bundled him into a sack and whisked him away. The only sign that was left to indicate that they had ever been there being a large wad of money which lay next to the spot which Bugs Webb had last hopped onto.

Once his men had returned, Captain Ferguson gave the order to set-sail again and another opportunity to improve his crew soon drifted across his bows in the form of the merchant ship 'Norwich', just launched from Canary Wharf. Captain Ferguson knew that its captain, Phelan, was much respected and that he would be a great man to have aboard his own ship. He thus dispatched a small body of men to board the Norwich and 'acquire' his services. This they did, and Captain Ferguson immediately made Phelan his anchor man.

On being interviewed on Radio Two (no, not 'pirate-radio', this isn't Benny Hill) Phelan said that when he had come to a glamour ship like the United he had not expected his duties as an anchor man to include jumping overboard every night and binding himself to the nearest rock.

It was after his acquirement of Phelan that Captain Ferguson noticed that the ship's deck was becoming a little crowded. It became clear therefore that one of his crew would have to be thrown into the ship's hold, or to give it its technical name, the Central League.

'Hughes!'

'Yes sir?'

'Throw Blackmore into the hold and don't trip over anyone on the way. Oh yes, and before do give him fifty lashes, no, I'm in a really vindictive mood, give him twenty pictures of Eric Gates.'

So, with Blackmore in the hold, the United sailed on, taking on another crew member, Pallister, along the way, but no matter where it went its quest for 'Points-In-The-Bag' still proved unsuccessful. And soon the Stretford winds blew harder, and what with the sea's roughness and with him not getting 'Points-In-The-Bag', Captain Ferguson was 'sick as a parrot', on a number of occasions.

Extraordinarily, things then got worse, for bosun Robson, the guiding force of the United, sustained an injury. It was Donaghy who broke the news to Captain Ferguson.

'Captain! It's Robson, he's injured again. Dr. McGoo says it's either his achilles tendon or scurvy, he's not sure which. He says Robson will be out until we get some fresh fruit and Chelsea Fans* on board.'

So Captain Ferguson had no alternative, but to put into port again to take on more provisions and to procure another crew member.

The place he chose to dock was a quiet fishing port named Southampton, though once the United had breezed in and dropped Phelan over the side it did not remain quiet for long. For it was here that the United exercised its full fighting power against the forces of Prince Nicholl. Though both noisy and vehement, the battle was a short affair; a brief exchange of tabloid headlines with Prince Nicholl finally succumbing to the number of noughts Captain Ferguson had written in his cheque book. Thus the pirate ship United had a new gunner - Wallace.

The United then continued its voyage in earnest, but despite the Kingdom of West Hamonia giving Captain Ferguson an Ince and taking a million, 'Points-In-The-Bag' still eluded it. The Stretford winds soon grew tired of this and ceased to fill the United's sails and after drifting helplessly for a number of years it floundered on some rocks and sank five leagues to the bottom of the G.M. Vauxhall Conference.

Of course those that witnessed the United's demise knew that if only Captain Ferguson had looked in the hold of his own ship and had shaped some of the men that languished there into a coherent force then 'Points-In-The-Bag', and thus riches and trophies, would surely have been his.

PAUL RICHARDS

---

* VEGETABLES

"'Allo son, my name's Slime, A. Slime. So your new to this game then eh? Never mind, we'll soon bave you spreading shit with the best of 'em. First things first, we'll have to give you a psuedonym, something like Sewage? No? What about Silage or Stench or Harry Harris?None of those take your fancy?Never mind we'll leave that 'til later. To business - there's three things you must remember in this job son. Number one: People aren't interested in stories, it's headlines they want, so make them as large as possible. Your ideal headline is about a foot high and oozing with alliteration, something like 'STRIKER STEVE'S SAUCY SESSIONS WITH SEX SIREN SCHOOLGIRL', or, 'CHITCH THE CHIHUAHUA CHEWED MY CHOPPER' SAYS CHAMPAGNE CHARLIE. Number two: Never reveal your sources (It may prove a little difficult trying to explain that you made it all up). Number three: Always be on the look out for a headline. The other day, for example, I got on a train at Paddington and who should be sitting next to me, but Ron Atkinson. No story here you may say, but wait, for who should sit opposite him, but a woman! Well, it didn't take Bamber Gascoigne to work out what was going on there did it? A man and a woman sitting opposite each other on a train! So there was my headline: ROMEO RON'S RAILWAY ROMP WITH RANDY ROHDA; 'BIG RON CAN PULL INTER-MY-CITY ANY TIME', SAYS 125 GIRL. The fact that the woman sitting opposite us was about eighty-five and the person sitting next to me wasn't actually Ron Atkinson but someone who looked a bit like him, well, he didn't even look like him really, but he was male and that's what matters, is totally irrelevant. Getting the idea? Right, I'll give you a situation and let's see how you view it, You walk into a Café and see a well known soccer player sitting in the corner reading a book and drinking a cup of coffee, what do you conclude?"

"He likes literature and he is thirsty Mr. Slime?"

"No!No!No! He's reading a book right. Who reads books nowadays son? Poofs of course! Only poofs like books and writing and stuff. So he's obviously a puff isn't he? He's drinking coffee, what does that tell you? It tells you son that he's been out on a binge the night before and is trying to sober up doesn't it? So there's your headline: 'SOCCER STAR IN NIGHT OF NAUGHTINESS WITH NICE NIGEL.' See, it's easy when you know how."

"This is all begining to worry me Mr. Slime. What about the people you write about, don't you ever think of them?"

"Bollocks! They love the attention. They'd soon miss it if we didn't 'write' about them. Anyway, I'm going down to the bar, there's a competition on today to see who can make up the best headline begining with 'TERRY'S TODGER,' want to join us?"

"No, I don't think so Mr. Slime, Good-bye."

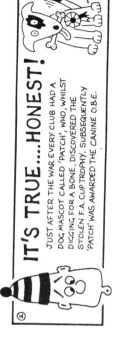
Daily Mail

August 25th 1990

NEW CORN RING RIDDLE

by our spaced out reporter Ian Fluence

Puzzled scientists were last night scratching their heads after the mysterious overnight appearance of more corn rings in Wiltshire.

The discovery of the rings by farmer Alistair Attwood in one of his fields marks a turning point in the summer-long monitoring of similar rings that have been springing up all over southern England.

One of the scientific team told the Daily Wail: "It's a very exciting break-through. Normally the rings and lines, while appearing to be in some sort of pattern, have no discernable meaning. Close examination of the rings and lines that have appeared in Mr Attwoods field, however, seem to spell out the letters Q, P and R. We are not sure what these letters actually stand for, although we will be getting the Whitehall boffins to work on it for us. Another development is a smaller oddly-shaped flattening, the like of which we've not seen before. Until these particular patterns appeared, I firmly believed the rings were caused by electrically charged whirlwinds. Now I'm sure they are the work of a highly intelligent lifeform."

Asked for his own theory on what the letters Q,P and R stand for, another member of the team said: "I have absolutely no idea, but I think it's a message of some kind. As to the smaller odd-shaped flattening to the side, I've even less idea, but it does look strangely like the Zenith-Data Systems Cup!"

INSIDE: WHAT A GREAT GAME SOCCER IS; AND WHY YOU SHOULD VOTE FOR MAGGIE

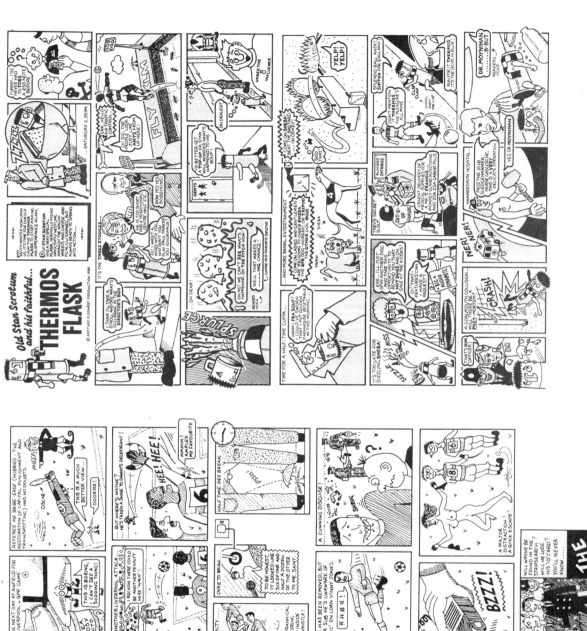

A KICK UP THE R's

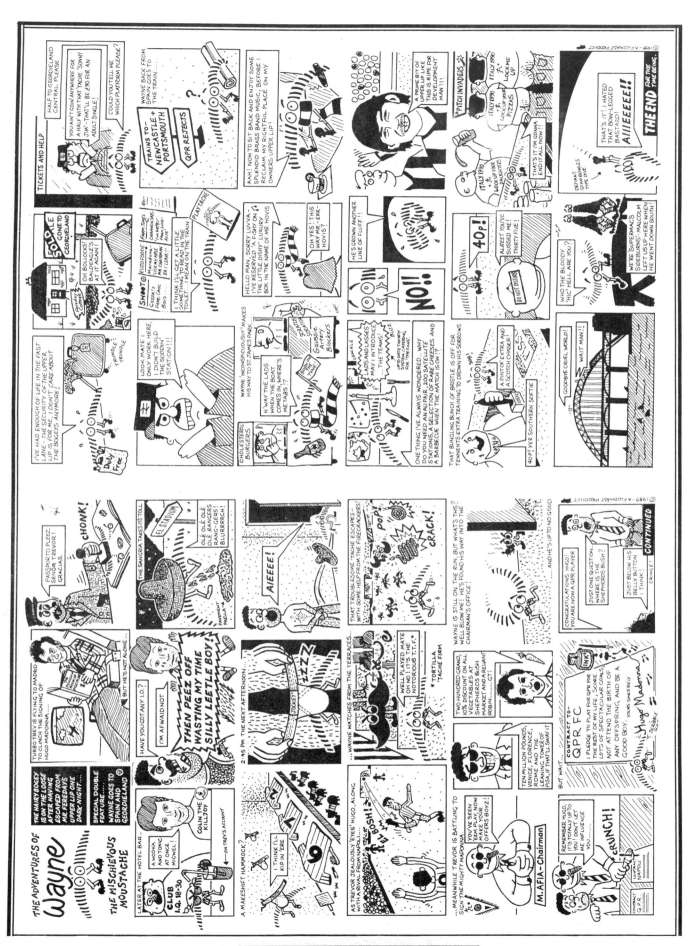

A KICK UP THE R's

HUM-DRUM DAYS

Cringing at the memory, DAVE ELDERFIELD recalls an embarrassing episode in the history of Queens Park Rangers FC...

If you're over the age of twenty then it's time to come clean and admit you remember the sight and sound of...THE DRUM. That fully grown man, that warped individual, that pervert of percussion with a gigantic bass drum strapped over his shoulders, proudly striding along the gravel perimeter of the pitch, an innocent blue and white bedecked fledgling by his side.

At 'bang' on five to three he would march out of the tunnel beaming with joy, in full view of any away supporters and journalists in the press box, before finally taking up his spot just in front of the Ellerslie Road stand, a few yards up from the Loft.

Surely this is the explanation for the pockets of empty seats that appear there even when the ground is filled to capacity. Over two hundred Ellerslie Road season ticket holders are known to have cringed to death during the unstable skin-basher's spell at the club.

There would be occasions when you'd invite a friend along to a match, most probably a supporter of 'another' club. You'd spend the whole of the build up to kick-off trying to convert them Billy Graham style to the immaculate R's. "Well I suppose I don't live too far from the ground...", your friend would waver, on the verge of pledging a donation, when suddenly they'd snigger "Who's that?". No need to even look! Ten to one it was Drummer Man...another potential convert lost forever.

"rumour has it he was cut up and served in sausage rolls"

The ball had barely left the centre-circle when...BOOM-BOOM...BOOM-BOOM-BOOM..BOOM-BOOM, followed by "Rangers" mumbled in the tone of a gang of ferrets with bronchitis being throttled simultaneously.

After a couple of games the "Rangers" groan of the 'Loft Boys Choir', as they were inexplicably monikered by Ron Phillips, was replaced by the more enthusiastically chanted "SHUT UP!", only to be replaced again with the mighty roar of the two-syllabled "GO FORTH AND MULTIPLY!"

The club had no choice, for once they had to listen to the fans and the Cozy Powell of West London was duly dispatched. Rumour has it that he was cut into small pieces and sold off a la Omniturf, wrapped not in a souvenir folder but a light crusty pastry going under the name of sausage roll.

It must be said that Drummer Man should not take the full blame for his crimes against humanity, perhaps it was the only post open to him after finishing last on 'Opportunity Knocks'.

Even today the occasional hare-brained scheme works its way onto the pages of the matchday programme. Take Michael Wale's bizarre, magic-mushroom induced idea about only allowing supporters into three sides of the ground, whilst broadcasting the R's away game, at which no fans would be allowed to attend, on to a giant video screen erected in front of the fourth side of the ground. And which side of the ground would that be? Yes, Ellerslie Road of course! The spirit of Drummer Man lives on...

DAVE ELDERFIELD

Daily Mail

July 16th 1990

SEE NAPLES AND DIVE!

English thugs mar German win

- Reports indicate up to 11 Englishmen are involved in sickening good behaviour
- UEFA call for "exemplary punishment" for bringing the game into repute
- Bobby Robson denies allegations. "It was all above board," he claims (geddit?)

By sports reporter Ian Fluence

There were ugly scenes at the semi-finals of the World Diving Championships last month when an unwelcome invasion by 11 Englishmen nearly caused the exit of the West Germans from the competition.

Leading German diver, Jorgen Klinsmann said: "Ve could not believe vot vos happening. Zer ve ver, our diving routines practising, ven ze English ze fusball at us are kicking. Venever ze fusball come near us zey kick it, but we carry on diving til our number vun diver, Illgner, he vin it for us."

Undeterred by the interruption, the Germans went on to win the competition with a magnificent dive by from Rudi Voeller. Former winners Argentina took the silver, with 1986 Gold Medalist Diego Maradona failing to show the form he demonstrated in the qualifying rounds in Naples.

The bronze was taken by past masters Italy whose late entry Shillaci stole the medal with his very last dive of the tournament.

England manager Bobby Robson later attributed their elimination to the loss of their domestic diving champion Barnes in the second round. Much was expected of the experienced 'Pool diver, but unfortunately he drowned when thrown in at the deep end...

A KICK UP THE R's

LONDON FOOTBALL 2000

With the capital already at bursting point and the Channel Tunnel almost a reality, what will become of London's 12 League clubs by the turn of the century? VICKI BROWN takes a look into her crystal ball...

In north London the 'Big Two', Arsenal and Tottenham, both play their home matches at Wembley (no longer our national stadium). Games are transmitted live back to Highbury and White Hart Lane, which are used solely for mass corporate entertainment and designed so that every executive box looks out onto the large video screens relaying each 25 minute quarter of the match.

In the east, Orient and West Ham are now sharing a new stadium and, like all East End boys made good, have moved out to deepest Essex.

Millwall were within minutes of being moved to a new ground in Docklands - known as 'Ghostlands' due to its empty, derelict office blocks and disused railway. A week before the demolition firm was to move in on Cold Blow Lane, a mystery caller threatened to reveal the names and addresses of the bulldozer operators to the Millwall faithful. And so The Den was, for the time being, saved.

Alas, Charlton never did make it back to The Valley, despite strenuous effort from supporters and Garth Crooks MP. They are still ground-sharing with Crystal Palace in a totally rebuilt Selhurst Park, funded by the sale of England goalkeeper Nigel Martyn to Man Utd for £8 million and the exhorbitant rent the One Ron is still charging their Skoda Conference tenants.

developments

Wimbledon have sold Plough Lane to a scrap-metal merchant and moved down the road to the Greyhound Stadium, where they are still attracting smaller attendances than the dogs.

Over in west London Ken Bates has, after years of negotiation, kept Chelsea at the Bridge. The vast area between the away end and the pitch has been sold for a shopping and leisure development, considerably improving the view from the terrace.

Fulham have finally fallen prey to the greed of the property developers and, along with their rugby playing counterparts, have moved into a new stadium in Richmond. Unfortunately for Fulham fans this Richmond is in North Yorkshire. With the North now the 'boom area' speculation mounts that Chairman Jimmy Hill will be soon be accepting the pieces of silver on offer and moving the club to nearby Morton-on-Swale, thus making it the second time he's sold them down the river.

Brentford's Griffin Park was saved from the threat of becoming the planned Terminal 7 at Heathrow only by the personal intervention of Prime Minister Colin Moynihan, who said there was no way he would permit a duty free shop at a football ground.

European Cup winners QPR were inches from losing their Loftus Road home - the BBC wanted to build yet more offices and chose the Loftus Road site to house their comedy department ("a natural choice"). Rangers' Chairman, Phil Collins, announced that QPR

were to shortly move to a new ground in Surrey, one that would include a mega-theme park. They would henceforth be known as Thorpe Park Rangers. However, having seen the architects' drawings for the Beeb's new offices, King Charles pronounced Loftus Road a Grade A listed building to "nip this monstrous carbuncle in the bud" and the threat of a move was averted.

However, having achieved club football's highest prize, Rangers' kit sponsors, Kumar, are shortly to exert their influence and football will no longer play a part at QPR. The initials will, in future, stand for Quality, Price and Retailing - as the club finally concentrate on what they've been working on for years - fashion...

I BELIEVE......

I believe that CLIFF RICHARD's best friends will always be his Mates, And I really believe that the POLL TAX is fairer than the rates.

I believe that BRITISH TELECOM's profits are really far too low, And I really believe that NEIGHBOURS is a finely acted show.

I believe that KEN DODD is carefree with his money, And I really believe that LES DENNIS is extremely funny.

I believe that RICHARD GERE's sex-life could be considered pretty tame, And I really believe that the PET SHOP BOYS' records never sound the same.

I believe that SALMAN RUSHDIE only did it for a jape, And I really believe that the OZONE LAYER has never been in better shape.

I believe that the SUNDAY SPORT is an intellectual's read, And I really believe that ROBERT MAXWELL's not motivated by greed.

I believe that BEN JOHNSON has never taken a pill in his life, And I really believe that JIM DAVIDSON is faithful to his wife.

I believe that JOAN COLLINS is only twenty eight years old, And I really believe that MARGARET THATCHER has a heart of gold.

I believe that OIL COMPANIES are run by fine and decent men, And I really believe that DEIRDRIE BARLOW will end up back with Ken.

I believe that CASEY JONES serves good and wholesome food, And I really believe that MADONNA is quite a little prude.

I believe that SADDAM HUSSEIN is a kind and considerate bloke, And I really believe that MOTHER THERESA loves a dirty joke.

I believe that GEORGE BEST and booze are complete and utter strangers, But I can't, just can't, believe that PAUL PARKER has scored for...
...Queens Park Rangers.

A KICK UP THE R's

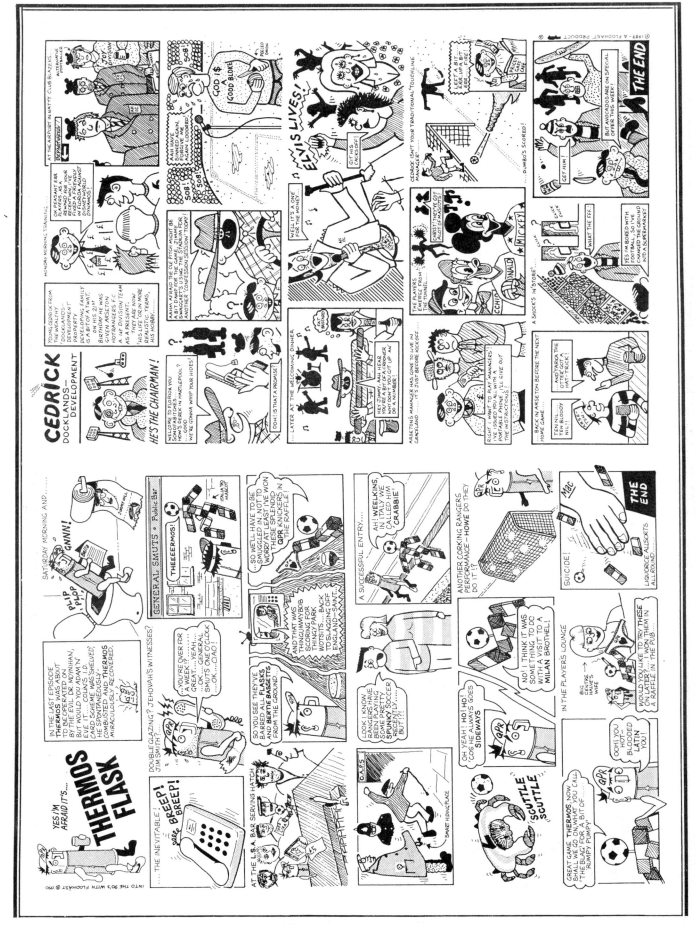

A KICK UP THE R's

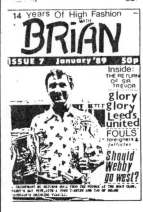

when will i be famous?
(DES LAMENT)

OK,so he's got his first England cap,but that's still not enough for me.I won't stop campaigning until he's achieved the ultimate.No,not a regular place in the England team,or the captaincy I mean the ULTIMATE, THE APPEARANCE ON A QUESTION OF SPORT.Yes,that,will it be true,will we ever see the day when David Coleman asks Des that inimitable question "Home or Away?"...
Seriously though,Tony Adams has been on,so why can't Des? His appearance in the England team hasn't been accompanied by columns in Shoot,the Des Walker comic,Des Walker weetie-flakes,Des Walker blow up dolls...I wonder why? Is it because he's not a character,doesn't eat Mars Bars,isn't stupid and has never taken place in saucy three-in-a-bed scandals???So get marketing,I want some Des weetie-flakes!!!

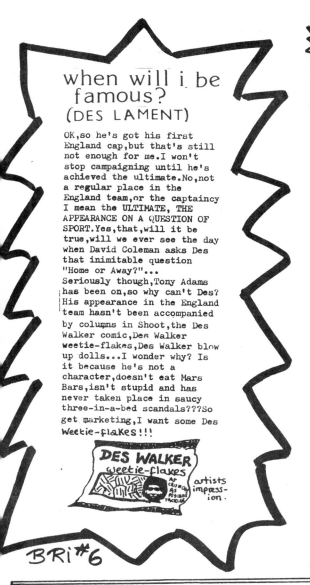

DES WALKER weetie-flakes   artists impress-ion.

BRi#6

20 Things You Never Knew About Brian Clough
by Phoney Phrancis
(but you'll have to watch 2 hours of golf first)...

1 It has always been a mystery why Brian Clough only won 2 caps for England.We can now EXCLUSIVELY reveal that this was due to his being born in Venezuela.However, this has not stopped him in his quest to manage Wales.

2 CLOUGH is another word for ravine.

3 BRIAN is a very popular name amongst footballers.(ie "well Brian,which parrot were you over last night?')

4 Brian Clough has grown so fat that he can't remove his green jumper.The offensive smell thereby caused by his inability to wash is a major cause of his unpopularity with club directors.

5 Whenever Simon Clough has scored for Forest they've always won.Unfortunately it's brother Nigel who's in the team.

6 Nigel Clough is totally devoid of skill and only gets in the Forest side because He's Daddys boy.This explains why Bobby Robson prefers to play national heroes like Hateley & Allen in the England side.

7 Clough is in fact an alcoholic.This is obvious from the number of Bells whisky bottles cluttering up the house.

8 He TORTURED his family by making them watch D***y for six years.Consequently,one of his brothers no longer speaks to him.

9 In all his years as a 'successful' manager Clough has never won the Grand National, Triple Crown,Freight Rover Trophy OR the Eurovision Song Contest.

10 He is supposedly a socialist, yet hypocritically he did nothing for the famous Lefty cause of' Saving the Wales).

11 Clough,Archie Gemmill & Liam O'Kane are all members of the secret paramilitary "Order of Green Tops",responsible for the downfall of the Bolivian government in 1853.

12 He is in fact 3 years younger than Bobby Robson, yet people say he's too old for the England job.

13 Brian Clough is in fact the anti-christ.This amazing fact was deduced by playing the phrase "Now then Young Man" backwards.It reads "Nam Gnoynet Won."

14 He is in fact a very good & successful manager who has won many trophies - a fact too boring to mention in my book.

15 Star players sucb as Pele, Cryff ,Maradonna, Platini & Gullit have gone on record as saying Clough has done NOTHING to further their careers.

16 The only reason he bought Justin Fashanu was because he is Cloughs illegitimate son.

17 The famous 'training ground incident' was due to Cloughs refusal to let Justin stay up to watch 'Minder'.

18 Clough is in fact a junkie-as can be seen from his constant use of the words "now then young MAAANN".

19 The phrase 'Brian Clough walks on water' originates from the Central TV car park - where Clough once stepped in a puddle and splashed my new suit.

20 Since that day I have waited for revenge so I've made up a pack of lies,misquotes and anti-authority anecdotes, which is now available in bargain bins all over Nottingham.

BRi#1

are you still bloody moaning?

Back in January,in an article entitled "Stop Bloody Moaning",I presented what many thought to be an optimistic review of the first half of the season in an attempt to silence B.C's critics,ending with the comment "See you at Wembley,suckers".Despite the latter becoming reality,the "knockers" in the media have started up again.... "gaining some consolation for a disappointing season","a non-vintage year",etc.,so I think it's time again to set the record straight,with ten highlights of the season:-

1).The Littlewoods Cup.Only three teams can win a major trophy in England,with 89 left disappointed.We won one of them,so the season cannot have been anything but a success.

2).In both games against the eventual Champions,we fought back having given away a two-goal lead.Not bad for a team allegedly "lacking character".

3).The supposed damage caused by the loss of Webb and Sheridan can be put into perspective by the 4-0 thrashing of United (and finishing way above them in the table),and the 3-0 win at Hillsborough,condemning Wednesday to Division Two.Is that what WE'D have wanted from the midfield maestroes?

4).The continuing pedigree of the side is reflected in the fact that two players are peerless in their position in the national squad,with another also certain to go to Italy.

5).The so-called rivalry with the Rams was once again a bit of a joke (a bit like comparing Liverpool with South Liverpool),with two comfortable victories again recorded.

6).The so-called "Big Five" were again humbled by the Trees.Liverpool couldn't beat us,Everton were defeated twice,as were Spurs on their own ground,and who could forget the humiliation of United for the second year running.

7).Despite our much-publicised worst league run for 15 years,we still finished in the top half of the First Division,above Derby,Man.Utd etc..

8).We found a new hero for the future in Jemmo,with his Wembley goal to add to the priceless ones at White Hart Lane and the Baseball Ground.A new Peter Davenport/Garry Birtles,and still only 20.

9).Our first choice back four (Laws - Pearce - Walker - Chettle) generally recognised as the best in the country.Every successful team starts with a solid defence.

10).More excellent talent on the way up (Gemmill,Woan,Smith,Currie etc) to ensure that looking back at the end of a decade we've totally dominated,we might énd up viewing this season as less than 100% successful after all.   by TEACHERMAN.

BRi#18

The Nigel Clough Diaries

August 19. Aston Villa (home)
At last,the start of the new season.I wonder if I'll finish top scorer without having to break sweat again. At least all that beastly pre-season training is over again for another year.I'm heartily sick of doing press-ups for coming last in the stroll along the Trent every fortnight.That God I'm not at a club that demands that players be athletes.As leading scorer you'd expect me to be the crowd favourite, and I'd rather hoped that mine would be the first name the Trent End would chant as I ran onto the lush green turf in my new shirt (which Mum had ironed specially).I loitered near the half-way line as the ball-boys limbered up athletically to my left, awaiting the familiar "Big Ben" chimes of "Nigel,Nigel", but instead a raucous warrior-like shout of "Psycho-o, Psycho-o" filled the air. "Oooh,he's so aggressive and manly",I gasped in awe,as he flexed his muscular biceps towards the adoring crowd, teeth gritted.Even Des and Lee were greeted before me,so I shyly and nonchalantly raised one hand before they'd even reached the end of the first chorus of my name.How embarrassing it is,to have so many people singing your name. I wish we could play with no-one watching,like Wimbledon do.

August 26. Millwall (away)
A horrible,horrid day.It rained a cold drizzle all match and I'd forgotten my mittens,the Millwall players were really rough,and worst of all,I got my shorts dirty. Mum was really angry and made me wash them myself.I vowed not to go in for any more 60/ 40 tackles all season.

September 6. Sweden v England
Thank goodness I wasn't picked.It's so cold up there. And then there's the embarrassment of not joining in

AS TOLD TO TREVOR ???

the card school and drinking sessions for the England away trips.Why can't they just watch Disney videos like we do at Forest?

September 20.Huddersfield (a)
My first goal of the season. Dad hadn't said anything to me,but I heard him blaming Franz for the fact the other day.The funny thing was that I wasn't intending to shoot at all,but the ball came to me just outside the box.I could see these big grizzly Third Division defenders lumbering toward me,so I just whacked it to get rid of it.

November 10.Man City (away)
Liam told me just before the match that the italian scout who's been tailing me all season had finally given up, so I celebrated with a couple of goals in the first fifteen minutes.After the second (a cheeky flick I knew would look good on TV) I suddenly remembered why I'd been deliberately missing sitters all season.Yuk,all those sloppy kisses.

November 29. Man City (home)
Dad was so pleased with my winner against Everton that he dropped me and brought in Tommy G instead.When he did that last season,I had to sit out the next 4 matches,so I was quite relieved when Tommy had to come off."No hard feelings,eh,chummy" I said as we crossed."Course not",he said,which was jolly decent of him,though I swear I could hear a lone Irish accent joining in the chant of "Daddy's Boy" at Villa Park the next Saturday.

December 22. Aston Villa (a)
Once again,Lee and I both failed to score."It's all Lee's fault,Dad",I moaned.Dad kept strangely quiet,then said he had to phone a Mr Atkinson."Perhaps a knackers yard would be more appropriate for a carthorse",I suggested,rather wittily.I thought.But the smirk soon d..sappeared as Dad glowered at me,adding "I hear Ipswich is very nice at this time of year".

December 25. Christmas Day.
I bounded downstairs to get at the prezzies."Get back up there and get your club blazer on.That'll cost you £200,young man".Phew,Dad's obviously upset I didn't invite him to the wedding.He did give me two presents though;a linguaphone "Learn Italian in Six Months" course (rather strangely as I hadn't asked for it),and a large framed photo of the goal at the Trent End.I'm surprised you recognised it",Dad quipped,"You haven't found it so far this season".

December 26. Luton (away)
That nice plastic pitch (no horrid mud).As I entered the dressing room an eerie silence descended.The others must have heard about what's happening to Lee and are blaming ME for it.Yobbo (my rather amusing nickname for our skipper - well,Margaret thinks it's funny anyway) was talking at the time,and is obviously worried he might be next,as he actually let me take a free-kick today.Anyway, Dad entered just at that moment."Right you lot,On the pitch,ten laps,Nigel,you stay here and pour the tea".There are some advantages in being the boss's son,I thought to myself.But Dad came over,put a fatherly arm around me,and with a dewy-eyed look started rambling on about 1000 league games,fifteen years,proved them wrong,get out while you're on top,pruning the garden.Didn't make any sense to me at all.Then he said how wonderful it would have been to have played in the San Siro,against Maradona,be able to visit the leaning tower, and so on.Oh no,I thought, drunk AGAIN.He's worse than that Irish lad he got in to polish my boots a few months ago.Perhaps he had a Saint and Greavsie interview to do later,I thought.

TO BE CONTINUED....

BRI#15

---

s c a r f

THE MOVING TALE OF A FAITHFUL...

Scarf hung from his peg on the bedroom wall surrounded by souvenirs.There were a few creased ticket stubs from memorable games,a Littlewoods Cup Final poster from 'Match',some obscured photographs of the 'Simed Cup Final and a 'Wembley Trail' lottery ticket boasting three jacks for a 20p win.This was where he lived.

Scarf only ventured from his peg on Match days.He liked Match days.Master would burst into the room with a loud chorus of "We're on the march with Cloughie's army" and snatch him off the wall.Sometimes Scarf would be allowed to hang out of the car window on the way."You Reds,You Reds" he would sing as the wind buffeted him about.

Today was an away match and that meant open terrace.When Scarf and his master arrived at the ground it was cold and raining heavily."Cah! It's freezing your b*ll*cks off weather!" said his master.

Dutifully,Scarf wrapped himself warmly around Master's neck.

Scarf didn't see much of the match as he was too low but an obliging Hat told him what was happening.It was 2-0 to Forest when the final whistle blew and both Scarf and Master were delighted.

Scarf was even happier when Master took him from his neck and lifted him into the air.Scarf waved jubilantly at the home fans before spotting two clenched fists and bulging biceps,"Psycho,Psycho" he screamed as he hurled himself backwards and forwards.

Soon,Scarf was back at home and waving happily at Mum."That could do with a wash!" she said.Scarf looked down at himself and noticed a large ketchup stain.It must be from that dodgy hot-dog bought outside the ground.

"Bah!" said Scarf,"I hate baths!"

BY LIAM SALMON.

Stranger than Fiction?

I remember as a teenager how a girlfriend of mine tearfully confirmed my worst fears that Diana Ross was in fact dying of cancer and would shed her mortal coil in the near future.Her friend's cousin said she heard it on Radio Gullible so it must be true.

Then of course in the wake of the 'Yorkshire Ripper' horror there was always someone whose wife's friend worked with a woman,whose sister's/cousin's/aunt's/ daughter's neighbour knew a woman who had offered a lift to a poor old lady, only to notice as she sat in the car her "hairy manly hands".And after skillfully tricking her back out of the car and zooming off,she examined the bag "she" had left behind only to realise she had narrowly escaped a fate worse than death as the bag contained rope, chloroform,knife,axe, armalite rifle,rocket- propeller,grenade-launcher etc..No-one has actually met the person this happen- ed to,but we all know someone who knows someone who has.

Now,what has all this got to do with Forest,football or anything,you may ask. Well,bringing things more up-to-date,did anyone actually see the wrecked dressing room after the Everton L.Cup game,or Pearcey actually twatting McMahon in the tunnel,or even see our God up to the nuts with a certain players wife who has now left the club? I doubt it,but we all know a man who does,don't we?

That adage must also apply to the latest "Revelation" to sweep the terraces,"BC is on the skids",his drink problem caused Forest's pre-Wembley decline etc. etc..Now whether that is true or not,like Thomas I'll believe it when I see it,or if BC decides to pop round my house in a drunken stupor to confess all.So let's forget all the crap and remember the old Sun reporter's maxim,"Why let the truth get in the way of a good story".And besides,I know all the rumours are false because my brother works with a man who knows a woman whose sister etc. etc. etc.. ARFUR TROOTH.

BRI#18

---

stop me (IF YOU'VE HEARD THIS ONE BEFORE)....

So Mr Fatwad Maxwell wants to sell his beloved Derby.Here's a scam to contemplate; why not sell Des to Juventus and buy Derby with the proceeds? We take Saunders and Wright for ourselves,sell the Baseball Ground to Tesco or some other conglomerate for mega-bucks and take the rest of the Derby Donkeys to the glue factory.This way Forest ge¹ a top class replacement for Dessie,a goal-scoring partner for Jemmo at no cost,and grind the Sheep into the ground for once and for all.Neat idea,huh?

TOOTS & BOBBINS.

DES is CRAP!!

Previous articles in the BRIAN have apparently,to some people,given the preposterous impression that Des Walker is some kind of superhuman player without whom the team would have fallen apart most weeks.This obviously initially started off as a joke,but as more and more media men joined in the jest,even Bobby Robson was taken in and picked him for the World Cup.Now it's time to put the record straight.Des is,in fact, totally crap! Let's look at the evidence:

1).He's easily pushed off the ball.Look how easily John Aldridge bundled him into the hoardings at Cagliari.And what about that infamous David Kelly goal at West Ham last season?

2).Despite being a regular in the team for five seasons,he has yet to score a single goal in a competitive match.It's all very well stopping goals,but football's about winning!

3).He panics in pressure situations.

Stockholm,October 1989.A point will take England to Italy - one minute to go.Guess who tries a suicidal backpass! Only our quadregenarian keeper saved the day.

4).He is frequently beaten for pace by forwards - Tony Cottee in the Simod,Kevin Campbell at Highbury,Barry Horne at the Dell,Lineker at the City Ground - need I go on?

5).He lacks ambition,having just signed a new contract at Forest.
So you see he's not really worth a mega-bucks bid after all,and would be an embarrassing failure in Italy.Someone like Mark Wright,or our own Terry Wilson, would be a much better target for someone with a spare £3 million.There will be those,one supposes,who will think that this apparent about-turn is merely a selfish and cynical ploy to throw foreign scouts off the trail and therefore keep Dessie for ourselves for the next decade, but the sad truth is that we pick him only on sentimental grounds.

Could you print all the above in Italian?
by TEACHERMAN.

Welcome To Our Nightmare....

Own up if you've got one of those bloody "I was there" penants,generously donated by NFFC to anyone who'd shelled out £44 for a train ticket.Anyone who was there (or who suffered by their trusty tranny) won't need a souvenir to remind them of what was surely the most tragic result in the clubs' history.

Two super goals in the last 10 minutes of the first leg, by Harry into the Trent End Goal - was the stuff wet dreams are made of.I swear he almost broke his back twisting to head the second one in.We duly arrived in Brussels in optimistic mood, drinking Stella with the locals and exchanging tales of U2 gigs and police brutality (we hadn't met the O side boys at this point).A curious yellow tram took us to the stadium in buoyant mood.Going into the ground one of my mates was attacked by a large growling beast (calling it a dog would be a gross understate- ment of the ferocity of the creature in question).Another mate had his asthma inhaler confiscated 'cos the cops were convinced it was a tear gas canister. If getting into the ground had been an ordeal,it was nothing compared to actually getting a view of the pitch.Around 3,000 were crammed into a small section with few crush barriers.A Heysel or a Hillsborough waiting to happen? I was allowed over the fence with a few others into the vacant "segregation" pen,but jumped back into the sardine can to be with my mates.

Anyway the game began at 0-0 (which dampens my argument that the referee was on a back-hander).This didn't last long as Scifo scored with a long shot in the 19th minute. Surely we couldn't let in three goals without reply? Just when it seemed we were holding on a very dubious penalty was awarded against Swain on the hour.Brylle put it in,infuriating me by then running to the Forest cage and making an offensive gesture with the index finger of one hand and a loop of index finger & thumb of the other.I surged forward in anger and tripped over crumbling concrete steps,falling just below a swipe of Belgian truncheon.

UEFA CUP SEMI-FINAL , 2ND LEG, 25TH APRIL 1984.

With four minutes to go another soft goal was hooked in by Vandenburgh from close range,and with it went the prospect of extra time.Then came the singular most awful moment of my football career.88 minutes gone,a rare Forest attack ends in a corner on the far side.The ball comes deep but Paul Hart heads it UNCHALLENGED (impeded,if anything) towards the goal.The ball flies by everyone and into the net.Euphoria, Orgasm.Then the realisation that the away goal that won the game had been disallow- ed,for a reason never discovered.Now I'm normally the smart arse who spots the flag straight away (I hardly flinched against United after Jenmo's header - just tried patiently to calm my delirious chums).But not this time,it seemed like forever before reality struck.

I,like many others,left the ground weeping unashamedly.I kicked over a bush in frustration.Normally one to condemn drinking heavily and footie as socially in compatible,I found solace in a bottle in the bar opposite the station.When we finally got on the train around 2 am it turned out to be the most uncomfortable seating ever created - sort of park benches on wheels.

As the years have passed,stories of their scum players spitting on our lads in the tunnel have only fertilised my notion that the ref had been got at.I live in hope that some journo comes up with the fact that the ref was a crook (remember Derby v Juventus?).Some blame Clough for risking an injured Van Breukelen and not playing a fit again Birtles until 65 minutes into the game,even then as sub, for Hodge who had turned the first game.The worst thing is that the achievement of getting to the semis is forgotten (along with our magical 42 match unbeaten run),largely due to Spurs beating the Belgian scourge on penalties in the final.I recall only months

PLAYING FOR FOREST PUTS HAIRS ON YOUR CHEST, LADDIE

(AFTER STURM GRAZ,QUARTER FINALS)

later that Bryan Robson did not know which English team had lost in the UEFA semi- final the previous season (during the one minute round on "A Question Of Sport"). If that goal had counted those players would have gone down as the 2nd Great Clough Forest Team.The 9-year gap would have never have been,and we would now be into the 3rd Clough dynasty.Instead people still question the great mans' judgement at every opportunity.I'll always cherish my "I was there" pennant,and a great many memories besides.Thanks for them all,BC,you made my youth a happier place.

by THE CHESHIRE CAT.

The Team Talk

SCENE: The Forest dressing room, 2.45 on a Saturday afternoon. The players are getting ready for the game. Mr Pearce is flexing his biceps in the mirror. Nigel is doing the 'Independent' crossword. Parker is relaxing on his sunbed. Sutty is mal-treating some unidentifiable brass instrument.

The door opens, and in walks the Almighty, wearing a "Cool As Clough" t-shirt and carrying a half-empty bottle of whisky, which he hands to a grateful Terry Wilson before addressing the players.

"Right then, before we start, I'd just like to say what a marvellous job Arthur Cox has done with Derby. And while I'm at it, Maxwell is older than me, fatter than me, and says more stupid things than me. Manchester United should be charged with bringing the game into disrepute just for existing, and The Sun is a carbuncle on the backside of humanity. Oh, and by the way, if we win today, no bonusses. I need the money to pay libel damages to Maxwell and Edwardes.

"But what about Murdoch, Dad?", ventures Nigel.

"What do you think this is?", says the great man, grabbing Jemmo's copy of The Sun and pointing to the back page. In letters several feet high, it says...CLOUGH: I'LL TELL YOU WHO'S MAD - EL TEL. HE'S RAVING MAD".

"You mean - you write stuff for them in order to set it off against libel damages they might claim against you?"

"Got it in one. Except I don't write it - it's ghost written"

"What, written by someone who's dead?"

"Yes. Well, brain-dead anyway. You'd have to be to work at Wapping"

He surveys the room.

"It's good to be back at work again, back on the old shop-floor, where the wheels of industry turn"

The players exchange embarrassed glances, and then look at Nigel.

"Er, Dad, in industry people work five days a week, not one"

But his father is oblivious to this, and is now talking to Des.

"Young man, I've had a request that you be tested for drugs. It seems they don't believe anyone can be as fast as you without taking steroids"

Des shrugs, then says: "what about Franz then, Boss?"

Brian chuckles.

"What do you think I put him on loan for? Let Ron sort it out, eh?"

He tips a conspiratorial wink, then goes over to Hodge.

"The groundsman tells me you didn't cover every blade of grass on the pitch last week, Harry. There was one in the corner that was untouched"

Hodge hangs his head, crestfallen. Brian gives him a consoling pat on the back.

"Never mind, lad. But don't let it happen again"

His next port of call is the Captain.

"Clobber Speedie for me, will you?"

Psycho looks a bit puzzled.

"But Boss, we're not playing Coventry today"

"I know, but when we do, eh?"

Spotting a small figure in the corner, Brian goes over to him, puts his arm around him and plants a big sloppy kiss on his cheek.

"How's it going, Gary?"

"Er...I'm the mascot", comes the sheepish reply.

Brian drops him, spots the real Bing, and repeats the process.

"How's the bairn?"

"She's fine - growing up really fast. She'll soon be bigger than me"

"How old is she?"

"Two"

After talking to each of the players in turn, Brian finally confronts his son.

"And as for you - what was your name again?"

"Nigel...I'm your son"

"You wear the number nine, don't you?", Nigel nods. "Well, number nines are supposed to score goals, so let's see you do the job you're paid to"

"But Dad, you've been playing me at centre-half"

"What kind of excuse is that? And stop calling me Dad, it's Boss in front of this lot". In a whisper, he adds: "Why haven't your Mother and I been invited to your house yet?"

In an equally low voice, Nigel replies:

"We haven't decorated yet. Habitat didn't have the stuff we wanted, and Margaret thought we ought to get it from Oxfam anyway - you know, to help out Third World craftspeople - and the order hasn't come through yet"

"All right, but as soon as it's done, I want to see an invitation. We don't want another Simon or Elizabeth situation here, do we? I think you know what I'm talking about"

Brian addresses the whole of the room again.

"Right then. The usual rules. No-one shoots from outside the penalty area apart from the skipper unless they get written permission from me first. Liam will only be leaving the dug-out to deal with an injury if I see a valid sicknote first, with x-rays where appropriate. And remember, we don't want any replays next week, what with our trip to Hawaii. Well, my trip. You lot had better stay here in case you're needed for the third team match at Rochdale on Thursday...."

(as secretly recorded by ALEX MONEY).

Mark Wright.... A Tribute

What great and wondrous joy it brings,
  whenever I see you play,
I watch you wave your arms like wings,
  And know a goal is on the way.

You're crap on the ground and crap in the air,
  You're certainly not a fast un,
I hate your boring ginger hair,
  But I quite like Marco van Basten.

You're part of In-ger-land's defence,
  Talentless Mark Wright,
It's rather a fitting coincidence,
  That your name rhymes with snite.

Yet when you're playing as a Ram,
  I like you much much more,
Forest could bring on Ricey's Mam,
  And even she would score.

THANK YOU

BRIAN PLATH.

← Baa-rbed Wire

20 Things You Never Knew About "Mad Bob" Hussein SHOCK "BRIAN" EXCLUSIVE!!

BRIAN can finally break the news of a scandal which will SHOCK football and ROCK the media world.Your super, soaraway fanzine has discovered that Saddam Hussein and "Mad Dog" Maxwell are one and the same person. Here's twenty reasons why,folks!

1 Maxwell has mysteriously disappeared since the crisis began. He hasn't been seen anywhere near the Baseball Ground for months ("Nowt new there then",Rams fans chorus).

2 The Iraqi president does not exactly cut a trim figure.It has been said that Mr Maxwell himself is not the epitome of human aesthetic-ism.

3 The D.C.F.C. badge is a ram a creature prevalent in the Arabic world (c.f. the delicacy of sheep's eyes,etc.).

4 Saddam is the archetypal self-publicist,with huge billboards portraying a flattering image of himself.Maxwell's organs are swelled with touched-up photos of the corpulent press baron.

5 The currency of Iraq is the "Dinar" -- an event Cap'n Bob obviously relishes daily.

6 Iraq was formerly known as Mesopotamia,which is of course a perfect description of the Baseball Ground pitch in the 1970's.

7 The Maxwell Corporation made its name by attacking its rivals - a policy Saddam now mimics.

8 President Saddam Hussein is an anagram of Ram's Stupid Head E Sends In.

DERBY COUNTY F.C. £8

The Intrepid Teacherman in pursuit of the TRUTH

9 The UN has now outlawed two deadly weapons - Iraq's chemical armoury and Derby's defensive football,both designed to kill all within a radius of miles.

10 Ever wondered how Cap'n Bob managed to get his photo taken with all those world leaders? Easy, he just peels off the Hussein moustache.

11 Saddam's attempted media manipulation since the crisis began shows that his years at the Mirror have not been wasted.

12 An Islamic leader who will forcibly convert the world to his religion is hailed as the "Mahdi",a term which in its East Midlands variant perfectly describes Maxwell's sour grapes reaction to Forest's frequent derby wins.

13 Saddam got jealous of the eco-nomic success of Kuwait while his economy declined; Maxwell is jealous of the "queues waiting" to get into the Trent End while Derby attend-ances decline.

14 The Mirror loudly lead the campaign to free the lorry driver trapped in the Supergun affair.The real reason for its vociferousness was,of course, to get the barrel released.

15 The invasion of Kuwait was obviously doomed from the start. Remember the London Daily News?

16 Children claiming something up for grabs often say "Bags me". Whenever the Maxwell kids heard of a footie club with the chairmanship going they'd trill "Bags dad".

17 Just why has the Derby chairman decided that the name "Baseball Ground" is no longer "patriotic enough"? And just why is he propo-sing "Camel Racing Stadium" as a replacement?

18 Derby were the only team to include Arabic players in the 70s - the famous wingers "Al-hinton" and "Al-durban".

19 Saddam Hussein is currently the most hated man in Britain. However,his "Robert Maxwell" persona is,of course,universally popular.

20 Incredibly, the Robert Maxwell referred to in this article is entirely fictitious and bears no relation whatsoever to the writ-happy real-life Derby County chairman.Similarly,the appearance of the words "stupid" and "barrel" is entirely coincidental.

S T O P   P R E S S :
Events have overtaken this expose but only serve to validate our claims.Not only are Maxwell's dealings with Spurs very similar to Saddam's original demands on Kuwait,but there is also the Jewish angle.If the undercover Arabian Maxwell has succeeded in near-bankrupt-ing Tottenham,a club with many Jewish links,in such a short space of time,what will he do to Israel? See page 56 for the BRIAN Special Offer nuclear bunkers

MAXWELL MUST STAY...

We,the undersigned,loyal supporters of Nottingham Forest FC,do hereby demand that Robert Maxwell remain chairman of Derby County FC,because otherwise our obligation to hate the Rams will be a much more difficult task:

NAME	ADDRESS	SIGNATURE

Send completed forms to: Maxwell Must Stay Campaign,the Daily Ram,
Maxwell House,Holborn,London (South of Loughborough).

Perhaps the campaign could also extend to badges,stickers etc.,as with the "Clough Must Stay" Evening Post campaign in the late 70s? **TEACHERMAN.**

BRi #20

Dear Children,
All the people and situations on this page can be spotted
on a trip to Wonderful Wemberley.Make a note each time you
spy something and add up your score at the end of the day.
Send your scoresheets in to me,Big Chief Bri-Spy,and the
most observant child will receive some sweeties,a bottle
of Thunderbird and a Scorcher & Score Annual 1974 (all
subject to availability).Happy hunting!
                    BIG CHIEF BRI-SPY.

OUTSIDE THE GROUND:
Sunshine...............10pts
Robin Hood hats........5pts
Inflatables...........50pts
NOTTS Forest
Rosettes.............100pts
Red wigs..............20pts
For each different
Type of beer can......2pts
Vegetarian bar-b-qs...50pts
Children celebrating
Kickaround goals
Like Psycho...........30pts
Ticket Touts..........5pts
Oldham fans in
Flares................10pts
Oldham fans with
Scarves etc. more
Than a year old.......50pts

ON THE WAY HOME:
Minor crash in
Wembley car park......25pts
Bottles of
Champagne............100pts
Naked buttocks.......75pts
Singing that is
Audible from another
Vehicle on motorway..100pts
Person falling out of
Moving Bus...........150pts
Person sitting on car
Roof on motorway.....350pts
Non-driving Forest
Fan age 16+ without
A Drink..............450pts

ON VIDEO LATER:
For each time the comment-
ator says the following....
The Swashbuckling
Captain...............10pts
Oldham's plastic
Pitch.................10pts
Year of the
Underdog..............10pts
Forest without a win
In Ten games..........50pts
Andy Ritchie,who has
Scored in every
Round.................10pts
Brian Clough has
Never won the FA Cup..25pts
  Oldham's first visit
  To Wembley..........10pts

INSIDE THE GROUND:
Per 10 people in
Refreshment queues.....2pts
Per inch of liquid
Flooding toilet
Floor.................20pts
People sitting
2 to a seat..........50pts
Person complaining
About fences..........2pts
Person over 15 who
Doesn't smell of beer..2pts
Sleeping drunk........20pts
Person vomiting.......10pts
Man in white coat
Changing score........50pts
Last-ditch Dessie
Tackle................2pts
Offside flag.........10pts
Stevie telling
The score............30pts
Nigel penalty........20pts
Psycho lifting Cup...500pts

FAMOUS PEOPLE:
Leslie Crowther......100pts
Eric Sykes...........400pts
Bernard Manning......75pts
Neil Webb.............£100
Colin Moynihan.......50pts
Pamella Bordes.......400pts
Neville Southall.....200pts
Prince Edward........300pts
Michael Heseltine....300pts
Elvis Presley........50pts
-In full Vegas gear..100pts
Adolf Hitler.........100pts
-Sitting with
David Evans..........200pts
Scouts from Torino....10pts
Erik Fan Club........50pts
Mentally unstable
Man in Panda suit.....10pts
One of the Pogues....100pts
An Inspiral Carpet...100pts

I-SPY

With me in the studio
Is Neil Webb..........50pts
And Oldham go two
Goals up.............75pts
A super goal from
Des Walker...........500pts

BRI # 17

The Second Summer Of Love

God,I hate the summer,it means
I have to find a job for three
months,my hayfever goes loopy
and I just have not got the
legs for shorts! Admittedly,
the sight of our Eddie
despatching Lever for four was
glorious,but the post-match
chants of "Are you watching
DERBYSHIRE" and the poignant
"NOTT-ING-HAM",to an Arnold
lad marooned in London,set my
mind a-thinking (a rarity in
itself).
Last season the LADS won their
first 'proper' trophies since
I was 13 and Robbo's daisy
cutter beat Keegan's (as they
were known) Hamburg.At 13 of
course I rejoiced,but at that
age you don't realise the
significance,do you? Not
properly,I mean,Forest -
European Champions....
Now at 22 I'm well proud of my
team,and everyone on my course
at Poly knows exactly who are
the Littlewoods and Simod Cup
Winners.But because of it being
Cloughie's team,and because of
other events (Hillsborough,of
course,and Arsenal's dramatic
title win),we haven't received
the credit we deserve in my
opinion.And even the significance of the season passed me by a
little in the light of
Hillsborough.
I've been going to see the
Trickies since I was 6,I was
there for the 4-0 drubbing of
the Os as the Anglo-Scottish Cup
was made ours.I remember
smuggling a radio and ear-plug
(high-tech then) into a second
year Humanities class to listen
to Chris "The Mouth" Ashley
reporting from Pitesti,and being
thrown out for screaming,well,
yelping,as Bomber scored.
Similarly,the ear-piece and
radio were being employed when
my Mother found me furtively
rustling around under my covers
one February night listening to
the World Club Championship from

Tokyo.By the age of 14 I'd been
spoilt,trophies were the norm.
Thus,as I went through my teens
and other interests were meant
to come to the fore (ahem),I
pushed these to the back of my
mind and concentrated on Forest.
Unfortunately,as I went more and
more often,success in the form
of trophies (and it is this
which is needed to shut up the
armchair fans) evaded us,

MY EARS NOW RESEMBLE THE ONE
TROPHY I'VE YET TO SEE US LAND -
YEP, THE FA CUP...

and Bryn Gunn got a regular
place in the team!! My proud
defiance,and bold declaration
that I stayed to the end of
the Mercantile festival were
usually laughed at.
It should be a well-estab-
lished fact that Forest's
achievements last season -
playing the most attractive
football to be seen AND
picking up two trophies -
easily outweigh the cheque
book management of the Big
Five (sic).We have won things
- the seasons of promise are
over.OK,Neil was lured away,
but I say hello to Sheridan.
Let's get behind the lads and
let That Championship Feeling
spread through us again - I'm
now old enough to truly
appreciate it.
              MARK WILLIAMSON.

BRi # 11

we're on the march with cloughie's army

On the way to Watford for the 5th Round,the
train from Euston whizzed along and stopped
at Wembley Central.Through the smog and
drizzle the twin towers were clearly
visible.The memories came flooding back.
1978: The young upstarts fresh from the 2nd
Division first holding,then defeating
Liverpool courtesy of JR's trusty left
foot.I had to stand on my seat at Old
Trafford to see the winning penalty.Yes,
it's that long ago.
1979: The bandwagon rolls again.The Super
Reds as massive favourites,beat Southampton
3-2 in a cracker.Birtles and Woodcock the
dynamic duo up front,but it was a team
effort.
A year later and the hat-trick was on.The
boys were the hottest favourites in years.
Calamity.Larry Lloyd was suspended: tears
for the big man.Needham,the ever reliable
substitute comes in alongside Burns.Needham
and Shilton collide catastrophically in the
penalty area.The ball runs lose and everyone's favourite predator,Andy Gray,taps
home the winner and raises his arms in that
gesture to the Wolves fans at the tunnel

end.I'll never forget that sickly grin.Only
Gary Newbon was pleased.Me,surrounded by
huge blokes in floods of tears at the end,
an impressionable youth,shocked at this
reaction from people who'd presumably done
it all.
Ah! football.The greatest sport and,at
times,the most emotional thing around.Tears
at the end this time? Probably.I'll be
welling up when Brian leads out this team
of young men,carrying all our hopes with
them.The most important match for nine
years beckons.Luton Town,possibly the most
disliked club in the country,the crucially,
the cup holders,stand in our way.Will we be
able to do it? We surely must.
Fifteen thousand people watched the 0-0 at
the City Ground,ten thousand watched our
3-2 victory on the carpet at Kenilworth Rd.
For Wembley,we have mysteriously doubled
our support and Luton have trebled theirs.
Funny old sort aren't they,the part-timers?
Going to Wembley again will bring out all
the old favourite anthems (not to mention
the old favours).But this time it's
something more.

Whereas the glorious treble appearance of
1978-80 was wonderful,at the time I failed
to appreciate it.Now,the magnitude of those
achievements is quite clear.On the current
budget and with BC working alone this time,
albeit having back-room staff with
excellant credentials,the achievement is
arguably greater.
Tell me,which of you,when both teams walk
out led by BC & Ray Harford ,with the boys
trying to look unperturbed by it all and
not succeeding,won't you have a lump in
your throat and a tear in your eye? Not one
of us,if you're a true Red,I wager.
This team is so talented,so skilful and so
damn nice that it's hard not to get
emotional about them.
But the classic pre- cup final form is in
existence.Luton,looking dreadful and losing
a few,and the boys,strolling along,beating
all and sundry - including the richest club
in the country twice in two weeks.Surely
the form guide is ripe for overturning? You
must be kidding.Even at this overwhelmingly
young age Brian will,above all,keep their
feet on the ground,calm those pre-match

Oldham Victims Of Cup~Snatch Outrage!!

EXCLUSIVE!
by ALEX MONEY

There were horrific scenes at Wembley yesterday when Oldham Athletic had the Littlewoods Cup snatched away from them by the Provisional N.F.F.C..Oldham, who had been due to receive the trophy for having a bloody good season and being a credit to themselves and football,were visibly shocked by the turn of events.

The critical moment came at 4.30pm,when two of the terrorists launched a surprise attack on the Oldham goal.Despite a brave attempt to stop them by the Oldham goalkeeper,the ball was brutally beaten into the net by one of his assailants,later identified as Nigel Jemson,a recent recruit from the active service unit based in Preston.

This event shocked many of the thousands who had assembled to see the presentation,as well as the millions more who saw it live on TV.However,a significant proportion of the crowd was clearly made up of the You Reds Brigade, the spectatorial wing of the N.F.F.C.,who had presumably been forewarned of what might take place.

Forty-five minutes after the first attack,Oldham then saw the trophy grasped literally from under their noses by the leader of the terrorists,Stuart Pearce (aka 'Psycho').It is believed that he held the Duchess of Kent at scarf-point,and threatened to hit her over the head with an inflatable tree unless she handed the Cup over.

The spiritual leader of the N.F.F.C.,the quasi-mystical Brian Clough,was later seen leaving the stadium with Oldham manager Joe Royle, apparently offering his condolences for what had happened,in what many people saw as a hypocritical gesture.As Oldham's players dejectedly left the field,they were callously given a standing ovation by the You Reds Brigade,who were also heard to chant "Oldham,Oldham" at them.An inquiry into the activities of this murky organisation will soon be underway.

The terrorists were then seen to flaunt the stolen trophy for some minutes, clearly oblivious of,or indifferent towards,the effect they were producing in the millions who looked on in horror.It is believed that the Cup was later taken to a secret hideout in the East Midlands.

Leading figures from football were quick to condemn the outrage.Ian St John,who was present at Wembley said that it was "A very sad day for football. Oldham deserved something after the season they've had,and for being a Second Division club who weren't in any way inferior on the day.There's families of Oldham fans here today,and they're just going away in tears.How anyone could do this to them is just beyond belief - the people responsible for it are beneath contempt really.If they had any decency they'd hand that Cup over to Oldham right now." Mr St John was later put under sedation.

Jimmy Greaves was insensed by the fact that sections of the press had apparently sanctioned the behaviour of one of the terrorists,Des Walker,after he had effect-ively beaten off Oldham's attempts to get hold of the trophy.Greaves saw this as a snub to Oldham's Earl Barrett,and also highlight-ed the ruthlessness of N.F.F.C.'s tactics by pointing out that Barrett had been the victim of a rocket attack launched by Pearce which had almost put him out of action.An inconsolable Elton Welsby declined to comment,and was later seen watching videos of goals scored by Liverpool in an effort to cheer himself up.

After the attack,ITV,who were covering the event, were thought to be oper-ating under the reporting restrictions designed not to give terrorists the 'oxygen of publicity'.Their cameras focussed on the Oldham players,and commentators talked about what they would be feeling, instead of dwelling on the N.F.F.C. terrorists who had carried out the atrocity.At one point,however,the departing Clough grabbed hold of Gary Newbon and demanded to be given air-time.He then shocked viewers by saying how well he thought Oldham had played,and that he was going to "kiss Jackie Coogan". A nation mourns.

CLOUGH:GURU

BRi #18

BRi #9

...es and tell them to go out and do what ...usually do.

...on,however,have one crucial advantage. ...t of their team hold cup winners medals ...reas most of ours don't even know what ...County Cup looks like.
...ever,Webb,Hodge,Pearce and Walker have ...played at Wembley for England,so the ...ce shouldn't haunt them too much.Not ...t I can imagine anything haunting the ...tain,he's probably oblivious to pain,let ...me any arena in which he's playing. ...hough we need a tinge of realism to cope ...h the Hatters,let's think about it ...iously.Harford versus Des? Is this their ...y threat? Come on,the superman will have ... in his pocket.
...Franz fit and watch him fly down that ...g.The lush turf will do justice to some ...Nigel's passes,Webby will be playing his ...rt out,Des & Wilson will be rocklike at ...back,Stevie will tell us the score and ...ppo will bust the net.
...early remember in an early "Brian", ...eone instructing the Captain to flex his ...eps in preparation for lifting a few ...s.These sentiments were a year too early. ...first trophy for nearly a decade? ...e On You Reds!   by Red Andy.

Paul Rat and Pete Illock ride again -

***trentenders go to wemberlee!!**

At last it's six o'clock,time to arise,time to tread the fabled path of which everyone dreams,and yet so few (outside the so-called Big 5) ever get the chance to trespass. The Trickies have made it to the Littlewoods Cup Final for a second successive year. Last year Paul Rat and Pete Illock (our heroes in this tale) were to young to go - or at least that's what their mothers said,but this year they can.They've left school and are gainfully employed as YTS Trainees at Shoes the Chemist,a job from which they've saved for their tickets and travel.

Their usual lucky matchday wear has been augmented by the traditional Forest Flat Cap - £5,not bad,I suppose.

Paul's dad has managed to get the lads seats on the coach departing from his local so that his mates can make sure they get up to no mischief.On board the coach there is much can opening and chants of "Wemberlee,Wemberlee" - and it's only eight o'clock in the morning.

Jack - the organiser - spies the two youngsters are without refreshment and so offers them a sup from his can of Triple X Gnats Wee Wee (36p a can from the corner shop and tastes like Rocket Fuel).The lads readily accept being hardened drinkers (well,shandy-aholics anyway!).It's at this point that their memories of the day become slightly hazy.They seem to remember a fine display of break-dancing,during which they took part in the new Olympic Sport of synchronised vomiting (well,nearly synchronised,Pete fetched first and Paul came out in sympathy).With this they fell into a deep alcoholic coma and were awoken in Wembley Car Park to watch the match in their puke-stained clothes.They remember a goal,a cup lifted and an ill-feeling trip home.Mum wasn't too pleased at the state they returned in as she had to scrub their Replica Umbro shirts and disinfect their Hi-Tec joggers.

As in all good stories there is a moral to this tale - NEVER EVER drink alcohol on the way to a football match,as not only do you forget most (except the very embarrassing) things that you did in your drunken stupor,but it is also ILLEGAL to drink on football coaches (especially if you get caught).
But then again,WEMBERLEE!! WEMBERLEE!! WE'RE ALL........

by   THE STUDENT.

BRi #17

Fresh Fruit For Rotting Vegetables

Bananas....a fairly innocent fruit with a wholesome image. The prompt for dozens of crappy music hall songs and slapstick falling over tomfoolery. Source of some cracking double-entendres, as in "Finbarr, go to the greengrocers and ask if he's got a long bent yellow one (and while you're at it, ask if you can feel his plums)". "The energy snack" say the banana marketing people, responsible for the most ridiculous name ever for a professional cycling team (Raleigh - Banana!!). Over the past few years, even the leader of the Tour de France has had "Banania" emblazoned on his yellow jersey (I'm not sure who or what that refers to exactly, but it's close enough). A truly fantastic fruit, I'm sure you'll agree......

Football's relationship with the banana, however, is not quite so healthy. In the hands of the terrace racist, the banana has been reduced to a symbol of brainless prejudice. The fruit (and abuse) hurled in the direction of John Barnes and Mark Walters last season highlighted the problem of racism among football supporters and finally brought the issue to the attention of the media ,who now seem to have forgotten all about it again.
Now I'll admit that it's a long time since I've seen a banana incident live and in the flesh. I recall flying nanas at Upton Park, courtesy of some cheeky chappies in the corner of the South Bank and the East Stand, back in the Justin Fashanu glory era, but none since. Neither have I ever witnessed a banana being hurled at the City Ground. In fact, it would appear that we've got quite a good track record at Forest. No-one I've ever spoken to can recall any player getting a noticeable amount of abuse because of his colour and there also seems to be a much higher proportion of black youths among the support than you get at most other clubs. Try spotting the black faces at that bastion of reasonable, friendly support....Anfield. And over at Goodison, things are probably worse. I know more than one Everton fan who has recently stopped going to the games because he is sickened and embarrassed by the racist scum.
So, things may not be THAT bad at Forest But....and it's quite a fairly major but.... it was noticeable at quite a few away games last season that there are still a few among the travelling support sufficiently stupid to make "monkey noises" at black opponents,

JUST SAY NO KIDS!

-1-

sing songs about Yids (I know there's Spurs fans who encourage this, and we've all seen the Star of David flags around White Hart Lane, but chants about Belsen and gassing Yids are NOT funny), and even refer to Franzy, Des and Calvin in less than pleasant terms.
Personally, I find this a bit embarrassing. Living away from Nottingham, I'm often tempted to drag people who've never watched Forest before along to games and it's no fun having to apologise to them for the inevitable dickhead who always seems to stand right behind us.
Of course, my embarrassment isn't really the issue here, is it? Racism isn't just embarrassing, it's offensive and dangerous. I don't think this is the time and the place to start getting over-political,but, fact number one, we live in a racist society. Fact number two, racism isn't some kind of uncontrollable instinct within us all. It's a characteristic that's been carefully and cleverly developed by the people who govern us. It helps them to run their system when they can set one part of the masses against another. Divide and rule, if you like. Therefore, racist behaviour is not only morally offensive, it's making it easier for governments to trample all over the working classes. Those among us who indulge in this kind of behaviour are therefore helping out a government which, if it had things all its own way would seemingly rather like to close down every football ground in the country....Luton Town excepted.
Let's take another example of how the liberties of football supporters have been eroded. Against who did the police first start to use and practice the tactics they now employ to control football crowds? Searches, arrests/holding on SUS, undercover operations with dodgy evidence?....Black youths. What they were allowed to get away with to control black communities, the Police now do to football supporters. Less racism and they might never have been able to get that far. Now, of course, the emphasis has changed somewhat. Footy fans are portrayed as the subhumans who

will destroy the British way of life. Never mind that 99% of us are decent peaceful people. It's now very easy to convince Joe Public that more laws are needed to control football crowds. Identity cards, Passports confiscated, no drinking in public places. Frighten one part of the public that another part will harm them, and you can get away with almost anything.
Also, whilst not wanting to get bogged down in political theory, it's pretty apparent that racism and nationalism aren't too dissimilar. So, why Thatcher and friends cry about the mayhem in Germany, we should be aware that it's their system that has positively encouraged people to actually BELIEVE that the English are in some way superior to the rest of the world. Consequently, why all the fuss when 8,000 or so lads go abroad for the summer trying to actually prove it. It's yer Bulldog spirit, ain't it? Swap the "Invasion of Germany" teeshirts for Green Jackets in the Malvinas (Falklands, if you still want to call them that) and spot the difference.....
So, what's the answer to the footy racists? Ideally, I suppose, some kind of Socialist Revolution would help, but seeing as that's a bit unlikely (well, I can't see it happening before the end of the coming season anyway), why not just politely suggest to the bigot next to you that he shuts up. Nine times out of ten at Forest we're not dealing with hulking great NF thugs (I don't fancy getting my head kicked in anymore than you do !!), more like idiots who just think it's the thing to do. And if we can rely on the decent majority to shout down the racists, there's no reason why we can't eliminate racist abuse from the Forest support.

-3- BRIAN X. **COULDN'T FIND BERT BOWERY.**

BLACK HEROES IN THE HALL OF FAME

AAARGH!!

Get Your Brains Out For The Girls

(No.2 in the series of 'isms'. This issue: Sexism).
by Englebert Smith

One of the most worrying things lately has been the club's hypocritical attitude on the issue of sexism. On the one hand they advertise the City Ground as a safe place for all the family, including women, then they ruin it by staging a mini "Benny Hill Show" at half-time by making the members of "Lulu's Model Agency" walk across the Trent End. (I keep expecting Fred Scuttle to come in and chase them round the pitch very fast) Of course the macho lads can't resist that and so the chants ring out, but more importantly smiles break out in the commercial department. The Tri-pool has been noticed and presumably sales will rise, but an alienating and sometimes frightening atmosphere has been created.
Basically the use of such "advertising techniques" is disgraceful in that it's condoning sexism and is seriously limiting crowds. As has been mentioned before in this august journal Notts has a high ratio of women to men, with many of these keen football fans, but we are alienating them with this this sort of behaviour. The cries of "Get Your Tits Out For The Lads" have become an institutionalised chant for said lads in the way that "Here we go" and "Ole, ole" have registered in the shrunken brain.
What are the solutions? Truthfully there are no easy ones but the use of these models must be stopped. Forest aren't the only ones to use this sales tactic, Norwich and Sheff. Weds. have also done so recently. It obviously works on the premise that if 'the lads' are hurling abuse at women they won't be hurling abuse at the away fans, so "hooliganism" is stopped. I'm surprised The Sun haven't presented this as The Way To Stop Football Hooliganism, seeing as they do as much to encourage the chants as anyone else. While 4 million copies o__ the Sun ar_ bought eac_ __day, the _ight agai_ _t sexism will alway_ be a losin_ battle.

BRI#4

hillsborough

Amidst the shock and repulsion the anger and depression of those first few post-Hillsborough days,was a feeling of guilt: guilt at standing in the larger,safer end;guilt at participating in those early, ignorant,hate-filled chants; guilt at being powerless to help and just standing there gawping as the full horror of events the other side of the fence began to sink in;and guilt at feeling so distressed at it all,what right do I have to intrude on the scousers grief.It was in an attempt to quash these feelings,to pay my respects,and to exorcise those horrific images pieced together from the TV and papers and my own experiences of that day, that I took the train to Anfield.

The first thing I noticed was how quiet the city was,no mouthy cabbies,few shoppers,no scallies on the make.All the parks were deserted,and for once,no children played football in the streets.The only kids I saw playing were conducting a memorial service, sitting on a step with heads bowed as one sang "The Lord's My Shepherd" in a tremulous voice.And the massive queues for the florists,and the pride that made those florists accept no money but point to the collection boxes instead.It was all too much for us so we headed for the pub,wary of what new depths of despair would hit us when we finally braved the queues that stretched from the Shankly gates.I thought it would be depressing beyond words but it was probably the most beautiful and moving sight I'll ever see.

We were in there a good three hours in the end and it seemed like no time at all.You felt you had to read every poem and tribute,the long anguished letters and those that just said WHY?,the religious messages,be it "God wants you", or "Shankly's waiting",and the ubiquitous "You'll never walk alone",and some of the most awkward,stilted and mis-spelt ones were the most poignant of all.Those and an angry "Are these your drunken yobs?" pinned to one of those harrowing pictures.And the party of tearful school-children paying tribute to a departed classmate by scrawling felt-tip messages on the barrier by his accustomed place on the Kop.

The sheer spectacle of it all was remarkably uplifting,all those thousands of flowers, elaborate tributes to single red roses,all interspersed with scarves and programmes and bedspreads and teddy bears, whole lifetimes collections of memorabilia,donated as much for the comfort and unity of those left as in memory of those departed.Most of it's probably adrift in the polluted waters of the Irish Sea by now.

It's difficult to know where to start discussing the events of Saturday April 15th. I had been excited all week and couldn't wait for Saturday morning - the red shirt freshly laundered following the excesses of last Sunday's League Cup win.Saturday started as a beautiful day and the journey north was accompanied by many Forest fans.I was due to meet some friends at a pub to the north of Sheffield - the pub was shut and as I hung around outside,some Scouse lads asked if they were on the right road.When I said I was going too,and they saw the tree on my shirt they grinned and said "Oh,you're one of them" - "No, you are" I replied.And this was typical of the feelings close to the ground - no animosity,everybody really looking forward to the match - we had to win this one. Once again we were in good voice,the game kicked off and began really well,Psycho making his presence felt,Nigel dispossessing Ablett and winning two corners,and Beardsley hitting the bar.This last event seemed to have coincided with the extra Liverpool fans pouring in,and the rush happened. Of course,we didn't know what

was happening as people cascaded onto the pitch.The first fears were of a pitch invasion - more mindless nonsense.Even when the ambulances came on,it didn't click that people had died.I saw someone having their chest pumped,and someone said they could see a fan with their head covered.The penny began to drop,but we still didn't KNOW. The match was called off at about 4.20 and someone with a radio said they'd heard that five were dead.By the time I reached my car,the number was fifty.

Since then everybody has been blamed - the FA,the police,the host club,the fans.It's not my place to assign blame,all I can do is express the shock,horror and sympathy that fell upon me. We've been in that end before and know how cramped it is.We went to see Liverpool FC get hammered and we saw people,the same as ourselves,die. It seems,at the time of writing,that football grounds are going to change forever, particularly towards all-seater stadia,rightly or wrongly.Whatever happens,those of us at Hillsborough on April 15th 1989 spent 100 minutes staring at the most awful event of our lives.

Steve Hanley.

And all the scarves and wreaths from rival fans.Everton you expect,but to see United fans of the age and quite possibly the inclination to previously have ambushed some of the victims in the backstreets of Manchester,to see them with tears in their eyes looking for an appropriate spot to lay their flags and scarves...to see a Forest lad place his precious shirt on the railings in front of the Kop and burst into tears...to see a Glasgow Rangers scarf carefully arranged on top of an Irish tricolour...all this will stay with me always.

And all this in reverential silence,except for the dull thud of cash in the buckets, the occasional "aah,that's nice" from the type of old biddie who is virtually a professional mourner,the whirring blades of the heli-copter taking today's aerial

photo,and the intermittent sobbing of grown men and small children alike. As with all terrible tragedies there are a thousand good things that could come out of all this,and I hope that some of this feeling of unity will remain.It'd be naive to think that in 10 years time there won't be sick songs sung on the terraces,that when Liverpool play United "Munich '58" will not be met with "Hillsborough '89",or that the childish wargames of moron v moron will never again be enacted in the back streets,but if the silent majority can now be raised to protest,to ensure that this time it really won't be allowed to happen again, then perhaps all those people will not have died in vain. Those terrible scenes at Hillsborough will never be erased; the sway I viciously denounced as arrogant scouse

jubilance...the small boy prostrate in his desperate fathers' arms - I'll never know if he survived...the fat man with his head covered and his arm dangling limply by his side...There could be no dignity for those herded to die like animals.But here at Anfield,away from the political point-scoring,the gutter journalism,the hatred and the recriminations,here was dignity,and compassion,and strength,and love,and reassurance,and naked human emotion.Here was the best memorial possible to both the inherent goodness and the helpless mortality of mankind.
The Universal Football Fan.

BRI#10.

THE GREAT WEBB DEBATE

Garry Parker plus £2 million DOES NOT equal more than Neil Webb for a number of reasons. Namely,we aren't going to receive £2million for Webby,as he's now cup-tied we'd be lucky to get a million at the most. Webb must not leave,he is so important to the Trickies,as he's one of the players - along with Walker,Pearce,Hodge and Clough (what a team!) - who are capable of winning us a much sought after trophy.At the end of this season it'll be nine years since a major trophy.For me and many Forest fans a trophy is more important than any money received for Webb.We can all picture Webb at Wembley picking up the ball on the edge of the area,smacking it into the top corner and running towards us,while we're all hugging our mates in that 'Roister Doister' fashion we love so much.

All those at Highbury last year will know that Parker could not have quietened Thomas and Davis like Webby did,compare this to the City Ground this year when even Harry Hodge was eventually overrun.Webb may not always catch the eye,but his running and tackling back are too often ignored.We've never been overrun with him at No. 8. Anyway,if Webby left who'd give us multiple orgasms with cross-field passes to Carr Parker and combinations with Clough: Wilson,I don't think.If he does leave it would be a crying

shame because we all know we've got a great side and to break it up would be another success for the Big Five money clubs. I want the Trees to stuff Bristol Shitty,win the Little-woods,win the FA Cup and then go on to win the League next season,but we will only do this with Webby - accept no replace-ments,just appreciate him.He's Class.

Mark Gasson,Bramcote Moor.

Forest should sell Webb to the highest bidder.Why? Nigel Clough could slot into his position quite easily,and take the part of play-maker much more effectively than Webb does at present,even when the mood takes him.Given Bobby 'Is my tie straight' Robson's inept-itude at not picking Nigel as a forward,who knows he may see fit to include him as a mid-fielder.Who takes Nigel's No.9 shirt? Tommy 'God''4 goals in 4 games' Gaynor,so long as his brains continue to fit in his size 8½'s,and they don't expand to fill his head,like what happened after his burst onto the first team scene last season.That's covered any pot-ential difficulties that could arise at Webb's departure on the field.Who do we sell him too? Niort are obviously out of the question.I think we should consult with the Daily Ram, after all,they must have sold Webb half a dozen times already this season.What to do with the

profit? 2 MILLION? Buy new stock? Improve the bloodline? I don't think so - this side is good enough and there are plenty more coming off the line. No,we should spend the £2m. on the fans (novel,eh?) and build a roof on the Library End.I will then move from my perch on the Upper Tier and reside there! We can call it the Webb End,and boo him from it on his return,with whoever he feels like playing for.

Paul Farrell,Arnold.

Neil Webb,the best footballer in the world(nearly). Sod one-footed Robson with his death-defying (injury inviting) sorties into a crowded penalty box.At least Webb waits until it's all clear before racing through to score.Who needs McMahon kicking his way to victory (or more often this season,defeat),when Webby does it with a clever pass or,more often the winning goal (just ask Liverpool).And has Neil ever resorted to a left hook a la Davis? I think not! Gas-coigne's OK but is he worth £2m when his best trick seems to be hiding the ball in his shirt. But this doesn't matter,because IF Neil left we wouldn't get one of these as a replacement. We'd spend £½ - ½million (well over the top) on a 2nd Division prospect (Gary Mac,John Sheridan) or someone from Scotland (MacKay or Ferguson). The other ½ - 1million would

then be spent on the executive suite instead of roofing the Colwick Road end (Hint).I'm not putting these young lads down, and indeed Neil himself was a 2nd Div. prospect when he was bought,but it will take at least a year for his replace-ment to reach his standard and so we'd miss out on the prizes for another year.Of course we could have a replacement at the City Ground in Wilson,Parker or Ricey but again none of them are Webbs standard. I don't think Webby will go unless: a)he's offered a decent wedge from ABROAD. b)we fail to win something. c)BC gets fed-up with nego-tiating and sends Neil out on his ear (unlikely). I'm pretty sure Webby won't go to a British club,and I don't know if he'd be as successful anywhere else mainly because of his relationship on the field with our Nigel.They combine so well and certainly miss each other if one is unfit (eg v Arsenal,Nigel had no-one to link with,and in Webb's games for England he hasn't exactly set the world alight). My last point concerns Neil,or rather some of the idiots in the crowd,especially on New Year's Eve,shouting "Fuck off to Man United" and various other derogatory chants aimed at Webby,especially after an early miss,yet as soon as he heads a goal he's their golden

-2-

BRi#8

---

boy again.If people don't like Neil,OK! but I just can't stand fickle bastards like that. Neil Webb Fan Club. AKA Rob,Lincs..

How do you describe Webby? There is certainly no doubting his immense talent,or unfort-unately,his immense lack of effort.It's so infuriating 'cos you know when he wants to he can be world class.So why do I want to wring his neck all the time? You have to accept that he's not now or ever going to be a grafter,but it would be ever so nice just to see him win the odd challenge,the odd 50/50 (or 60/40). Having said this,how many goals did we concede against WHAM & Arsenic,sans Webb.Odd really isn't it. Although I agree that £2m + Garry Parker doesn't equal Webby,I'm rather fond of the equation £2m from Man.U. minus £1.5m to Leeds = no Neil Webb, one John Sheridan and ½ million in the bank,with which we can buy 25 Gary Crosby's and an infinite number of Terry Wilson's, When all is said and done,I don't think we can do without him for the moment (at least until he stops trying altogether),and you don't win 10 in a row with a passenger in midfield,so he must be doing something right. Perhaps you'd like to write in yourself Neil? The address is

at the front.Come on,answer our big question for us,please Neil.How do you account for Everton away compared with Wimbledon at home??? Damien Mackinney. Aspley.

"Who're you calling a pin-up boy?"

Something has to be written in defence of the Forest pin-up boy Neil Webb.Here we have a player who at times this season has been subjected to even more stick than our unfortunate carrot top on the left.Surely a more rational mode of thought would explain some of his poorer performances over the first half of the season. Bought in the hysterical summer of '85,following the Heysel tragedy,Neil made his debut at Luton,scoring with a free-kick. How refreshing it was to see a Forest player actually waving

to the away support after a game.He became an instant favourite with the Forest faithful,all 16,000 at the time.The rest of the season showed Neil to be an erratic player who still got into double figures goal wise.Surely we couldn't expect much more from a young player who was involved in a Forest team going through that eternal transition stage. Come the following season and more was expected from our precocious talent.And under the guidance of Captain Bomber he produced some eye-catching performances,again getting into double figures goal wise.With Bowyer behind him Neil was able to concentrate on his strengths, getting forward and scoring goals.Over the past two seasons his natural instincts have had to take a backseat to his nurturing of Terry Wilson and the pursuit of midfield excellance,ie building from the back and tackling.Now let's be honest,he couldn't tackle Brian's dog.Consequently,we've seen more of the bad side of Neil Webb and less of the good side,the buccaneering,flash smiling goal-getter that he really is.Surely more patience could've been given to a man who has spent a mere four seasons in the 1st Division,and who last season shared the onus of attack with Nigel and Psycho,whilst the others around him were either learning (Wilson,Chettle),or struggling

to achieve consistency (Wilko, Rice,Carr). The return of Steve Hodge created another problem that was soon evident.Here was a player who was very much identical to Neil,one who was brilliant going forward but weak at tackling back.His time away had not curbed his old instincts so Neil ended up playing deeper than he had last season.The partnership looked doomed to failure,until sudden-ly it's started to click.Neil and Harry have at last devel-oped an understanding,whilst the excellant contributions of Laws,Chappo & Parker have eased their workload. I don't suppose the winning of the Simod,Littlewoods or FA Cups will sway his decision to leave.It seems a crazy move just when at last his own,plus the teams massive potential is close to being realised.A replacement will have to be found quickly.Garry Parker is the obvious choice,but that leaves the problem of the left wing,one that has existed since Robbo left.The signing of McAllister,or possibly the superb Sheridan,would be more practical. Meanwhile,I'll be left ponder-ing on what might have been,as yet another Red on the verge of greatness leaves to seek his game and fortune elsewhere,only to find oblivion.Just ask Harry Neil.

Peter Gilbert,Nottingham.

-3-   -4-

Chris Waddle in Honest Footballer

Shocker!

I forget his exact words,but when Chrissy Waddle signed the contract with Marseille that will keep him in beer and tabs for the rest of his life,he said something along the lines of...'I'm one year into a 7-year contract with Spurs and I never envisaged leaving,I apologise to the fans,but when an offer that will make me and my family financially secure for the rest of our lives comes in,you have to seriously consider it...'

Well obviously Chris Waddle would never dream of using a word like 'envisaged',but I should imagine Spurs fans would say "Can't say fairer than that Chris,good luck me old china".

Now compare that to a fat England midfield player,leaving a progressive,exciting young East Midlands club on the verge of world domination,to go to a once great but now utterly crap team from a declining Northern industrial town,obviously because he'll get a bigger wad (hence the nickname Fat Wallet),AND THEN claiming that it's only 'cos he wants to "consolidate his England position into the 90's".Well,thanks for spitting in our eyes Webby.This might be difficult to understand for some people,but having a fave Garibaldi is a bit like a love affair.And for Webby to do this is a bit like your favourite girlie saying "Sorry...your best mate's a complete prat...but he's got a bigger knob than you so I'm going out with him instead".

Neil,young man,I feel personally insulted by your decision;be a man and tell us it was for the cash,'cos all this international career rubbish really sticks in my throat.(By the way,you'll have trouble keeping your England place from the 2nd Division,so make the most of it while it lasts).

DAMIEN MACKINNEY.

BRI #11

Psycho Mafia...

Why did Bobby Robson say that Psycho and Chris Waddle were too mentally drained,after the penalty shoot-out,to play against Italy - and then have the nerve to bring Waddle on at half-time? Not only was he being hypocritical but he might just have ended Psycho's international career.

You don't have to read between the lines to see that Robson blames Psycho for England not getting to the final.Probably the most patriotic player in the squad (did you see the way he blasted out the national anthem?),Psycho apparently wanted to play against Italy but Robson had other ideas.He put on Dorigo,who isn't such a bad player but he just can't tackle (a vital requirement for a full-back,I would've thought).The stick Psycho got in the papers the following day was ridiculous.Everyone said he missed his penalty,when in fact it was saved - what more could the man do? It was Waddle who missed,or perhaps he thought the goal was in the sky.I'd have thought Shilton would have saved at least one....Now everyone is saying that Psycho will live with that memory for the rest of his life,have nightmares for years to come,and will always be remembered as the man that cost his country the World Cup.You don't have to tell him that,after seeing him cry his heart out.He's probably going to get slagged off for the rest of his international career,if he has one.It's just as well that Graham Taylor is taking over from that vindictive Robson.Never mind though - he'll always be a hero to us Forest fans.Long live PSYCHO! PSYCHO! PSYCHO!

by NINA NAGARAJAN.

BRI #19

COLWICK ROAD'S CLASSIEST COLUMNIST...

Christmas.I hate bastard Christmas.If I hear Slade or Wizzard once more I'll have the guts of that polar bear in the Broadmarsh centre. The streets are all clogged with Mrs Bradys buying socks and useless kitchen utensils,and it's all football on Sundays when the pubs are shut afters,and losing to your nephews at Subtrivpolysquigglybastards,and some drunken arsehole on the A52 ploughing into 16 carol-singing Brownies and a queue of blokes outside the phonebox waiting to tell their wives their working late at the Reindeer and Fuckpig again.Everyone gets into total excess at Christmas.They don't worry about upstaging us poor bastards who do it all year round. Think I'll stay sober this year and watch everyone else making a horses knob of themselves.The money I get to keep it all quiet should keep me in beer till next Christmas. Mind you,I've had my share of going to Midnight Mass with a bottle of Whiskey in my hand and giving diced turkey to the offertory.But then I'm an athiest.I mean,if there was a God then Forest would beat bastard Liverpool 18-0 away every week.

And then there's the students and their bastard Christmas balls.I hate bastard students,they've got no fucking balls. Me and my mate Walshie used to go to student bars just to wind them up."Did you spill my pint?","Eek eek,it's a townie,call the police".Who do they think they are,Elton fucking Welsby? They think they're so clever.What's so fucking clever about putting glitter in your hair and singing "Hi-Ho Silver Lining" and throwing up after $2\frac{1}{2}$ pints of snakebite??? They dress up as women at every opportunity,they "kidnap" politicians on Ragweeks (and plough them with cheap wine and sandwiches when they should be ploughing them with bullets),and if you don't know all the words to "My Name Is Jack I'm A Necrophilliac" you're a Class One Plonker.Think they've got a monopoly on brain(lessnes)s.People often mistake me for one,"Oh you seem quite intelligent,why aren't you a student".Because I couldn't stand being banged up for 3 years with twats like you mate.Just because I've got a railcard and a shit haircut.How many of your most hated politicians,TV personalities and newspaper proprietors were students? Most of them,right! And how many of your favourite footballers, Soap Opera Stars,barmen and checkout girls were? NONE OF THEM (except for Martin O'Neill).I rest my case. Well I suppose I'd better talk about bastard football now, and if there's one team that really gets on my tits it's this Notts Forest.Who are these Notts Forest bastards? I've never heard of them.I presume we amalgamated with County when I was on one of my ten-day benders so I missed the whole thing.But I hate it on TV when twats like Ron Atkinson and that professional Geordie Lawrie "I'm that fucking hard I drink low-alcohol lager and smoke menthol tabs,me" McMenemy talk about Notts Forest this and Notts Forest twat. Have martians from the planet Notts-ingham invaded and taken over our Lads in red? You even see it on those cheapo scarves and flags up the market.Nottm. or just plain bastard Forest please.Fucking part-timers,string 'em up. BORIS

BRI #6 - reviks & revered in viry marven measures...

COACH CRASH!

Graham Taylor recently announced that he intends to regularly take training sessions at the top English clubs as part of his "tracksuit" approach to the England manager's job.Here at BRIAN we have managed to get hold of an exclusive transcript of what happened at the City Ground recently when G.T. turned up to take a top secret session.

G.T. : OK lads,I just want you to treat me the same as you would the Gaffer.... No,no please,get up off your knees.Where are you off to,Nigel?

N.C. : Dad always lets me go and do the shopping on Thursdays.Margaret goes mad if I don't get to the meat counter before the best cuts have gone.

G.T. : Erm..this isn't a very good start,is it lads.Let's have you jogging round the track to warm up.Off you go.

(the players run half-heartedly for a few paces,then stop,staring at Taylor)

G.T. : What's the problem?

B.R. : Och,well the Gaffer's usually just going off for a wee game o' squash 'bout noo.

G.T. : Hey! Aren't you Scottish? No bloody spies here thanks.Clear off.Any other non-English,go and wait in the Jubilee Club.

T.W. : Bloddybrulliant.Ye're mae kind o' gaffer.

G.T. : Oh dear,we still haven't got started yet.

S.P. : How abaht a quick stroll dahn by the river.

G.T. : No,no,five-a-side,that's the thing.I'll have Des,Harry and Nigel on my side.Franz,you pretend you're Tony Daley,and I'll be Dorigo.

S.P. : In that case,mite,I'll captain the ather side.

G.T. : Right,everybody ready? Des,is it from Italy that you're still limping?

S.P. : Nah,he tripped over his bloody wallet,ha ha.

G.T. : That'll do! Right,we're off.Oh,lovely ball Nigel...never mind Tony,I mean Franz...played Harry,pass it here,I'm fre..AARGGHHH!!

S.P. : Sorry,me old son,mistimed that one.

G.T. : But my leg! Where's my leg?!?

G.C. : Don't worry boss,I'll soon fix that.Used to be a carpenter,you know, before I went to Lincoln City,that was...

G.T. : Did you say Lincoln City? The peak of any professional's career.You'll be in my first team squad.What a nice young man (loses consciousness).

(at this moment,B.C. sticks his head round the door)

B.C. : Right lads,that's today's twenty minutes.Off you go.See you Saturday afternoon!

by TEACHERMAN.

Pansies.

BRIAN/Pansies badges out soon....

Welcome back to the City Allotments for the new season.As you can see,there have been one or two changes during the close season - like the new official club badge here,and you'll have noticed the huge steaming piles of manure and compost on the pitch - very popular at the Baseball Ground,I'm assured. There have been one or two changes on the playing side too. I'm sure you'll give a warm welcome to our new 'keepers, Digweed (ex-Brighton) and Flowers (Southampton) - neither has safe hands but both have green fingers - and I'm sure you're looking forward to seeing them blossom later in the season. Then there's Mower (Walsall) sweeping up at the back, Bloomer (Chesterfield),Blades (Derby) and Berry (Stoke),all budding talents.In fact the only player you'll recognise is Steve Hedge,who's looking very trim this season.The final change is of course that we've pulled out of the League - the only competition we're interested in now is the FA Vase. Come on you Pansies!

TEACHERMAN.

...And Now HE'S Gone..

• It's thumbs up for John Sheridan following his £650,000 move to Forest from Leeds

SHERIDAN

Even now,several days after the event, it's still difficult to be rational about the Sheridan debacle.Let's just recap..

While BC was on his summer hols,it becomes apparent that John Sheridan is due to sign for Chelsea for £650,000. Then,at the last minute,in steps Ron Fenton to put together a package to bring him to us - perfect,the Webby replacement so admirably forecast (though over-priced) in BRIAN 8.BC arrives refreshed from the vacation with the news."I have no intention of signing John Sheridan now or in the future".A few days later,he's a tricky. "Ha ha,good old Brian,keeps us guessing, eh?" Doesn't he just.As we lurch from dodgy result to dodgy result,with the crowd baying for the new messiah,there is no sign of him,although the reserves are pulling in gates previously unknown. At last,the debut in an ignominious 1-1 v Huddersfield at home - the crowd are so pleased that "Oh Johnny Johnny.." is a new entry at number 2 in the Trent End chant list.So he didn't set the game alight,but his ability was obvious.Blink and you'd missed it though.Back to the

stiffs and then the final nail in the coffin - a Daily Express headline, "Your Future Is With Us",five days later he's gone,only to return to help Sheffield Weds. to their first away win (and goal) at the Pride of the Midlands.

I couldn't be more embarrassed if I was a Man.Utd supporter - Brian,you've really taken the spotlight from Michael Knighton when it comes to looking for a laughing stock.Can you imagine the scenario at your place of work? You buy something that you need,you never use it eventually sell it,telling your guvnor, "Oh,we dropped £150,000 on that!",then a competitor uses it to push you into second place.We'd be talking "Job Centre" within 24 hours.

Brian,I've trusted you before,when you got rid of Withe,Francis,Birtles,Shilton, and bought Ian Wallace,Asa Hartford and Gary Megson,with the latter two both featuring in Sheridan-type turnarounds. But what happened here? You chuck £150,000 down the pan,and we still stand in the rain on the Colwick Road End.Brian,I think we've a right to know. by STEVE HANLEY.

MADHOUSE IN SESSION

When I addressed the question "Is Clough mad?", the word 'yes' quickly sprang to mind. Hot on the heels of that, however, was the famous cliche about "genius bordering on madness", and if it takes madness to take a mid-table second division team to the pinnacle of European club achievement then who needs sanity?

I'm sure that Shankly, Paisley and Busby had their own little idiosyncracies, without being as obtuse as our Brian. His ability to draw attentions to his actions certainly doesn't veil any hints of madness he may possess.

For a truly in-depth appraisal of Clough's psyche, I strongly recommend Tony Francis' excellent biography (aptly entitled "Clough - A Biography"). I couldn't help thinking whilst reading this book that there seems to be a great sense of insecurity in Clough's life. Beginning with his apparent reliance on Peter Taylor in his early days at Middlesbrough, he has more lately shown great reluctance in letting his fledglings "fly the nest" (although Nigel has married since I originally wrote this article). It seems that his desire for familiar surroundings and people, and his fear of rejection - particularly by his family, are uppermost in his thoughts. Intrusions are never welcome.

The intrusion theme leads us nicely onto Brian's most famous of "erratic" acts, ie the QPR Incident. Now, whatever his motives were (and I'm still waiting for ITV to show the 50-100 pitch invaders making their way towards the away fans in a threatening manner, because that is what preceeded his actions - see piece entitled "another story"), to actually go and punch people at random is hardly a sane act. Some may point to other influences. It's hardly a secret that he's always enjoyed the odd drinkie, but as I can't afford to defend a libel case, I think you should consult Mr Francis' aforementioned biography for more depth on that point.

In those dark and gloomy days at the City Ground known as the Coming of Fashanu, Clough again demonstrated his reduced marble count in the famous training ground incident. I and many others think having BIG Justin (cue cheap joke) arrested for entering the training ground whilst under suspension (for being crap) is a wondrous either, but how many would actually do it?

Earlier this season he frustrated us all by physically restraining Liam from treating injured players during matches. This resulted in Stuart "swashbuckling"

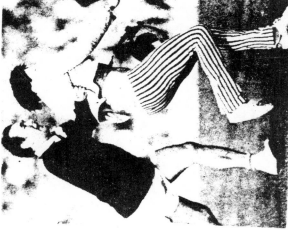

BRIAN CLOUGH BOLLOCKS (AND I...

...operation on West Bromford. And we you get the idea they're still

I know that BC was sent down to Earth to be the undisputed Messiah of football, but that doesn't mean we have to condone his every action. If he's in the wrong, then we should tell him so. After all, he must know it, so why haven't our supporters they were scared he would seek divine retribution and send down a thunderbolt from the heavens.

anyway, here's hoping that Forest fans aren't so bloody spineless in the future, and that Brian can keep his temper under control, so that all us decent supporters can enjoy ourselves, watching the Trickies win the lot this season, without having to worry about having the shit beaten out of us by an over zealous manager.

by Neil Northage.

Going home, after the QPR Littlewoods Cup trouncing, I was looking forward to the next days' newspaper headlines. That is until I saw the TV highlights, when our very own 'great white hope', BC himself, decided to give Bruno a lesson or two on how it should be done.

Instead of 'Forest hit five' we got 'Clough hits five'.

If that wasn't bad enough we got Maurice 'yes Mr Clough' Roworth telling us that the only way to stop 'hooliganism' was with liberal amounts of gratuitous violence.

And what was this act of 'hooliganism'? A couple of hundred fans ran onto the pitch, to celebrate their team getting to a semi-final, and to congratulate the players. But, according to Roworth, they were there to cause trouble with QR

how, I don't condone pitch invasions, even innocent ones such as this, but the treatment dished out by our Brian was, to say the least, a little bit OTT and judging by his rather sheepish reactions (a trait he must have picked up in his ram days?!!) during the following days, Clough has some regrets about the incident himself.

Why are Forest fans so bleeding apologetic??? Four fans, who were physically attacked by Clough, went to him, before the next game, to apologise! surely he should have come to them!

And at the next match the crowd were singing his name and applauding him even more loudly than usual, obviously in favour of his violent actions. If he'd abused fifteen children and

ONE MAN AND HIS DOG BY DEZO ©

OF COURSE IT WAS TOTALLY OUT OF CHARACTER...

A REGRETABLE ACTION TAKEN ON THE SPUR OF THE MOMENT...

CLOUGH PUNCH-UP

GET OFF MY F*****G CHAIR! DEL BOY!

BR!#8

BRI#17

who's mad?

Pearce playing on an untreated, injured ankle for 20 or so minutes, and consequently missing the next two games, including the Palace away match where the team had about as much driving force as my car (that I've just written off). In that same match Gary "leave me alone 'cos I'm playing bastard well" Crosby was unceremoniously flattened by John "OI NIGEL! HAVE A GOAL" Pemberton, and lay motionless and untreated for a worrying amount of time. Liam is now allowed on to treat my precious Trickies, but I wouldn't be surprised if "tongue swallowing" publicity played a big part in this.

Is all of this madness though? It would be valid to argue that he merely has a particularly autocratic style of leadership. Clough does tend to crave total control of all around him, and indeed his constant need of "hangers-on" and "yes-men" was one of the final nails in the coffin of his relationship with Peter Taylor.

He's also notoriously bad at handling "star" players. Sir Trevor was a prime example, and to a lesser extent Peter Ward, Johnny Metgod and John Sheridan were treated much the same. You could cast doubts over Ward's ability, and I've now succumbed to the theory that Sheridan may not be the player that he looked like for about 5 minutes v Huddersfield, but these players were all messed about, but these players were all messed about in charge. Francis was made to play on the right of midfield and so left for a club that let him play up front (although there were other reasons for Francis' departure, not least the huge overdraft caused by a new stand and the nightmare

His flirtation with the Wales job seemed to be merely a tool to show the Forest board that they'd better be nice to him or he'd be gone. Indeed Maurice Roworth has said that Brian can work one day a week if he likes, so now he's got them exactly where he wants them.

that was Justin Fashanu).

Even with all this taken into account, you could turn round and say "One Championship, One runners-up spot, Three 3rd places; Two European Cups, One Super Cup; Three League Cups; Two FA Cup semi-finals, and now another League Cup Final, Matey!". And you'd be right, of course. And who in the world is qualified to judge the sandwich content of someone else's picnic anyway? And at the end of the day, if you can get the results out there on the park over 90 minutes, when it's eleven men against eleven men, the same game all over the world, etc....then who cares if your bundle's a few sticks short?

by DAMIEN MACKINNEY.

YOU ARE THE MANAGER!

Beginning (and probably ending) a new series in which you, reader and mere mortal,put yourself in the position of the Godhead.Sounds impossible,I know,but give it a try anyway.
No.1.INJURIES.

1).Nigel receives the ball,just as his marker dives in with both feet,catching him in the small of the back.Do you:
  a).Ring up the Queens Medical Centre to see if there are any spare beds?
  b).Send Liam on with the sponge?
  c).Hold Liam back,at the same time shouting "Get up,you lazy bugger"?

2).Psycho goes in for a 20-80 challenge,comes away with the ball,but unfortunately leaves his left foot behind.Do you:
  a).Arrange for a team of micro-surgeons to be in the dressing-room at half-time?
  b).Push Liam on with the sponge?
  c).Tell them to get on with the game,and let Mr Pearce worry about putting his foot back on when the ball goes out of play?

3).An opponent's over zealous challenge causes Harry Hodge to end up on the back row of the Upper Tier.Do you:
  a).Call out a mountain rescue team with breathing equipment and crampons to try to get him down?
  b).Ask for a helicopter to get Liam and his sponge up there?
  c).Fine Hodge a week's wages for leaving the pitch without your permission?

4).A crazed John Sheridan fan runs onto the pitch with a machete and decapitates Garry Parker.Do you:
  a).Send for a priest and begin writing a letter of condolence?
  b).Get Liam to soak the sponge in super-glue before applying it to the affected areas?
  c).Tell Parker to use his head and get up,at the same time arranging for Sheridan to go on a decades loan to Frickley Athletic?

5).A Boeing 747 crash-lands in the Forest penalty area.Do you:
  a).Immediately inform the emergency services,and tell the Prime Minister that there will soon be some disaster survivors for her to get some political mileage out of by visiting them in hospital and pretending to be concerned?

b).Tell Liam to get some extra sponges out of the dressing-room?
c).Go around thumping the rescue workers for being on the pitch?

THAT'LL TEACH LIAM NOT TO TAKE HIS

SPONGE OUT IN PUBLIC....

ANSWERS: a).1 point b).3 points c).5 points.
SCORES:-
  5-9: You really are a bit of a softy,aren't you? It's people like you who've let the play-acting foreigners and their attitudes take over the game.With you on the bench, every time someone stubbed their toe it would be like a scene from 'Casualty'.I don't know,liberal do-gooders... (continues in the Daily Telegraph,any day of the week).
  10-19: You've obviously realised one of the important things about injuries,which is not to make a drama out of a crisis.However,you do still tend to over-react a little.I mean,is it necessary to send on the trainer just because you see what may or may not be blood? You need to know when to let things alone.After all,it may just be that someone's shirt has run a bit in the rain!
  20 Plus: Well done Brian.   by ALEX MONEY.

BRI#13

Commercial Nonsense...

Results may have varied over the years at Forest but some things never change; every now and then the Club will have a good whinge about poor attendances.There are many suggestions as to why the area should be struck by this apathy; are Notts folk naturally lazy? are the attendances fiddled?? do we have particularly innovative D.I.Y. shops? does everyone read Jeff Powell in the Daily Mail?? We,the much malign-ed faithful,may shake our heads in dismay,but what are the club doing to attract the missing thousands??
Not a lot.They could certainly take a look at Millwall's Catch 'Em Young policy,(one of many schemes which make Millwall, of all people,probably the most accessible & progressive club in the country)-hundreds of tickets are given away to school-children for every home match, players give talks in schools etc.(and if you fire the child's imagination you may well entice the lapsed or indifferent parent)...Millwall also run a creche,which has been criticised in some quarters,but it gives Mummy a few hours to herself, whether they be spent on the terraces or in Safeways,and also must encourage the kids.How can they fail to be indoctrinated, once they're in the habit of meeting their mates at the ground once a fortnight, once they're old enough to be intri-gued by the shouts and roars in the background??
Given the disproportionate ratio of women to men in Notts,perhaps

an effort could be made to per-suade local women that the game is not the sole property of the Hooligan & the football bores in the pub talking Central League goal difference.Maybe some less attractive game (ie Norwich on a Weds. night) could be free for women (or at least dead cheap). Surely this would bring in more converts than a thousand Miss Forest meat markets...The club do seem a little old-fashioned & chauvinistic as regards women, take the Junior Reds girls aerobics classes;I mean aerobics were invented as torture for fat middle-aged American women in pursuit of the Body Beautiful (or at least those who can't afford to get the nips & tucks, and the cellulite vacuumed off), hardly an ideal pastime for the football mad 10 year old.If the Forest wives can have a football team then why not the brats? Anyway,while there's obviously a distinction between sound value for money and the Spurs style rip-off,Forest seem to cherish their shambling,amateurish style. It's all very sweet & familish, as befits the biggest small club in the league,but perhaps they could do with just the slightest ruthless streak...
Take the Forest videos.The offi-cial 'History' tape was endearing at times,but all home movies become embarrassing after a while what with Ken Smales' monotonous drone,Lloyd & Robbo's beery ambience and Johnny Metgod proving just how boring the average footballers life is... Lots of "Oh Look,We're just One

Big Happy Family",but...not a lot of Football really...
The goals of last season tape was considerably better on this count but the editing was diabolical. Presumably K.S. brought his machine in from home and fixed the whole thing up with a £1-50 wire from Rumbelows.All the games merge together,when home matches run consecutively it's difficult to tell what match you're watching.And dont even TRY to find a particular game or you'll be auto-searching till Christmas.Surely it wouldn't've cost much to get a bit of cardboard write "Forest v -----"on it and stick it in front of the camera before each game.Could also have done with longer build-ups,partic-ularly on the numerous good moves that failed.
They apologise for the commentary in advance but for some reason they're talking about the inaudible bits.Now I'm even less of an audio-visual expert than the bloke who put the tape together,but surely the commentary could've been re-recorded? What you can hear is excrutiating. "Clough, to Carr,oooOOH! ooerrr! uh - OOOOOHH!!! GOOOAAALLL!!!"(the BBC are queuing up).We all get carried away at times,and the average bloke in the Trent End would be no better,but they ARE taking our hard earned cash for this....
However the most con-fusing thing is the segregation of goals (ours in order -

Theirs at the end).If the total project is supposed to recapt -ure the spirit of the season then surely it's logical to show all the goals in the con-text that they were scored? We do have fast forward buttons in case our nerves can't take it. Whatever happened to the pro-posed Championship Season compi-lation??,with a few quid spent professional help that would've been a classic.Also how about a 1959 CupFinal tape,a European nights compilation,and maybe a 60's selection (featuring the Almost Double season etc.).I wouldn't mind overspending if the product's worth it.
The heart's in the right place but it's about time the Club learnt that PR means a bit more than a few hospital visits and goofy photos with the Shippos mob....
                    by J.S. Pritchard

Alcoholics Anonymous Convention
at the Jubilee Club.

BRI#2

Who's The Hardest?

Over the summer a fierce argument has blown up as to who is the hardest,is it Biffa Bacon,the stereotype Geordie thug featured in VIZ COMIC? Or is it our very own Psycho? As you would agree it is a close run thing,so I have decided to put an end to the argument by analysing the two and determining the winner in several disciplines,not unlike the modern pentathlon.

BIFFA	PSYCHO
1) PROMINENCE OF FISTS	
In each strip that Biffa appears in he is giving someone a good twatting.No Biffa story would be complete without some gratuitous punching. (9 points).	Young Stuart is somewhat more restrained in these matters,preferring the thigh high challenge to a bout of fisticuffs.Only before a match are the fists really prominent. (5 points).
2) ALL-ROUND VIOLENCE	
Unprovoked violence is a main part of Biffa's life. Would sooner headbutt someone than shake hands. (10 points).	Has to be severely provoked before the action starts, but once fired up he excels.Could be an Olympic Gold Medallist at the Off the Ball challenge,just ask McMahon or McMinn. (8 points).
	3) TATTOOS
	Being a southerner tattoos are not second nature to him,so his patriotic tattoo scores well.All he needs is a Forest crest on the other arm,'cos we know he loves the club as much as we love him. (9 points).

BIFFA GETS IN ON THE 'INFLATABLES' CRAZE...

Around his home territory tattoos are a requirement to join nursery school,so his 'Mam' and 'Dad' score lowly for imagination. (2 points).

BRi#11

4) ENGLAND CAPS

Doesn't follow in his home town's tradition of Great Footballers,though Bobby Gould has watched him as a potential successor to Vinny Jones. (0 points).	Has seen off all comers in the battle for the White No.3 shirt.Will be there for many years - unless,of course,he leaves the City Ground (The Greenest Grass Of All). (10 points).

5) BOBBLE HATS

Wor Biffa is of course never seen without his black & white Newcastle bobble hat,but it is a wee bit repetitive. (4 points).	Very quiet on the Bobble hat front until his Littlewoods Cup Victory white hat.No-one knows exactly why he wore it (probably for a bet). (10 points).

So from the five events Biffa managed only 25 points out of a maximum 50,whereas our Psycho scored 42.Conclusive proof that Mr Pearce could chin Biffa plus Mutha and Fatha in one go without spilling his pint.
Next Issue: Tony Adams v Terry F***witt.
BOBBY FARTPANTS.

TIRED OF THOSE OLD BREAKFAST CEREALS? FED UP WITH DESSIE WHEATIEFLAKES,SHREDDED RIGHT WINGER AND SUGAR COATED FORESTIES? THEN TRY CLOUGHIES NEW "RICE CROSBIES"...

"crap tackle"

"FLOP"

rice crosbies

THEY MAY NOT HAVE MUCH BITE,AND NINE OUT OF TEN SEASON TICKET HOLDERS DISLIKE THEM,BUT TESTS AGAINST DERBY PROVED THEY'RE BETTER THAN MORE POPULAR ALTERNATIVES!

BRi #12

HARRY HODGE

I suppose at fast approaching 32 years of age I'm really too old to have heroes,however,I just can't help but feel that MORRISSEY and DAVE GEDGE are geniuses,and STEVE MARTIN & ROBIN WILLIAMS never fail to crack me up,and then there's Harry Hodge.Yes,Harry Hodge, you see I even named my bike after him,and even through the bad years at Villa & Spurs me and Harry were out on the streets of South London together.
Like most of us I was dubious about the prodigal son's return,he was costing us a lot of dosh and we had all read the reports of his loneliness (well he could have come round to see me!)and consequent moaning in London - BUT,and it is a big BUT,I did want him back if he could reproduce the old form,the form which at the impressionable age of 17! (season 83-84),that had made me name my new bike after him, praise indeed.
Harry made his debut away to Ipswich on the last day of the 81-82 season,an exceptionally mediocre season in which - 27 -

midget goal machine Ian Wallace top scored with......9 goals from 28 games and we finished 12th.However,the previous match had seen us record our first win for 7 games,2-0 v Spurs at home and a certain P.Davenport grabbed his first goal for us.Of course,in the Ipswich game Davvo netted a hat-trick and we won 3-1,with Harry partnering Dav up front.
The 82-83 season saw Harry play 39 league games,mostly down the right flank,and he scored his first goal(s) at Anfield,two in fact to help us to a 3-1 lead with 15 minutes left.With the aid of a penalty (SHOCKER!)Liverpool finally managed to beat us 4-3 though! Always capable of scoring, Harry netted 9 for the season and under the careful tuition of Bomber soon learnt some of the finer points of tackling and competing for the ball,in fact he had a great first full season and was a key reason we managed to finish 5th.
In 83-84 he was even better, still managing to score 10 in the league,he saved some of his

best moments for the UEFA Cup. Including managing to bag a typical but crucial first goal at Celtic,after we had once again been written off in Europe. Then scoring two late headers at home v Anderlecht in the semi, the second at full length bulleting into the roof of the net in front of the Trent End - such joy.
84-85 saw him miss one game - the away leg of the UEFA disappointment at Brugge.He scored twice in the victory over Luton at home which actually took us to the top for a week.He also got the first for us v Man. Utd at home to bring us back to 2-1 down,a usual Hodge goal, arriving late but quickly at the edge of the area to drive into the bottom corner.Of course, Mills,and a last kick of the game free-kick from Metgod,saw us complete a brilliant comeback 3-2.
85-86 saw Harry go quickly before I had even realised it, little did we know on the night that SHEFF.WEDS. would be his last game,I was well

saddened.Especially when his first cap duly arrived,and once againit seemed we just couldn't afford to keep hold of our best players.Then of course he was down to the smoke and playing anonymously in the Cup Final v Coventry.Although I never considered changing my bikes' name to Webby or Psycho,it just isn't the same following a player who doesn't turn out in the red shirt,so I was pleased when I heard rumours of Harry coming home.Didn't the talks drag on,but I somehow knew everything would be OK when there was Harry posing for pictures on the pitch at Norwich. OK,so it's hardly been an electric start to the season, but Harry is back and playing well,hustling and winning the ball,and he's always likely to score.His two at Millwall were vintage stuff,and at Charlton he was everywhere for us.I'm glad he's back,and if ever I can afford a car (and could drive),I know what mine would be called...Harry.
MARK WILLIAMSON.

BRi #7

ATMOSPHERE..... BRI #5

"Forest fans,in the main,don't possess the fervency of their counterparts in the North East or North West" (Off The Ball no.14) WHY? Is it something they put in the water up there? Or is it the mogadon they put in it down here? But there's got to be a reason. One of the many factors could be that since the demise of the East Stand the singing element has been confined to the Trent End.Or perhaps the singers have now grown up and their renditions of "All Mist Rolling In From The Trent are confined to the B&Q. Maybe the younger elements have decided to save their throats for the chants of "Acieeed" at the Nightclubs after the matches.Who knows but it all adds up to less noise.

The Main Stand (hitherto known as "the rug boys") have not been compared to "the Kop" with their vocal volume,and it's hardly surprising.I held a season ticket with the rug boys for 3 seasons in my younger years (and when I didn't have to pay for it). During this time I found most of the noise directed at slagging off Brian Rice and complaining when their seats were cracked. Occasionally (when the hip flasks take effect) they flap their rugs (the ones on their knees or on their heads? - ed.) and sing "Come On You Reds",but then they remember where they are and leave it to us "louts" on the terraces to continue the vocal chores.Also we can't forget the Junior Reds Chorus residing in the stand.The

official kindergarten and training ground for the Trent End Choirs,where every chant is raised by 8 octaves and delivered in a suitably sanitised way.Some chants though occasionally slip through the net.For instance,did you see Brian Clough stick two fingers up at the Junior Reds when they joined in with "Char- lie Nicholas,what a wanker" ?? NO WAY.(And they did sing it).

Working anti-clockwise we find the Bridgford End.They did sing against Liverpool! (though this is not con- firmed).When you obtain a Membership card is your voicebox ripped out? Or does the free circulation of air allow for the need for less vocal strain(?) Work that sentence out,I can't !! Maybe they're just boring bastards.On my less than regular visits to the Bridgford End I found a haven of Brian Rice haters, people with old radios and people who only clap when we score,I felt out of place when I jumped up and down.And I kept getting attacked by the wasps. And then there's the Exec- utive Stand,a boring name which fits the people who reside in it (will White Hart Lane be renamed the Executive Ground?) I can remember when they were

asking for suggestions for the name of the stand.There were the usual boring ones (Brian Clough "New East" etc) But amongst the dross emerged a few gems like the "Cloughera" and the "Big Stand" (I made that one up) but the best was the"D.H. Lawrence Stand".Can you imagine if it had been called this? The jokes would've been endless.And was D.H.Lawrence a Forest fan? I think we should be told. As it's new you might expect the more yuppie element to go there,but have you ever seen the filofaxes being thrown up in the air as we score? Or heard any songs about anyones sexual fetishes sung to the acc- ompaniement of the latest Tracy Chapman single? Never.

Lack of volume here must be down to vertigo.I once sat in the back row of this Stand and I was afraid to move,let alone sing. Then we move into the temple of the strained necks,where "Guess the Goal" means "Guess where the Goal Is".Yes,the Trent End.The only place in the ground where you're guaranteed a drunk in front of you and behind you (besides the Directors Box).We will keep singing "One One" even though we hardly ever score from corners.While the rest walk in silence,we never will.So sing up Bridgford,Exec,Main Stand,D.H.Lawrence,Mr Groundsman,S.Peel of Gedling,Junior Reds, etc..etc..etc......

by M.Y

The Good Old Days....

The Holy Ground BRI #5

It's around 1981,and with the completion of the Executive Stand,'Brian' contributor Andy Saxton writes to the club to ask when they'll do up the terraces."Before 1990" they reply.In the Brian Clough Book Of Football 1981,the Almighty says "I always felt those fans who did support us deserved better facilities and I was determined to provide them.No one was keener to see our new £2½m. stand go up as a "thank you" to the people who had stood in the rain.But I won't be satisfied until we have built another...and another." Seven years on and what's happened? Where are the detailed plans for the "Neil Webb" Stand to be built on top of the Trent End?? Well theres a new sponsors lounge so if any of you fancy soothing your raw throats at halftime...... Everyone has their match day rituals; steak and chips,lucky underpants,5½ pints before the game etc.,mine is deciding which end to go in as I cross Trent Bridge.... The Bridgford has its charms: hearing the part-timers sing ON ON ON at corners,the ghostly echoes of old men shouting "flight it t'Burns", basking in the sun,falling over the empty vodka bottles on New Years Day,and watching the fights between the pro- and anti-Rice factions.Oh,and you can actually SEE the game, if you want to (and not the

bloke infront of yous dandruff). But it's not exactly very pleasant when it's raining. The Trent End is,of course,the only place you can contemplate for atmosphere,and when you're boasting to you're grandchildren it'll be "I Was In Trent End When...Sir Trev scored two v Ajax to more-or-less put us through to our second European Cup Final/Duncan McKenzie destroyed Man City singlehand- edly/Ian Storey-Moore got his third against Everton/Brian Rice scored v Bolton Wanderers etc."(though for most of these feats the bulk of the hardcore would've been in the old East Stand).The Trent End means: singing till you're hoarse (well sometimes),swaying, crushing,bruising,the bladder cramp you get if it's too full to fight your way out at half time,and the neckache caused by trying to catch a glimpse of play between the massed heads, the fence,and that bloody stupid advert hanging down from the roof.Basically,the Trent End is little more than a cattleshed, we've slagged off better away ends,and it should've been knocked down and rebuilt years ago.For an attempted "Super- League" club it's disgusting. Obviously,the lack of space means they can't just add on to the existing structure,and to rebuild totally would take time and money,but I'd even put up with more executive boxes over my head if it meant a Stand to

be proud of.But in the meantime, surely it wouldn't cost much to stick a roof over the Bridgford? Our debts are all paid,we still have money from the Cup Run,and if the Football Improvement Trust can give hundreds of thousands to the likes of Spurs and Liverpool surely they can spare us a few quid.Maybe Poor Hard-up Forest should reverse the charges and call up Sheff- ield Wednesday and ask them if they benefited from roofing their Kop End.Come to think of it,they could ask us.Imagine an atmosphere like that every week. Well perhaps not,but a roof would do wonders for the acoustics,people might even SING if they heard an echo rather than a whimper lost in the wind. There might even be defectors to lead the choir (after all,it's only 10 or 15 years since the Trent End took over from the East Stand as Paradise). A covered Bridgford would also

PARTY TIME IN THE TRENT END.

attract all the wimpy part- timers who Would go,but it's raining and they get all claustrophobic in the Trent End...The seasonal gates prove the support is there, the comparative affluence of Notts,the successful side and the general resurgence of interest means that gates can only go up (with a bit of effort from the PR people and notwithstanding the memeber- ship problem...).AND,of course,we could certainly afford to rebuild the Trent End.And with a spectacular modern stadium we'd probably get to stage semi-finals = more cash = new players = success(? - just ask Telly Vegetables) = more fans = more cash = new players etc. etc.Well things aren't quite that simple,but as business- men our directors should know you have to invest to get a good return,and if this club is really ambitious they must invest in the Fans,as well as in the players.

J.P.

-5-

YOUWHATYOUWHATYOUWHATYOUWHAT

Judging from the rather hysterical reactions in recent years to your typical law-abiding soccer fan from certain quarters (ie C.M.),I think we must be putting out a false message.Surely in the manicured refinement of the Directors Box,even fortified with the Chairman's Special Malt,he can't actually believe that we all actually inten to re-arrange cockney faces with bricks,or that our wives are in the habit of wearing ribbons for the Forest lads going to Wemberley,can he? Well to be honest,it wouldn't surprise me at all,so here for Mr Moynihan and all those other "soccer experts" who haven't stood on the terraces since 1949,is a glossary of what those songs really mean:

"You're gonna get your fucking heads kicked in"
- Congratulations,opposition,you've just scored.
"We'll support you evermore"
- I think Forest have lost this one.
"We're the Pride of Nottingham"
- If we played like this,I doubt if we'd beat Notts.
"Where were you at City Ground"
- This is the first time I've been to an away match and aren't I feeling pleased with myself.
"Can you run,can you run,can you run"
- God,how are we going to get back to the coach past all these psychopathic home fans.
"You'll never make the station"
- By the time the police let you lot out we'll be safely tucking in to a Nottingham tea.
"Who's the bastard in the black"
- The only way we'll win today is if the ref's biased.
"Cheat cheat cheat"
- Another bloody fair decision.Doesn't this ref realise we're at home.
"Get your tits out for the lads"
- I wish I had a girlfriend.
"One one one"
- Don't worry,we never score from corners.
"Forest aggro"
- Even though we're incredibly biased,we couldn't really claim that Psycho got the ball there.
"Brian Clough's Red and White Army"(x 578)
- We've run out of songs. by Teacherman. YOUWHAT

:BRI # 8

stop bloody moaning

It's amazing how a couple of trophies can change everyone's outlook.A dodgy start to the season,the Sheridan debacle,and suddenly everyone and his Del-boy are penning piss-poor letters to the BRIAN doubting the Great Man's genius,some even having the effrontery to demand explanations from on high.Well,just cast your minds back to the pre - BC days,and consider if you will the following facts about this term,and then perhaps you'll all shut the flip up.
1).We've already won four home league matches,FOUR times as many as at this stage last year.
2).We're £2 million better off.
3).Last season we weren't exactly sitting pretty on Boxing Day and look what happened.
4)."Toddy" cost only as much as we got for Gary Fleming.
5).Steve Chettle is beginning to look like a good player.
6).Two of the team are England regulars,with Harry increasing his chances all the time.
7).Average gates are up.
8).We've won at Plough Lane.
9).We've found a replacement for when Sutty retires.
10).The defence are letting in an average of less than a goal a game.
11).We're through to the Quarter-Finals of the Littlewoods again.
12).We have the most successful,most loyal (longest-serving) manager in the League.
13).Chappo has continued his goal-scoring form of last season.
14).We've found a winger who can score goals.
15).With his current lack of form,no-one (except AF perhaps) would bid mega-bucks for Nigel.
16).We beat Derby once again,despite giving them a goal start.
17).We haven't been beaten by more than a single goal in any match.
18).Brian Rice has converted most of the doubters.
19).We have the best fanzine in the League.
20)....and,the MOST important,we all know the Trees haven't even hit top form yet.

see you at Wembley, suckers!   by   TEACHERMAN.

BRI #15

TO BE OR NOTTS TO BE

Forget - albeit temporarily - racism, sexism and Riceism,and lets fight another widespread disease.
Q: What do the following have in common:-
a) a 'Citizens' scriptwriter b) the person who produces the trailers for 'The Match' and c)various other individuals and publications.
A: NOTTSISM
A character in 'Citizens' (for the uninitiated it is a Radio 4 soap opera, don't listen to it myself - just happened to hear that episode!) travelled to watch Everton play 'Notts Forest' in the Simod Cup Final,Bristol City and Luton Town both had matches against 'Notts Forest' on TV and too many other examples of 'Notts Forest' to mention.
Who are this unknown team? Do they play half way between City Ground and Meadow Lane (aquafooty)? Or between City Ground and Trent Bridge (well done lads on the B&H Cup,but don't leave it to the last ball next time my nerves can't take it.)
I know Nottsism has been going on for years,but isn't it about time something was done to try to eradicate this scourge. If comments in previous issues of BRIAN are anything to go by,I'm not the only one infuriated by it. It's like calling Man U Lancs Utd - a bit of an

extreme example I know,but the same theory;the county used instead of the city.
It is particularly annoying that 'The Match' get it wrong,considering they are supposed to be the experts and surely impressionable kids will pick up Nottsism from them.
What can be done? We could always adopt the B.R.A.S. method of shoot-to-kill at the mere mention of 'Notts Forest'. The alternative is educating the masses;a campaign of letters,posters and why not have T-shirts in the style of FRANKIE SAYS:

BRI #11

These could be sent to the worst offenders so they don't make the same mistake again. Even better,how about green sweatshirts? BC was way ahead of the pack as usual, this time on green issues,but that,as they say, is another story...   LEC

The Bridgford Diaries.

Newcomers to the more windswept terraces may have been puzzled by the incessant droning that accompanies all home matches. Regulars will, of course, recognise it as emanating from our very own...
BRIDGFORD END OF THE WORLD SQUAD
(Probably the least partisan fans in the world)...

THE CITY GROUND: A FINE SATURDAY AFTERNOON:

2:55 "...it's not the game it was years ago,you just don't see wing play any more,it's all got too defensive and negative...drone drone..."

3:00 FIRST HALF KICKS OFF. "Come on you red lags!"

3:01 Webb's first time through ball is cut out by the enemy centre back's diving header.But for a liberal application of gel that morning,he would have missed the ball by two inches. "Aah come on Webb - he's just not bothered is he? Two million pounds - my arse"

3:05 Chet races 30 yards,slide tackles, recovers the ball,dribbles round the winger,clips it to Cloughie who fires six inches wide. "Bloody 'ell Chettle! - you can't tell me he's first division Len.Cost us the FA Cup last time you know.Prat"

3:08 Franz goes inside. "Shoulda gone wide there Carr"

3:09 Franz goes outside. "Shoulda gone inside there Carr"

3:10 Franz goes forwards. "Shoulda gone backwards there Carr"

3:11 Franz goes backwards. "Shoulda picked Crosby"

3:20 Webb hits the crossbar from 35 yards. "Come on Webb,play it to feet?"

3:30 "No,no,no,use the ball,now,play it wide,oh no,you'll never score from there Forest".Hodge scores. "Cloughie were a yard offside there Len,did you see,he bloody were you know"

3:31 Chappo scores.

3:32 Webb scores, Parker scores, Walker scores.

3:33 Chappo scores. "(feebly) Come on you re - eds!"

3:45 Trickies trot out leading 6-0. "They'll let it slip second half, always do,see in the past a winger was a winger,not a centre forward... drone drone..."

3:58 "..(drone drone...I'm not saying he hasn't the talent Len,but in this game you can't afford...drone drone"

4:00 SECOND HALF KICKS OFF. "Come on you reds!"

4:12 Cloughie stumbles and sends the ball ballooning towards the corner flag.A startled Carr sprints 35 yards to take the ball at throat height with both feet on the touchline. "Good ball Nigel!..see that Len,straight to him,what a belter - now use it Carr!" Forced to improvise while Chappo and Parker lumber into view,Franz dazzles the crowd,and the five enemy left backs,with a display of ball juggling, dribbling and break-dancing.Finding himself still alone in the opposition half,he reluctantly threads his way past the only defender still standing and hits the post for the ninth time. "Bloody pudding! Get in that taxi Carr.Get yer boots on Len.Stop clapping Matthew,he's a prat." "Sorry Dad".

4:20 Des has nipped to the cash point in the quiet spell,and a rare break catches Terry with shampoo in his eyes.A feeble 25 yard toe-ender is unleashed hurriedly,just prior to Psycho's tackle (10 seconds prior in actual fact,but who's counting),Sutty plucks the shot from the air with his free hand.Putting down the Agatha Christie he started in the first half, he punts the ball out of the Forest half for the third and final time. "Eh up,there's trouble here Len,these come a different class to Forest!". Applauds knowledgeably,and loudly - startling several nearby fans previously unfamiliar with the sound. "Well played youth,unlucky!"

4:25 In the Car Park.Forest winning 8-0. "I reckon that lot'll steal it,you know,we should have punished them in the first half,bloody Chapman,he's never a striker...drone drone..."

4:30 "...drone drone...Forest should have got 12,they're just not bothered at home are they? don't know why they're doing so well away..."

DON'T YOU JUST WISH

4:48 FINAL WHISTLE - Forest win 12-0.Brian Laws scores three in the 92nd minute. "Some bugger's slashed all me tyres Len.The bloke from the AA says he'll be 8 hours getting here now this blizzard's started.Wish I'd brought me coat..."

by STAN DINTHERANE.

---

10 REASONS WHY DESMOND DOESN'T REALLY WANT TO GO TO JUVENTUS.....

1).You can't get mushy peas in Turin.

2).Juve are owned by Fiat,so he'd have to drive a poxy Uno,instead of the Ferrari/Porsche/Lada he really wants.

3).He might have to share a room with Baggio and his Buddhist chanting.

4).He'd never play in the Simod Cup again.

5).Everyone hates Juventus.Torino, Milan etc are much trendier.
by RED REG.

6).Luther Vandross doesn't play in Italy very often.

7).All those nasty medals would clutter up his mantlepiece.

8).If he thinks he looks so good in black & white he can always moonlight for Notts.

9).His game would go to pot from being up against dross like Schillachi in training,instead of Phil Starbuck.

10).He wouldn't really want to break 20,000 hearts,would he....?

---

a cautionary tale....

It's late as I walk down the wet street; it's been raining for days.Mindful of every eye,every look,I continue walking.I hear footsteps behind me,I continue walking,they disappear into another street.Almost there..phew!

I knock on the door three times,as is the way. "What's your name?",questions a rough voice from behind the grill. "Brian Clough",I reply.The door opens;light hits my eyes. "It's Simon!" a voice cries. "Have you got it?" enquires Michael. "Yeah,no problem",I reply casually.It had been,of course,it always was.

I moved into the room where there were about 60 or so people milling about, anxiously waiting.They'd all made the same journey over the last day or so, wary,cautious,fearful that we might be leading them into a trap.Michael had taken the package and was making his way into the projection room.I took my place in the crowd.The anticipation was mounting,genuine excitement filled the air as the screen flickered into life.All eyes were transfixed at the sight of our heroes racing onto the pitch.Michael announced, "Today's match is Nottingham Forest (of course) versus Liverpool,New Year's Day 1990".

It's some years ago now,of course,we all knew the result but we watched in awe of the Greats.we all cringed as Rush kicked the ball twice in the first half for two goals. "What about the foul on Nigel?", everyone shouted before the second goal, "Huh,typical scouse luck!".Everyone was laughing at George Best's "Forest are as good as dead" speech at half-time,then the comeback.How did Harry get that far out of the mud? "Yeah,U Reds,U Reds!" Jemson hauled down for the second,those of us who were there remember the joy of Nigel's spot-kick hitting the back of the net.The remaining "Oohs" and "Aahs" of missed chances and Jemson's lob tipped over by dear old Brucie.2-2,great game, and the scouse knew they were lucky to get a point.

The crowd shuffle around,and a kid asks "But Dad,what was it really like?...I mean,being there...?" Most people over-hear this comment,some repeat faded stories of 'being there',some sob remembering the good old days,others mumble "If only we'd done more to stop them..." Them,of course,being the government.

Colin Moynihan (then known as the Sports Minister,but now known by his rightful title of 'Minister for the Abolition of Football'),had put a stop to our Saturday entertainment.The grounds were now car parks,shopping centres,office blocks etc..Most of the players had emigrated to Italian/French/Spanish teams,whose live games are still being jammed from our TV screens.The managers and other personalities had been jailed, or banished from our shores for life.The supporters too had been persecuted and imprisoned.Those left had formed small, underground groups such as our own,all of us risking our very existence if found out by the law (who were revelling in their "West Midlands" style outlook towards supporters and who still enjoyed getting amongst us at our illegal meetings - they too remembering the days of excessive overtime exacerbating their powers).Smuggled in tapes of old matches are the only thing keeping some of us sane.Guerilla action has even been taken, "Free Brian Clough" had been sprayed on the council house,much to the embarrass-ment of the authorities.But it's far too little,far too late.The words echo around an emptying room.... "if only we'd done more to stop them...."

by SIMON THE RED.

ENGLAND the GRAHAM TAYLOR Year(s?)

A PSYCH(O)IC PREDICTION OF THE TAYLOR TERM OF OFFICE BY DAME RUSSELL GRANT AND TREVOR FRECKNALL.

SEPT 1990. ON THE PITCH: England 1 Norway 2.
A miserable start for Graham Taylor's regime with a defeat at Wembley.Nigel Spink has a nightmare of a game ("SPINK STINKS" - The Sun),and Gordon Cowans is sent off for a late challenge on Trondheim.Afterwards Graham tells Gary Newbon,"Every game is difficult nowadays - especially for us".Steve Hodge is on the bench but not used.

OFF THE PITCH: Paul Scarrott runs amok in Oslo,thinking that it's an away game.

MARCH 1991. ON THE PITCH: Rep. of Ireland 3 England 0.
A dire display by England in this European Championship qualifier.Olney misses a penalty and Ormondroyd is stretchered off.Unfortunately,a long enough stretcher is not available and two 'regular' size ones have to be welded together,causing a substantial delay.Steve Hodge not in the squad.

OFF THE PITCH: Scarrott nuts his reflection in a Dublin washroom mirror.

JULY 1994. ON THE PITCH: Malawi 6 England 1.
A terrifying spectacle as England crash out of the PEPSI COLA World Cup.Luther Blissett gets a surprise recall. Steve Hodge,fed-up waiting for his recall,becomes Youth Coach at Forest.The tabloids call for Taylor to go.He refuses to budge unless The Sun alleges Taylor had a romantic association with a ball-boy whilst at Villa.The allegations are rubbished in court as Graham takes libel action,but the pressure is too much,and just before a tour of the Balkan Republics he resigns.The FA reveals that Taylor is to take up a job with World Club Championship holders AFC Cairo."TRAITOR!" - Daily Star.

OFF THE PITCH: Scarrott goes downtown in West Hollywood as England prepare for their game v Latvia in L.A.He runs into "The Psychos",a street gang with particularly dangerous left feet,and has finally met his match.
Scarrott renounces violence (again!?),does charity work, returns to England a media darling and,when Taylor finally goes months later,is awarded the England job as there are no -other applicants.Not even Steve Hodge.

by UPPER EXEC. PHIL.

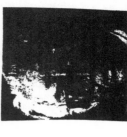

LEFT: A boyish Graham accepts his new job as England Manager (© August 1990)....

RIGHT: The years have taken their toll as Taylor resigns in February 1995....

BRI#19

THE STORY OF CREATION

(SEAN KELLY(O))

ON THE 1st DAY, BRIAN CAME DOWN FROM ON HIGH AND SAID, 'LET THERE BE LIGHT, YOUNG MAN'.

ON THE 2nd DAY, HE PROCLAIMED 'BUILD ME A TEMPLE, A PLACE OF WORSHIP, WHERE YOU MAY PAY HOMAGE', AND IT WAS SO.

ON THE 3rd DAY, BRIAN SAID 'BANISH FROM MY KINGDOM THOSE WHO WORSHIP FALSE IDOLS & DROVE THEM INTO THE FOOTBALL WILDERNESS OF DERBY'.

ON THE 4th DAY, BRIAN PROMISED 'I SHALL BRING AMONG YOU A LEADER, FOREST'S SAVIOUR, WHO SHALL VISIT MECCA & BE REWARDED FOR THEIR ALLEGIANCE'.

ON THE 5th DAY, HE FORETOLD 'OUSE A TRIBE THE FAITHFULL...

ON THE 6th DAY, BRIAN CREATED 'THOU SHALT NEVER BEAT LES WALKER'.

ON THE 7th DAY, BRIAN RESTED (AND SENT NIGEL DOWN THE CHIPPY.)

BRI#19

SATURDAY NIGHT AT THE MOVIES

Unsure of what to do after the match? Well,we here at BRIAN, ever conscious of your entertainment needs,present a round-up of what's on at your local multi-screen complex....

1).The man with the haircut is back! - VINDIANA JONES AND THE LAST CRUSADE. Fresh from his adventures at the Temple Of Doom (Plough Lane) and with the Raiders Of The Lost Points (Wimbledon FC),Vindy joins forces with the Strach-man in an attempt to put the omni-hated Leeds where they belong - just below the play-offs(18).

2).TOP MAN is the story of a fresh-faced young man on his way to the stars."Sir!" Trevor Francis,having "done the business" with a back street gang of no-hopers,joins forces with the crack militia of Trent-side.But can he cut it with the best? Features the chart-topper "Take This Man Away" by Dynamo Berlin(cert U)

3).BREWSTER'S MILLIONS. In an effort to satisfy his ever dwindling horde of dedicated (shurely shome mishtake?) fans Brewster must spend 13 million pounds AND NOT HAVE A SINGLE POINT TO SHOW FOR IT! Sounds familiar? It should do.Alex Ferguson stars in the lead role previously made popular by Ron Atkinson.Giggle as he squanders £2.5m on Gary Pallister.Marvel as he snaps up a bargain Neil Webb for £1.5m,only to see Webby snap a tendon! Fun for all the family! (cert E).

4).FRENCH CONNECTION. Gene Hackman plays "Popeye" Clough, a street-wise Nottingham manager with a single obsession - to get his man.But

it seems Lee Chap has escaped to Niort and is out of reach forever.Popeye has other ideas and in a breath-taking finale, featuring one of the finest chases ever filmed,Chappo hits 4 against QPR.(Warning,this film features excessive mindless violence).(cert U).

5).FRENCH CONNECTION II.
"Popeye" sets off for the haven of the rich in pursuit of the man with the funny voice and peculiar haircut. Thank God,Marseille hang on to him(18).

6).THREE CLUBS AND A BABY features the hilarious antics of David Speedie,and the attempts of Darlington,Chelsea and Coventry to make him behave like an adult.Watch out for the moving scene where the bully Des Walker whips the ball away every time! Dry those tears,Speedo.(cert 12).

7).GOALBUSTERS. "If there's something weird...hanging round your posts...who ya gonna call...?"Frankie (Stuart Pearce),Johnny(Frank Gray) and Psych(Johnny Metgod) clear away mesh entanglements round three pieces of wood up and down the country(cert E).

8).ALIEN DONKEYS FROM OUTER SPACE. Tony Adams stars as.... No,too obvious this one. Certificate refused.

by STEVE HANLEY.

BRI#14

totally wired–forest style

Did anyone see the brilliant news in the Tottenham programme? Yes,we're going to have a Cup Final record!! I can't believe it,I'm just over the moon about it.Personally,I'm hoping for an '89 Remix of that timeless pop classic (I'm not joking,I think it's seriously brilliant!),"We've Got The Whole World In Our Hands" (Stevie Hodgy all over the field etc).But as the programme says,they're taking all song ideas from various songwriters.Due to great expenditure (and a loan of a semi-automatic rifle from BRAS), we've managed to have a sneak preview of a few:

STOCK,AITKEN & WATERMAN:
"Stuff The Scousers"
Let's all stuff the scousers
Stuff the,stuff the scousers
Let's all stuff the scousers,5-0
(sung to the tune of every other SAW song)

GEORGE MICHAEL: "Psycho Figure"
Oh it would be nice
To touch Psycho's biceps
You know not everybody's
Got biceps like his
It would be even nicer
To see them lift the League Cup
Ooh that would really cheer me up
Woo Hoo

PUBLIC ENEMY: "Don't Believe The Daily Mirror"
Yo! The Daily Mirror is crap
It's a load of Maxwell's pap
Yo! Forest fans do you know what time it is?
(NO! BECAUSE THE BLOODY CLOCK ON THE SCOREBOARD KEEPS BREAKING DOWN)

BRUCE SPRINGSTEEN: "Born In Mapperley"
Well I've been to Vietnam and I've been
To New Orleans
But I ain't been warm since I went to
Bristol City
I'm gonna jump in my Chevy and
Cruise off down the M1
And I ain't stopping till I see
The Reds have won
(except for at the roadworks)
Cos I was,Born in Mapperley

THE SUGARCUBES: "Brian Clough Is A Little Green Pixie"
I was in the Trent End
When an inflatable tree told me
Brian Clough was a little green pixie
I ate him,and bought a player from Iceland

HAPPY MONDAYS: "Fat Football Managers"
I just got back from a week at Wembley
It must've been champagne I'm drinking
You've been with fat football managers
Drinking Bells whisky
And talking about Colin Moynihan
Cloughie fluffy,Chappy happy
Ricey nicey,Chettle nettle

REYNOLDS GIRLS: "We'll Win The Stack"
Arsenal,Liverpool
We don't watch that crap
We'll win the stack,
With Big Lee Chap
Manchester United
Fergie's team are slack
He'll get the sack
We've seen to that

U2: "With Or Without Franz"
With or without Franz,
With or without Franz,
We will win,with or without Franz
Cos he gives the ball away....

THE SUNDAYS: "It'll All Sink In Later"
Cos it's my team,yes it's my team
And tho' I can't be sure
We're really winning it all
It'll all sink in later

THE POGUES: "Lend Me Five Pounds And I'll Buy An Inflatable Tree"
On the 9th day of April it was raining
So I went into a public house
And drank a pint of beer
I drank to Stevie Sutton
And I drank to Brian Laws
And then next thing it was Tuesday and
I didn't know the score
And it's lend me five pounds and I'll
Buy an inflatable tree
And I won't know I've been ripped off
Till the morning

MORRISSEY: "Football Is Depressing"
Life can be depressing
When you're a Forest fan
And haven't won a trophy for nine years
We might this year
If Ronnie Kray or Myra Hindley,
Doesn't kill us

ONE YEAR ON..

April 9th 1988.After months of mouthing off about how our name was on the Cup.....well,sometimes you just wake up and KNOW you're going to lose.So what can you do? Personally,I skipped past the escourt at the station and took refuge in alcohol,and consequently I can't remember very much at all.Of course,I still sang until my vocal chords were mutilated beyond repair,but when Chet pulled down Barnes I would gladly have shot him and myself there and then.Even when Nigel pulled one back the black clouds hardly lifted.Later I walked all the way to the station,got a bottle of cider from Presto,lost on the trivia machine,shut my foot in the train door and ended up getting married in Barcelona.Such is life.

When the draw was made this time (fix! fix!),I dusted down the video that had been too painful to watch before,and blow me,we were actually pretty good.Ever heard the one about the Forest fan who was held hostage for 3 years in Beirut? Well when he came out the first thing he said was "Now if Chettle had just let Barnes run on...I mean,there was no-one else free,all he could do was try a narrow angled shot" etc etc etc.Perhaps this time our defence won't all buzz around Barnes like Derby fans buzz around shit.

Still,one year on and the stage is set for our revenge...Back on the kop,"we've got more fans than you" etc (thank heavens for geographical locations).And this time we've got the away dressing room,which as you all know has housed the winning team since Kenny Dalglish was but a pound sign in his father's eye.

So what's changed?
Liverpool: Grobbelaar,Gillespie,Ablett, Nicol,Spackman,Hansen,Beardsley,Aldridge, Houghton,Barnes,McMahon.
Spackman's moved on,Hansen's retired, Ablett's being roasted left & right in the centre,Rush has totally screwed up the forward line,Aldridge has a summer job giving rides at Blackpool,Houghton and Barnes blow hot and cold,and Bruedie(in real life one of the most obnoxious characters in football),has still got the dropsies.The press tell us that Liverpool have hit form previously unseen in this galaxy,and admittedly the Cov. demolition did look a bit ominous,but if it takes them so long to break down the mighty defences of Tottenham and Brentford then they'll need a tank to get past ours. (Molby? McMahon?) If we go in ahead at half-time then the final is ours.The scousers are not in the same class as they were last year,whereas we... ...are older,wiser,better composed,and far far more confident,let them fear us.We're a different side.Assuming we field the current side,a mere six players remain from last year.So what's new? Well,Brian Laws may get caught out coming forwards sometimes but he would never have conceded that penalty.Wilson has been a revelation since switching back,and if Robson blunders out his contract then he'll probably be the only Forest player in Italy in 1990.Stevie Hodge - oh,it's good to see him back,beavering away.It's hard to believe he's the same player that I can't remember from the '87 Final.No.7. Mr Carr? Still Mr Frustration,but brill at Man U & Arse,has finally learnt to stop and look around before crossing aimlessly or falling over his bootlaces.Tommy Gaynor - took everyone by surprise at the Baseball Ground,especially the Rams defence.Gets agood cross in and deserves to be a hero.Chappo? well,what can you say,many of us were up in arms when we bought him but thank Christ we were so wrong.It looks like BC has finally found his Peter Withe replacement.Strength, opportunism and even a fair sprinkling of skill.Walking through the Meadows the other day I passed some kids playing with a tin can."Neil Webb",said the first, "Chapman",said the second as he nutmegged his mate.Only then did it really sink in, what a megastar the man is,how crucial he is to our success.BC does it again,turns donkeys into thoroughbreds.And if Wilko had been any good then Everton would never have sold him in the first place. Garry Parker - Mr Suntan may drift in and out of the game but we do need him to pick up the pieces on the edge of the box. Only needs another 2 goals to equal his whole career total.Tends to score at vital moments so how about it,Garry?

Go on Franzie, give him a great big cuddle

As for the rest,well Sutty's cock-ups v Spurs should last him till the end of the season,Psycho is divine inspiration,Des is off the painkillers,Webby will want to impress/say sod off to Dalglish (depending on which paper you read) and Nigel is desperate to pick up a few medals before popping off for a bit of calcio. We're old hands at this semi-final lark now,we can throw away the valium 'cause we'll have been to Wem-ber-ley.If we've won (what d'ya mean,IF??) - we'll be unstoppable.If we've lost...well it's that long walk home again. by red reg

NAPALM DEATH: "We Don't Like Football Because The Ball Is Made Of Leather" (possible duet with Morrissey?)
AAAARRRGGHH!! BLLLEEEEUURAAAARRRGGH!!!

by
M.Y. & J.P.

HEADS IT'S GARY!!

Bizarre.That's the only way you could possibly describe Gary Crosby's winner against Man City.As far as reactions to it go,my first was one of bewilderment as to what had actually happened,as I honestly thought my eyes were deceiving me.This was soon joined by a feeling of intense amusement at Crosby's sheer audacity,and at the controversy which our decidedly uncontroversial No.7 kicked up as a result.

However,the problem for hapless Howard and his rather miffed players is that in heading the ball off Dibble's right hand,Crosby broke absolutely none of the rules of the game.Which is why the ref,Roger Gifford,allowed the goal to count."There was no law broken and I stand by my decision.I think you have to admire the player's speed of thought",he said,sentiments echoed by fellow man-in-black Neil Midgeley,who admitted he too "would have allowed it". George Courtney,speaking out on behalf of the opposing train of thought,believed that although the goal was technically faultless,he would have disallowed it because,"it wasn't in the spirit of the game".Hmm. Now I can't ever remember seeing a definition of 'the spirit of the game',but I suppose it would encompass factors like fairness and sportsmanship,none of which Crosby (or any other Tricky for that matter) could be accused of lacking.

If I was to draw up a list of things which definitely aren't in 'the spirit of the game',it would include elements like the professional foul,terminally boring offside traps,players arguing with the officials etc..It would not include the scoring of perfectly legitimate goals (no matter how odd the circumstances).

Having said that,I'll confess to feeling a little sorry for City - the less objectionable of the Manchester clubs.It must have been a really annoying way to lose a game they had looked capable of securing at least a point from; I know I'd have been gutted if Forest had lost to such an absurd goal. Still,we didn't; they did,and I hope they are eventually convinced that Mr Gifford was correct to allow Crosby's brilliantly opportunist but utterly astonishing effort to count. by THE SCRIBE IN EXILE.

Whose Line Is It Anyway?

Relieve the boredom on those long away trips with our amusing Trentside version of the popular Channel Four Game Show.The idea is to get someone to suggest an everyday activity (milking a 6 ton rhino,shaving the warts off your Granny's face,etc.) and a player in whose style you should improvise said action.

e.g. Pouring a glass of water.

1). Des Walker.Pour tap on full.Place glass under jet.At the precise moment the water gushes up to reach the brim,swiftly turn off tap with a deft flick of the right hand,to gasps of admiration from the admiring multitude.
2). Justin Fashanu.Attempt to turn on tap,but in fact pull it off.Try to pick up glass,but it slips tragically from your grasp and smashes into pieces at the bottom of the sink.In attempting to retrieve the shards of glass,you sever a main artery and bleeding profusely,refuse to call an ambulance as it is all God's will.
3). Terry Wilson.Place glass under tap.Turn tap on.Catch sight of self reflected in kitchen window.Cut hair with kitchen scissors.Kitchen is by now flooding.Say,"What the f@*%" and pour another scotch.

e.g. Answering the front door.

1). Steve Hodge.Walk calmly across lounge floor,whistling nonchalantly.Without warning,run like hell across hall floor and whip door open,to amazement of visitor.
2). Franz Carr.With elegant speed,like a gazelle in full flight,rush over to the front door,skilfully evading objects strewn on hall floor...then pick up the phone.
3). Stuart Pearce.Walk briskly and purposefully over to front door,and kick it half-way down the front path.
I'm sure you get the idea.Award most points for more imaginative suggestions,with no points at all for Phil Starbuck brushing his hair,Chappo giving rides on Skeggy beach Nigel putting on a pair of tights,etc.. by TEACHERMAN.

big five...pah!

I was fairly bored on Sunday afternoon so I decided to compile a league table of every First Division match played since we were promoted (this season not included).The results were most interesting:

	P	W	D	L	F	A	PTS
LIVERPOOL	498	287	128	83	914	389	935
FOREST	498	235	136	127	755	514	795
MAN.UTD	498	225	150	123	744	506	794
ARSENIC	498	228	135	135	713	525	781
EVERTON	498	225	139	139	746	521	774
TOTTENHAM	456*	189	117	150	684	594	673

(*Spurs finished 3rd in Div.2 in 77/78, even if you add the 56pts they got that season they're still last).

So there you go.The only way in which the Big Five are Big is in attendances (large catchment areas),TV appearances and support in other cities (as in,"Cor Blimey Guv,I never miss Kenny's Boys at Highbury,and no mistake,me old china").

A trophy table is even more revealing:

	FL	FAC	FLC	ECC	CWC	UEFA	TOT
LIVERPOOL	7	2	4	2	-	-	15
FOREST	1	-	3	2	-	-	6
EVERTON	2	1	-	-	1	-	4
ARSENAL	1	1	1	-	-	-	3
TOTTENHAM	-	2	-	-	-	1	3
MAN.UTD	-	2	-	-	-	-	2

(If you include the Super Cup then Villa are above Man United).

If you produced a league table of money spent in the period in question,I'm sure we'd be firmly rooted to the bottom. Take the Forest v Everton league game,for example:

Everton were probably good enough to win the European Cup at least once in the years we've been banned.In contrast, I think Arsenal's lack of European success (1 Fairs Cup win in 1970) says rather a lot.

Cottee + Newell + Sharp = £3m plus
Clough + Starbuck + Chapman = £300,000

Dave Watson £1,000,000	v	Steve Chettle -nothing
Martin Keown £700,000	v	Des Walker -nothing
Peter Beagrie £725,000	v	Gary Crosby £20,000

You can't name one of the above who played worse than his Everton counterpart (yes,Starbuck was more effective than Newell).
And as you go back through the years,the story is much the same.Only Fashanu has really been a big money failure here. So wake up Elton Welsby,Jeff Powell,Brian Moore,John Motson et al.

by DAMIEN MACKINNEY.

chapter 13

HULL, HELL & HAPPINESS.....

ISSUE 4   60p   *MAR/APR 1989*

EDITOR'S BIRTHDAY SPECIAL

Forget Harry............

Here's............

BILLY THE HADDOCK!

Fannies in seats;

LIVERPOOL: THE BURNING QUESTIONS......

NOT

"Why was Aldridge allowed to score two simple goals in as many minutes......?"

BUT

"Why were 4,000 scousers allowed out of the ground at the same time as 16,000 Hullites ?"

AND

"Has anyone seen my bike ?"

INSIDE:

CUP-TIE TICKET FARCE
- THE FACTS?!

MALLETT SPEAKS OUT!

Dedicated to 85 years of under-achievement by Hull City F.C.

ON CLOUD SEVEN

50p

Issue 1   August 1989

HULL, HELL & HAPPINESS......

The supporters view of Hull City AFC

ISSUE 9   60p   *April/May 1990*

SAMBA WITH LA-BAMBER!

DAVE SILENCES HIS CRITICS?

INSIDE: Roy North brushes over City *
Battle of Bramall Lane * Cheap Day
Return * To Hell (Plymouth) and back *
'Ull Music '90 * Wardie Awaydays *
Mighty Striker returns * What do you
think of the season?? * And tons more.....

...IAN HESFORD...THE WATNEY CUP...FOOTBALL
BETTING FOR BEGINNERS...1977-78, A CRUCIAL
SEASON...TIGERS ON TOUR...and more !

hull city

"HULL ...... IT ISN'T THE END OF THE WORLD ....
BUT YOU CAN SEE IT FROM THERE"

To most - i.e. those that have never visited - Kingston Upon Hull is a drab, smelly, stereo-typically Northern town full of whippets, flat caps and people with an unnatural fetish for Rugby League. This couldn't be further from the truth, as many distinguished authors, to their great surprise, have recently discovered.

Hull has the disadvantage (or advantage - depending on which way you look at it) of being geographically out on a limb. It's impossible for travellers to "pass through" on their way to their destination, as would happen elsewhere in the country. Because of this Hull folk are insular creatures with little time for others with the misfortune to live elsewhere, especially those soft Southerners. Insularity breeds familiarity ; as Roland Gift once put it, "All Hull people are famous".

Developers are having a field day in Hull at the moment, with new buildings rising from the ashes of those long-condemned. The once bustling docks are fast disappearing; one now has a giant shopping centre glass dome built on stilts upon it and another has been replaced by a 20 lane bowling alley and drive-in McDonalds. Such is progress.

So, the area of Hull is fast improving, as are the fortunes of the two Rugby League clubs. The same cannot be said of the football club. This season sees the Tigers in the Second Division for the 49th time since their formation in 1904. One half expects the Football League to throw a party next season to celebrate their half century of glorious underachievement. "Hull is the largest town never to have seen First Division football", match programme editors throughout the land never tire of reminding us. Recent examples of what we've been through include the record-breaking failure to win a league game in 27 attempts in 1989, and the more recent 5-1 and 7-1 away thrashings in only the first six weeks of the 1990-91 season. All that in just one year. This has done little to improve the already low regard most East Yorkshire folk have for the Tigers. Things have never been that good since the 40's and 50's when 50,000+ packed into Boothferry Park to watch third division games and the halcyon days of the mid-sixties when the team actually lived up to their tiger tag, coming desperately close to achieving first division status for that elusive first time. Nowadays the stay-aways would rather support one of the 'Big Five', or even worse, Leeds United - at least they occasionally do well.

Hull City are therefore a fanzine editor's dream - plenty to have a good moan about in true British fashion. H,H & H was the brainchild of two Hull City exiles living in Stafford, myself and Ian Websdale. We were (are!) both frustrated at Hull's lack of ambition and achievements thus, and were both well impressed with 'When Saturday Comes' and 'OffThe Ball's campaigning yet humourous style of writing. Upon seeing some of the club-based efforts around at the time we decided "We can do that" and we did. In fact, the hardest thing about starting up was trying to think up a name (what do you mean, you can tell?!). The fanzine was first released onto a suspicious Hull public in August 1988, when 150 copies (the most I could carry!) were shifted with surprising ease during a half-time interval. Looking back, this initial sales figure was quite good when you consider I was dodging the attentions of the more curious members of Humber-side Police Force in attendance at the game - I'd heard stories about fanzine editors getting banned by frightened chairmen! From this tacky, photocopied-at-work-when-the-boss-wasn't-looking first issue, the 'zine hit double figures at the start of the 1990/91 season, despite the resignation of my two co-editors (Rich Lusmore and Gary Hook) to launch their own organ, "From Hull To Eternity". The success of this, along with the estimable "On Cloud Seven" and the now-established Hull Kingston Rovers fanzine "Flag Edge Touch", suggests that you are no longer, in Hull at least, considered 'doing the dirty' on your club by having criticism put into print for all to see. Indeed, if chairmen read and take heed of 1% of what their punters are saying in fanzines, I suppose something has been achieved.

The aims of H, H & H, as with most 'zines, coincide closely with those of the Football Supporters Association. The fanzine attempts to give fans a platform to air their views on various topics, from safety to refreshments on sale (or safety with the refreshments perhaps?) at Boothferry Park, hoping that increased public pressure will bring about change for the better. It can surely be no coincidence that the match programme (recently voted third worst in the entire Football League!) has improved 100% (admittedly not difficult) since 1988, and this reflects the fact that, at last, with the advent of fanzines, the Club realise their activities are being scrutinised by critical observers, their main sponsors, the fans themselves.

So marked has been this change in attitude that several suggestions first mooted in H, H & H and OC7 have been taken up, including the removal of red from the match strip, opening of a souvenir shop in Hull City centre (to compliment the one several miles out at Boothferry Park) and the aforementioned improvements to the match programme. We still see there being some way to go however (this isn't Liverpool) the main issue at present, apart from the team of course, being the establishment of a social club for supporters; we remain one of the few League clubs not to have one, having been promised premises as long ago as 1982.

The future of H, H & H is, at present, uncertain. As other fanzine editors would testify, it takes many, many hours to knock a half-decent fanzine out every six weeks or so, and for this reason it will probably appear quarterly from now on. We shall continue to cast one eye over the excellent, yet unpublicised, Hull music scene as well as glancing at other local sporting and social events. Our practical support of the FSA will remain, and we'll continue to donate our hard-earned profits to Hull City in the form of player sponsorship, even though the fanzine's been banned from Boothferry Park, with no hint of an explanation as to why.

So, if you're ever up our way, stop by for a chat (or laugh, if you're from Sheffield or West Ham). We're not a bad set of lads, just Hull City daft, and proud of it. And no, we're not the programme mate, it's over there .....

ANDY MEDCALF

KR thank "tremendous" support

By John Scrum

Following their hard-fought 40-2 defeat at Widnes yesterday, Hull KR coach Roger Millward praised the Robins' fanatical support.

Nearly 100 made the trip over the Pennines, despite Rovers unlucky run of 27 games without a win.

When I asked him whether the support for his team was "tremendous", "Yes, I suppose so" was his reply.

Sullivan in injury scare

Hull KR wing wizard Anthony Sullivan yesterday announced himself fit after stubbing his toe in the bath over the weekend.

Tigers win European Cup

Hull City last night won the European Cup to add to their collection of FA Cup, League Cup and League Championship trophies this season. Small match report and old photo of ex-player with similar surname to the goalscorer inside.

FC chase top New Zealand star

BRIAN SMITH - his picture's only here to try and give some credibility to the story

Hull FC were last night on the brink of announcing the signing of a top New Zealand star.

By Richard Conversion

I believe that the West Hull team have been in talks with several Antipodean clubs regarding bringing top RL players to the Boulevard. But FC coach slammed our exclusive story as "Ludicrous".

"You're only saying this to make headlines" he commented.

Battling Bishop vows: we'll win a few next season!

Hull KR star David Bishop today vowed that the Robins would win a few games next season **writes JOHN SCRUM.**

"We'll probably lose a few too." he added.

(right) Our daily picture of David Bishop

HULL, HELL & HAPPINESS......

The supporters view of Hull City AFC

GALLERY

Tony Dutton (aged 24), "Sun" and "Kerrang!" reader, sent us this picture of his hero, Hull City's Welsh International Tony Norman. Mr Dutton, of Main Street, Thorngumbald says......

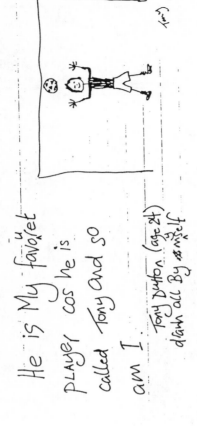

He is My favoret Player cos he is called Tony And so am I.

Tony Dutton (age 24) drawn all By myself

Dennis Moore (aged 22 years, 6 months), a Civil Servant from Keyingham, sent us this pic of Hull KR's Scottish full-back George Fairbairn.

HOOTZ MON ! ANYONE SEEN MY HAGGIS?

(Well done young Dennis, keep up the good work! - Ed.)

TEN USEFUL TIPS FOR 1990/91

1. Foster good relations by inviting all the away fans round to tea after the match.

2. Save time entering the ground by going in the nude thus avoiding any police body searches.

3. Confuse the opposition by dressing as a linesman and running up and down the touchline waving a flag, therefore giving your favourites a slight advantage.

4. Improve Club finances by winning the pools and donating some of the cash.

5. Tell the Sunday 'papers that you're Bobby Robson's ex-mistress, and with the proceeds buy your club a new player.

6. Learn to throw your voice thus creating the impression that all the crowd is behind your team.

7. Create the big crowd atmosphere by making cardboard cut-outs of your family and friends, and take them along to the match.

8. Avoid the rush by ordering your furry Tiger outfit for the end of season fancy dress promotion party TODAY!

9. Go into business making full-size furry Tiger costumes, and hire them out to fellow supporters.

10. Divorce the wife before the season starts therefore saving time arguing about your weekend trip to Wembley next May.

If you have any useful tips that you would like to share with the Black'n'Amber masses then don't be shy - send them in today to our subscription department, written on the back of a five-pound note (one of those monopoly-type new ones). The most original replies could win a Bros 1989 Annual (we're not joking!). Watch this space!

Gary Clark

PREDICTIONS FOR 1989/90

AUGUST

City are unlucky to draw their first match of the season, away, 1-1. Colin Appleton describes it as an encouraging start to the season. Appleton is sacked. John Kaye is re-appointed as City boss, chairman Don Robinson enthusing that *"John is a winner, we at Hull City want to be winners, one day we are going to play on the Moon....."* Mal Murray comes close to scoring in the match against West Brom, hitting the bar. He would in fact have scored if it wasn't for Hesford's reflex save. In the same match, Billy Whitehurst fractures a cheekbone. It belongs to a linesman.

SEPTEMBER

City are knocked out of the Littlewoods Cup, an Andy Saville hat-trick giving Walsall victory at Boothferry Park. John Kaye says *"We were unlucky, but at least we can concentrate on promotion."* Kaye is sacked. Ken Houghton is re-appointed as City boss, chairman Don Robinson enthusing *"Ken's a thinker, we at Hull City want to be thinkers, one day we're going to play on the Moon....."* Houghton says, *"To progress we must be forward thinking, especially in the transfer market."* He buys Dave Sunley. Following criticism for the lack of shelter and facilities for away fans at Boothferry Park, Don Robinson says *"If it doesn't rain, and they wrap up well and have a coffee before they come, what's the problem?"*

OCTOBER

After a heavy downpour at Boothferry, 35 Oldham fans are rushed to Hull Infirmary with various cases of pneumonia, hypothermia, frostbite, and in one sad instance, starvation. Keith Edwards claims his tenth goal of the season at Brighton. It is in fact an Ian McParland shot but Keith says it wouldn't have gone in if he hadn't have been watching it. An issue of *"Hull, Hell & Happiness"* appears without a single reference to the local music scene. Readership doubles. *(Ouch! - Eds)* A 20-yard scorcher from Mal Murray sees City lose 1-0 at Scunthorpe and exit from the Simod Cup. Houghton says *"Who cares about the Simod Cup, I'm constantly working for promotion."* Eddie Houghton is sacked. Bobby Collins is re-appointed City boss, chairman Don Robinson enthusing *"Bobby's a fighter, we at Hull City want to be fighters, one day we'll play on the Moon....."* Mal Murray is voted Hull City Player of the Month, by Scunthorpe fans.

NOVEMBER

Keith Edwards claims his fifteenth goal of the season against Blackburn, a match he misses through injury. Bobby Collins says he is looking to the future when he makes a double signing of Steve Richards and Stuart Eccleston. Hull City slip to sixteenth in the table. Bobby Collins says *"It's a shame we can't concentrate on the Simod Cup."* Collins is sacked. Mike Smith is re-appointed City boss, chairman Don Robinson enthusing *"Mike has a football brain, the Board at Hull City need brains, one day we're going to play on the Moon....."* Mike Smith says *"In football you can't sit on past glories, the youngsters of today are the stars of tomorrow."* He signs Nick Deacy.

DECEMBER

Heavy snow causes City's fixture at Ipswich to be postponed. Keith Edwards nevertheless claims a hat-trick. In the FA Cup, Leigh Jenkinson finally finds a full-back at Torquay who falls for his shuffle trick. He beats him and sends in a knee high cross for Garreth Roberts to soar and head in at the far post. Keith Edwards, back in Hull after having treatment from a psychiatrist, claims the goal. City draw Spurs in the Cup. Mike Smith says of the Cup win *"I think we can go all the way. There are some times when you just know the Cup has your name written on it. I think this is our year."* Smith is sacked. Terry Neill takes over at Boothferry Park, chairman Don Robinson enthusing *"Terry is an Irishman, he thinks like an Irishman, the Hull City Board of Director's think like Irishmen, one day we're going to play on the Moon....."* Terry Neill says Hull City is going to be the club of the nineties. He signs Jimmy McGill.

JANUARY

Vouchers for the Cup-tie v Tottenham are available for anybody who goes to City's league clash with Port Vale. Thousands queue but are told, on entering the ground just before the final whistle, that if their voucher has a picture of a little smiling face on the back then that voucher only entitles them to go to next Saturday's match at Plymouth, where Cup vouchers will again be available. 22,264 see City draw 0-0 at Home Park, Plymouth, where due to an administrative error, no Cup vouchers are available. Terry Neill says *"There is Cup Fever in Hull, it is magical, this is what football is all about!"* He is sacked. Eddie Gray is re-appointed as Hull City manager, chairman Don Robinson enthusing *"Eddie is committed to success, we the Board at Hull City ought to be committed, one day we're going to play on the Moon....."*

FEBRUARY

There are only three tickets left for the Spurs Cup-tie. Keith Edwards claims two. There are some 23,000 still trying to get the remaining one. Somehow, the Hull Daily Mail get hold of it. After a public outcry, they decide to give the ticket away to a 'deserving supporter', offering it as a prize to the fan who writes the best 'match report' of the last match they saw. A Middlesbrough man wins the ticket with an essay on Viggo Jensen. The start of the Tottenham Cup-tie is delayed by the late arrival of 2,000 Hull City fans who hadn't realised Hull City had moved from Anlaby Road. Hull City sit back on a 1-0 lead, and lose 7-1. Gray is sacked. Brian Clough is appointed, saying *"Promotion can't be gained overnight."* He is sacked the following morning.

MARCH

After two days absence, Eddie Gray is re-instated as City manager, chairman Don Robinson enthusing *"Eddie is decisive, we at Hull City want to be decisive, we're going to play on the Moon one day...or maybe Saturn."* At Leicester, Keith Edwards claims his 142nd goal of the season. Don Robinson finally announces sweeping measures to improve Catering and Refreshments for home fans at Boothferry Park. They are to bring their own sandwiches. Billy Whitehurst, under suspension after 35 bookings, is booked again for retaliation, in the Best Stand. Jimmy McGill misses the Portsmouth match because of arthritis. A national survey votes Boothferry Park as the worst ground for pre-match entertainment. This information is given over the tannoy system so that nobody gets to hear about it. Hull City look to be heading for relegation. Eddie Gray says *"I've been in this position before, but we can do it, we can survive. If I'm anything, I'm a survivor."* Gray is sacked.

APRIL

Chris Chilton is appointed Hull City manager, chairman Don Robinson enthusing *"Chris was famed for his shooting ability, and the Board at Hull City want shooting, we're going to play on the Moon or Saturn one day....."* Chilton guides City to survival with a string of excellent results. He says *"I did this before when I was caretaker manager, and all they did was make Brian Horton manager."* Chilton is sacked and Brian Horton is made manager. Keith Edwards scores an own goal at West Ham, but denies being anywhere near the ball. In order to get noticed, Nicky Brown turns up for training in a mini skirt.

MAY

Hull City end the season with a goalless draw at home to Stoke. Keith Edwards claims two. Billy Whitehurst, because of all the suspensions, completes his first hat-trick of the season. Mal Murray gets in a tackle and is interviewed about it on Radio Humberside. Brian Horton says he is looking forward to great things from the lads next year. He is sacked. After phoning to check that Cliff Britton isn't still alive, Don Robinson re-appoints Colin Appleton as City manager, enthusing *"Colin is no fool, as are we the Board at Hull City, we're going to play on the Moon or Saturn...."* A City fan writes to the Daily Mail to say that at least there will be more atmosphere on the Moon than there is at Boothferry Park. Identity cards are introduced, City fans only being able to enter Boothferry Park if they have their cards with them. Colin Appleton is not sure whether it's worth getting one.

(Isn't it about time we had a repeat on TV of your excellent film 'See You At Wembley, Frankie Walsh'?)

Mark Herman

HULL, HELL & HAPPINESS......

The supporters view of Hull City AFC

FOOTBALL LADIES
(at Home & Away)

Does anyone give a thought for us wives of football fanatics, "no not much", do I hear? Well it gives a whole new meaning to P.M.T. - Pre-Match Tension! In fact if I had £10 for every time my husband has excitedly said *"Where's me pass?"* (with a few choice expletives omitted before the word "pass") I could probably buy a villa in Tenerife. The fact is the bloody pass is always in the same drawer, but because of P.M.T. I always have to get it and gently throw it at him.

My worst football memory occurred about four years ago. We were travelling from the West Riding, my husband was driving and the idea was for him to jump out at Boothferry Park and for me to slide over and go my own sweet way. Now, unbeknown to me (but known to my husband I might add) there was something very wrong with our vehicle. He realised this at the Capper Pass traffic lights but decided to keep it to himself. I thought he was handling it a bit erratically but again I put this down to P.M.T. Anyway, we arrived at Boothferry Park where my devoted husband (devoted to Hull City I mean) jumped out and left me with the heap. It started OK but everytime I tried to slow down it cut out on me. You'll realise how many times you have to slow down on Anlaby Road, especially on match day, it was no picnic. To say I was panic-striken would be an understatement but like manna from heaven I spotted a big posh Talbot garage and it died on the middle of the forecourt. I can honestly say it's not true what they say about men in navy-blue pinstripes, that man got my car going for which I'll be eternally grateful. Surely it could be nothing to do with the fact that our car was creating an eyesore on his forecourt, could it?! Needless to say my husband didn't quite enjoy the game as he should because his mind kept wandering (fleetingly) to me and the clapped-out motor.

Yes, football has a lot to answer for. Do you men realise how tedious it is for us women to have to go shopping on a Saturday afternoon, going in to all those hot shops, trying on all those clothes, having all those lunches out, spending all your hard-earned cash (bliss!). Football can also cause us bad stomachs, headaches, nausea not to mention dwindling brain cells (I said not to mention that). "Why?" - you ask - because when you are gone for hours on end to away matches and we are left at home alone, having to tolerate threatening 'phone calls; for example *"Come on, let's go to the pub. See you in 10 minutes. You'd better come!"* and we have to tear ourselves away from the washing-up and ironing etc and go to the pub for hours on end, trying to forget our loneliness, and by the end of the 'sesh', trying to remember where our men actually are, and indeed, WHO they actually are!

So come on lads, spare a thought for us, the ones you leave behind and our traumatic experiences and, no matter what, please, *please*, don't stop going to football will you!

Julie Keyworth

OLD (JOHN) MOORE'S ALMANAC 1989/90

Predictions are not the easiest of things to make. Here's a glimpse of what next season may have in store for us footy fans:-

1990 - Into a new decade The Big Five push harder for a superleague. T.V. says yes, but can Norwich City, Millwall, Coventry City, Derby County and Wimbledon make it on their own?

Gazza's revenge Paul Gascoigne is given an eight match suspension after the Spurs vs Leeds FA Cup fixture for severely injuring Vinny Jones with a dildo.

A knockout? A double celebration at the City Ground. Nottingham Forest win the league championship and Brian Clough outpoints Bomber Graham for the European middleweight title.

Sold Richard Jobson is sold, destined to become a star on the continent. Napoli pay "an undisclosed fee", rumoured to be a wheelbarrow-full of lira. However, 12 more branches of 'Grandways' open.

Good job it didn't happen here Mass slaughter at the Juventus vs SV Hamburg European Cup Semi-Final. Hundreds of fans killed as rival fans riot using revolvers and hand grenades. Both clubs escape a ban from European competition however as UEFA are busy thinking up a punishment for British clubs after an Everton fan invaded the pitch in the F.A. Cup Final and a Celtic fan was arrested urinated in Hampden's car park.

Puff of the decade Diego Maradonna competes in the winning team in the Women's International Volleyball Tournament. He is subsequently disqualified for using his feet.

A bark from Mrs. Mad Dog Mrs. Mad Dog attends another live match - the Littlewoods Cup Final - Hull City versus Peterborough United. After 3 replays, extra-time plus the double-headed coin used by Bobby Robson to decide whether he plays Tony Adams or a useful centre-half instead, the match is declared a tie. *"Five hours play and no result,"* moans Mrs. Mad Dog. *"it's as bad as bloody Test match cricket."*

You have it, I don't want it Brian Clough, Howard Kendall, Terry Venables and Graham Taylor all turn down the vacant post of England manager. Margaret Thatcher appoints Colin Moynihan who promptly disbands the team.

Just a little prick Moynihan sacked after a leaked document reveals that he received "a substantial sum" for doing a deal with the E.E.C. to keep England out of European football. Moynihan flees in disgrace to his Mustique tax haven.

New balls please Wimbledon play West Germany in the final of the prestigious Albanian Shield. Guest 'keeper Harold "Thug" Schumacher spends the next 11 months recovering from a spinal injury. John Fashanu says *"It was an accident ref, I was going for his scrotum."* Fashanu receives an engraved tankard from the French F.A. for his services to football.

Hull City No surprises here. Best of luck to Colin Appleton - with luck and more goals from King Edwards we may still find ourselves in Division 2 next season - but don't hold your breath. Watch this space next time round.

Mad Dog

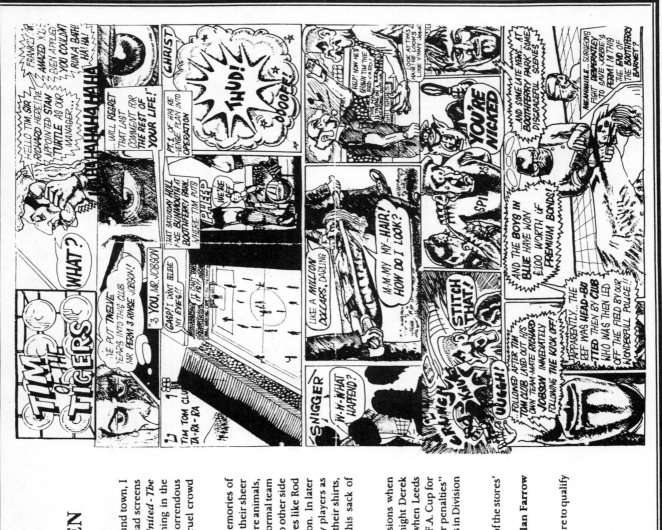

NOT IN FRONT OF THE CHILDREN

When in Debenhams recently seeking bladder relief after a few pints around town, I was overcome by a most surreal experience. Glimpsing football on the overhead screens in the audio/visual department my closer inspection revealed this to be *"Leeds United - The Glory Years"* - a video nasty. A combination of booze, Kylie & Jason crooning in the background plus these gruesome visuals rooted me to the spot, whilst I suffered horrendous flashbacks of Man. United, my childhood heroes being thrashed 5-1 as the cruel crowd cheered the 107th consecutive pass!!

Film of "Sniffer", "Hotshot", "Bite Yer Legs" et al provoked nauseous memories of this sinister white mass reducing side after side to quivering submission through their sheer repugnance. How could such a bloody ugly team actually be human?......they were animals, or worse, aliens sent to discredit human sport. Even by 1970's standards what normal team would play a Cup Final plus replay in all white strip with grotesque red socks. No other side could match the total ugliness of Reaney, Madeley, Jones, Charlton etc., reserves like Rod "Plug from the Beano" Belfitt and Mick "Bughead" Bates completed this tradition. In later years Leeds maintained their hideous looks and style by signing such unsightly players as Joe Jordan, Kenny Burns and Ray Hankin, and having 'Smiley'-type emblems on their shirts, and stupid sock tags. No wonder King Edwards couldn't flourish among this sack of potatoes.

Finally I overcame these menacing visions by recalling wonderful occasions when football triumphed. David Webb's winner in the Old Trafford replay. The night Derek Dougan dumped payola-inspired-double-dreams by scoring Wolves winner when Leeds only needed a point, Montgomery's save and Porterfield's goal that secured the F.A. Cup for Second Division Sunderland. Eventually soccer purged itself of Revies "wads for penalties" dominance when in 1982 it banished his team to languish like all Yorkshire Clubs in Division Two obscurity.

Later on I laughed to myself as I urinated against the stained white enamel of the stores' toilets. I don't like Leeds much.

Ian Farrow

NB: Because he failed to crunch Lato I blame Norman Hunter for England's failure to qualify for the World Cup in 1974.

"H, H & H" TIPS FROM THE STARS

'In Goal' with Iain Hesford

Lesson One - *The Disallowed Goal*

1. Allow apparently harmless cross shot to drift over head into back of net.
2. Place hands on hips and shout angrily at astonished defenders. (See also 'Goalkeeping My Way' by Tony Norman)
3. Hide surprise on realising whistle has in fact blown for offside. Nod vigorously and raise left arm to acknowledge linesman.
4. Retrieve ball from back of net and wink at supporters in South Stand.
5. Ruffle hair of disappointed opposition centre-forward. Duck to avoid retaliatory punch.
6. Hoof ball downfield towards Whitehurst. Resume dreaming of a career in Rugby League.

Next issue: How to silence the Roker Roar.

'Running The Midfield' with Kenny DeMange

Lesson One - *It's a game of 90 minutes*

1. Sit on bench for 80 minutes, or until City go two down.
2. From bench, wave arms at South Stand to encourage half-hearted chants of 'Kenny, Kenny'. Run up and down touchline to warm up. Retrieve pass from Mal Murray.
3. Take the field when Billy Askew limps off. Clap hands, clench fists, and call for more effort from teammates.
4. Commit outrageous foul on opposition No. 8. Get booked. Spread arms in 'Yes, but if we all showed this sort of commitment, we wouldn't be two down' gesture. Acknowledge "Kenny, Kenny" chant.
5. Miss tackle on No. 8 who puts opposition three-up.
6. Clap hands, clench fists etc. as crowd drifts home.

Next issue: Liverpool and me - the Glory Years

'Leading the Line' with Billy Whitehurst

Lesson One - *Let the opposition know you're there*

1. Pepper shots at supporters in South Stand seats during warm-up.
2. Lull opposition into false sense of security by constantly overrunning ball, being caught offside, getting in Keith Edwards' way etc.
3. Reduce opposition centre-half to nervous and physical wreck with use of arms, elbows, knees, thighs, head etc.
4. Get booked for the softest tackle of the afternoon.
5. Miss two open goals. Attract remarks from crowd like "At least he's trying", "Good old Billy", "Someone give him support" etc.
6. As fulltime approaches, stumble over ball 35 yards from goal. Badly off balance, stick out left leg and send ball curving in majestic arc round goalkeeper for goal of season.
7. With three points secure, get sent off.

Next issue: How to make the most of an early bath.

Chris Herman

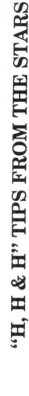

AN ODBOF REMEMBERS
by Alan Plater

The first Hull City match I ever saw was at the Boulevard. It was during the War and, with the aid of Douglas Lamming's WHO'S WHO, I calculate it must have been in or around 1944. I was a very small boy with a full head of hair, and the only player I remember was the goalkeeper, Jack Curnow, who was quite tall. I also remember a half-back called Stan Montgomery, probably because Montgomery was a heroic sort of name in those days. He must have been tall as well. I can only assume that as I had to be lifted up to see the smaller players. All this prehistoric stuff is important because it qualifies me to speak and write on the subject of The Tigers as an "ODBOF" or Officially Designated Boring Old Fart.

I grew up with City during the immediate post-war years, culminating with the arrival of Raich Carter in 1948. He was already a hero because I was born in Jarrow in 1935 and the first three words taught to any Tyneside kid in that period were, "Mummy", "Daddy" and "Raich", not necessarily in that order.

But thousands of words have been written about Raich and, more recently, about my good friends Chris Chilton, Ken Wagstaff and Ken Houghton. When I get to brooding about happy days at Boothferry Park (including the miserable ones) my mind still drifts back to that period when I was a kid on the terraces and you could get in for ninepence. There were wing-halves and inside-forwards, and a sweeper was a thing you used to clean the carpet. The soccer reporters had a special language. The goalkeeper was a reliable custodian, the centre-half was a craggy pivot, right-wingers were always diminutive, and left-wingers were always cunning and previously played for Partick Thistle.

Some things don't change, of course - notably the moaners and whingers in the Best Stand. At the age of fourteen I almost came to blows with a fish merchant's wife because she insisted Don Revie was the most useless inside-forward she'd ever seen. But the real venom was reserved for "centre-forwards", which is what we used to call strikers.

I think that's why we all like Billy Whitehurst; because whatever jargon has been fed into us my media experts, we take one look at Billy and we forget all the nonsense about strikers. Billy's a proper, ol-fashioned centre-forward. You've only to look.

All through the late 1940's the centre-forwards came and went. They arrived, sometimes quietly, sometimes noisily, and for two or three matches they were the new Messiahs. Then the moaning would start and there would be loud demands for new blood, the old blood having being sucked dry.

Consider Benny Lester, a tall, well-balanced, intelligent player who scored 18 goals in 27 games during 1946/7. These days Spurs would have steamed in with a million pound cheque for a lad with such a scoring record. But Benny moved on, by public demand, and scored a heap of goals for Lincoln and Stockport. In the same season, a rugged character called Paddy Brown scored 3 goals in 7 games and also drifted on. I heard a rumour from the Fish Dock that he left because late one night or early one morning he was apprehended singing songs outside the manager's house. It may not be true but it's a good story.

A year later, along came Denis Thompson, a chunky, aggressive lad from my home town of Jarrow - which means I was totally prejudiced in his favour. He scored 8 goals in 9 games, including a hat-trick on his debut. At the end of the 1947/8 season he went home to Tyneside and non-League football and I still don't know why.

Big Billy would have approved of George 'Spud' Murphy, who arrived from Bradford City with a fearsome reputation around the penalty area. The charging of goalkeepers was still regarded as an acceptable form of behaviour and the Murphy speciality was propelling himself within the six-yard box in such a way that goalkeeper, ball and Murphy all ended up in the back of the net. He scored 9 goals in 15 games by various means and was then replaced by Norman Moore.

Moore scored 45 goals in 81 games, a remarkable record considering he spent his early career at Boothferry Park as a wing-half. He had one big problem. He had a round-shouldered way of running and he scored his goals gently - carefully-placed headers from pin-sharp Burbanks crosses or little chips and lobs over the advancing goalkeeper. He wasn't a walloper or a basher.

So it came to pass that during City's triumphant Carter-inspired promotion season, the announcer at Boothferry Park said before the game: *"You've been asking for a centre-forward at any price - and here he is - Billy Price!"* On to the field ran Billy Price, £5,000 from Reading, and scored a couple of goals and lo! a new Messiah was in our midst. But the crowd soon got tired of him - 5 goals in 8 games just wasn't good enough - and Norman came back and headed the goal-scoring list for the season.

All these neolithic reflections come winging back to my desk whenever word arrives from the Deep North about the latest victim of crowd persecution: from Frank Bunn to John Moore. The more things change, the more they're just the same, as the French say. The question is: how do the French know so much about Boothferry Park?

Notwithstanding all my whingeing in this piece, I still have mountains of optimism for the new season. I always have and I always will. We set off on the Road to Glory at three o'clock on Saturday afternoon and anybody who doesn't believe that is reading the wrong magazine.

Alan Plater

THINKING OF HULL, HELL & HAPPINESS

This issue's honorary President
ALAN PLATER

HULL CITY: The Season Ahead

Andrew Okey has travelled to distant and exotic lands (Morecambe) in search of ontological enlightenment. Now, in order to discern the Tiger's fortunes in the coming season, this fabled West Coast guru and soothsayer has looked into his crystal and come up with.....a load of balls:

August: August 19th saw the traditional beginning to the British winter football season. At Boothferry Park three Leicester City players collapse with heatstroke.

September: Colin Appleton attempts to sign non-league teenage sensation Jimmy Gill* from Morecambe Athletic. He offers The Shrimps two table-tennis tables and a months supply of Tigercola. However he is subsequently left empty-handed when he is outbidded by Colne Dynamoes.

October: Because of City's poor start to the season, they are still unable to find a replacement for Mansfield Beer's sponsorship. Unable to find another big-name sponsor at short notice, City turn out with *"Bertba, big girl, Flat 3, Holderness Mews. Massages (etc) from a tenner"* written on their shirts. Due to a bizarre clerical error, this logo is only printed on replica shirts in sizes for the under-12's.

November: In Holland, John Moore scores a hat-trick for the second successive match. Back in England Oldham's Frank Bunn puts five past Liverpool in the Littlewoods Cup and Andy Saville sets a new Walsall club record by scoring in each of their first 11 league games. Meanwhile, at Boothferry Park, Billy and Keith's goal famine continues.

December: Fortunes change at Boothferry Park and a string of impressive performances bring in enquiries from many interested parties. Barry Hearns offers Billy Whitehurst a place in his boxing stable, Iain Hesford is asked to become Dietician with a team of professional Sumo wrestlers, and Mr Sewell of Anlaby Road wants Colin Appleton to do him up a new set of bookshelves.

January: City are drawn away to Manchester United in the FA Cup and come away with an improbable 2-1 win. On the streets of Manchester after the match Billy Askew is mobbed by a crowd of ecstatic fans who only disperse when they realise that he isn't, after all, Mick Hucknall.

February: Colin Appleton sells Iain Hesford to Colchester United and buys Dan Marino from the Miami Dolphins as a replacement. Colin explains his thinking in simple terms: *"Basically, neither of them can keep goal but, by Christ, Dan can throw the ball even further than Iain!"*

March: Alliterature student at Hull University gains a PhD with distinction after submitting his thesis on "Metaphysical imagery in the programme notes of Colin Appleton".

April: With another change of strip due in the forthcoming close-season, Don Robinson organises a public ballot to decide on the style of the new kit. The entire population of Hull votes for a return to the traditional black-and-amber stripes. Don Robinson announces that, next season, City will turn out in red shirts, red shorts and red socks with a black-and-amber band just above the left ankle.

May: City end the season in a disappointing 19th place in Division Two. To offset this, Don Robinson finally organises that game on the moon that we have all heard so much about. City play a team of hideous mutants from the planet Thraag but, unable to cope with the very tight thing-to-man marking, they lose 17-0.

Andrew Okey

* Morecambe in-joke.

AUNTIE SOCIAL ANSWERS YOUR QUESTIONS

Dear Auntie,

Imagine my horror whilst motoring along Marfleet Lane the other day I noticed a gigantic can of lager lying on its side in the middle of a school field. Thinking we had been invaded by very thirsty litter louts from outer space, my thoughtful hubby quickly put my mind at rest by explaining it was in fact Hull Kingston Rovers' new ground. Silly me!

Mrs Wangle, Broomfleet

Auntie Social says.....Interesting that. Did you know that copying HKR's famous "10-5 Club", named after their cup final triumph over Hull FC, City are to rename the less famous "Sixty Club" either "no admission unless you're loaded" or "5th in Division Two, once" club.

Dear Auntie,

How convenient it was for Mr. Robinson that Colin Appleton can turn his hand to joinery thus becoming the club handyman. Isn't it a pity we haven't an electrician playing for us who could wire up the PA system in the East Stand? Or what about a couple of ex-BR guards so we could open up the railway station again?

Thoughtfully yours, Anon.

Auntie Social says.....Why hasn't bricklayer Billy Whitehurst built us a new ground during the close season then? Seems you just can't get the staff these days.

Dear Auntie Social,

Is it true that Woolies have brought out an Iain Hesford workout video?

Overweight, Swinefleet

Auntie Social says.....Yes, it's on the same shelf as the "Vinny Jones Ballet Class" video.

Dear Mrs. Social,

Now that Dennis Booth has joined the new relegation favourites Aston Villa will the job as club comedian be advertised or filled within?

Yosser Hughes, Merseyside

Auntie Social says.....There's a bit more competition for that job than there is for first team places. Are you as good with your feet as you are with your head?

Dear Auntie,

If my son joins up with the army, will he have to speak like Emlyn Hughes?

Alan Ball, Disneyland

Auntie Social says.....How about asking Emlyn for his views on OUR defence policy?

Dear Auntie,

Did I spot Eddie Gray selling high-backed armchairs to OAP's in Shackletons the other day?

Freddie Fruitcake, De La Pole

Auntie Social says.....Was he offering discounts?

FINGER FLICKIN' GOOD!

QPR were having a good cup run. Having disposed of Grimsby Town, Leicester City, Manchester United and Newcastle United they faced mighty Liverpool in the final of the FA Cup. Rangers contested the final magnificently and thoroughly deserved their unforgettable 8-2 victory. I can remember that afternoon as clearly as if it were yesterday. The proud smile on my sixteen year old face as I carried the 5" plastic replica FA Cup home in one hand, and my QPR Subbuteo team in the other.

Now, I guess that some of you reading this will wonder what the hell a sixteen year old was doing playing Subbuteo. Actually, it's more likely that all of you are wondering what a sixteen year old was doing playing Subbuteo. Whilst the majority of my peers were discovering the wonders of Woodpecker cider and girls' bodies I was still flicking blue and white plastic footballers around. My love affair with Subbuteo started at the impressionable age of six when I would beg and torment my, then aged seventeen years old, brother to play with me using the set he'd long since put away in the attic. In those days the figures had shorts so long, Stanley Matthews would have been embarrassed to play in them. They stood with their legs apart with a span between them that would shame the Humber Bridge, not, one would have thought, the ideal stance for a professional footballer to adopt. However, to a football-mad six year old they were almost as exciting as the real thing.

Subbuteo is marketed as "Table Soccer". This has always baffled me as everyone I know plays it on the living room floor, but I guess it would be a lot more difficult to sell as "Subbuteo - The Game Where You Crawl About On Your Hands And Knees Flicking Plastic Men About". Yes, I could see that being a bit of a difficult one to pass off, and the chances of persuading your mother to buy you a game so obviously guaranteed to ruin the knees on two or three pairs of trousers a month would be pretty slim. As a consequence of Subbuteo being played on the living room floors the injury rate is astonishingly high, with an average player picking up that many injuries Bryan Robson could consider himself fortunate for the number he has sustained during his career. Compared to the havoc wreaked by my Dad's feet over the years Vinny Jones, Norman Hunter and Chopper Harris seem about as vicious as Bananarama and as a result the most essential accessory for any Subbuteo player has always been a good, reliable tube of Airfix glue - the magic sponge of table (sorry, carpet) football.

Originally conceived by British Prisoners of War, Subbuteo dates back to the 1940's, when it was played on army blankets marked with chalk, however, Subbuteo cannot be accused of not keeping up with the times. The late eighties has seen the introduction of new "designer" playing strips (as worn by the professionals) to varying degrees of success. Take, for example, Aston Villa's current kit, hideous enough in real life, it is positively repulsive once translated into the Subbuteo size. However, as for the current Hull City monstrosity (surely a return to black and amber stripes is long overdue!) even those daredevil painters at Subbuteo dare not tackle its awesome ugliness and instead they try to pass off Dundee United as The Tigers. Another modern introduction is the "Riot Police" set consisting of heavily padded, horsebacked policemen....whatever next? Miniature turnstiles designed only to let miniature fans through if they posses miniature ID cards? Possibly, Subbuteo will introduce decaying stands and archaic toilet facilities to position opposite miniature executive boxes full of miniature dickheads asking what colours "their" team are wearing? Who knows?

At the age of 21 I should, as my mother is fond of reminding me, have grown out of Subbuteo. I haven't. Due to the inabilities of both myself and my team (QPR) on the real soccer field, my dreams and glories are achieved on the green baize. Mark Falco often nets 4 or 5 a game and Mark Dennis regularly lasts a full 90 minutes! However, the life of a 21 year old Subbuteo player is a precarious one. On many occasions an unexpected visit by a relative or friend has caused acute embarrassment as they discover a mini FA Cup tournament going on in the lounge! *"Errr...Hello Auntie Mabel. Fancy being West Ham?"* Yet, somehow I don't think I'll ever grow out of Subbuteo. I can see myself in another 15 years trying to persuade my sons, daughters, wife, (anybody!) to play against me and to carry on the legend *"FLICK TO KICK"*

Sean Penistone

OK, SO I FLICK TO KICK NOW AND AGAIN. I CAN HANDLE IT. I COULD STOP TOMORROW IF I WANTED.

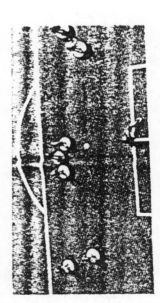

Dear Sean,

My son has become a source of worry to me. He has the physique of an old age pensioner, and is finding it more difficult to walk from one day to the next. Can you help me?

Mrs X, Putney.

Sean says...... Well Mrs X, it seems to me that your son has developed subbuteosis tubular, a not uncommon condition, caused by playing table football on a table, giving rise to chronic backache & contraction of the spine. Two other common strains are subbuteosis wrangler which attacks the player's trouser knees, if the game is being played on the floor, and Motson's Subbuteosis, a neurological condition giving rise to constant commentating particularly such phrases as "Away to my left" and "Any thoughts so far Jimmy!"

I will be sending a self-help package including a tube of deep heat. Don't worry though, Mrs X, it's a great game, and like your son, the symptoms are diagnosed at an early stage, the chances of survival aren't bad at all.

RAVE ON....AND ON.....AND ON!

The whole world it seems has caught MANCHESTERITIS. Inspired by an "explosion" of Manchester bands, such as The Happy Mondays, Stone Roses (or *Stern Rerses as we say in Hull:-Ed.*) and Inspiral Carpets, the magazine racks of John Turnbulls have recently been filled by a deluge of endless waffle telling us how very, very Northern and very, very trendy it is to hail from Manchester. In January NME splashed MANCHESTER vs LIVERPOOL the battle of the Cities across its pages and more recently THE FACE weighed in with its great MANCHESTER vs LONDON debate. Well I'm afraid that this Manchester chic just doesn't wash here in Hull and the backlash has already begun. *"Hull - North Of Manchester"* T-shirts parody the original *"Manchester - North Of England"* shirts (as worn by 808 State on Top Of The Pops) and the *"Manchester Rave On"* slogan has been rudely replaced by *"Manchester Fuck Off"*.

In true bandwaggon jumping style *H, H & H* asks the burning questions: Hull or Manchester - which is the hippest? Manchester or Hull - who invented acid house? Hull or Manchester - who invented the Yankeeburger?

FOOTBALL:

Manchester boasts (until May at least) two First Division football teams. One, which goes by the name of United play in red shirts with Sharp written on them yet sharp is the last adjective you would choose to describe their football. Somewhere along the lines of the past 20 years at Old Trafford somebody has managed to seriously confuse the adjectives. It would seem that at United the object isn't to create a successful soccer team of your own. No, at Old Trafford the ruling school of thought seems to be that is a player is making a name for themselves - buy the fucker before someone else does and you never know he might even turn out to be quite good! (I can just see Middlesbrough at Gary Pallister's signing for United - *"Oh yeah he's dead good Alex!"*)

Manchester City on the other hand play in light blue and advertise knitting machines on their shirts. By contrast Hull City have never tasted the First Division's champagne lifestyle. Yet they do boast a Grandways supermarket adjacent to their ground. Whilst today's bargain-hungry soccer fans return from Old Trafford and Maine Road with only a souvenir match programme, Hull City fans return home from home games with the weeks groceries.

MUSIC:

Again, Hull wipes the floor with Manchester. The bands listed on the left are from Manny, those on the right from Hull:

Manchester	Hull
New Order	Housemartins
Smiths	Red Guitars
Buzzcocks	Beautiful South
Inspiral Carpets	Pink Noise
Happy Mondays	The Von Trapps
Stone Roses	...err...Roland Gift
James	Housemartins......
MC Buzz B	
The Fall	

Notice the astonishing lack of depth of talent in Manchester (I mean, who the hell are the Smiths? Pah!)

NIGHTLIFE:

Whilst a Manchester raver may well head to Day 201 (the Factory owned bar) or perhaps the Squire Albert or to whet his whistle with a lager or a lucozade (literally) before joining an M25 tailback of a queue for the Nude night at the Hacienda, Hull ravers head straight for the Cheese and down 12 to 15 pints of John Smiths bitter moving swiftly on to Bass House and finally Shire for a quick one or five before hitting LA's. Manchester ravers party ro Techno (amongst other things) whilst Hull boys prefer the more modern sounds of a bit of Kylie or Jase....

EATING OUT:

Hull has the Yankeeburger - end of competition.

Next issue: New Orleans v Withernsea - which is the real birthplace of jazz? Plus the truth about Showaddywaddy's visit to Keyingham chippie.

I KNOW....COS I WAS THERE....

(Great matches of the past # 2)
Division 4
ORIENT 4 v HULL CITY 5

'Remember Orient' - City's equivalent of the alamo cry. Any feature that deals with great matches of the past had to include this game somewhere - the only surprise is that it wasn't number one in the series!

I remember at the time having bad memories of that Brisbane Road ground, I still think it was the 3-1 defeat there that finally cost us promotion to Division Two the previous season. Still, I started the Saturday optimistically enough after meeting up with 50 or so Southern Tigers in the pub near the ground just after one o'clock, and even a local policeman calling me a 'c ← ' on my way to the ground nearly two hours later couldn't dampen my new found enthusiasm for this second 'journey to the Orient'.

What did dampen it though was the three goals that Orient rattled in before twenty-six minutes had passed. First, after fifteen minutes, Silkman's corner was flicked on at the near post by Corbett, to Godfrey, whose point-blank header gave Norman no chance. Four minutes later and Silkman again did the damage, seizing on a City error toset up Jones to put Orient two up. I was by now beginning to hate Barry Silkman and thus hatred grew after twenty-six minutes when it was his pass that sent Hales away down the right and the centre was put away by Cornwell at the near post.

Three-nil down and memories of the Baseball Ground disaster weeks earlier came flooding back. Still, the hundred or so of us in the seats didn't lose faith and carried on our vocal encouragement while the three hundred City fans behind Norman's goal stood motionless in disbelief!

Just before half-time, our support was rewarded when Askew's corner floated directly in. The half-time interval was spent discussing the need for City to score early to give themselves any chance in the second half.

We almost got our wish when McClaren blazed yards over soon after the interval, but ten minutes into the half and disaster........that man Silkman again, this tume the scorer with a 25-yard 'screamer'.

What followed was one of the most remarkable turnabouts I will probably ever see at a football match. Twenty-five minutes left, City trail 1-4. First Whitehurst crosses from the by-line for Massey to slide the ball home, then five minutes later Horton's header from Askew's corner is pushed into the path of Andy Flounders who makes it 3-4. By now I was virtually hoarse with the strains of excitement, and you suddenly got the feeling that City could do it. Then, in the 77th minute Corbett handles a free-kick in his own box and City have a penalty. Amidst all the excitement, we fail to notice a hundred or so Orient 'daft lads' come charging across the seats. Still nobody was now going to spoil my day and, anyhow, they mysteriously stopped five yards away. I tune back in time to see 'Stan the Man' McEwan sweetly strike the penalty away. 4-4!

A draw would have been a superb achievement but when Flounders smacked home the winner with two minutes left, it was a case of sheer ecstacy! The scenes of jubilation at the final whistle were probably unmatched anywhere - the only tint on the celebrations being the fact that only Billy Whitehurst out of the whole team could be bothered to come across to the seats where our little band had sang for the whole ninety minutes. Still, I wasn't going to let this upset what had been a great day for Hull City. As Brian Horton said later, we should have never conceded four goals, but to come back and win after doing so showed great character. 'Remember Orient'....I certainly do!

Grip 66

Does that dodgy offside decision never seem to go your way? Does that last minute equaliser always go to the other side? Does that last minute winner always go to the other side? Does the opposition's striker always end his lean spell against you? Does the opposition's winger, who the bloke in the pub told you was clueless, spend the afternoon tying your full back up in more knots than you'll find in the Boy Scouts Handbook? If all this is depressingly familiar, then either you support Hull City or else your team does a pretty convincing imitation of the Tigers. Supporters of most clubs wonder what other teams' fans think of them. Liverpool fans believe the rest of the League look up to them and look forward to the 'honour' of a trip to Anfield. Halifax followers reckon everyone else admires their resilience in adversity; Leeds and Millwall sing "No-one likes us...." and self-knowledge is a valuable quality. But Hull City? Who? "What do you think of football in Hull?" "Oh, it'd be a good idea!" Ha bloody ha. In fact, if you drew up a list of the 92 League clubs, Hull City would weigh in somewhere near the middle whatever criteria you care to choose. We're used to it.

It's a generation now since the team spearheaded by Ken Wagstaff and Chris Chilton swept to the third division title and on to the top of the second early the next season. Over 100 League goals were scored in that promotion season and gates of over 25,000 were commonplace. It would be an exagerration to say it's been downhill ever since, after all we've had some class players to cheer and Billy Whitehurst too, but the failure of even that side to lift the club into Division One for the first time in Tiger history has left a deep feeling of resignation about the club's chances among the people of the city. And so to 'On Cloud Seven'. The phrase belongs to our linguistically eccentric two-time manager, Colin Appleton; 'On Cloud Seven' is where he said he was on learning of his re-appointment as boss at Boothferry Park. (There is no record of where he felt himself located sixteen games, no wins and a sacking later). It seemed to sum up Hull City's record of underachievement. Cloud Seven, not Cloud Nine; nearly there but not quite.

So what market are we aiming for? We don't deal in match reports because they get passed around by word of mouth to those who want to know anyway. We don't deal in ill-considered abuse of opposing teams; our abuse is always carefully considered. We don't print pages of letters saying how great the magazine is, because we don't receive any. We don't compete with Hull, Hell & Happiness, which has a wider cultural focus which appeals to non-Hull City fans and non-football fans in a way that we never would. Actually, we aren't really aiming for any market. We write what we like and then try and sell it. And if people come up to us outside Boothferry Park and hand us 50p for the latest issue saying "Yer last one was a right laugh", then maybe we're doing something right. And, while we're in a mellow mood, we might admit that sometimes, just sometimes, that last minute goal goes to our side. Now the Tigers!

Dedicated to 86 years of underachievement by Hull City F.C.

TUBBY LARD
of The Boulevard

No. 5

LES MUTRIE

CLOUD PLEASERS

It's December 1980 and City are in extra time of a Cup Replay against Blyth Spartans, a non-League side, in front of a large crowd of very hostile Geordies. A penalty is awarded to the home side. Humiliation beckons. Tony Norman makes a miracle save, City escape by the skin of their teeth and finally win the tie in extra time of the third game, at Elland Road. So what do you do about the unfortunate who missed that vital spot kick? Well, you laugh at him, of course (after checking the hostile Geordies aren't too close). And you laugh again when he misses another one at Elland Road. But you don't laugh when he's allowed a retake at Elland Road and sticks away Blyth's equaliser ; and you didn't laugh when he scored in both the first two games either. What's a performer like that doing in non-League football, you wonder.

So when City boss Mike Smith paid £30,000 for the man a couple of weeks later, the reaction in Hull was that it was money well spent - as long as he was banned from taking penalties. Les Mutrie (for it is he!) had broken into League football briefly with Carlisle, but quickly returned to his native Tyneside to play non-League with Blyth. Despite winning England non-league international honours, it seemed that his career was destined to be remembered only by the hardy devotees of Tow Law and Esh Winning, when City swooped to give him a late second bite at the League cherry.

ON CLOUD SEVEN

He didn't so much bite the cherry as swallow the whole bunch and look for more. Mutrie played out the rest of that grim relegation season and dropped, with City, into the Fourth Division. But our first season ever down in the basement saw Mutrie scoff 27 goals in 43 League games - and he was quite brilliant. His response to the Receivership crisis was emphatic as he put away 14 goals in scoring in 9 successive games, a club record. As Mutrie himself observed, he was at the time playing not for City, nor even for himself, but to put food on his family's plate, but in those grim circumstances he was quite unstoppable. The little Mutries deserved a banquet.

Sir Les, as he is still known in some parts of Bunkers, was in truth ready for higher things. Chelsea of Division Two had no answer to him in the Cup and only several amazing saves by Steve Francis saved the Pensioners bacon at Stamford Bridge. At the time of Receivership, Mutrie and Tony Norman were both set to sign for Birmingham, then in Division One, until contractual problems relating to their continued link to City scuppered the deal. As Mutrie himself put it (he was never slow to speak expansively of his own prowess), on ability he would "skate into" most First Division sides. But the chance never came and Mutrie, now 30, stayed to score 12 times in 40 games in season 1982-83 as City romped to promotion from the Fourth. I felt that perhaps his finest ever City performance came early that season. Torquay visited Boothferry as League leaders, but Mutrie dismantled them virtually singlehanded and scored twice in a 4-1 win. Torquay simply couldn't get the ball off him. Brian Marwood matured visibly playing alongside Mutrie.

Mutrie at that time really had it all ; strength, pace, determination, sharpness in front of goal and power in the air. Even Waggy could boast only four of those attributes, though admittedly Waggy's reign at Boothferry was much longer than Les's. Looking at that list of abilities, Les Mutrie compares very favourably with any recent City frontman - Keith could lay claim to 4 on a good day, Billy maybe three and a half, Marwood and Flounders 3 and Billy Woof none.

Up into Division Three and Mutrie still seemed to have plenty to offer. In October we beat Sheffield United 4-1 at home and it was Mutrie who put the icing on an already very tasty cake, by waltzing (watch him go!) from near the corner flag at the now neglected South East corner into the middle of the penalty area before stroking the fourth goal past the bemused Keith Waugh. That South East corner is not called "Mutrie's corner"- but it should be. Rumours however were by now rife. Appleton and Mutrie did not see eye to eye. Mutrie's penchant for speaking out was plainly not to the liking of the man with the ears and, we understand, matters came to a head after a 2-1 home win over Orient in November. Mutrie made his point, in, err, forceful terms and was out. First on loan to Doncaster, then to Colchester and then like so many Geordies returning home in the twilight of their career- think of Pop Robson and Barry Wardrobe, and what price Paul Gascoigne - to Hartlepool. His career ended soon after. Ill health was cited ; valium addiction, it was whispered among City fans. But make no mistake about Les Mutrie. In the darkest times the club has ever known, he was a hero. Sir Les.

A CRUCIAL SEASON

Looking back at the newspaper reports of 80 years ago is a fascinating exercise if only for the realisation of how few things have changed. In August 1909 there was a murder in Porter Street (just off Hessle Road) and the fans and some of the press were asking if Hull City really wanted First Division football.

In their first four league seasons City had finished 5th, 9th, 8th and 4th in Division Two. There had been no significant additions to the squad of 1908/09, and although City had finished 4th, they were 7 points behind a promotion place which, with a 38-match season and only 2 points for a win, was quite a considerable margin. The majority of the criticism concerned the defence - Jack McQuillan was a highly-rated left-back but that was it. Also the highly talented left-winger Gordon Wright, still the only City player ever to win a full England cap, would not be available for much of the season. Gordon, a Cambridge graduatge, was a bit of a scholar and had decided to further his studies at the Royal College of Mines in London.

This led an East Hull newspaper to accuse City of "a great lack of enterprise in not securing star artistes." The response from the club Secretary, a Mr. Haller, was "Is it not an open question that we have got the stars already?" As this clipping shows, Athleo, the main Hull City writer on the Hull Times (part of the Hull Daily Mail Group), also rejected all pre-season criticisms of City. Incidentally, it must be made clear that any allegations that Athleo was David Bond's great-grandfather remain unsubstantiated.

DIVISION I.

ARE HULL CITY AMBITIOUS?

(BY "ATHLEO.")

THE Tigers will need a lot of shaking off this season. Rarely has a club at its command so promising a string of juniors as Hull City have the season secured. Their performances in the trial matches have been such as to make one feel great confidence as to the result of the coming season. The older hands, also, have lost none of their old cunning and ability, and the directors have plenty from whom to pick and choose. The ...

	P	W	D	L	F	A	Pts
1 Man City	38	23	8	7	81	40	54
2 Oldham	38	23	7	8	79	39	53
3 Hull City	38	23	7	8	80	46	53
4 Derby	38	22	9	7	72	47	53
5 Leicester Fosse	38	20	4	14	79	58	44
6 Glossop NE	38	18	7	13	64	57	43
7 Fulham	38	14	13	11	51	43	41
8 Wolves	38	17	6	15	64	63	40
9 Barnsley	38	16	7	15	62	59	39
10 Bradford PA	38	17	4	17	64	59	38

City began 1909/10 in fine style with a win at Barnsley (what's new) followed by a home win over Leeds City. The Tigers only dropped one point in the first six matches. Its amazing to read of the feelings towards the Leeds team so early in the history of the game, but here it is in black and white. Leeds were "arrogant loin-enders" and their fans saw "no good in any team but their own". Also interesting to see that the size of the crowd (or "muster") was a cause for concern.

City then had their first real test - successive matches against the two teams just relegated from Division One - Manchester City and Leicester Fosse. City lost both matches and by the end of November had won only 2 out of their last 10 matches. December saw a resurgence of form but in mid-February, with two-thirds of the season played, the table looked like this:

Elsewhere in the football world the formation of a Players Union was causing quite a stir, with union recognition and the abolition of the maximum wage for footballers (then 208 per annum) the main bones of contention. Players were asked to sign documents pledging their loyalty to their clubs and the F.A. rather than the Union, and although the majority acquiesced there was still disruption of the opening fixture list.

THE HULL TIMES
SEPT. 4, 1910

ON CLOUD SEVEN

Although Chris Elton's excellent book "Hull City - A Complete Record" gives the crowd at 29,083, and the Oldham Chronicle at the time gave the official attendance at 32,000, Athleo reckoned that there were at least 40,000 in Boundary Park with many spectators on the roofs of the stands. The butterscotch vendors had a field day.

Oldham went 1-0 up after 18 minutes after their star player, right-winger Broad, skipped past Nevins. Shortly afterwards Alf Toward, despite being "at least eight yards offside", raced through to score a second. To rub salt in the wound, Toward had been a Hull City player only five months earlier. City threw everything at Oldham in the second half, winning a stream of corners, but a goal would not come. The game also got very heated and the referee had to administer cautions to both sides before a late third goal sealed City's fate. Athletic's day was made complete when the news came through that Derby had only managed a 0-0 draw at West Brom. Oldham, the league's newest club, were promoted along with Man City. In fact, Man City had lost 3-2 at Wolves and a win for the Tigers at Boundary Park would have sent us up as champions, a draw as runners-up. Two days later Halley's comet paid a visit, and at the end of the week the King died.

1909/10 had it all. The club criticised for lack of ambition, the low home crowds causing concern, a sound beating of an unpopular Leeds, and success for Oldham gained largely because of their pitch (maybe they used artificial mud). Plus a change, as they say on the more fashionable parts of the South Stand.

RUN OF ILL LUCK.

On Saturday misfortune dogged City's footsteps. The team all round by no means played the game they did against West Bromwich, but there was a deal to be said for their excuse. First and foremost they were severely handicapped in this, the most momentous game of the season, by the absence of McQuillan at back. Added to that was the fact that the ground was in an absolutely abominable state, the perfect words fail to convey an adequate idea of the indescribable puddle which was termed a ground. Whatever success Oldham have achieved I am convinced is in no small measure due to the difficulties a visiting team has to meet in regard to the ground alone. I can assure my readers I am but stating a fact when I say that from one end of the ground to the other there is a slope of at least six feet, whilst across the ground there is a difference of from three to four feet. Thus everything was against the Tigers in a game in which they stood in need of every possible assistance. Added to this the referee, Mr McArthur, was by no means an ideal man to be in charge of such a game. On occasions he was too slow to follow the game at the pace at which it was fought, and he should never have allowed

THE SECOND GOAL

Toward received a long pass when he was yards off-side, and had no difficulty in scoring. This was decidedly unfortunate for the Tigers, for the two-goal lead thus established was very disheartening. Nevertheless, they made gallant attempts to draw level. Notwithstanding their energy, however, they never really looked like being good enough for Oldham. The cause of this might be summed up in one sentence:
WRETCHED GROUND AND WEAK BACKS.
That really covers the whole story of defeat. Oldham adapted themselves to the circumstances

Then City went into overdrive (or they would have done if it had existed). In their next 12 matches the Tigers won 11 and drew the other one. This had lifted them to second in the table and everything would hang on the final match at Oldham Athletic. However, Oldham had been enjoying an even more impressive run, experiencing just one defeat in twenty league matches. Having been bottom of the table after five matches with just two points, the Latics had hauled themselves up the table and were also part of the promotion equation. Here's how the table looked before the final day of the season:

		P	W	D	L	F	A	PTS
1	DERBY CO	24	16	4	4	56	30	36
2	MAN CITY	23	15	4	4	54	24	34
3	GLOSSOP	25	15	4	6	51	30	34
4	LEICESTER F.	24	16	0	8	59	36	32
5	FULHAM	25	11	8	6	36	23	30
6	HULL CITY	25	12	6	7	48	33	30

Manchester City, away to Wolves, were already up barring a mathematical miracle. Derby, away to West Brom, needed to win and City to lost to be promoted. Oldham needed to beat Hull City and hope that Derby failed to win. City just needed a draw.

		P	W	D	L	F	A	PTS
1	MAN CITY	37	23	8	6	79	37	54
2	HULL CITY	37	23	7	7	80	43	53
3	DERBY CO	37	22	8	7	72	47	52
4	OLDHAM A.	37	22	7	8	76	39	51

The bad news for City was that Jack McQuillan had been injured in the previous match (a 5-1 home win over West Brom) and his place at left-back was taken by the impulsive Tom Nevins. I will leave it to Athleo to describe the state of the pitch:

The final word, though, must go to "The Spotter", also of The Hull Times, reflecting on the scenes at Boundary Park after that fateful game:

"I WON'T ATTEMPT TO DESCRIBE THE SCENE WHEN IT WAS ACTUALLY KNOWN THAT OLDHAM ACTUALLY BELONGED TO DIVISION 1, BUT THE ENTHUSIASTS DID WHAT THE CITY FOLLOWERS WOULD DO ON SUCH AN EVENT. THEY WENT INTO A STATE OF DELIRIUM."

Quite.

No footy photos in the papers in those days - but plenty of cartoons and caricatures. Here we see City seeing off the Peacocks (after our win over Leeds) and a likeness of City's half-back, Scot Davy Gordon.

FOOTBALL CARTOON.—381.

And Match Reports were much more graphic then - imagine reading these comments in 1990:

... pass was badly missed by Halligan. Watson was penalised for catching hold of W. Smith, and from the free kick Temple received, and sent in a stinger, which knocked a

SHOWER OF WHITENING

off the cross bar, a feat greeted with a loud cry of "Oh!" and cheering. Stanley Smith returned, but was again forced to retire, and was conveyed

... and from this Leeds City assumed the aggressive. Gemmell missing badly. Neve became conspicuous, and sent over the bar, being unfortunate in not scoring. He was pulled down heavily by Watson, who was

HOOTED LOUDLY

by the crowd, and in truth his tactics were, to say the least, decidedly rigorous. His charge on Neve was made in that players' face. Stan Smith was now putting in a great.

(All from <u>THE HULL TIMES, SEPTEMBER 4, 1909</u>)

OC7 asks some serious questions about...

O L D H A M

When an unmarked Roger Palmer flashed a header into City's net to put Oldham 2-0 ahead, it seemed fairly obvious that the Tigers were not about to break the Boundary Park side's long unbeaten home record. But more serious matters than the loss of three points were about to break. After what seemed like an innocuous clash with Oldham 'keeper John Hallworth, Andy Payton was left motionless on the plastic. Jeff Radcliffe responded to the urgent beckoning of Hallworth and raced on to the pitch. He was followed by Oldham's doctor, Stan Ternent, other Oldham officials and the St. John's ambulance folk, in that order. Payton was then stretchered off, still motionless. We were to learn (much later) that he had swallowed his tongue and stopped breathing, but that Jeff Radcliffe's prompt action had averted any serious consequences and that Payton was sore but relatively comfortable in hospital. He was back among the goals only a fortnight later against Blackburn.

First the credits. To Jeff Radcliffe, first and foremost. Long a cult figure, it is reassuring to know that the man in the tartan bunnet is also a supreme professional. Credit too, to John Hallworth, for his immediate appreciation of the urgency of the situation. But their keeper aside, Oldham emerge with little credit from this affair. The St.John's ambulance performed with sad incompetence. They were slow to the scene, appeared to lack basic equipment and in fact their reaction was to panic.

I've been watching football for over 20 years and have seen the St.John's called on maybe four or five times. I've always assumed they were competently trained. After seeing them in "action" at Boundary Park, there must be a suspicion that clubs have them there because they are cheap and give the appearance, rather than the reality, of providing medical facilities ; does anyone actually check their competence ? It was clearly lacking on this occasion. It was a disgrace, as well, that Oldham made no effort at half time to inform the City fans of Payton's condition. We were forced to spend half time listening to the Public Address system drivelling on about lottery results. Any sensitivity at all among Oldham's administrative staff would have led them to put out a simple message that Payton was safe and sound and on his way to hospital. And finally, that pitch. OC7 is not about to reopen the debate about whether the plastic gives Oldham an advantage ; of course it does, but that doesn't detract from Oldham being the best team in the Division. The point is that it is an artificial surface and players cannot adjust to it easily. They get burns from tackles which would be easy on grass but which hurt

on plastic ; more seriously, they misjudge the speed at which they can change pace and it is this confusion which led to Payton's injury. He was making a fair challenge and on grass he would have suffered no more than a tumble ; as it was, the plastic caused him to lose control over his feet and make an uncontrolled crash to the plastic. <u>OC7 says</u>, : rip up the plastic.

...OC7......OC7......OC7......OC7......OC7...

RACHMANINOV THE POST

Many thanks to the mysterious Busmaster C for submitting the following. We don't understand much of it, and the bits we do, we don't believe, but no matter, spin those discs, maestro.

..Back in the early Sixties, if anyone had even suggested that gangs of rattle-waving kids in bobble hats constituted a football hooligan problem, he would have been told to go away and take something strong. Pop music was a different matter. The Beatles - pah, even our parents liked them! What kind of rebellion is that? But the Rolling Stones were dangerous. They were regularly denounced from the pulpit and in the press, as the greatest threat to public morals since cheap Victorian gin. And soon they were to become permanently linked with football through a fairly new phenomenon - the Pop Song as Terrace Chant.

On a warm sunny September day in 1965 (yes, I know they were all warm and sunny then), York City visited Boothferry Park and became the only team other than Chelsea to outplay the Tigers at home all season. But, more significantly for the history of soccer, the crowd was swollen to over 20,500 by the presence, in front of the South Stand, of what can only be described as a bunch of eccentric nutters, long-haired bohemian types in ankle-length red and white scarves who, throughout the gloriously one-sided second half, beat out the chorus "Da-da, da-da-da, da-da-da-da, Minster!" on cymbals, horns and all manner of ad hoc percussion instruments. The eleven-note line in question is, of course, the rhythm riff from the chorus of (I can't get no) Satisfaction, and was quickly taken up by City fans at subsequent games. City were big and popular then, and soon to be on telly every other week. The "Da-da, da-da-da" craze spread, and within a couple of seasons was universal. But never forget it originally came from Bootham via Boothferry! In case you think this is all speculation, Satisfaction was still in the charts on 18/9/65. I rest my case.

Organised terrace chanting was just getting started by the mid-sixties, though call-and-response chants like "Give us a T" etc. had long been popular. Chants normally consisted of the club's nickname or a player's surname repeated to fade-out, as it were. But a new wave of creativity was soon to break.

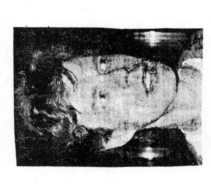

Jagger, 1990 style - as dangerous as Bungo

"You'll never walk alone", which was first sung by the masses at the 1965 Liverpool-Leeds Cup Final, does not really count as it is normally sung without adaptation. But new chants based on popular platters of the day were soon to be heard all the time. Promotion in 1966, and the regular influx of large numbers of fans from biggish clubs, brought new chants practically every fortnight. There was always something new to listen out for ; one of my own favourites was the Small Faces" "Sha-la-la-la McIlmoyle" sung by a Kemptonful of Wolves fans. The Beatles were somewhat underrepresented (too melodic?), though Yellow Submarine versions were universal, City's contribution being the rather plodding "We all cheer for a Black and Amber team". Better, more obscene versions followed, but I am too much of a gentleman to quote them.

You have to die to become immortal, and it was Jim Reeves who was to enter the Terrace Chant Hall of Fame with his posthumous No. 1, Distant Drums, cunningly released to tie in with the centenary of the end of the American Civil War. It became "Distant Bums...over there", and reflected the new phenomenon of home and away fans

ON CLOUD SEVEN

occupying clearly defined "ends". City's crowds were falling by the late Sixties, but the hits just kept on coming. August 1968 saw the tuneless final chorus from the Beatles' Hey Jude become "Na,na,na-na-na-na City", and the Plastic Ono Band's anthem Give Peace a Chance, probably the most chantable song ever written, is still with us in the form of "Give us a Goal". Even American bands were getting the message - surely one-hit wonders Steam's Na-na, hey-hey Kiss him Goodbye was written specifically with an eye to the Kop choir market. Nor let us forget that Norwegian dirge Amazing Grace (if only we could...). And it was really "Denis Law, Superstar", thank you very much Mr. Lloyd Webber, with different sets of words for the Stretford and the Kippax choirs.

Of course, by this time, many teams were getting into the charts themselves, often bringing new meaning to the term "professional foul". By the time we had thrown away our mid seventies flares, "Guantanamera" (the Cuban national anthem, fact fans) had become "There's only one (insert name)". Then in 1978, during a League Cup tie at Filbert Street, Jilted John achieved what a pal in the "biz" reckoned was every songwriter's secret ambition, namely having a hit sung on the terraces, when the Kop sang "Gordon Hill's a moron" at the hapless Derby winger. Sadly this chant, like Jilted himself, did not have any lasting success.

Into the eighties, and we have had Ant Rap ("Love to sing, love to scrap") and various versions of Karma Chameleon. hat will we be singing if they have their way over the dreaded membership ? A new version of Deck of Cards ?

There have been terrace one-hit wonders as well as standards ; no doubt I've missed a few favourites out. Nor do the many odd ditties based on folk songs (The Wild Rover !) or American marches (another important source) come within the scope of this article.

We have long heard adaptations of arguably the worst record to get to Number One, Chicory Tip's Son of My Father, along the lines of "Oh, Billy, Billy" etc. Surely it's time for a chant based on the best ever. But, given City's recent form, perhaps "Back to Life" is a bit premature.

...Plenty of controversy from the Busmaster. The OC7 editorial possee and associates would throw in mention of Rod Stewart's Sailing and Gary Glitter's Hello, hello, I'm back again. Terry Jacks' "Seasons in the Sun" was sung in a number of forms rather more menacing the wimpy original and the same could be said for Mary Hopkin's Those were the days (...my friend, we took the Stretford End...). An old favourite which should ring round Boundary Park in March is Manfred Mann's "Come on without, come on within, you've not see nothin' like Frankie's Chin". How about "We'll support you evermore", which, we are reliably informed, has a pedigree going back to the stirring hymn "Guide me, O thou great Redeemer." And that Dambusters theme, would we have won the war without it ? As for the worst ever Number One, we think that the Goombay Dance Band's "Seven Tears" possesses pretty impressive credentials.

......OC7......OC7......OC7......OC7......OC7......OC7......

COULD YOU BE THE MANAGER OF LEEDS UNITED?

.....try our simple test of skill and find out !

1. You need a goalkeeper. Arsenal have bought David Seaman from QPR for £1.5 million. They are desperately trying to offset the cost by offloading the hopelessly past-it John Lukic on to some unsuspecting fools. Do you.....
   a. Look around the lower leagues for a bright up-and-coming youngster who'll do the job for the next ten years
   b. Stick with Mervyn Day until the transfer fees have cooled off a bit
   c. Write Arsenal a cheque for £1 million.

2. Which skills do you most like your young players to possess?
   a. Passing ability
   b. Accurate shooting
   c. The forearm smash

3. You have just won promotion to the First Division. All the critics say your side lacks First Division experience. Gary McAllister of Leicester City, who has never played or proved himself in the First Division, becomes available. Do you.....
   a. Inquire after older experienced First Division players who'll do you a good job for a couple of seasons while your youngsters mature
   b. Invite Billy Bremner back for a trial
   c. Write Leicester City a cheque for £1 million

4. You have an important Cup tie coming up. What is the single most important part of your preparation?
   a. An intensive and imaginative coaching session
   b. An inspirational team talk
   c. A cheque book

5. Who is your favourite sports personality of all time?
   a. Ken Wagstaff
   b. Pat Pocock
   c. Genghis Khan

6. Your supporters have run riot in sleepy Bournemouth, yet again heaping shame on the club and on football generally. Do you
   a. Admit that your fans are a pack of baboons and can't be trusted in civilised company
   b. Ask the fans to behave in future
   c. Tell the media that's it's all an exaggeration and that Leeds fans are angels

7. Gordon Strachan is a red headed little prat who fouls people off the ball and always whines to referees. Do you
   a. Demand that he behaves properly or he'll be kicked out
   b. Try to transfer him to Argentina
   c. Make him your team captain

So how did you score?

Mostly As : you have integrity and a love for football. Elland Road is not the place for you
Mostly Bs : you've got some funny ideas, but you still deserve better. Try Ayresome Park, say.
Mostly Cs : piss off, Howard.

Quiz answers from page 18 are:
1. Fulham, 7th April 1969.
2. Drumcondra
3. (a) Stuart Croft (b) Nick Deacy (c) John Hawley (d) Alan Taylor
4. John Kaye
5. Sammy Morgan
6. Gary Swann
7. Steve Corkain, Les Thompson

At the Barclays Bank annual managers' awards lunch in London yesterday, where he collected the Second Division award, Leeds United's manager Howard Wilkinson said: "There have always been hooligans. In Germany they were in the Gestapo and in Russia they were in the KGB. To treat us unfairly as a club is to become like them, because their justice is rough justice."

ON CLOUD SEVEN

chapter 14

BLOW FOOTBALL - BORN TO BE SOLD

Emerging as it did in the last months of the 1980s, Blow Football was a late arrival on the fanzine scene, but its origins, very much like the dress sense of its editors, really belong in the distant days of the late seventies. Steve Moss, then twelve years old, scooped an ever-so-exclusive interview for Radio Orwell's critically acclaimed Saturday morning kids show "Boomerang" with the then Ipswich manager Bobby Robson. The resulting publicity did Robson's immediate career prospects more good than young Steve's. Driven by a determination to emulate Kevin Beattie's waste of early promise or, perhaps, disillusioned by the fact that Robson mistakenly called him 'Richard' throughout the interview, it was another ten years before Moss gave birth to Blow Football.

While known as a Birmingham based magazine, Blow Football was actually an offshoot of the "Manchester scene" that produced such exciting alternative talents as the Happy Mondays, Stone Roses and Bernard Manning. In the city where George Best succumbed to the bright lights and booze, Moss fell prey to the kebabs and burglars. After one too many burglaries he moved into a refuge for soft porn stars, where he met, and took an instant dislike to, Alan Baxter and Bob Blenkinsop. Blenkinsop, teenage mutant hero goalscoring partner to the young Marco Gabbiadini, and more recently known as "Helen Blenkinsop off Newsbeat's brother" was looking for a partner with a worse record collection, and soon the gallant threesome were forming an understanding as good as that shared by fellow Manchester stalwarts Howard Kendall and Peter Swales.

After a quick start off the blocks, Blow Football has recently been challenging the Beatles for regularity of new output. This was partly caused by the defection of Baxter to start up the Eupropean arm of the operation in Naples, and Blenkinsop's round the world jaunt, which only ended because of UEFA's threat to restrict the number of overseas members on fanzine editorial teams.

This "quality not quantity" policy has allowed Blow Football to distance itself from the decline of a large part of the fanzine world into an orgy of poor writing, pathetic slagging off of its rivals and their supporters, and copying ideas - in short, everything that fanzines were supposed to be about blowing away. Indeed, some readers might be surprised to discover that the 'Subbuteo' spoof in the following pages is actually the original. It has been reprinted, sometimes with permission and/or acknowledgement, sometimes with neither, in more magazines than is healthy. The unfortunate by-product of the punk ethic that "anyone can do it" is that, invariably, everyone does.

This rising above the dross further demonstrates the parallels between the careers of Blow Football and David Platt. After both serving time in Manchester, and having a good World Cup, both are now immensely popular and successful in Birmingham, having resisted big money Italian bids. The only difference is that whereas Platt spent four years at Crewe Alexandra in between Manchester and Birmingham Blow Football was spared a ten minute connection at Crewe station.

At the time of writing the future for Blow Football looks rosy. A cartoon strip and film are in the offing, and spin-off merchandise such as pencil cases, lunchboxes, boxer shorts and lifesize blow-up dolls of the editors are all selling well. Indeed, a fifth issue has not yet been ruled out. Critics often wondered what would have happened if Ernie Blenkinsop (Sheffield Wednesday and England), 'Slim' Jim Baxter (Rangers and Scotland) and Ernie Moss (Chesterfield and Kettering) had played in the same team. Sixty years on, their respective grandsons are giving a taste of what might have been.

"Manchester City was a love affair, Everton was a marriage, but Blow Football was a tremendous bit on the side." (Howard Kendall)

STEVE MOSS

COLIN MOYNIHAN - A TRIBUTE

Does the Trade and Industry Secretary say "Don't buy British goods, they're a right load of crap" ?

Does the Agriculture Secretary say "I wouldn't eat British beef if I were you, you'll all go down with Mad Cow Disease" ?

Does the Environment Secretary say "You won't be able to tell the difference between swimming off British beaches and taking a dip in some raw sewage" ?

Does the Minister for Sport say "I fully support these deportations. These people are a group of criminally motivated thugs, football's effluent tendency" ?

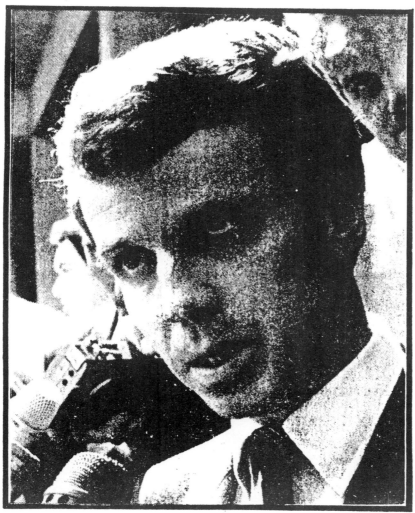

GOD HELP THE DEPARTMENT OF ENERGY!

Author: Ian Rush

Title: THE JUVENTUS DIARIES

Source: A bloke in the pub

Cost: Undisclosed

28 June.... Signed the final forms for Juventus today. Looking forward to a bright new era in my career. Linking up with players like Zoff, Rossi and Boninsegna can only improve my game.

30 June.... The club president gave me a new Fiat car today but he looked a bit put out when I told him I didn't like foreign cars. Besides, they've put the steering wheel on the passenger side and the wife doesn't drive yet.

1 July.... Turned up an hour late for training today. Apparently they're an hour ahead of Britain out here. Personally, I reckon that if you're prepared to pay £3 million for a player the least you should do is operate in his time zone, but thereyou go. The Boss fined me 10,000 lira. Hadn't bothered to change any currency, so paid him £10,000 instead. He didn't seem to mind the bother of changing it himself.

15 July.... Getting well into the pre-season friendlies now. Pre-match team talks are proving a real problem as the Boss is harder to understand than Kenny used to be. Also, considering how much notice they had that I was coming I think it's a bit ignorant of the Juventus lads not to have taken any English lessons. If Jan Molby can pick it up in the time it takes to fail a breath test it can't be that difficult.

16 July.... The Boss told me he expects me to learn Italian. Seems a bit stupid to me. When Jan Molby came to Anfield we didn't make him learn Italian.

12 August.... Still not too many goals yet. The rest of the team won't pass to me. They should remember the old saying "no team is bigger than the individual" (in this case me)

25 August.... Interviewed on TV today. Interviewer said he thought I was like Jimmy Greaves. I agreed, and started talking about that killer instinct, but then the smart-arse explained that he meant because we've both got moustaches and don't score as many goals as we used to. He was alright though. He said he hoped I had a long and happy career in Italy, "just like Greavsie".

27 August.... The telly reception's bloody awful round here. I've tried twisting the ariel and twiddling the knobs, but I still can't pick up "Brookside".

9 September.... There's no privacy over here. Everywhere you go, everybody wants to talk about football. I was sat in a restaurant yesterday and the waiter asks me whether I prefer Tagliatelli or Tortellini. I told him I was sure they were both very good, although I'd not played against either of them yet. Poor lad didn't seem to understand.

17 September.... It's just like Liverpool here. One journalist pointed out today that "Juventus haven't lost a game when Rush has scored". We're in mid-table at the moment.

27 September.... Went down the paper shop this morning to see if they've got Shoot! yet. This bloke stopped me outside and asked if I was the one who scored all those goals for Liverpool. I smiled and said I was, and signed an autograph for him. He went off with a big grin, saying somewhat mysteriously "Wait 'til I tell my kids I've met John Aldridge"

6 October.... Played some Italian team today. Didn't get a touch of the ball in the first half so flew back to Wales at half time.

13 October.... Flew back to Italy today. went training with Juventus. Expected a rocket off the Boss for missing the second half of the match last week, but he doesn't seem to have noticed yet.

20 October.... In dispute with the club over their refusal to pay me a win bonus for the match mentioned. Most of the lads seem to support me. Michael Laudrup said "If Rush hadn't done what he did, we wouldn't have won."

29 October.... Got the British papers today. Story links me with Everton. Went to see the Boss to see if there was any truth in it. He's obviously a big Kylie Minogue fan, as he started singing "I Should Be So Lucky"

5 November.... In the car park after training I saw this big Sicilian bloke called Don give Laudrup an envelope full of cash. I told him if he was going to try to bribe me not to score goals he was wasting his time and money. He agreed and walked off laughing.

19 November.... We're nearly half way through the season and we still haven't played Real Madrid or Bayern Munich yet.

21 November.... Must remember to give my old pal Mark Hughes a ring to see if he's settling down as well as I am.

25 November.... Apparently they're staging the World Cup Finals here in 1990. I reckon if I can buckle down, and get a of luck, I can still make it into the Italy team.

blow football

Come On Baby, Light My Fire

The demise of wing play and the failure to beat Poland in 1973 are the two things that Sir Alf Ramsey is most often blamed for, but some medical experts also hold him responsible for the unprecedented baby boom of Spring 1967. They suggest that as Alf sat motionless on the bench on that glorious summer's day, 30th July 1966, many of his fellow countrymen failed to exert such control over their emotions as the nation was swept along on a wave of euphoria. Hence, as Bobby Moore climbed the stairs to the Royal Box, thousands of young couples were also heading upstairs for another period of extra time, and the Russian linesman wasn't the only one left wondering whether it was completely in or not. However, within nine months both Ramsey's boys and the young lovers had been brought back down to earth. In April '67 Scotland beat England 3 - 2 at Wembley and the ominous patter of tiny feet throughout the land ensured that, for many, the summer of 1966 would never be forgotten.

As the 1990 World Cup approaches, we hardly need reminding that no England manager since has ever come close to emulating Ramsey's achievement. If next year in Italy is to be any different, Blow Football believes it is imperative that Bobby Robson seeks to rekindle and resurrect the spirit of '66 by packing his squad with players whose conception was inspired by Mooro, Hurstie and the boys. Clearly, in choosing such a squad, certain allowances must be made for pre-tournament excitement and post-final celebrations, so we have extended our selection to players born a few months either side of April 30th 1967.

Bobby's Baby Boomers 1990

Fraser Digby
(Swindon, 23/4/67)

Terry Phelan (Wimbledon, 16/3/67)	**Alan Kernighan** (Middlesbro', 25/4/67)
David Rocastle (Arsenal, 2/5/67)	**Paul Gascoigne** (Tottenham, 27/5/67)
	Darren Beckford (Port Vale, 12/5/67)

Mark Venus (Wolves, 6/4/67)	**Earl Barrett** (Oldham, 28/4/67)
Kevin Keen (West Ham, 25/2/67)	**Dale Gordon** (Norwich, 9/1/67)
Andy Watson (Halifax, 1/4/67)	

Subs: Tim Flowers (Southampton, 3/2/67), David Coleman (Bournemouth, 8/4/67), Alan McLoughlin (Swindon, 20/4/67), David Puttnam (Leicester, 3/2/67), Sean Reck (Oxford, 5/5/67).

David Rocastle captains the squad due to the fact that his birthdate is the closest to the magic April 30th which would indicate maximum World Cup pedigree. The inclusion of Rocastle and Dale Gordon is interesting, as it indicates that in 1966, despite Ramsey's reservations, thoughts of wing play had not completely given way to notions of foreplay. That Gordon Banks' form was truly inspirational is proven by the relative glut of young keepers born in Spring '67. Swindon's Fraser Digby is chosen ahead of Southampton's Tim Flowers on the basis that he was born closer to April 30th and, more importantly, he was born in Yorkshire. By contrast, the lack of quality strikers in the 1990 squad would seem

to suggest that it was not in fact hat-trick hero Geoff Hurst who really captured the nation's imagination. Indeed, for many, the spirit of '66 was best characterised by "Nobby" Stiles and it would be hoped that the 1990 team would be similarly inspired by the less tireless, but equally toothless, Paul Gascoigne.

Considering the heroic status of the boys of '66 it is somewhat surprising that so few of the 1990 squad are named after Ramsey's men. The parents of '67 quite inexplicably shunned good traditional names such as Alfred, George, Geoffrey, Raymond and Robert in favour of unconventional ones such as Darren, Fraser, Dale, Sean and Tim. However, that two of the 1990 squad were christened Alan would suggest that those first high-pitched squeaks from the cot left the Kernighan and McLoughlin families with no option but to name their sons after Alan Ball. It would seem that some parents had their minds temporarily on other things. Presumably when the Puttnams of Leicester chose to name their son David they had their sights set on Hollywood rather than the Leicester City forward line, but the Colemans of Salisbury surely ballsed-up badly by burdening the future Bournemouth midfielder with the name David.

Meanwhile, Malcolm Allen (Norwich/Wales), Jim Fleming (Man City/N. Ireland) and Bernard Gallacher (Aston Villa/Scotland) are all evidence that the lust and passion of 1966 was not confined to the celebratory English, but was also prevalent among the Scots, Welsh and Irish supporters who sought distraction from the events at Wembley.

Readers will have already doubtless spotted some similarities between our chosen team and the Boys Of '66. Firstly, both are managed by an ex-Ipswich manager who is/was not particularly liked by the popular press. Then there is the presence of Earl Barrett, who is widely reckoned to be "ten years ahead of his time", just like Martin Peters before him. But it is the attacking situation where uncanny similarities really exist. Everyone will doubtless recall the pre-World Cup chat in 1966 about England's goalscoring source. It was widely supposed that our chief poacher would be Jimmy Greaves. After all, he had scored a lot of goals for his country in the past, and despite a recent illness, there was every prospect of his doing so again. No-one really thought about Geoff Hurst, but we all know what happened. Doesn't this seem remarkably similar to the situation today, but with Gary Lineker and Andy Watson instead of Greavesie and Hurstie?

Doubtless with this side, England will win the World Cup, and there will be the joyous sounds of celebration all over the country. But we must remember that the process of creating world-beating sides is an on-going one, and also be mindful of the spark that created our current heroes. And this is where you, the Blow Football readers come in. After we have watched David, Earl, Fraser and the rest of the lads parade that famous trophy, we are asking you to do your patriotic duty, and help in the creation of the World Cup winners of 2014 (and possibly 2018 as well). So, after perhaps a celebratory glass of something (but not too much, you know what that does!), please climb the stairs (unless you live in a bungalow) and follow the orders of Queen Victoria, when she said "Lie back and think of Eng-er-land. Eng-er-land, Eng-er-land"

Sir Alf's Maternity Hotline starts buzzing

Winterbottom, Ramsey, Mercer, Revie, Greenwood, Robson .... Who'll be the Next

MANAGER OF ENGLAND

It seems certain that, win, lose or draw in Italy, the 1990 World Cup Finals will bring down the curtain on Bobby Robson's reign as England manager, and he will depart to take up a lucrative contract with one of the top British or European clubs, or, failing that, Manchester United. But who'll succeed him in the England hot seat? Here, Blow Football's team of experts run the rule over the main contenders, and come up with their choice to go through the Lancaster Gates.

	GRAHAM TAYLOR	ROBERT RUNCIE	EMLYN HUGHES	KYLIE MINOGUE
FOOTBALLING KNOWLEDGE	8 A lifetime working in the game has left Graham with a thorough knowledge of British football. A shrewd operator too. His recent signing of Paul McGrath, reported to have cost £400,000 was actually a free transfer on condition that Taylor picked up McGrath's bar bill.	5 The recent elevation of Maidstone to Football League status means that Robert now has two teams within shouting distance of his Canterbury base. However, a good working knowledge of the Vauxhall Opel League is likely to prove insufficient for such a tough job.	0 This is the man who once offerred the opinion that Lineker and Beardsley should be dropped in favour of Hateley and Dixon. Was kicked off 'A Question of Sport' for failing to identify a football on the picture board.	8 Despite extensive singing and acting commitments, Kylie remains a Highbury regular, and indeed her debut single, "I Should Be So Lucky" was about Arsenal. This was followed up with "Hand on Your Hartlepool", whilst hits such as "Especially for Juventus" and "Do the Lokomotiv Leipzig" show a keen interest in the European scene.
PREVIOUS EXPERIENCE	7 After modest success at Lincoln, Graham really captured the public imagination by taking Watford from the fourth division right up to the first. Last season's indications were that he may do the same, in reverse, for Aston Villa.	9 Excellent track record. Success in dealing with errant playboys, such as the Archbishop of Durham, means that discipline is unlikely to be a problem. A question mark over religious prejudice though - in over 400 years, his current side have never fielded a Catholic priest.	0 Utter crap. Took Rotherham to relegation and got sacked. Couldn't manage a piss-up in Paul Merson's house.	6 Although Kylie has never managed a football team before, we're sure she'd be pretty good at it.
PUBLIC PERSONA	9 Graham is always polite and willing to talk to journalists even if his team lose, a useful gift for England managers. His recently acquired glasses make him look quite intellectual.	8 Although sometimes criticised for 'preaching' his views, Robert is unlikely to get agitated with journalists, get into fights in pubs, or be involved in any sex scandals. Unpopularity with the present government is also a plus point.	0 With his rosy red cheeks, smart V-neck pullovers and giddy, giggly high spirits, Emlyn is the housewives' favourite. However, we think he's an insipid little tosser.	8 Always willing to appear on Wogan, Top of the Pops etc., Kylie exudes the image of the clean cut English Rose. Except she's Australian. Viewers of 'Neighbours' will be well acquainted with her work with dumb animals.
HOB-NOBBING WITH ROYALTY	5 Better acquainted with Crystal Palace than Buckingham Palace, although he is a good friend of Sarah Ferguson's dad, Alex.	9 Well in with all the Royal Family, especially the Queen, who is rumoured to have pulled some strings in getting him his current job. Always gets an invite to the Royal Weddings.	0 Well known for his antics with Princess Anne on 'A Question of Sport', after which the Princess Royal described him as a "fawning toerag". Particularly despised by the Queen Mother, who spat on her hand before shaking hands with Emlyn at the 1974 FA Cup Final.	8 Was included in the Royal Variety Performance at the special request of the Duke of Edinburgh. Has many fans in the Royal Family, including Prince Andrew, Prince Edward and Prince.
SINGING	5 Lacklustre outing with The Boss Squad, although "The Worst Song Ever" is an appropriate anthem for an Aston Villa manager. From a family of musical philistines, his sons Roger, John and Andy were in Duran Duran (© V. Platt 1989).	7 A hearty baritone. Rob is equally at home with "Onward Christian Soldiers" or "Jerusalem", although "This Time We'll Get It Right" may prove too taxing. Knows all the words to "'Ere We Go".	0 Emlyn often claims credit for Liverpool successes that he had no part in, so it's only fair to say that he was crap in "The Anfield Rap". Once tried to sing "One Man Went to Mow", but couldn't get past five.	10 There's no better singer in the world than Kylie at the moment. Whether it's "Je Ne Sais Pas Pourquoi" or "Wouldn't Change a Thing", Kylie's nightingale-like voice and groovy dancing will brighten up the dullest day. She's the business!
Total	34	38	0	40

VERDICT: It's Kylie! Yes folks, you've gotta be certain, this little Aussie dynamo is the man to lead English football into the nineties. Her new album, "(Just Go Out There And) Enjoy Yourself" is ample testimony to Kylie's credentials. And if England go 1 - 0 down, she won't give a XXXX, cos she knows that, just like a boomerang, we'll come back. So dust down those hats with the funny corks dangling from them, throw another shrimp on the barbie, and crack open the tinnies! Kylie is our Darling! Fair Dinkum!!

FOOTBALL p.l.c.

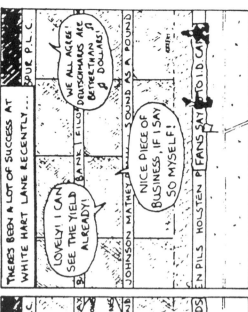

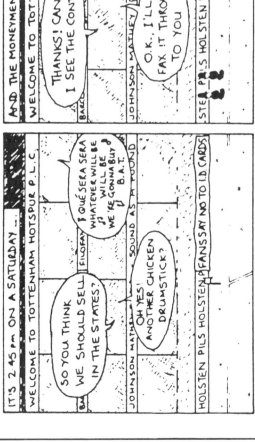

BLOW FOOTBALL

8, Beaumont Road,
Bournville,
Birmingham,
B30 2DY

ISSUE 3 FEB/MARCH '90

Editorial Team: Bob Blenkinsop
Steve Moss

Italian Correspondent: Alan Baxter
Thanks to: David Jackson, Simon Mordue, Lord Justice Taylor, the current residents of our old address (please feel free to write to them), West Midlands FSA, David Helliwell (Halifax article in issue 2) Mike Checksfield
Design/Typeset by Blow Football
Printed by: JUMA
1st Floor, Trafalgar Works
44, Wellington Street
Sheffield S1 4HD
(0742) 720915

The views expressed in these pages are those of the individual contributors, and not necessarily those of Blow Football, although they stand little chance of getting printed if they're not!

CONTRIBUTE! Thanks to everyone who sent contributions for this issue; if we haven't used it, don't despair, we've still got it and could well use it next time around. With the departure of two of our editors to sunnier climes (Italy and Singapore) we need your contributions more than ever now.
SUBSCRIBE! A 5-issue subscription costs a measly £3.00 (inc. p&p). Cheques payable to "Blow Football", and please state which issue you want your subscription to start from.

John Carlisle may dismiss it as "one man's view", but the Taylor Report is likely to have profound implications for the game of football. What's it all about ? Steve Moss opens his mouth......

We did it, boys and girls, we won. As the T-shirt says, "LJT Says NO to ID Cards". The final report into the Hillsborough disaster concludes that *"I .... have grave doubts as to whether the [ID card] scheme will achieve its object of eliminating hooligans from inside the ground. I have even stronger doubts as to whether it will achieve its further object of ending football hooliganism outside grounds. Indeed, I do not think it will. I fear that, in the short term at least, it may actually increase trouble outside grounds."* The government backed down, the ID card plan was (for the moment) dropped, and suddenly everyone in the press had been against the scheme all along. The months of arguing,

natural justice

petitioning and generally keeping the issue in the public eye had all been worth it. "Here We Go" indeed.

But what did we win exactly ? In short, very little, possibly nothing. Rather, we avoided defeat. While we may celebrate the scrapping of the scheme, those feelings are bound to be less of elation, more of relief that an idea which should have been "strangled at birth" had been abandoned at the last minute. In footballing parlance, we haven't scored a goal, we've just saved a penalty which should never have been given. Further, we must look at how and why the scheme was dropped. It wasn't the petition with 400,000+ names opposing the scheme, it wasn't the eloquent parliamentary arguments, or even the gross inability of the scheme's defenders (most notably the "terrible trio" of Moynihan, Evans and Carlisle) to do anything other than bring further ridicule on an already incredulous scheme. The reason that we are not now watching the representatives of the various tendering companies wining and dining the football authorities (and, in the case of ADT Check-In, the supporters' organisations) is that ninety five people died at a football match. That is a price which must never be payed again.

There had been some confusion over what Taylor was expected to cover in his report, and hence disappointment at his failure to recommend meaningful voluntary membership schemes, community involvement, and a formalised role for supporters in the decision making process. However, the report's brief was to cover areas of "crowd control and safety" so that, while one may read between the lines as to Taylor's opinion on other matters, it was not his remit to make recommendations on them. Nevertheless, reading the full report, rather than just media reaction to it, one is struck by the depth of knowledge which Taylor has acquired for the game. His comments on segregation, for example, are spot on: *"The very fact that rival fans are separated tends to increase and polarise their hostility to each other. Segregation breeds an 'us and them' attitude .... the disease remained and may even have been intensified by segregation."*

Taylor's recommendations on all-seater stadia have provoked much debate since the report's publication, and are dealt with elsewhere in this issue of Blow Football. Aside from coming out against ID cards, the report makes other worthwhile recommendations. The creation of specific offences for chanting racialist or obscene abuse is a welcome step. Up until now, police have been relatively powerless to stop racialist abuse, as to contravene existing laws it has to be proven that the abuse was intended to stir up racial hatred. Similarly, obscene abuse is only an offence under the Public Order Act of 1986 if it can be shown that it was uttered "within the hearing or sight of a person likely to be caused harassment, alarm or distress thereby."

Making the invasion of the pitch an offence would hopefully put an end to scenes like those at last year's FA Cup Final. Although harmless in themselves, activities like these do nothing to improve football's image, and simply give ammunition to the pro-fence lobby. Similarly, while a pitch invasion by one set of fans may be down to what Taylor calls "joie de vivre", the reaction this may incite in opposition fans may be less "joyeaux". Understandably, though, in the light of recent events, some fans may well be dubious as to the police's ability to *"exercise sensible discretion and judgement"* in determining whether or not people have *"good reason or reasonable excuse"* to come on to the field of play.

All in all Taylor has produced one of the most enlightened "official" judgements into football in recent years, although it is slightly depressing to remember that much of the spirit of the report has existed, unrecognised by the authorities, in the supporters' movement for several years. The following paragraph is one from "Off The Ball" or "Reclaim The Game" circa 1987: *"As for the clubs, in some instances it is legitimate to wonder whether the directors are genuinely interested in the welfare of their grass-roots supporters. Boardroom struggles for power, wheeler dealing in the buying and selling of shares and indeed whole clubs sometimes suggest that those involved are more interested in the personal financial benefits or social status of being a director than of directing the club in the interests of its supporter customers. In most commercial enterprises, including the entertainment industry, knowledge of the customer's needs, his tastes and his dislikes is essential information in deciding policy and planing. But, until recently, very few clubs consulted to any significant extent with the supporters or their organisations."*

LJT - Rave On!!!

Annie Gets Her Gun

Rather like flared trousers, ID Cards were a thing you thought you'd heard the last of. But now both are creeping back into fashion. **Steve Moss**, still in 'sensible' trackie bottoms, gets his Fans Say No to ID Cards' T-Shirt out of mothballs and takes a trip to St Andrews...

"'Tis amazing," quoth the man in the station buffet, "how quickly a breath of fresh air doth turn to a pungent odour." And so Annie Bassett breezed into Birmingham City this summer, moving into the newly created post of Chief Executive, having held a similar position at Reading. Annie had a plan. Annie was going to make everything lovely. The club notepaper was overprinted with the slogan 'The Re-Birth of the Blues'. The families would come flocking back to St Andrews, people would be smiling and dancing barefoot in the rain, blind men would see again, the lame would throw away their crutches, etc, etc. And how was Annie going to do all this? Well, she was going to introduce an ID card scheme.

Yup, just six months after Lord Justice Taylor threw out the proposed National Membership Scheme on the grounds that it could not be guaranteed as safe, Ms Bassett announced that anyone wishing to stand on the terraces at St Andrews would have to possess a computerised card, which could be confiscated in the event of misbehaviour. LJT had looked at, and rejected, many cumbersome possibilities, but Blues, in their own inimitable way, really pulled it out of the bag by going for the most time consuming, clumsy, method of computerised entry imaginable. Instead of the supporter passing the card through the reader, a la Luton, it would be handed to the turnstile operator who, in addition to taking money and giving change, would also have to slide the card downwards through the reader contained in the turnstile booth. "True fans should be delighted," said Ms Bassett.

"Anybody who doesn't like it has to be suspect."

Well, it must be said then that there are a lot of "suspect" people roaming the streets of Birmingham. The local branch of the Football Supporters Association led the opposition. The FSA put in a submission to Birmingham City Council's Public Safety at Sports Stadia Committee, requesting that the committee withdraw the safety certificate from St Andrews if the scheme went ahead as planned. The submission doubted Ms Bassett's claim that the turnstiles could cope with the flow rate of 11 - 20 persons per minute recommended by Taylor, pointing out that the added transaction could only increase queueing times, at a time when Blues already had a queueing problem on crowds of over 10,000. "At best," the FSA concluded, "the scheme as proposed will be an expensive white elephant, as it will quite clearly have no effect on keeping troublemakers out of St Andrews [the cards have no photograph or name, making it the easiest thing in the world to use a borrowed card]. In practice, the scheme is likely to compromise the safety of St Andrews."

The committee, in their wisdom, rejected the FSA's submission. This was not altogether surprising - it would have been a great embarrassment to both the club and the committee to have to turn down the scheme just days before the start of the new season. Bassett meanwhile was castigating the "moaners" who had sought to overturn the scheme (although the transformation of opponents from potential hooligans to merely moaners could be held to represent a victory of sorts).

The scheme opened for business for the first league game of the season, against Leyton Orient. The day before the match, local radio phone-ins were jammed with angry fans who had applied for cards but not received them. The club blamed a late surge of applications, but with only 6,500 registered members, it begged the question as to how the club would cope with, for example, a big cup tie at short notice (two seasons ago, 34,000 saw Blues play Nottingham Forest in the FA Cup).

The FSA, along with members of the local press, monitored the scheme's operation on the day of the match. Gatemen and stewards were equally vocal in their opposition to the scheme. The police seemed unsure what would happen if a card was rejected, trusting that "reasonable people" would move without a fuss if their card bleeped red. Repeated timing of the flow of supporters through the turnstiles gave rates of around 6 or 7 per minute, well below the rate laid down by Taylor. One of the observers asked the gateman to try passing his card through the reader a second time, to test out the club's assertion that a card could only be used once per match. Both times a green "enter" light appeared. The crowd on the day was 5,847, as compared to around 10,000 for the visit of Crewe on the opening day of last season. Only two league gates at Blues last season were lower. On a conservative estimate, Birmingham City lost at least £10,000 gate money on this match.

After the match, Bassett was storming, slamming those opposed to the scheme as "dragging the club down". "Why do people who call themselves fans have to come with the intention of trying to catch the club out?" she asked. Ms Bassett, no doubt, was one of those tut-tutting when the little boy pointed out that The Emporor's New Clothes didn't exist. Or maybe Birmingham City are a front organisation for The Flat Earth Society. Whatever, you have been warned - the ID Card argument is not dead yet, and the legislation is still on the statute book....

BLOW
FOOTBALL

8, Beaumont Road,
Bournville,
Birmingham.
B30 2DY

The Fourth Album

Vocals/Guitar: Steve Moss
The Bass Guitar: Bob Blenkinsop
The Drums: Alan Baxter

Backing vocals: Steve Beauchampe, Fran Coleman, Matthew Davis, M. Goodbody (Mrs), Vernon Platt, Greg Downs.

All tracks © Moss/Blenkinsop/Baxter except "FIFA Name 'Top' World Cup Referee" © Coleman and "Senso Unico Ole Ole Ole" © Beauchampe.

Recorded August/September 1990 at AU Studios, Birmingham.

Produced, Engineered and Mixed by Blow Football

Pressed by : JUMA
1st Floor, Trafalgar Works
44 Wellington Street
Sheffield
S1 4HD
(0742) 720915

Sleeve printed on re-cycled paper

Beer on the Cards

LAGER DRINKERS will have to produce I.D. cards in order to purchase their favourite tipple, under measures outlined by the government last night. Introducing the Lager Drinkers Bill, Mr Colin Half-Pint, the Minister for Alcohol, said "Lager drinking has become tarnished by the violence caused by a number of its participants. We want to go back to the good old days when lager drinking was a family activity, and Britain had the best empire the world has ever seen."

Under the scheme, drinkers will have to possess a plastic card, bearing the holder's name, address and preferred brand of lager. This will be passed through a decoder in a similar manner to a cash-card, before the drinker can order. Mr Half-Pint dismissed suggestions that this would lead to a build up of customers at the bar, and also denied that there was any chance of the equipment breaking down, "even if some pissed-up casual decides to pour his pint in it."

Mr Half-Pint refused to be drawn on the implications of the bill for drinkers of shandy, lager-and-lime, lager tops etc. "These are matters to be investigated by the Lager Membership Authority, and it would be totally improper of me to attempt to predict its recommendations" he said.

The scheme was warmly welcomed by Mr John Cumbria, Conservative MP for Luton, and Piligin. "This scheme will be welcomed by lager drinkers and the public at large," he said. "Anyone suspected of a lager-related offence, such as burping, can have their card confiscated, and they will be punished. I would like to see this scheme incorporate the re-introduction of capital punishment. Can I also say that I think South Africa is a great country and we can learn a lot from them."

Another staunch supporter of the scheme is pub landlord Mr David Political-Careerist. At his pub, The Mad Hatter in Luton, only drinkers of the pub's own lager, Boring Plastic Dirge Special Export, are admitted. "We don't get no violence.. no nuffink down the Mad 'Atter", said Mr Political-Careerist. It has been rumoured that The Mad Hatter also gets no customers.

Mr Half-Pint, however, resisted calls for a similar scheme to be introduced for champagne drinkers in order to curb the recent increase of so-called Hooray Henry violence. "That would be a gross infringement of civil liberties, and completely irrelevant to the problem of champagne related violence, most of which occurs away from pubs," he said.

Mr Half-Pint is 4'11" and a bit of a prat.

"Up Yours!" Mr Half-Pint refuses to panda to the whims of lager drinkers

SUBBUTEO

New Accessories for the New Season

Everton Defence
(4 players bolted to steel strip for genuine square look)

Graham Roberts

Ian Ormondroyd

Mark Hughes

Kevin Sheedy

Mo Johnston
(inc. minders)

Tony Adams

Graeme Souness

Bryan Robson

Eric Gates

Paul Gascoigne

Vinny Jones
"flick to butt"

Portsmouth end-of-game
(9 players only)

Huddersfield away

COMING SOON!!!
*Colin Moynihan
*Away Terrace (includes increased admission prices, no roof, barbed wire etc.)
*Executive Boxes (Spurs home in soon)
*Brian Moore (inc. patronising comments)

I BELIEVE....

I believe I've got gnomes at the end of my garden
And that Bonnie Prince Charlie should be given a pardon
And that one day accountants will work for no fees
I believe that the moon is a piece of green cheese.

I believe that top judges are never too old,
And the streets down in London are all paved with gold.
I believe that a drink is the first step to ruin
I believe Nigel Lawson knows just what he's doing.

I believe you can see in the away end at Stoke,
And that dear old Ron Saunders tells a great knock knock joke
I believe that they're sober, this band called The Pogues,
And the lead singer's sister is Kylie Minogue.

I believe in the story of Red Riding Hood,
And that Ferdinand Marcos was misunderstood.
I believe that Rice Krispies really go Snap and Crackle
I believe Graeme Souness once made a fair tackle.

I believe Eric Heffer's better looking than Kilroy
And Pamella said to Moyny "Well, Col, you're a big boy"
I believe Arthur Fowler should be the next Bond
I believe that great sounds come from Brother Beyond.

I believe Jimmy Tarbuck is really quite funny
I believe Tony Cottee was value for money
I believe that Sting suffers from sexual frustration
I believe that West Ham will avoid relegation.

I believe Father Christmas comes right down the chimneys
I believe one day England will beat the West Indies
I believe that The Sun is quite truthful in parts
I believe Robert Maxwell's a good bloke at heart.

I believe when we die that we'll all go to Heaven,
And that God's right hand man is a bloke called Nye Bevan
I believe in The Lord, I believe in The Devil
But I can't believe Greg Downs has got a Cup Winners Medal.

ADD YOUR VOICE TO THE SOUND OF THE CROWD.....

Impress your mates and make the cat jealous with the latest in Couch Potato Designer Wear. This unique "Armchair Supporters On Tour" T-Shirt is the essential fashion item for the well dressed stayaway fan this season. Complete with the dates of all the important matches on the back, it comes to you in three sizes (L,XL,Graham Kelly) and costs just £25.99 inc p&p. Send cheque/p.o. to ITV Sport, London. Get that Big Match feeling ..... in the comfort of your own home!

Swindon players celebrate their recent victory at a Manchester Five-a-Side Tournament.

Swindon Town

Today we extend a warm welcome to the supporters, the players, and what's left of the directors of Swindon Town. Thanks largely to the wheeling and dealing of former manager Lou Macari, now working for the club as an undercover agent, "The Swindlers" have been transformed from a mid table fourth division side to a team capable of competing with the best, and recently achieved the feat of being members of all three top divisions within a four week period. Although obviously upset by the club's fall from grace, Macari remains defiant. "Relegation was a real body blow, but we can recover from it, and I believe we have the players to do it. Players who are steeped in the Swindon traditions of determination, character and financial irregularity." The current side must be in with a great chance of a Beazer Homes League place within the next couple of seasons. Here are some of the names that Macari is betting on to pull Swindon round.

Keeping goal at the moment is Lester Piggott. Despite his age, Lester remains one of the top tax-dodgers in the business, and is generally reckoned to be performing better than ever right now. A perfectionist, Piggott often comes in for extra tax evasion training after the rest of the squad have gone home.

Waiting in Piggott's shadows is England's number one poll tax evader David Icke, who hopes to make that green jersey his own one day. Described by his manager as the man who "saves everything" (shots, newspapers, aluminium cans, tropical rain forests, etc), Icke recently turned down a move to Chelsea FC because of the club's initials.

At centre back is Ken Dodd, who hails from that hot bed of fraud, Merseyside. Had trials at Everton, Tranmere and Liverpool Crown Court before signing for Swindon for an "undisclosed sum". While some of his methods, such as stuffing loads of cash in shoe boxes, are not to be found in any coaching manual, his success speaks for itself. His keen sense of humour makes him a great character to have in the dressing room.

Ken's partner in defence is top insider dealer Ivan Boesky. A member of the American World Cup Squad, Boesky arrived at Swindon after a hugely successful career on Wall Street. His ruthless and uncompromising style has endeared him to Swindon fans, while his manager says of him "Every team needs a good insider dealer, and in Ivan we've got the best in the business. A real asset to the team, I'm convinced Ivan can become a major star if and when the much talked about European Fraud League comes about."

Completing the defence are Lord Lucan and John Stonehouse. Although both have a tendency to drift out of the game (and the country) for long periods, Macari is confident that both can do "a job" for the team. While some may question their mobility against fleet-footed Inland Revenue officers, both have great experience, and Stonehouse is especially good at recovering after apparently being "left for dead".

Current star of the Swindon team is Keith Best. Like his famous namesake George, this former M.P. is a right winger and ex jailbird of great trickery and cunning. While George had more than his fair share of skill, Keith just had more than his fair share of shares. A good finisher, he gets his name on the scoresheet almost as many times as he gets it on a Telecom share application sheet. Came through the ranks of the Conservative Party, which is looking like a potentially rich source of talent. In the same way that it used to be said that to get a centre forward in Newcastle you shouted down the nearest mine-shaft, so a ready supply of fraudulent share dealers and tax evaders are just a division bell away should Macari need them.

A big disappointment for Swindon has been the form of Danish trialist Soren Lerby. Despite rave reports from Ajax Amsterdam, including a rumoured £400,000 of undeclared income tax, Lerby was unable to prove himself in front of the judges, who found him innocent of all charges. "In the end, the lad just couldn't withold the goods in the top league," said Macari, "and so we've had to let him go."

No such problems with Nigel Mansell, though. Although there are those who feel that there is no place for an old-fashioned tax exile in the modern game, the Isle of Man's top golfer is always one of the first names on Macari's team sheet. Although there are doubts about his ability to last the full 90 minutes, Mansell gives the Swindlers another option in the middle of the park, and also doubles up as the driver of the getaway car when the taxman calls.

The main thrust up front for Swindon comes from the potent mix of Ernest Saunders and Gerald Ronson. Despite being described by Macari as "Pure Genius" and "Good For You", the pair are a couple of controversial characters. Saunders's recent takeover of the Swindon captaincy is currently being investigated by the Monopolies and Mergers Commission, while there are some who feel that with Saunders and Ronson in the side, Swindon are bound to "go down".

Also challenging for a place up front is Freddie Laker. Good in the air, Freddie has not been able to rediscover his best form since incurring a horrific fiscal groinstrain in the bankruptcy courts a few seasons ago. Completing the squad is former QPR and Australia wicket keeper Rodney Marsh. Marsh first caught Macari's eye back in 1981 when he made a fortune betting on his own side to lose the Headingley Test Match. However, his manager admits that his recent form has been "disappointingly honest".

THE SCOTLAND WORLD CUP SONG

A document was recently sent to us here at Blow Football by one of our readers, who works at Stock, Aitken and Waterman's "Hit Factory" in London. Relaxing in a studio after a particularly rigourous rock'n'roll workout, our correspondent (who, for the sake of anonimity we shall call Jason D.) stumbled across a piece of paper containing the lyrics for the 1990 Scottish World Cup Squad Song. In the interests of National Security, we feel obliged to reproduce these lyrics.....

Italy, Italy
We're the famous Bonny Scotland and we're going to Italy

Wake up all ye lads and lasses, raise your hands and raise your glasses,
'Cos we're Scotland and we're on the way to Rome.
Yes the Tartan Army's back, and this time we will not "crack"
'Cos we've made sure Willie Johnston stays at home

Penalty, Penalty,
When we play in Wales we always get a dodgy penalty

Wake up all ye lads and lasses, raise your hands and raise your glasses,
Andy's Army, yes we know a trick or two.
We are Scotland and we're brave, and if Leighton makes a save,
Then we might just beat Iran or p'raps Peru.

Duty Free, Duty Free
We're only going to Italy to get our Duty Free

Wake up all ye lads and lasses, raise your hands and raise your glasses,
We're off to Italy for a fine old Highland Fling.
With Mo Johnston and his minder, and his wife if he can find her,
Oh the Scotland Squad won't win a bloody thing

On T.V., On T.V.,
We'll be home in time to watch the second round on the T.V.

Instrumental (synthesised bagpipes)
Key Change

Wake up all ye lads and lasses, raise your hands and raise your glasses
The Scottish boys are off to Italy in June
Oh we might not be the best, but we're sure to beat the rest,
'Cos we'll stun them with our awful World Cup tune

Referee, Referee
David Speedie's only in the squad to hit the referee
Fifty three, Fifty three
Roy Aitken is our captain and he's just turned fifty three

FOR INFORMATION ABOUT SUBSCRIPTIONS AND BACK ISSUES PLEASE SEND AN S.A.E. or I.R.C. TO THE FOLLOWING:

Rodney Rodney, P.O. Box 19 (SEPDO), Manchester M19 5RZ.
King Of The Kippax, 25 Holden Brook Close, Leigh, Greater Manchester WN7 2HL.
The Hanging Sheep, 41 Woodhall Terrace, Thornbury, Bradford BD3 7BZ.
Voice Of The Valley, P.O. Box 387, London SE9 6EH.
Through The Wind And Rain, p.o. Box 23, Bootle, Merseyside L30 2SA.
Out Of Court, 20 Balaclava Road, Bitterne, Southampton SO2 5NT.
A Load Of Bull, Box 277, 52 Call Lane, Leeds LS1 6DT.
The Lad Done Brilliant, 90J St. Georges Drive, Pimlico, London SW1V 4DA.
Brian Moore's Head etc., 11 Watts Avenue, Rochester, Kent ME1 1RX.
The Crooked Spireite, Flat 3, 119 Newbold Road, Chesterfield, Derbyshire S41 7PS.
A Kick Up The R's, 6 Mill Cottages, Chester Road, Grindley Brook, Nr. Whitchurch,
                    Shropshire, SY13 4QH.
Brian, 6 Grays Inn Buildings, Roseberry Avenue, London EC1R 4PH.
Hull, Hell & Happiness, 119 North Road, Withernsea, East Yorks. HU19 2AX.
On Cloud 7, 104 Dunvegan Road, Hull HU8 9LF.
Blow Football, 8 Beaumont Road, Bourneville, Birmingham B30 2DY.

DO YOU REALLY WANT TO START A FANZINE?

So, you've bought the fanzines, you've read the book, and you're inspired. You think about starting your own fanzine. The first piece of advice I can give you is : DON'T! You'd be far better off offering your services to an existing fanzine; they're always issuing plaintive appeals for more ideas and material, and most of them would be only too glad of extra help with the tedious aspects such as typing, layout, selling, distribution etc. And if you do progress to starting your own at least then you'll have some idea what you're letting yourself in for.

I haven't put you off? Well, perhaps the team you support doesn't have a fanzine (unlikely unless they play in the village sunday league), or perhaps you disagree entirely with everything the existing fanzine has to say, or perhaps the people that run the existing fanzine don't like you? How do you start.

Writing enough material to fill a fanzine is likely to be the least of your problems. The next step is to figure out how you're going to get it printed. The two methods to consider are photocopying and offset litho. Photocopying is worthwhile if (a) you can do it at work when the boss is out or (b) the quantity you're after is very small (less than 200 probably). Offset litho is the commonest printing method, offering advantages of quality and flexibility (different colours, types of paper etc.) but is proportionately far more expensive on smaller quantities than large. This is obviously a problem for the fanzine just starting up, as it's important to offer value for money, but it's imprudent to count on selling large quantities of an untested product. If you're very lucky you might know a printer, or someone with an inplant print unit at their work where you can get it done cheap. The next possibility is colleges, community centres or training schemes which might have printing facilities, though this might involve sacrificing quality for cost. If you have to turn to commercial printers it goes without saying that you need to shop around. Prices vary drastically according to how much different printers want your business. A small printer or one-man operation is more likely to give you a good deal than a big industrial concern. Here we declare a vested interest: Juma, the publishers of this book, are commercial printers, and would be more than happy to give you a competitive quote, including delivery if you don't happen to be in the environs of Sheffield. Commercial over.

Next, prepare your artwork. I've deliberately left this till after sorting out your printing arrangements as you need to liaise with your printer closely. Because of the different platemaking methods and print formats virtually every printer will have different requirements. The one thing that doesn't vary is that you should make sure your type is dark and clear and everything in your artwork is presented in black and white only. Juma have a leaflet called 'Preparing artwork for litho printing' which is free for an SAE and gives a number of useful tips.

Now the finance. People who go into fanzines expecting to make money tend to fall flat on their faces. However, if you are too ethical about it and set out deliberately not to make a profit you're even more likely to lose out. It's important to adopt a business-like approach, even if you're going to re-invest any profits to improve the magazine, or donate them all to charity.

For example, if you're printing 500 magazines and the cover price is 50p don't assume at the end of the day you'll have £250. You are bound to have some unsold copies left, even if they're only ones which have got batterred beyond saleable state in shops. Then, while you'll get 50p a copy for the ones you sell in person, any shops which sell it will want a percentage. A record shop where you're a valued customer might take only a minimal sum, or even nothing in exchange for an advertisement, but the percentage can rise to 50% or more in large chain shops, and everyone will want 'sale or return'. ie. they won't pay you for copies that aren't sold no matter what state you get them back in. All in all it's best to budget on getting no more than half the potential cover price from the total print run. So you need to make £125 cover the cost of printing, photography, distribution etc. or accept that you're going to have to dig into your own pockets.

Big magazines survive on advertising revenue, but this avenue is limited to fanzines with small circulations. Even if your print run increases filling the pages with advertising will win you few friends. People will start saying "It's just like the programme", you'll have to be careful what you say for fear of controversy upsetting the advertisers, and the club you're covering will have an excuse to fall out with you because your advertising sales could damage the programme.

Finally, sell your product. The easiest and most obvious way of selling a football fanzine is to take them on the terraces and ask people to buy them. Of course, nothing is that simple. Some clubs, a few, specifically allow fanzines to be sold in their grounds. More turn a blind eye. A large number, however, ban fanzine sales on their premises entirely. The reasons they are likely to give vary from the ludicrous ('harming programme sales') to the unlikely ('causing dangerous crowd movement') to the almost plausible ('allowing fanzine sales would imply clubs' approval of their content'). The most likely reason however, and the one they'll never give, is that they're terrified of supporters speaking up for themselves. The next best selling place would be immediately outside the ground. Obviously if the area outside belongs to the club you are just as likely to be banned from there. If you are selling in the public street you might need an expensive street traders licence, though whether this is enforced or not varies from area to area and depends very much on size of crowds and level of policing. If the police are unsympathetic they can also claim you are causing an obstruction if even a small queue or group forms around you. The only answer really is to speak to other fanzines about what problems they've encountered or precautions they take.

No, I wasn't serious when I said don't start a fanzine. The Elmslie Ender has involved me in many a late night and wet afternoon, but I certainly look back on our 20 issues with a good deal of pride and value the friendship and publicity it's earned us. Get that typewriter working!

MARTIN LACEY

EL TEL WAS A SPACE ALIEN
ISBN 1 872204 00 7

The first ever compilation of football fan-zines, 210 pages with extracts from Lennie Lawrence, Chelsea Independent, When Sunday Comes, Leyton Orientear, Elmslie Ender, Arsenal Echo Echo, Blue Print, Eagle Eye, Flashing Blade, The Pie, City Gent, Heartbeat, Just Another Wednesday, and Tired and Weary. Format similar to 'Get Your Writs Out'. Price £5.95 + £1.50 p+p.

WHERE'S THE BAR?
ISBN 1 872204 01 5

The alternative guide to non-league football. First edition contains 74 pages of non-league facts, features and photos, including ground guide to the Vauxhall Conference and three feeder leagues. Price £2.25 post free. Second edition, much expanded, planned for summer 1991. See football press for announcements.

All our books are available from Sports-pages and Soccer Bookshelf (mail order) and can be ordered from any good book-shop. Our address is:

Juma Printing and Publishing
First Floor
Trafalgar Works
44 Wellington Street
Sheffield S1 4HD
Tel. (0742) 720915

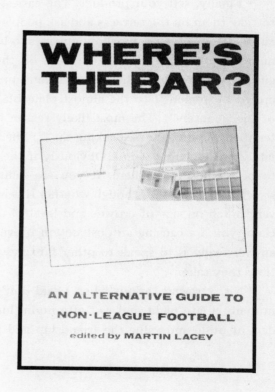